CLASS IDEOLOGIES & EDUCATIONAL FUTURES

CLASS IDEOLOGIES & EDUCATIONAL FUTURES

David W Livingstone
(Ontario Institute for Studies in Education)

The Falmer Press

A member of the Taylor & Francis Group

First published 1983

ISBN 0905273 39 7 limp
      0905273 40 0 cased

Jacket design by Leonard Williams

Printed and bound by Taylor & Francis (Printers) Ltd
Basingstoke
for
The Falmer Press
(*A Member of the Taylor & Francis Group*)
Falmer House
Barcombe, Lewes
Sussex BN8 5DL
England

Dedication

To my mother and father who taught me how to care for humane causes.

To the road construction crews of Dawson Creek and Prince George and the line workers in the Vancouver bakery and dairy plants, who gave me my best lessons in what working class culture is all about in the contested terrain of the workplace.

To the members of the Oak Street Community School Association in Regent Park who began to show me how working class parents could struggle for the educational liberation of their children.

Acknowledgements

A project of this kind can only be completed with the help of a very large number of people. In the first place, I never would have been in a position to consider such an inquiry without the support of many of my own teachers, most notably Bill Derpak, S.J. Schwieg, Yunshik Chang, Terry Nosanchuk, Art Stinchcombe, and Roy Breton. Just as important was the practical education in the highly contradictory competitive and co-operative tendencies of capitalist societies that was provided by experiences of my hyperactive youth, much of which was spent in innumerable sports teams and the scouting movement. Among all the friends, and coaches, leaders, teammates and opponents, Gloria Bingham, Bob Porter and Lance Richardson probably had the most lasting influence. In more immediate terms, my colleagues in the Department of Sociology in Education at the Ontario Institute for Studies in Education (OISE) have created a most supportive setting for the pursuit of critical social inquiry. In particular, Andy Effrat and Michael Fullan offered much encouragement of my early work, and more recently Mary O'Brien has provided the inspirational example of her rigorous feminist scholarship.

The several research studies on which much of text is based required the participation of thousands of people. The several hundred people who were involved in the group discussions and open-ended interviews on which the various opinion surveys were based, and the advisory committees of each of the surveys, all played essential roles. The larger studies from which the empirical data were drawn have been funded by OISE, and by the Social Sciences and Humanities Research Council of Canada. In particular, Clifford Pitt, the former director of OISE, was instrumental in facilitating the more recent opinion surveys through the research priorities that he established for the Institute.

The people who have worked on the staff of these surveys deserve a special vote of thanks. Mark Holmes made useful contributions in the preparatory and design phases of the most recent surveys. Cecilia Green, Aminur Rahim, Ingrid Wellmeir, and Bertrand Wong have all been very helpful graduate research assistants. The secretarial work which has been done by Gail Buckland, Mildred Landry and Judith Walters, has been uniformly excellent; I am especially grateful to Gail and Mildred for their very fine typing of the present manuscript. Research officers have co-ordinated the day to day work on each of the large-scale surveys, Jutta Keylwerth and Doug Shattuck on the 1973 survey, and Doug Hart on all the later studies. Doug Hart has played an invaluable role in all phases of the empirical research reported here. Doug has not only conducted all of the computer-based analyses presented in the text, he has made substantive contributions to many analytical aspects of this inquiry, and in particular has done most of the documentary research for and the first draft of the thematic analysis of class-based educational ideologies in English Canada that appears in Chapter Three.

A number of the student colleagues who have engaged with me in critical dialogues focused on their own related projects have provided some of the provocation for work on several aspects of the current study. I am most grateful to Patrick Healy, Richard Mason, Satu Repo, Sandy Siegel, Ric Williams, and especially Wally Seccombe in this regard. Don Lake was similarly helpful, and in addition did the library research for the discussion of guild socialism that appears in Chapter Five. My colleagues in the Critical Pedagogy and Cultural Studies Group at OISE (Madan Handa, Mal Levin, Paul Olson, Roger Simon, Ed Sullivan, Jack Quarter, and Gordon West) have offered constructive criticisms of parts of the manuscript. Michael Apple, Phil Corrigan, John Harp, Phil Wexler, and Paul Willis have also made helpful comments.

I owe a very large debt to Phaedra and Stephanie, who have done a good share of my domestic labour and kindly tolerated my absences while this manuscript was being written. Most of all, I am inexpressibly grateful to Angela Nall-Livingstone who has shared in all the struggles, and who has taken much time from her own work so that I might finish mine. History may well judge me harshly for serving to delay her recognition as one of the finest artists of ceramic sculpture.

Contents

Introduction   I

Chapter One: Educational Facts and Intellectual Interpretations   5

Chapter two: Class Structure in Advanced Capitalism   43

Chapter Three: State Schooling and Class-Based Educational Ideologies   89

Chapter Four: Mass Opinion in Education Crisis: A Class Analysis   143

Chapter Five: Intellectual and Popular Images of The Educational and Social Future   179

Chapter Six: Notes for Educational Praxis in Advanced Capitalism   225

Index   243

List of Tables

Table 1   Post-war Trends in Educational Participation   9

Table 2   Public Expenditure on Education as A Proportion of Public Expenditure and of Gross National Product   11

Table 3   Selected Indicators of The Economic Performance of Major Industrial Market Economies   12

Table 4   Class Structure of The World Capitalist System (1975)   53

Table 5   Class Structures of Major Industrial Market Economies: Economically Active Male Population   60

Table 6   Estimates of Class Structure of The United States and Canada: Economically Active Population   61

Table 7   Class Structure of Ontario: Economically Active Population   62

Table 8   Class Position by Age, Ontario 1978–80   68

Table 9   Class Position by Sex, Ontario 1978–80   69

Table 10   Class Position by Ethnicity, Ontario 1978–80   69

Table 11   Class Position by Father's Main Class Position, Ontario 1978   72

Table 12   Class Position by Spouse's Class Position, Ontario 1978   73

Table 13   Class Position by Trade Union Membership, Ontario 1978–80   74

Table 14   Father's Main Class Position by Respondent's Educational Attainment, Ontario 1978   78

Table 15   Class Position by Educational Attainment, Ontario 1978–80   80

Table 16   Class Position by Assessed Usefulness of Own Formal Education for Work, Ontario 1978   81

Table 17   'Which of The Following Should Have The Strongest Claim on Tax Money?' (1978–1980)   152

Table 18   Strongest Claim on Tax Money, 1980   153

Table 19   Desired Level of Public Spending for Education in The Next Budget Year, 1980   154

Table 20   Views on The Use of 'Surplus' Teachers, 1980   155

Table 21   Perceived Representation of Class Interests in the Development of Community Colleges, 1980   157

Table 22   'Students From Families of All Occupational Backgrounds (Such as Managerial, Professional, Clerical and Blue Collar Levels) Have an Equal Chance of Getting A Higher Education in Ontario Today.' (1979)   158

Table 23   Extent of Perceived Bias Against Working Class Students, 1980   159

Table 24   Support for Greater Emphasis on Business Rights and Workers' Rights in Ontario Schools, 1980   160

Table 25 Orientations to High School Discipline, 1979   161

Table 26 Preferred High School Authority Structure, 1980   162

Table 27 Preferred Locus of Control of High School Testing, 1980   163

Table 28 Preferred Freedom of Student Choice in High School Course Selection,
          1980   164

Table 29 Views on Teachers' Right to Strike, 1980   165

Table 30 Preferred Organization of The Elementary School Learning Process,
          1980   167

Table 31 Highest Priority Educational Objective for Secondary Schools, 1980   168

Table 32 Preferred Curricular Emphasis in University Programs, 1980   169

Table 33 'Compared to Twenty Years Ago, Do You Think The Work Most
          of The Canadian Labour Force Does Now Involves More or Less
          Skill and Independent Judgement? (1980)   170

Table 34 Regulation of The Educational System to Match Job Opportunities, 1978 171

Table 35 Frequency of Thinking About The Societal Future, International
          Comparisons   197

Table 36 Frequency of Futures Thinking, Ontario 1973   198

Table 37 Clarity of Image of The Future, Ontario 1973   198

Table 38 Influence of Scientists and Technologists in Society by The Year 2000,
          Ontario 1973   199

Table 39 Expected Future Influence in Public Affairs, International Comparisons 201

Table 40 Expected Future Influence in Public Affairs, Ontario 1973   202

Table 41 Expected Future Equality in Society, International Comparisons   204

Table 42 Expected and Desired Future Equality of Incomes, Ontario 1973 and 1978 204

Table 43 Expected and Desired Extent of Future Change in Educational
          Institutions, Ontario 1973   206

Table 44 Expected and Desired Future Public Influence in Educational
          Planning, Ontario 1973   211

Table 45 Desired Freedom of Choice in Future Education, Ontario 1973   213

List of Figures

Figure 1   Main Objective Positions in Advanced Capitalist Production Relations   54

Figure 2   Graph of Dominant Relations Between Typical Positions in
The Class Structure of Advanced Capitalist Production   59

Figure 3   General Class Structure of The 18+ Ontario Population, 1978–80   66

Figure 4   Historical Class-based Educational Ideologies in England   108

List of Figures

Introduction

The primary purpose of this book is to contribute to understanding of the influences that class relations in contemporary advanced capitalist societies have on educational practices. A framework is suggested for the development of systematic historical materialist analyses of class relations generally in such societies, and in educational settings in particular. Most of the book represents an effort to begin to apply this framework in a *macro* level analysis of how major class forces help to generate, reproduce and change what goes on within the school systems of advanced capitalism. While the focus of the current study is on class relations, it should be stressed that this historical materialist framework remains open to the consideration of other irreducible aspects of social reality – namely sex, ethnicity, and age-based social relations – both generally and in terms of their own unique influences on educational practices.

There is now a substantial body of historiographic research on the development of schooling in capitalism over the past one hundred and fifty years, and a similarly rich body of ethnographic literature on class relations within contemporary school settings. But the theoretical formulations emerging to date from such studies, as well as from those inquiries more abstractly couched in a nascent Marxist political economy of education, have remained quite vague or assertive about the composition of the class forces effecting the schools, and the fundamental dimensions of educational relations that are involved in this process. The current study attempts to make several specific contributions in this regard. First, an empirically grounded analysis of class relations and class structures in advanced capitalist societies is offered as a basis for studying class differences in educational practices. Secondly, primary dimensions of educational relations (that is cultural ownership of the schools, and the social and technical relations of the schooling process) and the respective educational interests of different classes are identified; the recent educational ideologies articulated on these dimensions by spokespersons for major class groupings in one advanced capitalist setting are analyzed in some detail. Thirdly, the expressed popular sentiments of people in different class positions with regard to issues bearing on these three primary dimensions of schooling, especially in the current crisis, are also analyzed. The basic intent is to move beyond both mechanical structuralism and cultural subjectivism to begin to identify the real historical class force largely outside the schools that are shaping the educational future.

In Chapter One, some of the most apparent features of the current economic and educational crisis in advanced capitalism are summarized. Recent types of intellectual interpretations of education/society relations are then reviewed in relation to the changing historical context and researchers' own contrasting social alignments. The main part of the chapter sets out the basic assumptions, method of inquiry and model of social totality of the historical materialist approach to be used in the present study. This approach is then applied to begin to interpret the current educational crisis.

In Chapter Two, the historical basis for the existence of classes is discussed, especially in relation to the development of material production. Advanced capitalist societies are situated within the world capitalist economy, and the main class positions in advanced capitalist production relations are identified and empirical profiles considered. The empirical focus of much of the remainder of the text is on Canada and especially on English Canada's 'industrial heartland' of Ontario, largely because in several respects my own empirical studies provide the most relevant sources of evidence. In the rest of Chapter Two, the particular development of the Canadian class structure is reviewed. Classes are then considered more inclusively as lived associations constituted in household and community relations as well as in production; in short, as social circles involving both cores and peripheries. Finally, relations between class position and school attainment are examined and implications for differential class support of the established form of schooling are suggested.

Chapter Three attempts to provide a conceptual basis for critical analyses of class-based educational ideologies. First, ideologies are situated generally as aspects of social reality, and distinguished from both lived cultures and ideological domination or 'hegemony'. The history of class conflict over education in capitalism is briefly noted and the three previously cited primary dimensions of educational relations in advanced capitalism are identified. With reference to these underlying dimensions of everyday educational practices, the educational interests of capitalist and working classes are then compared. The rest of the chapter characterizes themes expressed in current class-based educational ideologies in terms of these underlying dimensions. This empirical analysis relies on the public discourse of spokespersons for the most organized cores of the capitalist and working classes in English Canada.

The purpose of Chapter Four is to provide some indicators of the current subjective dispositions of those in different class positions regarding acceptance of, or support for, changing existing educational provisions. The primary means of this assessment are recent mass opinion surveys in Ontario – perhaps the only large-scale opinion surveys in the advanced capitalist world in recent years to deal in a sustained way with organizational alternatives for education. The design and limitations of such surveys and the immediate historical context of the most recent one are first briefly outlined. The remainder of this chapter presents the survey findings on class differences in attitudes concerning educational financing, and issues related to the primary dimensions of cultural ownership and the social and technical relations of the schooling process.

Chapter Five offers critical inventories of alternative images of the educational and social future that might be considered, especially by working class and other subordinate groups, in efforts to initiate change. First, the sorts of visions of the future that have been articulated by both bourgeois and socialist intellectuals are reviewed, and a number of limitations noted. Then, on the basis of the only available international survey and my own Ontario survey, empirical assessment is made of the images of the educational and social future held by ordinary citizens and particularly by rank and file members of different class positions. The limitations and 'latent potentialities' of such popular sentiments about the future are noted.

Finally, Chapter Six briefly raises some strategic questions that are invariably implicated in the development of progressive educational and social movements in advanced capitalist societies, and which frequently have been given little attention. Any movement that aspires to sustained progressive change must have an adequate critical understanding of the existing society, a vision of a desirable future, and a carefully thought out strategy for getting there. The chapters in this book are intended to offer some resource materials for such purposes.

Chapter 1

Educational Facts and Intellectual Interpretations

This chapter begins with an inventory of some of the most evident features of the current difficulties or 'crisis' in state-run, mass-based school systems and in the relations between this form of education and its societal context in the major industrial market societies.[1] Then an attempt is made to characterize, in very general terms, the different types of intellectual interpretations of education/society relations that have been developed in the post-World War II period and to suggest the association of such respective interpretations with the changing historical context and the divergent social alignments of educational researchers themselves. Next, the basic elements of the historical materialist approach that will be used in this book to interpret education/society relations in advanced capitalism are presented.[2] In the final section, this historical materialist approach is applied to begin to develop a critical analysis of the current educational crisis.

The Current Educational Crisis

School is not dead in advanced capitalist societies, but it is certainly not very healthy. Over the past generation, the incidence of such individual student acts as classroom violence, truancy, vandalism and dropping out has generally increased in the state-run, mass-based school systems of all western industrial countries. More collective expressions of unrest with existing school provisions and related social institutions have frequently appeared in such forms as rebellious youth cultures, student political movements, increasingly militant teachers' organizations often bonding together with other state workers and clients to fight budget cuts, and parent and other interest group movements pressing for various types of reorientation of the schooling process. Mass opinion polls document a growing general sentiment of dissatisfaction with the schools. Educational debate in both Western Europe and North America has become increasingly focused on basic organizational concerns. Among the fundamental issues on which there is now visible, persistent dispute in most countries are the following: whether control of the school system should be more centralized or more localized; whether the learning process should emphasize 'the basics', rigid discipline and universal standards, or curricula built from children's actual experiences and cultural differences; whether equality of educational opportunity should be more fully provided through affirmative action measures for disadvantaged groups or, conversely, whether merit criteria should be more exclusively emphasized in the light of growing economic demand for highly trained scientific and technical personnel; and whether specific job skills or more general adaptive skills should be emphasized in linking school programmes more effectively with the world of work. While the particular character of existing school provisions and the growing patterns of criticism may differ substantially, in each of these countries a number of institutional features of schooling that were previously taken for granted by all are now being questioned by many. Government commissions to propose the institutional reorganization of various levels of the school system have recently been established within most countries. In short, we are in the midst of an 'educational crisis'.

In many respects, such a situation is not unique. Even the most cursory glance at the history of public schooling since its inception, less than two centuries ago, reveals recurrent periods of intense criticism of the adequacy of established forms of schooling to meet evident social and economic needs. Revisionist educational historians have now extensively re-examined some of the major nineteenth century periods of educational conflict and documented the often divergent interests of leading business and professional groups involved in criticizing and transforming the dominant institutional forms of state schooling. Within the twentieth century, such conflicts have been somewhat less evident and more muted, as they have been largely encapsulated within a single, taken-for-granted general form of schooling. As the leading revisionist, Michael Katz, noted for the United States that by 1880:

> American education had acquired its fundamental structural character-
> istics, they have not altered since. Public education was universal,
> tax-supported, free, compulsory, bureaucratically arranged, class
> based, and racist.[3]

Moreover, within this general form of schooling a number of more specific organizational features have been quite fully institutionalized over the past hundred years with little serious dispute. These include: full-time attendance; age grouping; an increasing reliance on teacher-dominated classroom instruction of age groups, with declining assistance by home instruction or student monitors; the graded curriculum; extensive and standardized supervision of students; expansion of the size of schools, school systems and administrative hierarchies; and the extension of the school day and of the extra-curricular responsibilities assumed by school staffs.[4]

Nevertheless, periodic educational crises have remained discernible. Marxist scholars, in particular, have begun to analyze systematic connections between economic crises and educational reform movements in this century. The most seminal work, by Samuel Bowles and Herbert Gintis, focuses on the progressive education movement at the turn of the century and the current period of 'educational change and ferment' in the US, as well as the nineteenth century era of the common school reform. They conclude that:

> ... the main periods of educational reform coincided with, or immediately followed, periods of deep social unrest and political conflict. The major reform periods have been preceded by the opening up of a significant divergence between the ever-changing social organization of production and the structure of education ... The three turning points in US educational history which we have identified all correspond to particularly intense periods of struggle around the expansion of capitalist production relations.[5]

While subsequent critics have justifiably scored the simplistic formulation of Bowles and Gintis' 'correspondence principle', their major empirical conclusions remain largely unassailed.[6] Indeed, at least in the most recent periods of economic crisis, some of these connections have become clear enough to many educators themselves. As Merle Curti observed in 1935, in his historical review of the social ideas of leading American educators:

> The depression of 1929 and subsequent years ... like the World War, made educators of every shade of opinion more socially conscious and more willing to assume new responsibilities for building a better and more truly democratic order. The depressions of 1837 and 1857 had stimulated some educators to assume special responsibility for preventing such catastrophes in the future, but the debacle of 1929 had more far reaching effects. The economic crisis, as Judd reminded his educational colleagues, 'has made us all aware in a new and vivid way that schools are a part of the general social order and that the curriculums of schools and their methods of dealing with pupils are largely determined by the conditions of life outside the schools'.[7]

A similar awareness has re-emerged in the current period. As the Swedish comparative researcher, Torsten Husen, puts it:

> The most evident symptom of changed attitudes towards education is the wave of criticism from both left and right that swept many countries in the late 1960s. The former consensus about the benefits of traditional schooling and the conviction that education always represented an intrinsic good were gone. So was the belief that education was the main instrument for bringing about a better society ... A by-product of the debate was the growing awareness that the schools of a given country operate within a given social and economic framework, whereas prior to the 1960s school problems were often conceived of as purely pedagogical ones that emerged in a socio-

economic vacuum. This widening of the perspective has been beneficial to the debate, because it has led to the realization that problems besetting the educational system are in the last analysis social problems which cannot be solved simply by taking action only within the walls of the school.[8]

Typically, it has been some time after the onset of such economic crises that educational leaders have been moved to reassess established educational practices. Curti further observed that:

> ... it was only in the later stages of the depression, when business support was increasingly withdrawn from the schools, that educators were thoroughly aroused regarding the educational, social and economic crisis: and that even then their attitude and program, with some exceptions, was more conservative than that which the Federal Council of Churches took in September, 1931.[9]

Similarly today, it has been some years after the onset of the current period of economic stagnation and fiscal crisis, and in the face of substantial education budget cuts, that educational leaders once again have become concerned enough about such symptoms to consider seriously any basic reforms of established organizational forms of schooling.

However, the current 'educational crisis' is also quite distinct in several respects. It is much more extensive and more sustained than previous periods of educational conflict. In reviewing the history of conflict in the British educational system, Tapper and Salter conclude that:

> Although past educational issues have resulted in bitter controversies ... they appear to have been successfully contained in terms of their duration, the range of the interested parties involved, the confining of the debate to established elites, and the limitation of its wider societal impact. This is in direct contrast to the present situation for the conflict is continuous, it is not confined to the elite levels of a few interested parties, and the issues being raised have direct implications for the overall character of the society.[10]

While Tapper and Salter may have seriously underestimated the role of subordinate groups in stimulating earlier educational reforms,[11] there can be little doubt that the current 'debate' involves far more active participants than any previous crisis period. In contrast to the 1930s, the vast majority of the 'eligible' age group are now enrolled in secondary schools, higher education has expanded very rapidly to include at least a quarter of the 20 to 24 age group in most advanced capitalist societies, and the majority of the older population have attained some measure of secondary schooling and come to regard continuing access to advanced schooling as an entitlement for their children. Post-World War II trends in participation rates are shown in table 1. Clearly, a far greater proportion of the population stands to be directly affected by persistent cutbacks and reorganization initiatives than in prior crises.

Table 1   Post-War Trends in Educational Participation

Country	Secondary School Gross Enrolment Ratio*					Higher Education Gross Enrolment Ratio+				
	1950	1960	1970	1975	1978	1950	1960	1970	1975	1977
United States	77	86	99	98	97	20	32	49	58	56
Japan	71	78	91	92	93	5	9	17	25	29
West Germany	–	53	66	–	94	5	6	13	24	25
France	38	46	74	84	83	6	10	20	24	26
Italy	17	34	61	70	73	6	7	17	25	27
United Kingdom	51	66	73	83	83 (1976)	5	9	14	19	–
Canada	31	56	76	91	89 (1977)	8	16	35	39	38

Source: UNESCO *Statistical Yearbook*, Paris: UNESCO, 1980 and various years; and for 1950 higher education ratios, OECD *Development of Higher Education 1950–1967: Analytical Report*, Paris: OECD, 1971.
* This ratio represents the total enrolment of all ages divided by the population of the specific age group which corresponds to the age group of secondary schooling in the respective country. The figures are not directly comparable across countries because of varying age limits.
+ This ratio represents the total enrolment of all ages divided by the population of the 20–24 age group.

Indeed, whereas in previous economic crises the secondary schools served only a minority of those eligible and higher education remained an elite preserve, the schools in the post-War period have become the central institution for socializing and selecting virtually all the young people of advanced capitalist societies into their adult pursuits. To reorient such a pervasive institution in response to economic crisis has become an extraordinarily difficult and delicate matter. In the wake of the post-War economic expansion, public expenditures on schooling in many of the industrial market economies of Western Europe and North America were permitted to increase their share of the GNP from two to three percent in the 1950s to six to eight percent in the late 1960s, including massive capital outlays to build new universities, colleges and urban schools. Educational expenditures grew much faster than economic productivity and considerably faster than total goverment revenues. The educational infrastructure established in the 1960s facilitated the unprecedented growth of higher education enrolments which continued throughout the early 1970s. With the economic stagnation of the 1970s, the increased productivity and enhanced life chances long associated with advanced schooling were gradually perceived to be false promises as more and more educated youths faced unemployment and extended underemployment. More generally, as growing numbers not only heard the many promises but experienced the reality of advanced schooling, various inadequacies and contradictions became widely evident. The situation had reached the point that, by the early 1970s, radical criticisms directed at the false identity between schooling and education as a generic human activity, and at the dominant general form of schooling, as well as proposals to abolish schools and create alternative forms of education for young people, began to be listened to seriously for the first time in over a century.[12] But by the early 1980s, the deschoolers have been largely forgotten. In a context in which the most palpable alternative to the current institution of schooling appears to be a reduced and reprivatized version of the same general form, popular sentiment in the advanced capitalist societies now appears to be preoccupied with trying to protect established levels of use of the schools. Indeed, after slow or negative enrolment growth in the late 1970s and in spite of growing financial constraints, new students are once more flocking to higher education in record numbers in some of these countries. In spite of their acknowledged inadequacies, these state-run, mass-based institutions remain widely regarded as the best available means to equip young people for life in these increasingly complex technological societies.

In the 1970s, with secondary schools established in virtually every large community and higher education institutions dotting every region in these societies, capital expenditure on schooling was much reduced. But aspirations for advanced education had become deeply rooted and, even though the job market contracted, educational certification remained a central criterion of occupational selection. Among the more direct constraints on any sustained initiatives to reduce current expenditures or enrolments in advanced schooling have been the commitments to existing teaching staff and to students already enrolled in existing programme streams, as well as the prospect of strong reactions by many others manifestly denied 'career' opportunities by such cutbacks. Table 2, which suggests general trends in public expenditures on schooling in relation to total government spending and to GNP during both the economic expansion that prevailed in the 1960s and the stagnation of the 1970s, is indicative of such constraints. The relative fiscal priority given to public education by the state has generally declined since the late 1960s as governments have been forced to intervene in the economic crisis by pouring funds into areas perceived to be in more urgent need, such as economic development and other social service programs. But even with deep cuts in capital spending on education, recurrent payroll expenditures for established teaching staffs have continued to grow. None of these countries was able significantly to reduce financial allocations to education in relation to economic productivity during this decade.

The major quantitative measures of economic performance have been consistently indicative of stagnation throughout the past decade in the major industrial market economies. Unemployment rates, however restrictively defined, have risen to the highest levels since the 1930s; unemployment rates are considerably higher. Inflation rates have generally doubled or tripled in comparison with the 1960s, while the growth of domestic production, especially

Table 2   Public Expenditure on Education as a Proportion of Public Expenditure and of Gross National Product.

Country	As per cent of Public Expenditure				As per cent of GNP				
	1960	1970	1975	1977	1950	1960	1970	1975	1977
United States	22.6	19.4	18.1	17.7	3.1	5.0	6.4	6.2	6.4
Japan	–	20.4	17.5	16.5	4.8	5.5	3.9	5.5	5.4
West Germany	13.5	12.0	9.1	8.8*	3.2	3.7	3.4	4.4	4.2
France	–	–	–	–	2.0	3.2	4.7	5.7	5.8
Italy	19.6	17.4	11.7	9.3*	2.4	4.9	4.3	5.0	5.1*
United Kingdom	20.0	14.1	14.0	14.3*	3.2	5.3	5.2	6.4	6.2*
Canada	–	–	–	–	3.1	6.1	8.5	7.9	8.0

* 1976 figures
Source: UNESCO, *Statistical Yearbook*, Paris: UNESCO, 1980 and various years.

in manufacturing, has been cut in half. The rate of new domestic investment has dropped even more sharply, to virtually zero growth in some countries. Meanwhile, the burgeoning of credit that had fuelled the post-war 'boom' has continued unabated in spite of tight money policies by some central governments, leading to a liquidity crisis increasingly expressed in terms of business failures and personal bankruptcies. Most of these tendencies are documented in table 3. It should be stressed here that such ten year averages simply indicate long-term trends, and mask the substantial cyclical variations within each period. On virtually all counts, economic conditions have worsened appreciably within the past several years.[13]

As implied above, state expenditure has continued to grow quite rapidly in spite of such private sector trends. The established universal entitlements not only to public schooling but also to medical care and various other social service programs have been major factors in the intractability of public finance to fiscal conservatism. The growth of interest payments on the public debt, a rise of military spending, the demand for economic development funds both to stimulate private investment and to bail out failing corporate enterprises, and the consequent growing failure of tax revolts and the ineffectiveness of the reprivatization strategies that have occurred to date in some countries to reduce the costs of government services, are also now quite widely regarded by analysts as important contributors to a quickly deepening fiscal crisis of the state.[14] The continuing decline of public confidence in all social institutions as detected by opinion polls, and the mounting emotional collective protests by small businessmen, homeowners, the unemployed, trade unions and others against these economic conditions and the lack of more remedial government actions, the riots of inner city youths, as well as the proliferation of both strident and escapist reactions to such rebellious social acts are all confirmations in more palpable human dimensions of the depth and extent of this general crisis in the major industrial market societies.

Table 3 Selected Indicators of the Economic Performance of Major Industrial Market Economies

	Average Unemployment Rate		Average Annual Inflation Rate		Annual Growth of Manufacturing Production		Average Annual Gross Domestic Investment Rate	
	1960–70	1970–80	1960–70	1970–79	1960–70	1970–79	1960–70	1970–79
United States	5.2	7.1	2.8	6.9	5.3	2.9	4.8	1.9
Japan	1.4	1.8	4.9	8.2	11.0	6.2	14..0	3.2
West Germany	1.1	3.5	3.2	5.3	5.4	3.0	4.1	0.9
France	1.6	4.6	4.2	9.6	6.6	3.7	7.3	2.0
Italy	2.9	4.6	4.4	15.6	7.2	3.0*	3.8	0.1
United Kingdom	2.2	5.0	4.1	13.9	3.4	0.6	5.0	0.8
Canada	5.7	7.7	3.1	9.1	6.7	3.5	5.8	4.5

* Estimate

Sources: For unemployment, calculated from OECD *Labour Force Statistics*, Paris: OECD, 1981 and various years; and OECD *Main Economic Indicators*, Paris: OECD, 1981 and various years.
For other indicators, the World Bank *World Development Report 1981*, London: Oxford University Press, 1981, Tables 1, 2 and 4.

How this generalized economic, fiscal and educational crisis will be resolved remains quite uncertain at this point. It is only in the last few years that the cumulative effects of economic and fiscal crises have become so serious that educational authorities have been compelled frontally to challenge assumed educational entitlements, not only by making large budget cutbacks and closing some state colleges, but also by openly contemplating the wholesale reorganization and reduction of established forms of schooling. This is a much more perilous pursuit than in previous educational crises because never before have the schools been such a pervasive bulwark of the existing social order.

Vantage Points, Alignments and Paradigms

Few of the preceding 'social facts' may be directly disputed by educational officials and researchers, but the pertinence they are granted and the interpretive uses to which they are put in explaining educational processes differs greatly among such intellectuals. Divergent interpretations of social reality generally become most evident in such periods of protracted social crisis, as does the tendency for such interpretations to be associated with different *vantage points* and *group alignments*. Vantage points denote actual locations within work relations and other spheres of social activity. Those in dominant, subordinate, and marginal or intermediate positions typically have different arrays and ranges of experience. Usually those securely lodged within a dominant group or tightly locked into a subordinate one have many restrictions on the range of experience upon which they draw to interpret society as a whole. Historically, the relatively comfortable material existence of dominant groups rarely appears to have provoked sustained efforts to interpret social life in their societies in penetrating terms, while the most subordinate groups – however intensely troubling their life experiences and however strong the impulse to make deeper sense of them – have hardly ever possessed the means to record their reflections for posterity. In any case, the most necessary condition of authentic social interpretation is a deep commitment to take social historical reality as the centre of attention, including an openness to the experiences of people in different locations from one's own, and to portraying this perceived reality in the observer's own terms rather than under patron's, market's, or state bureaucrats' criteria. To practice such inquiry is to think what many people have thought, to see what a lot of people have seen and, in some sense, to resonate what everybody already knows.[15] Thus, the most sensitive and enduring observations on the human condition have frequently come from among those who are most marginally or ambiguously placed within their societies (for example, petty bourgeois intellectuals, emigrés) and are thereby most open to their contradictory realities.

However, to have an intermediate vantage point is not necessarily to be objective, neutral, or non-aligned with particular social interest groups. Indeed, intermediately placed intellectuals have traditionally been most likely to produce works that either assume or complement the viewpoints of dominant groups, while they continue to insist on their own non-alignment. In this regard, Antonio Gramsci's distinction between organic and traditional intellectuals is highly relevant. Organic intellectuals align themselves with the interests of definite social groups or classes in their work and engage primarily in reflecting, organizing and directing the ideas and aspirations of that class, whereas traditional intellectuals take for granted the autonomy of their own work from any particular social group or class interests.[16] It should be clearly recognized that alignments are not fully constrained by vantage point and that, in particular, intellectuals with marginal vantage points can, and to varying degrees often do, align themselves not only with dominant groups and interests but also with subordinate ones. Intellectual interpretations are always socially contingent. It is therefore important to distinguish intellectuals both in terms of the dominant, subordinate or marginal vantage point from which they work, and in terms of whether they align themselves with their own social class, another one, the intellectual community *per se* or assume non-alignment, in order to appreciate their interpretations of social reality. While such alignment distinctions are applicable to all intellectuals, they are especially pertinent to appreciating scientists' and researchers' interpretations of social reality today, with large scientific institutions operating largely from intermediate social vantage points and with the non-alignment, autonomy and neutrality of science widely and often vehemently asserted as an article of faith.

The main point to be stressed here is that intellectuals aligned with major social groups can not only be genuine scientists but, indeed, often have been the most influential of scientists. Certainly, scientific contributions that have contradicted received knowledge and vested interests have often had to resonate the experience or interests of emergent social groups in order to be considered seriously both within the scientific community and society at large. Such associations are somewhat more easily observed over long historical periods and for the social sciences in particular. The reciprocal relations between the works of philosophers and political economists supporting capitalist relations (such as Bentham and the Mills, Adam Smith and David Ricardo) and the rise of the industrial bourgeoisie in Europe for example, represent a relatively well documented case.[17] Similarly, the alignments between the theoretical perspectives of the 'sociologists of the chair' and US corporate business interests around the turn of this century have also now been analyzed in some detail.[18] The few case studies of actual contemporary social relations of scientific practices strongly suggest that serious development of potential contributions to scientific knowledge is often very much a matter of the group interests and experience they resonate.[19] One of the most evident current examples is the array of research consultants attracted to the Trilateral Commission who, while clearly aligned with trans-national corporate capitalist interests, are carrying out detailed, empirically grounded investigations of the world capitalist economy and its governability in the current crisis.[20] Despite their narrow alignment and whatever propagandistic use may be made of their findings, such researchers themselves can remain primarily scientists rather than ideologues for capitalism. By the same token, those researchers who align themselves with broader subordinate groups are not necessarily disqualified as scientists by such alignments. While scientists who presume their neutrality are probably the preponderant majority in most fields, the development of science in achieving general social truths should be properly understood as the result of the cumulative works of aligned and non-aligned scientists using inter-subjectively verifiable methods *and* critically assessing the concepts, hypotheses and findings of those scientists with other 'values'; that is, other vantage points and otherwise aligned or non-aligned. All contemporary science remains class based in some sense, but a growing self-consciousness about the effects on past and present scientific work resulting not only from diverse particular methods and individual differences in perception but also from different vantage points and alignments can aid scientists in establishing real truths about the world.[21]

More specifically with regard to educational analyses, it is relevant to note that most school officials and researchers owe their own typically intermediate position to their success as students in the existing school system. While they commonly have remained non-aligned, they tend to have vested interests in maintaining the general form of this system for both themselves and their offspring.[22] Indeed, from the intermediate vantage point of most educators, it is generally considered both inappropriate and impolitic to assume anything but a neutral stance. Of course, as previously noted, in periods of economic crisis educators have often been pressed to make more explicit political choices. But interest alignments are actually much more pervasive. It has been one of the seminal contributions of the 'new sociology of education' of the past decade, most notably the work of Michael Young,[23] to begin to document the extent to which different social contexts and social interests have affected the nature of problem selection and the production of knowledge in ostensibly neutral educational research and practice.

Educational researchers, as all social analysts, may be classified most broadly in terms of the emphasis their interpretations tend to put on two fundamental dimensions of social reality, namely the relative pertinence given to social *structures* and to human *agency* and, secondly, the tendency to characterize society as a *consensual social order* or as comprised by *opposed interest groups*. With regard to the structure/agency duality, Alan Dawe has noted:

> ... the basic dualism of modern social experience, to which those voices from everyday life have testified, has been articulated in sociology in the form of a basic dualism of sociological thought and analysis on which the entire history of the discipline has turned. Throughout that history, there has been a manifest conflict between two types of social analysis, variously labelled as being between the organismic and mechanistic approaches, methodological collectivism and individualism, holism and atomism, the conservative and eman-cipatory perspectives and so on. The debates about these issues are central and perennial in sociological discourse and, at root, they are all different versions of the fundamental debate about the abiding conflict between the domination of the system and the exertion of human agency.[24]

To put the polarity most starkly, in the structural approach 'social actors are pictured as being very much at the receiving end of the social system. In terms of their existence and nature as social beings, their social behaviour and relationships, and their very sense of personal identity as human beings, they are determined by it'.[25] In contrast, the human agency approach '... con-ceptualizes the social system as the derivative of social action and interaction, a social world produced by its members, who are thus pictured as active, purposeful, self-and socially creative beings'.[26] There appear to have been predictable inclinations among analysts to stress structural perspectives in periods of social stability and human agency in periods of crisis.

Cross-cutting this duality is another one between consensus and conflict perspectives.[27] In consensual order approaches, individuals are regarded as generally sharing common value orientations toward their society and attention is devoted to identifying the functional requisites of social equilibrium and the mechanisms through which such homeostasis is established and reproduced. A central assumption is that 'given the necessity of order and the reality of consensus, all members of a society are expected to conform, adapt, or adjust to these legitimate social requirements'.[28] In conflict perspectives, the opposed interests of different groups or classes are stressed and primary attention is given to distinguishing the conditions and concerns of particular groups and to the ways in which they relate to more dominant or subordinate groups. The contrasting central assumption is that 'given the necessity of change and the reality of constraint, the legitimacy of social order is in question. Conformity, adaptation, and adjustment become problematic'.[29] While consensus perspectives have prevailed in western social science throughout most of this century, conflict approaches have become increasingly emphasized within the past generation.

Paradigms refer to models of inquiry that guide scientific work, providing a conceptual framework for understanding the phenomena to be studied, indicating the sorts of questions that should be asked and the relevant types of relationships, methods of inquiry and bodies of evidence.[30] In the realm of educational research, the only fully developed and applied paradigm in the post-war industrial market societies has emphasized the structure/order combination. This mode of social interpretation, which has commonly been labelled as '*structural-functionalism*', has predominated until very recently in the social sciences generally and has typically been practised by traditional, non-aligned intellectuals. As Christopher Hurn has characterized its use in education:

> Until a decade or so ago one major interpretation of the role of schooling in modern society prevailed almost unchallenged. This theory, which I shall call the *functional paradigm*, offers both an explanation and a justification for the role of educational institutions. In simplest terms, the functional paradigm argues that schools are essential institutions in modern society because they perform two crucial functions: first, schools represent a rational way of sorting and selecting talented people so that the most able and motivated attain the highest status positions; second, schools teach the kind of cognitive skills and norms essential for the performance of most roles in a society increasingly dependent upon knowledge and expertise. The functional paradigm is largely an elaboration of these two apparently straightforward propositions.[31]

Interpretations of schooling within this paradigm have generally assumed 'business values' of pyramidal authority and methods of efficient management, and have often utilized an explicit conceptual model of systems analysis – with the raw inputs (children) to be shaped into required 'outputs' (efficient workers and responsible citizens); structural Marxist analysts of schooling, while critical of the capitalist social order, have tended to make comparable assumptions.[32] But, as the current crisis has deepened, the functional paradigm has faced growing intellectual criticism for its failure to account for many of the social facts referred to above.

Thus, while both traditional intellectuals and those aligned with dominant groups have typically continued to assume a consensual order model of society, they have devoted growing attention to questions of human agency. For the most part this has involved detailed consideration of more effective mechanisms of management and control by educational authorities.[33] Such a 'top down' preoccupation with consensual order assumptions also remains evident in the critical analyses of schooling offered by those traditional intellectuals who have become disturbed enough by dehumanizing and inequitable conditions of institutionalized schooling to make populist appeals for its abolition. This critical perspective, which persistently stresses *elite domination*, Hurn rather glibly terms the 'radical paradigm' and notes that it:

> ... portrays schools not as more or less rational instruments for sorting and selecting talented people, but as institutions that perpetuate inequality and convince lower class groups of their inferiority. In the radical paradigm what is important about schooling is not the cognitive and intellectual skills schools teach, but the class-related values and attitudes that they reinforce. In this view, schools are instruments of elite domination, agencies that foster compliance and docility rather than independent thought and human values.[34]

Many traditional intellectuals are thus now quite prepared to criticize strongly the existing school system or the management practices of administrative agents as well as to contemplate basic reforms which could overcome current problems. But they still show little inclination to admit the existence of divergent social interests or actively opposed social forces either inside or outside the school.

Among those researchers who have explicitly aligned themselves with subordinate groups, a conflict perspective which regards society as constructed from opposed interests has usually been emphasized. During the stability, or quiescence, of the immediate post-war period, this perspective was commonly combined with a strong emphasis on the immutability of the social system, in the works of the rare scholars who were clearly so aligned. The study of the popular culture of the English working classes by Richard Hoggart offers a classic example. Hoggart looked at education and culture in a more inclusive sense than that of formal schooling, and he observed such phenomena from his own working class background. He noted that:

> There has been plenty of violent action by the authorities in England, especially during the first half of the nineteenth century. But on the whole, and particularly in this century, the sense of 'Them' among working-class people is not of a violent or harsh thing ... Yet there exists, with some reason, a feeling among working-class people that they are often at a disadvantage, that the law is in some things readier against them than against others, and that petty laws weigh more heavily against them than against some other groups ... Towards 'Them' generally, as towards the police, the primary attitude is not so much fear as mistrust; mistrust accompanied by a lack of illusions about what 'They' will do for one....
>   When people feel that they cannot do much about the main elements in their situation, feel it not necessarily with despair or disappointment

or resentment but simply as a fact of life, they adopt attitudes toward shadow, a life without a constant and pressing sense of the larger situation. The attitudes remove the main elements in the situation to the realm of natural laws, the given and raw, the almost implacable, material from which a living has to be carved. Such attitudes, at their least adorned a fatalism or plain accepting, are generally below the tragic level; they have too much of the conscript's lack of choice about them. But in some of their forms they have dignity.[35]

This perspective, which might be termed the *systemic subordination* tradition, saw little relevance in scrutinizing the institutional processes of formal school systems directly. Rather, it was preoccupied with examaning the distinctive adaptations of the working classes to such 'natural' laws as were presumed to prevail in dominant societal institutions, as well as with documenting the persistence beneath or beyond them of residual working class cultures.

With the expansion of post-secondary schooling, educational researchers of working class origins have become somewhat less rare. As the generalized crisis since the early 1970s has made many inequities and inconsistencies of established educational organizations and practices more obvious, growing numbers of intermediately-placed intellectuals have also aligned themselves with subordinate groups in their work. The increasing evidence of problematic and contested aspects in educational and social relations has lead such researchers to search for a more active theoretical perspective which incorporates working class and other subordinated groups as agents in the continuing construction of their own and the larger social reality. A leading example is the work of the Centre for Contemporary Cultural Studies at the University of Birmingham which was founded by Richard Hoggart himself in the mid 1960s. Under the later leadership of Stuart Hall, the Centre has increasingly tried to conduct cultural analyses that are more organically linked with the full experience of subordinate groups in capitalist society and that focus on explaining how particular orderings of collective cultures come to be produced and sustained as a result of concrete sets of practices and relations. Such practices include both the constituting of a particular cultural order as dominant *and* '... the active subordination of alternatives – their marginalization and incorporation into a dominant structure: hence, also, the resistances, antagonisms and struggles which result from regulation'.[36] The Centre's most recent analysis of post-war English educational policy offers the most fully developed expression of this perspective. As the authors summarize:

> Human beings are implicated in these social relations, but *actively*; because the relations are unequal or asymmetrical, activities involve struggle. For this reason, the power of dominant interests is never secure; it always has to be won. Following Gramsci, we use the term 'hegemony' to sum up this process on a societal level. Hegemony involves securing both the conditions for future capitalist production and the consent of the subordinated population to the social and

cultural implications of 'progress'. It is exercised not only through law and coercion, but also through 'educative' processes in a larger sense, including schooling, the media and, centrally, political parties. It necessitates the building of alliances that may be active in promoting new solutions. Hegemony is not uniquely a product of 'the state' but involves the institutions of 'civil society' too.

If hegemony refers to the overall relations of force in a society, we wish to use the term 'educational settlement' to refer to the balance of forces in and over schooling. Settlements entail, at this 'regional' rather than 'global' level, some more or less enduring set of solutions to capital's educational needs, the putting together of a dominant alliance of forces, and a more widespread recruitment of popular support or inducement of popular indifference.

Settlements are highly unstable and deeply contradictory arrangements which easily pass into crises. One way to understand the history of educational policy is in terms of the succession of crises and settlements.[37]

Similar approaches, also emphasizing a conflict model and the role of human agency in constructing and reproducing educational institutions, are being developed in other advanced capitalist societies as well.[38] This perspective, which could be called the *contested subordination* view, would appear to be the one most 'in tune with the times'.

All four of these general types of interpretive tendencies then are evident in the social scientific study of education today. Such tendencies are seldom as starkly distinguished as suggested by the polar cases cited here; many current works can be read as tentative admixtures of these elements. Indeed, as the contested subordination perspective itself implies, both structure/agency and order/conflict remain persistent dualities of social existence. Which of these alternative emphases the next dominant paradigm of educational thought will assume and what sorts of leading propositions will be involved now depend very much on ensuing historical events, and upon the effectiveness of intellectuals in developing such respective types of interpretation in relation to the major social forces involved in these events.

A Historical Materialist Approach

My own vantage point is that of an intermediately placed university intellectual[39] with a petty bourgeois ancestry of Irish emigré farmers and English Canadian shopkeepers, and direct personal origins in the family of a similarly ambiguously located, and highly scrupulous, municipal civil servant. I have consequently been occupied for as long as I can remember with contradictions between choice and constraint in social existence and especially in political practice. I developed, very early, strong sympathies for the life conditions of subordinate groups in Canadian society and abroad, and increasingly have aligned my work with their social interests. The intellectual tradition that I have found to be most compatible with such predispositions has been historical materialism. I will attempt to convey my general understanding of this perspective in some detail in this section.

Historical materialism had its most vital intellectual origins in the works of Marx and Engels in the mid-nineteenth century. Many marginalized intellectuals chose to align themselves with subordinate groups in this period of widespread social unrest. Karl Marx's particular vantage point as a petty bourgeois German intellectual who became an occasionally employed emigré in France, Belgium and England did facilitate a unique intellectual synthesis which drew on primary sources from German philosophic, French socialist and British political economic modes of thought. Such intellectual origins of historical materialism have often been cited. But the historical material origins of this intellectual perspective have been much less widely appreciated. Most critically, the formative years of Marx's thought were at the historical conjucture in which working class movements in major European countries made their first sustained appearances.[40] In particular, Marx began to study political economy and to develop the basic features of his materialist theory of history in Paris in the early 1840s at the same time as he came into intimate contact with the artisanal community there, especially revolutionary organizations of French and German workers. At the same time, Engels lived alongside the English working class in Manchester and in contact with the most advanced working class movement, the Chartists. Marx and Engels' experience of this real social world of concrete materiality and struggle was later deepened most notably by engagement in the German workers' strike of 1848 and participation in the International Working Men's Association of the 1860s. This observation is not intended to deny the genius involved in Marx's critique of political economy, but rather to recognize that central categories of his inquiry, such as surplus value, could only be recognized and systematized from the standpoint of the working class and on the basis of its experience.[41]

The historical materialist tradition regards social reality in terms of the ensemble of relationships that people have established, and continually either reproduce or modify, with each other and with their non-human environment. Humanity's relations with what it produces, including material objects, techniques, institutions and ideologies, are seen as the central problematic of human life. The most distinguishing substantive feature of this perspective has been the view that the relationship of the owners of the means of production to the direct producers provides the essential basis for the social construction of historical societies. Marx's most general expression of this view was probably the following:

> The specific economic form, in which unpaid surplus-labour is pumped out of the direct producers, determines the relationship of rulers and ruled, as it grows directly out of production itself and, in turn, reacts upon it as a determining element. Upon this, however, is

founded the entire formation of the economic community which grows up out of the production relations themselves, thereby simultaneously its specific political form. It is always the direct relationship of the owners of the conditions of production to the direct producers – a relation always naturally corresponding to a definite stage in the development of the methods of labour and thereby its social productivity – which reveals the innermost secret, the hidden basis of the entire social structure, and with it the political form of the relation of sovereignty and dependence, in short the corresponding specific forms of the state. This does not prevent the same economic basis – the same from the standpoint of its main conditions – due to innumerable different empirical circumstances, natural environment, racial relations, external historical influences, etc., from showing infinite variations and gradations in appearance, which can be ascertained only by analysis of the empirically given circumstances.[42]

Marx came to regard the task of scientific history to be the determination of the tendential laws regarding the movement of different epochs of history. He clearly recognized that general, abstract, historically indeterminate laws do not exist in history. A scientific conception of history could only be developed through the process of establishing the historically determinate laws specific to each epoch, and their corresponding concretely developed categories. In this perspective, human societies are generated, shaped, reproduced and transformed by historically specific processes of class struggle. Such conflicts stem from the *particular* nature of relationships between those who do the work of producing the society's means of subsistence and material development and those who claim the right to determine and allocate what is surplus in these production activities. The capitalist mode of production clearly prevails in societies in which workers generally do not possess the active means of production themselves but must sell their labour power in the labour market in order to reproduce themselves. In such societies, the major means of production are owned by the buyers of labour power and the production process is organized so that they can claim the new value created by labour power and accumulate part of it through the sale of the resultant goods and services commodities. At the most fundamental level, capitalist societies are driven and sustained by the extraction of this *surplus value* (in the form of unpaid labour time) from workers producing saleable commodities, and by the allocation of much of the surplus value realized (in market exchange as monetary profit) into activities to produce more surplus value rather than unproductive consumption.[43]

As Marx saw it, the most essential contradictory relationship in capitalist societies is therefore the *class struggle between capital and labour*, with capitalist owners attempting to take over ever more potential means of production and to claim more of the surplus value produced by labour, while workers try to retain control of the production process and keep for their own consumption as much as possible of the value produced. A second basic contradictory relationship is *inter-capitalist competition*. Private firms must sell their commodities against those of other firms and so must limit their operating costs accordingly; but each firm must also try to avoid unrestrained competitive pressure in order to ensure sustained capital accumulation, with resulting tendencies toward monopoly concentration, price leadership, and governmental market regulation. Thirdly, both class struggle and inter-capitalist competition impel capitalists to encourage the *development of the capacity of the society's productive forces* (that is the relation between human labour and the means of production to transform nature) while striving for private control over this production process. The amount of human labour required to produce a given amount of commodities tends to be reduced through replacement by more cost-efficient and dependable mechanized means of production. Such machines can, until their obsolescence, only transmit into the commodities the same amount of value already embodied in them. Therefore, even as the mass of surplus value produced with expanded capitalist production grows, the relative amount of surplus value to value invested and the related of profit will tend to decline.[44]

Marx's own major task was to identify and explicate these dominant *economic* forms and relations of the capitalist epoch of production. His scientific study of this epoch, culminating in *Capital*, was as Jairvs Banaji has summarized:

> . . . nothing else than the rigorous, systematic investigation of the laws of motion of capitalist production, in the course of which a series of simple abstractions ('wage-labour' money, etc.) were historically concretized as bourgeois relations of production, or abstractions determinate to capitalism as a mode of production; that is, reconstituted as 'concrete categories', as historically determinate social forms. It follows that modes of production are impenetrable at the level of simple abstractions. The process of 'true abstraction' is simultaneously a process of 'concretization,' of the definition of specific historical laws of motion . . . Taken as a whole, across its various stages, the substance of Marx's analysis lies in its definition of the laws of motion of capitalist production: the production and accumulation of surplus value, the revolutionization of the labour process, the production of relative surplus value on the basis of a capitalistically-constituted labour process, the compulsion to increase the productivity of labour, etc. The 'relations of capitalist production' are the relations which express and realize these laws of motion at different levels of the social process of production . . . As modes of production are only the definite totality of historical laws of motion, relations of production become a function of the given mode of production. The character of any definite type of production relations is, in short, impossible to determine until these laws of motion are themselves determined.[45]

This persistent effort to identify contingent, historically determinate abstractions underlying and animating simple abstractions distinguishes Marx's method of inquiry from that of most other social scientists, friend or foe of his revolutionary commitment to the working class. On the one hand are all those preoccupied with simple abstractions *per se*, ranging from social relativists such as ethnomethodologists concerned with reconstructing common sense interpretations of social reality to naturalistic materialists who regard intellectual concepts as naively realistic impressions of objects themselves. On the other hand are all those formalist approaches that have reified particular concepts into universal abstractions and timeless logics which are then presumed to underlie surface appearances in varied historical phenomena; this has been the dominant intellectual tendency of bourgeois science as well as both Western and Soviet Marxism throughout most of the twentieth century.[46] Certainly many intellectuals who profess to work from explicit historical materialist premises tend to turn the determinate abstractions that were Marx's points of arrival into points of departure of timeless validity for widely varied social studies and hence into formalistic abstractions.

This is not to suggest that exhaustive historical studies are required whenever determinate abstractions are to be used. Many of the concrete economic categories and laws of motion that Marx discerned in the 1860s, largely on the basis of the English case, may still be very operative as capitalist relations of production have taken more fully developed or 'adequate' forms in the advanced sectors of the contemporary world economy.[47] The point is to *continue* to regard laws of motion as historically contingent, not merely to seek the 'facts' to further apply or verify them but, in studies of whatever historical or contemporary scope, to assess whether the extant social forms and simple abstractions actually do correspond with such previously established determinate abstractions. Thus, historical materialist studies of contemporary capitalist societies can draw on the analytical distinctions and determinate abstractions established by Marx, but should always verify and be prepared to modify them through reference to concrete social reality, and never presume that any *a priori* set of abstractions is adequate to reproduce this reality.

Indeed, historical materialism is more accurately regarded as a methodological postulate than as an intellectual paradigm claiming to comprehend fully, or to provide timeless concepts capable of comprehending, concrete social reality. It is in this methodological sense that one should understand Marx's oft-quoted statement that 'it is not the consciousness of men that determines their existence, but their social existence that determines their consciousness'.[48] As Alfred Sohn-Rethel has aptly observed:

Read as a statement of an inherent truth Marx's sentence is worth less than nothing. It is to link up two questions each begging the other. To know how to judge consciousness we are referred to social existence, but to know about social existence we are referred to consciousness. Understood, however, as a methodological postulate the sentence says

23

everything. For this interacting reference is precisely the movement we have to carry out in our actual search. The Marxist method in *Capital* is the continuous reference of concept to reality, of reality to ideology . . .

The reality, then, to which Marx critically opposed the various forms of consciousness of men is the historical one of their own social existence. It is not 'matter' or the 'external material world independent of any consciousness'. Our notions of things and the concepts in which we undertake their systematization are historical products themselves. So are science, mathematics, natural philosophy, etc.[49]

Whatever the subsequent variations in historical conditions of social existence, Marx's use of this method has left an irredicible legacy to those who wish to understand – from the standpoint of subordinate groups – both the antagonism *and* the unity that have been inherent in the social reality of all historical societies. What he did was to uncover the pivotal basis of the existence and contradictory development of classes in the distinction between necessary and surplus labour and in the extraction and appropriation of surplus labour. As Goran Therborn has recently summarized Marx's view of economic classes:

[Classes] are the bearers of one and the same exploitative mode of production. The two [polar] classes of such a mode of production presuppose and precondition each other, and their relationship is not just logical, but material – between exploiter and exploited, oppressor and oppressed. The classes are the two necessary poles of a common, specific mode of exploitation and oppression. Their interrelationship and their struggle are therefore determined by the development of this mode of production, a development which occurs in and through the struggle between the classes, as Marx demonstrates in the first volume of *Capital* (struggles over the working day, the introduction and use of machinery, wage levels, and the accumulation of capital). An exploitative mode of production, then, is contradictory in the sense that it is at the same time both a specific unity of opposing classes, of immediate producers and appropriators of surplus labour, and a conflict and struggle of these opposing classes.[50]

In sum, Marx's mature work has been of such enduring relevance because its analysis does not depend on speculative philosophical concepts but on real historical abstractions regarding the material production basis of society. He can thereby proceed to comprehend, and we can continue to build from his exposition of, fundamental animating aspects of actual social relations in capitalist societies. These are the real determinate abstraction of surplus value (which is predominantly thought of in capitalism in the guise of 'profits', and which wageworkers have sometimes identified in such terms are 'getting a bit of our own back') and the tendential historical laws of its extraction from labour power.

There have been a great many creative developments as well as sterile departures in historical materialist thought since Marx's time.[51] The most significant development for Marxist scholarship in the past generation probably has been the flowering of historiographic and ethnographic studies. The great numbers of new historical and empirical studies taking the vantage point of subordinate groups are providing a much more comprehensive basis for historical materialist analyses. The recent flourishing of such Marxist and non-Marxist historiography and ethnography is undoubtedly related to the increasingly evident difficulties these groups have in reconstituting themselves in such crisis conjunctures. These conditions have led some critical Marxist scholars to question seriously the adequacy of their established intellectual perspectives and categories for fully reflecting working class vantage points on social relations in capitalism. As Stanley Aronowitz poses the issue:

> ... the result of most Marxist theory is to focus on the systematic coherence of late capitalism, an approach that corresponds at the metatheoretical level to a social physics. But unlike the most recent controversies within natural sciences, the moment of indeterminacy is missing. Marxism, in its logical manifestations, is geared to explanations of the past by means of formal criteria and to predicting the future on the basis of them. Subjectivity is constituted by a definite logic whose external parameters are fixed within a relatively narrow range of probabilities ...

> The class struggle is no longer understood as the confrontation of two historical actors, each obeying different, but mutually conditioned logics. The class struggle is recuperated by capital, becomes a condition for the reproduction of capital on a new level, involving both a displacement of labor as well as shifts in the location of production.

> In order to show the limitations of paradigmatic explanations and thus allow for the undecidability of historical development, to show its jagged side, *we must have another starting point – namely the notion that the working class is self-constituting as much as it is constituted by capital.* This viewpoint takes the class struggle seriously and restores the perspective of capital as a social relation in which class is not understood merely as the location of a social group within the production process, even a contradictory *location*, but is understood as the underlying logic of the undecidability of capitalist development. In order for this logic to function as a regulative principle, we must investigate the specific *praxis* of the working class ...

> By recognizing multiple logics, corresponding to Marx's concept that the capitalist mode of production is a system of *multiple determinations*, we refuse one of the metatheoretical assumptions of recent Marxist theory: that the structuration of the mode of production is tied to the classificatory logic of identity ... The spread of workers' resistance in the 1960s and 1970s ... is the result of an oppositional

cultural logic of the working class and the middle strata, the movements of women and youth that refuse the authoritarian logic of capital accumulation.[52]

Both historiographers and such critical Marxist theorists have increasingly emphasized what I have previously termed the 'contested subordination' perspective. Certainly, the self-constituting of the working class of advanced capitalism by its own material and ideational activity should now be recognized as one of the essential ingredients in an adequate account of social reality in such societies, including the reality of public schooling.

Gender and age-group as well as ethnic relations have also been increasingly recognized as essential features of social totality which are not simply reducible to or derivable from class relations *per se*. Women, minority ethnic groups, and young and old people all also experience particular forms of oppression and have had their vantage points submerged in advanced capitalist societies. All four forms of oppression (that is, class, gender, ethnic and age-based) are now experienced as an active totality. More generally, biological differences in sex and age always provide potential material bases for gender and age-based subordination in all human societies. Environmentally-founded differences in physical distinguishability, language, religion, or other ways of life always offer bases for ethnic subordination of distinct 'peoples'. Humanity's appropriation of its needs from nature and the attendant allocation of the material product always provide yet another potential basis for subordination within human collectivities. As previously suggested, the distinctive scientific contribution of historical materialism to date has been: (1) to show that in all historical societies in which the products of social labour are appropriated either unilaterally or reciprocally by non-labourers, the extraction of the surplus product always generates forms of class subordination; (2) to identify tendential laws of motion of such production processes, especially for the capitalist mode of production; and (3) to begin to examine the connections of these economic forms to other aspects of social structure. While most of Marx's own work and the subsequent 'orthodoxy' have been preoccupied with the production process and – to widely varying degrees – with the vantage point of the subordinate producer classes in the direct relations of production, *historical materialism remains essentially open to being combined with subordinate gender, ethnic and age-group vantage points for more comprehensive description, analysis and explanation of social totalities*. There are now some promising initiatives toward clearly establishing these vantage points and drawing such links, both in contemporary social movements and intellectual work.[53] It is beyond the scope of the present study to do anything more than document some empirical connections between class relations and indicators of age, gender and ethnic relations. But it should be stressed that, for those of us whose primary interest remains in understanding class relations *per se*, the significance of these developments is at least twofold. First, they underline that classes themselves are constituted in other material spheres of life as well (for example, the

household) rather than simply derived from production relations and reproduced elsewhere; and secondly, they indicate that these other (that is, gender,
ethnic and age-based) essential features of social relations, however entwined
with class relations, are likely to have their own historically determinate effects
on both class existence and the overall structure of social totalities, as well as on
historically specific forms of education.

While historical materialist appropriations of history from the standpoint of
subordinate groups are thus still very far from thorough, the recent development of historiographic and other empirical research should now facilitate the
sifting out of more inclusive sets of *transhistorical* categories to *orient* historical
analysis of social totalities. In this regard, I would suggest that there are at least
six general categories that are invariably involved in the ensemble of human
relationships: namely, the non-human environment, human biology, enduring
material institutions and modes of thought, and the practical activities and
consciousness of individual social beings.[54] A satisfactory historical model of
social totalities, then, in addition to recognizing the environmental and biological constraints on social activities, must encompass these four basic aspects
of social reality *per se* – the historical material institutions in which people act,
the modes of thought they use to think and communicate, their individual
efforts to interpret the world to themselves, and their own material acts. By the
same token, the minimal criterion of adequacy of any historical account of
advanced capitalist societies, and of educational phenomena within such
societies, would be consideration of all four social aspects and their interaction.

Within the domain of materially-located social institutions, we can begin
with *material production* and with Marx's premise that the social production of
the means of subsistence is the central problematic of human existence and the
most fundamental historical act. But the social act of *reproducing* the capacity
for material production through consuming the results of such labours and
regenerating the species in both daily and generational terms is equally
essential. In addition, a third material activity essential to all human societies is
communal relations, interactions across co-residence domestic groups which
create and modify languages, customs and social order, and thereby permit and
facilitate the continuing production and species reproduction of human
collectivities. The particular forms of institutions in which material production,
species reproduction and communal relations are materialized may differ
immensely across time and space, but institutions involving all three of these
generic social activities serve as the irreducible material basis for the continuation of all social totalities.

In fact, empirically-grounded Marxist inquiry outside the sphere of
material production relations is still largely at the level of comprehending
history and identifying simple abstractions. In the past decade, however,
significant new analyses of determinate material forms of class relations in
particular historical periods have once again begun to emerge. Such analyses are
occuring in the context of a growing general recognition – again stimulated by
subordinate group social movements and documented by historiographic and

ethnographic research – that the irreducible material basis for the continuation of historical social totalities resides in the antagonistic constituting of institutions involving not only production but also reproduction and communal relations. At least five distinguishable material sites of class relations are now being analyzed, namely the *workplace*, the *household*, and the *community*, as the major sites of everyday social existence where most essential production, reproduction and communal relations occur, as well as the *marketplace* and the *state* as 'second-order' (that is, not of irreducible necessity to the continuation of social life) institutions which have developed mainly from primary produc tion and communal relations respectively to achieve increasingly pervasive influence in class societies.[55] Such material sites are intimately interconnected and, particularly in pre-capitalist societies, may even be fused. But it is the comparative analysis of the different historical forms of these respective material institutions, from the locus of advanced capitalism where they are most fully developed, that currently provides the leading edge of Marxist theory in general and class analysis in particular.

However, it is not only enduring material institutions that provide the social context for particular individuals' and groups' existence, but also established patterns of thought. Such thought patterns include both cognitive processes of how people think (for example, perception, reasoning, imagination, abstraction and generalization, deduction and inference) and substantive forms of consciousness (for example, signification structures, prevailing themes). The historical materialist method of social inquiry must continue to begin with reference to material social existence and to analyze mental life on this basis rather than disconnected from material context. But particular historical modes of signification and modes of cognition always characterize mental life and should be regarded as just as essential as modes of production categories to an adequate analysis of the pre-existing social context for historical individuals' activities in all human societies.[56]

In the most transhistorical terms, then, such material institutions and modes of thought represent the general set of circumstances given and transmitted from the past that are encountered by individual social beings. But it is always individuals who make history. The actual starting point of Marx's inquiry was the individual in society, individuals relating to each other and mutually constituting society as a whole. As he stressed at the outset of his inquiry:

> Above all we must avoid postulating 'society' again as an abstraction
> *vis à vis* the individual. The individual is *the social being*. His life, even
> if it may not appear in the direct form of a *communal* life in association
> with others, is therefore an expression and confirmation of *social life*.[57]

Material institutions and modes of thought are always historical social structures – not disembodied things but emergent summaries of social relationships which are continuously either reaffirmed or modified through individuals' *acts*, even though the mediated effects of human agents' acts are often remote from their intentions.

Individual acts involve the use of innate or acquired capacities or potentialities, whether as direct capacities or as capacities to acquire new capacities. The development of personality always entails *a complex dialectical relation of acts and capacities.*[58] Individuals as unique personalities are constituted at any point in their life cycles by the structure of their activities, the time devoted to combinations of direct relations with oneself and interpersonal relations using already existing or previously untapped capacities. At all points, concrete individuals should be analyzed as the environmentally, biologically and especially socially mediated structures of such activities, rather than being *reduced* to skeletons hidden behind a wall of general contradictions of productive forces and relations of production or to empirical contingencies within universal schemas of human needs or psychoanalytic themes.

At the level of the individual social being, then, material existence and consciousness are interwoven in highly complex ways. Nevertheless, if we accept historical materialist methodological postulates, we must begin analytical inquiry of individual subjects by situating their practical activities in the material world, most essentially their material practices in institutional settings centred on production, reproduction and communal relations. Individual consciousness, then, can be comprehended in terms of contextuating societal and individual material conditions as well as extant modes of cognition, individual phases of cognitive development, and modes of signification including prevailing patterns of 'philosophy' (or ideology) and 'common sense'. While rarely attained by Marxist cultural analysts to date, this would be a matter of 'grasping patterns of belief as they are lived in combination by concrete social individuals'.[59]

The reader may well ask what direct relevance the preceding general discussion in this section has for the specific topic of the book, state schooling in contemporary advanced capitalism. First, jt is intended to make clear basic assumptions that I take to characterize the historical materialist method of inquiry, namely a materialist epistemology, the centrality of history and the requirement of empirical verification. This particular combination is not only quite contrary to the prevalent pattern of methodological assumptions of traditional western social science but is also contested by numerous contemporary Marxist scholars.[60] Not to illustrate such assumptions in this context of 'paradigm shift' would be to invite confounded appreciations by readers of the later presentation of findings.

Secondly, the transhistorical conceptual categories of social reality that serve as the general analytical framework for the subsequent interpretation of educational phenomena have been established and the *limited* focus within this framework on class relations has been identified. Thus, the analytical portions of the text will have little to say about age, gender or ethnic relations in education. Education is regarded as a phenomenon constituted at material sites, permeated by particular modes of cognition and signification including class-based patterns of belief, and constituted through the consciousness and practical activities of particular individual subjects. More specifically, state schooling in advanced capitalism is perceived to be constituted primarily as a communal institution, characterized by both dominate and subordinate as well as intermediate class cultures, and constituted, reproduced and transformed through the consciousness and practical acts of particular capitalist, intermediate and working class subjects. In terms of the current interpretive perspectives on schooling and society referred to in the previous section, this approach has most affinity with the 'contested subordination' view. But, while the present study takes a similar alignment with a working class standpoint on education, it is more explicitly concerned than the former view with structure/human agency dualities, and with unifying as well as conflictual aspects of class relations. As Gramsci recognized, socialist revolution under modern conditions of capitalist hegemony in advanced industrial societies requires the development of a critical consciousness in subordinate groups that comprehends the fullest dimensions of their condition. Aligned intellectuals must strive for the analytical appropriation of this *contradictory* existence while also being as clear as possible about perceived limits of their analyses.

Thirdly, and most importantly, a general rationale for following an analytical and interpretive process that is consistent both with this historical materialist perspective, and with the current limited extent of identification and verification of the determinate abstractions and tendential laws of motion of contemporary capitalist societies, has been pre-figured. More precisely, Marx's developed method of inquiry is seen to involve at least six interrelated moments including:

a   comprehensive observation and/or experience of concrete historical materials in terms of their surface appearances and empirical details;

b   analytical division of these materials into constituent abstract elements including trans-historical categories, simple historical abstractions and determinate historical abstractions;

c   exploration of the connections between historical abstractions, and definition of specific historical laws of motion in the materials;

d   reproduction of concrete social reality in thought through the interplay of multiple abstract determinations, a collectivity of historically tendential laws of motion;

e   practical empirical verification of these analyses (that is, b, c, and/or d) in the movement of concrete history;

f   discovery of additional empirical materials and new historical abstractions and connections through continuing practical activity in and critical inquiry into the complex social totality.[61]

Considered in these terms, broadly historical materialist studies of state schooling in advanced capitalism have been largely occupied with describing schooling processes and effects, primarily in terms of their reproductive functions for the capitalist economy and often in terms of abstractions formalistically read into education from Marxist analyses of production relations.[62] To my knowledge, no thorough Marxist historiography of working class educational practices in a capitalist society has yet been written.[63] Indeed, we may still be at a stage in critical educational studies of 'the products of learning' comparable to that of Marx's critique of political economy when he began to look at the simple abstraction 'commodity'. However, a number of recurring simple abstractions (for example, specific themes of dominant and subordinate educational ideologies, and distinctive educational practices of working class youths) can be drawn from the ethnographic and historiographic studies conducted with a 'contested subordination' approach in the past few years.[64] Such works offer an experientially grounded and potentially fruitful basis on which to *begin* to build more systematic historical materialist analyses of education in capitalism. The current attempt at such an analysis will begin by outlining general class relations in advanced capitalist societies, starting from material production relations – or, in other words, by exploring the material structural context of the class forces potentially active in education. Then basic material dimensions of the relations of such classes in public educational institutions will be suggested. Typical contemporary expressions of class-based educational ideologies in terms of these material dimensions of educational activities then will be documented and analyzed. In the final steps of this preliminary analysis, empirically-based efforts to assess the current expressed consciousness and practical activities of adult citizens in different class locations concerning education are made in terms of these same material dimensions and recurring ideological themes. One must always be wary of reifying analytical divisions (for example, material/ideational; structure/human agency; class and other irreducible individual features, etc.) which continue to be experienced as totalities within social existence. But making grounded analytical distinctions and tracing real connections between them are necessary steps in the critical reproduction of concrete social reality in thought, as well as potentially vital aids to transformative social practice.

Hopefully, then, the basic assumptions, conceptual framework, and method of investigation of the historical materialist approach explicitly outlined here in the most general terms may be referred to for clarification when the reader becomes involved in the specific details of the empirical analysis of education and society which comprises the core of the book.

Toward a Historical Materialist Analysis of the Current Educational Crisis

The tendential laws of motion of the capitalist mode of production, and most directly the long-term tendency toward a falling average rate of profit, have led periodically to a declining collective willingness of capitalists to re-invest in productive activities. Such unwillingness usually has been coupled with the over-production of and greatly reduced mass demand for durable commodities as well as with increasingly speculative paper investments. In these *accumulation crises*, capitalists typically have relied more heavily on such measures as increasing the intensity of the labour process (that is, speed-ups and lay-offs for both productive and non-productive workers), drawing on surplus populations to weaken the labour movement and depress wages beneath the value of labour power, widening public formal stock ownership, harnessing major new technological innovations and carving out entirely new commodity markets, in order to counteract this structural tendency and start a new round of sustained accumulation.

Over the past decade, the world capitalist system once more appears to have become engaged in an intense accumulation crisis which had lead to increasingly extensive efforts at reconstituting social relations. At this point there are at least three possible general options for resolving this crisis, the first two of which remain within a capitalist framework: (1) intensified direct exploitation of productive workers and cutbacks of non-productive workers and state sector social services; (2) massive investment in and reorganization of public social services to enhance human creative capabilities and social productivity, coupled with increased worker self-management of means of production and at least short-term continued reductions in the average rate of profit; (3) a socialist revolution that expropriates concentrated private property in the means of production and distribution of goods and services.[65]

The outcome will likely be determined by the organizational strength and social consciousness of the class forces and alliances involved in this struggle. In most of the advanced capitalist societies, the relative strength of corporate capitalist interests *appears* to be sufficient at this point to implement the first option – as indicated by growing attacks on subordinate class living standards, conditions of work and trade unions, and on 'unproductive' state expenditures, and by the largely defensive reactions of most of the labour movement. However, as the accumulation crisis continues to show signs of deepening,[66] the worsening material conditions of subordinate classes could give rise to more radical socialist consciousness and practice.

The development of public, state-provided systems of education in capitalist societies can only be adequately understood within this more general context.[67] Whatever the limitations of the 'correspondence principle', educational institutions in advanced capitalist societies do exhibit an essential comparability of form with capitalist production. This is so both because educational practices are also generally shaped by class struggle,[68] and because the specific relations of ownership of major means of cultural production and the relations within the educational process itself have become increasingly incorporated into a fully generalized capitalist social form of production (characterized by concentration of both capital and labour, systematic intervention of the state in the economy and educational system, and growing reliance on sicentific knowledge-based forms of production) and more directly subject to the fluctuations of the capital accumulation process.[69] While educational practices have their own specific contradictory relations and remain only indirectly influenced by (and influences on) social relations in the material sites of commodity production, they cannot escape the constraints imposed by accumulation crises.

Thus, the current accumulation crisis and capital's 'corrective' tendencies have led generally to: (1) declining rates of real investment in state education with educational expenditures falling behind levels of inflation; (2) 'overproduction' of and restricted demand for graduates in many programme areas; (3) speed-ups of teachers' work coupled with layoffs and increasing temporary use of a growing educational reserve army of the unemployed; (4) cut-backs especially of 'alternative curriculum' options which had been developed primarily during the 1960s and early 1970s in response to subordinate culture and minority community needs; (5) a growing emphasis on standardized, routinized curricula focused on basic skills for most students, coupled with intensified efforts both to select out an educational elite for more comprehensive professional, managerial and advanced scientific training as well as to expand numerous educational services in the private sector under the guise of 'informal adult learning' packages.[70]

The recent state-centred initiatives in nearly all advanced capitalist societies to initiate a more major reorganization of educational institutions can be understood as responses to a deepening accumulation crisis as well as to the more apparent related problems such as declining enrolments and increasing drop-out rates. Whatever the recommendations of particular public commissions, it remains the case in education as in the sphere of production that the solution to the current crisis – whether some form of renewed 'educational settlement' or a revolutionary change – is most centrally a question of the social consciousness and organizational strength of the class forces and alliances involved. Much of the remainder of the book is therefore concerned with assessing contemporary clas forces and classbased educational ideologies and attitudes.

Notes

1 The term 'major industrial market societies' refers here to the United States, Japan, West Germany and France, as well as the considerably smaller economies of Italy and the United Kingdom and, most marginally, Canada. The tendencies noted below are common to nearly all of those countries with fully generalized capitalist relations of production, essentially the full members of the Organization for Economic Co-coperation and Development (OECD). The focus on these particular countries is based on their status as the largest industrial market economies at the moment. According to the most recent available statistics (THE WORLD BANK (1982) *World Development Report 1981*, New York, Oxford University Press, Table 6, pp. 144–45), the value added in manufacturing in these seven countries still represents about *two-thirds* of the total value added in the entire world economy, excluding the Soviet bloc countries.

2 A more detailed discussion of the assumptions, method and conceptual model

involved in this approach is developed in LIVINGSTONE D.W., (1981) 'On Class Existence and Intellectual Interpretations of Social Reality: A Historical Materialist Perspective' Paper presented to the Critical Pedagogy Seminar, Ontario Institute for Studies in Education, Toronto, September.

3 M. KATZ (1971) *Class, Bureaucracy and Schools: The Illusion of Educational Change in America*, New York, Praeger, pp. xix, 106.

4 For further discussion of such developments, see, for example, T. HUSEN, (1979) *The School in Question: A Comparative Study of the School and Its Future in Western Societies*, London, Oxford University Press, pp. 36–46.

5 BOWLES, S. and GINTIS, H. (1976) *Schooling in Capitalist America*, New York, Basic Books, p. 234.

6 For the most substantial of such critiques, see HALL, S. (1981) 'Schooling, state and society,' in DALE, R. *et al*, (Eds.), *Education and the State, Vol. 1. Schooling and the National Interest*, Barcombe, Falmer Press, pp. 3–29, and HOGAN, D. (1979) 'Capitalism, liberalism and schooling' *Theory and Society* 8 pp. 387–413. For Bowles and Gintis' most recent response, see their 'Contradiction and reproduction in educational theory' in BARTON, L. *et al.* (1981) (Eds), *Schooling, Ideology and the Curriculum*, Barcombe, Falmer Press.

7 CURTI, M. (1935) *The Social Ideas of American Educators*, Paterson, NJ, Littlefield, Adams and Company, (1959) p. 573.

8 HUSEN, T. (1979) *op. cit.* p. 11.

9 CURTI, M. (1935) *op. cit.* pp. 573–74.

10 TAPPER, E. and SALTER, B. (1978) *Education and the Political Order: Changing Patterns of Class Control*, London, Macmillan, p. 194.

11 For the most extensive historical examination to date of the roles of subordinate groups in British educational reform, see SIMON, B. (1974) *Studies in the History of Education*, 3 volumes, London, Lawrence and Wishart. Local case studies to document such influences carefully are much needed. For a good American example, see WRIGLEY, J. (1980) 'Class politics and school reform in Chicago' in ZEITLIN, M. (Ed.) *Classes, Class Conflict and the State*, Cambridge, Winthrop, pp. 153–71.

12 The leading advocates of deschooling were ILLICH, I. (1971) *Deschooling Society*, New York, Harper and Row, and REIMER, E. (1971) *School is Dead*, New York, Doubleday. For an indicative exchange between Reimer and a variety of critics of deschooling, including myself, see the special issue of *Interchange*, 2, (1), (1971).

13 For documentation of the most recent economic tendencies, see ORGANIZATION FOR ECONOMIC CO-OPERATION AND DEVELOPMENT, *Main Economic Indicators*, Paris, OECD, quarterly.

14 In the US federal budget, for example, between 1974 and 1980 interest payments on the federal debt grew by 156 per cent, education, health and human services spending by 121 per cent, and military spending by 71 per cent. See SEIDEN, S. (1981) 'Interest is eating up the budget', *Business Week*, February 9 (1981). For a useful recent overview from a neo-Marxist perspective, see O'CONNOR, J. (1981). 'The fiscal crisis of the state revisited: A look at economic crisis and Reagan's budget policy', *Kapitalistate* 9 pp. 41–61.

15 See, for example, WILLIAMS, R. (1980) 'The writer: Commitment and alignment', *Marxism Today* (June), pp. 22–25.

16 The traditional/organic intellectual distinction was developed by Gramsci in his cryptic prison writings. He placed major emphasis on the creation of strata of intellectuals who were closely or 'organically' aligned with dominant classes, and on their role in giving such classes homogeneity and awareness of their own social functions. See HOARE, Q. and NOWELL-SMITH, G. (1971) (Eds), *Selections from the Prison Notebooks of Antonio Gramsci*, New York, International Publishers, pp. 5–23 and *passim*.

17 See, for example, MACPHERSON, C.B. (1962) *The Political Theory of Possessive*

Individualism: Hobbes to Locke, London, Oxford University Press, and HIRSCH-MAN, A.O. (1977) *The Passions and the Interests: Political Arguments for Capitalism before its Triumph*, Princeton, Princeton University Press.

18 SCHWENDINGER, H. and SCHWENDINGER, J. (1974) *The Sociologists of the Chair: A Radical Analysis of the Formative Years of North American Sociology, 1883–1922*, New York, Basic Books.

19 See, for example, LIVINGSTONE, D.W. and MASON, R.V. (1978) 'Ecological crisis and the autonomy of science in capitalist society: A Canadian case study', *Alternatives* 8, (1) Winter, pp. 3–10, 32; LIVINGSTONE, D.W. and MASON, R.V. (1980) 'On the social context of Science' in SCHRECKER, T. and HOOKER, C.A. (Eds), *The Human Context for Science and Technology*, Ottawa, Social Science and Humanities Research Council, pp. 128–33; and especially MARTIN, B. (1981) 'The scientific straightjacket: The power structure of science and the suppression of environmental scholarship', *The Ecologist 11* (1) January-February, pp. 33–34.

20 See, for example, SKLAR, H. (Ed) (1980) *Trilateralism: The Trilateral Commission and Elite Planning for World Order*, Montreal, Black Rose Books. Among the prominent social scientists associated with the Commission are economist Fred Bergsten, sociologist Michael Crozier and political scientist Samuel Huntington.

21 See, for example, LEVINE, R. (1981) 'Class science and scientific truth,' *Working Papers on Marxism and Science* Winter, pp. 9–22, for a discussion of the relations between class science and scientific insight with particular reference to Euclidean geometry and Newtonian physics.

22 The critical role of intermediate class elements generally in reproducing the dominant schooling structure has been stressed both by Basil Bernstein (1977) 'Classes and pedagogies: Visible and invisible', in KARABEL, J. and HALSEY, A.H. (Eds), *Power and Ideology in Education*, New York, Oxford University Press, pp. 511–34, and by Pierre Bourdieu and Jean-Claude Passeron (1979) in the epilogue of *The Inheritors* Chicago, University of Chicago Press.

23 See especially YOUNG, M. (Ed) (1971) *Knowledge and Control: New Directions for the Sociology of Education*, London, Collier Macmillan, YOUNG, M. and WHITTY, G. (Eds) (1976) *Society, State and Schooling*, Barcombe, Falmer Press; and WHITTY, G. and YOUNG, M. (Eds) (1976) *Explorations in the Politics of School Knowledge*, Nafferton, Nafferton Books.

24 DAWE, A. (1979) 'Theories of social action' in BOTTOMORE, T. and NISBET, R. (Eds) *A History of Sociological Analysis*, London, Heinemann, p. 366.

25 *Ibid.*, p. 367

26 *Ibid.*

27 The distinctive assumptions of order and conflict approaches to social analysis are elaborated in virtually every recent introductory sociology textbook. A particularly systematic comparison appears in REASONS, C. and PERDUE, W. (1981) *The Ideology of Social Problems* Sherman Oaks, Alfred Publishing, pp. 4–14. See also HORTON, J. (1966) 'Order and conflict theories of social problems', *American Journal of Sociology* 72 (May), pp. 701–13.

28 REASONS, C. and PERDUE, W. (1981) *op. cit.*, p. 6.

29 *Ibid.*, p. 10.

30 The seminal formulation of scientific paradigms is by Thomas Kuhn, (1962) *The Structure of Scientific Revolutions*, Chicago, University of Chicago Press.

31 HURN, C. (1978) *The Limits and Possibilities of Schooling: An Introduction to the Sociology of Education*, Boston, Allyn and Bacon, pp. 30–31.

32 The early dominance of this paradigm in educational administrative practice in the US while Progressivism still prevailed in the thought of educational theorists has been well documented by CALLAHAN R. (1962) *Education and the Cult of Efficiency*, Chicago, University of Chicago Press. For a classic expression of the paradigm, see PARSONS, T. (1959) 'The school class as a social system', *Harvard Educational*

Review 29, pp. 297–318. For more recent examples, see HERRIOTT, R. and HODGKINS, B. (1973) *The Environment of Schooling: Formal Education as an Open Social System*, Englewood Cliffs, Prentice-Hall; and GRAMBS, J. (1978) *Schools, Scholars and Society*, Englewood Cliffs, Prentice-Hall. The most influential Marxist work emphasizing structure/consensual order concerns has been that of Louis Althusser. See especially ALTHUSSER, L. (1971) 'Ideology and ideological state apparatuses' in *Lenin and Philosophy and Other Essays*, London, New Left Books.

33 While works emphasizing educational management techniques *per se* have burgeoned over the past decade, a shifting emphasis toward the human agencies involved in managing educational change and the incorporation of dissatisfied groups is also clear in the studies of social order theorists who had previously stressed quite dehumanized systems models of schooling, as well as in the major themes of conventional survey textbooks. See, for example, HERRIOTT, R. and GROSS, N. (Eds) (1979) *The Dynamics of Planned Educational Change*, Berkeley, McCutchan Publishing; and JAROLIMEK, J. *The Schools in Contemporary Society*, New York, Macmillan.

34 HURN, C. (1978) *op. cit.* p. 31. Hurn cites not only Illich but, rather inappropriately, Bowles and Gintis as exemplars of this approach. In contrast to those analysts who assume elite domination, Bowles and Gintis place explicit programmatic emphasis on class *conflict* as the basis of educational change (for example, *Schooling in Capitalist America,*, *op. cit.*, p. 224–41). In fairness, however, it is Bowles and Gintis' occasional overestimates of capitalist class economic and political powers (for example, p. 238) and their more persistent lack of specification of working class cultures or actions concerning education (for example, distinctive residual cultures, forms of resistance) that permit Hurn's (pp. 49–53) interpretation of the substance of their work without reference to conflict. More representative exemplars are the revisionist historians, such as KATZ, M. (1971) *op. cit.*, KARIER, C. SPRING, J. and VIOLAS, P. (1973) *Roots of Crisis*, Chicago, Rand McNally, and VIOLAS, P. (1978) *The Training of the Urban Working Class*, Chicago, Rand McNally, who have constantly stressed the role of elite domination in educational change. For representative examples of contemporary analyses by radical critics of elite domination of the schools, see USEEM, E. and USEEM, M. (Eds) (1974) *The Educational Establishment*, Englewood Cliffs, Prentice-Hall. I would also consider the main tenor of Bernstein's work on class communication codes and schooling (*Class, Codes and Control*, 3 volumes, London, Routledge and Kegan Paul, 1973, 1974, 1976) to be conducted from this perspective, as well as that of Bourdieu and Passeron on 'cultural capital' (*Reproduction in Education, Society and Culture*, Beverly Hills, Sage, 1977 (1970); in both instances, as in Bowles and Gintis' work, there is also a clearly underlying structuralist conception.

35 HOGGART, R. (1959) *The Uses of Literacy: Aspects of Working Class Life*, London, Chatto and Windus, pp. 62–63, 77–78. See also the early work of Raymond Williams, another British scholar of working class origins, especially *The Long Revolution*, London, Penguin (1961), in which persistent historical differences between engrained working class educational ideals and those of other social classes are examined. For a more recent American work which takes a similar perspective, see SENNETT, R. and COBB, J. (1973) *The Hidden Injuries of Class*, New York, Vintage Books.

36 HALL, S. (1980) 'Cultural studies and the Centre: Some problematics and problems', in HALL et al. (Eds) (1980) *Culture, Media, Language*, London, Hutchinson, p. 27. This article provides an excellent summary of the general intellectual sources and historical development of the Centre's work. The original influences of Hoggart, Williams and E.P. Thompson and the later influences of continental Marxists, especially Althusser and then Gramsci, are all duly recorded.

37 Education Group, Centre for Contemporary Cultural Studies, (1981) *Unpopular*

Education: Schooling and Social Democracy in England Since 1944, London: Hutchinson, p. 32. The most insightful ethnographic works on social relations within the schools from this perspective has also been conducted through the Centre. See especially WILLIS, P. (1977) *Learning to Labour: How Working Class Kids Get Working Class Jobs*, Westmead, Saxon House.

38 Notable North American examples are the recent works of Michael Apple (1981) *Culture, Class and the State: Reproduction and Contradiction in Education*, Boston, Routledge and Kegan Paul; and Henry Giroux (1981) *Ideology, Culture and the Process of Schooling*, Philadelphia and Lewes, Temple University Press and Falmer Press.

39 It is perhaps worth noting here that I agree with Gramsci that 'All men are intellectuals ... but not all men have, in society, the function of intellectuals.', HOARE, Q. and NOWELL SMITH, G. (Eds) (1971) *op. cit.*, p. 9. Intellectuals in this functional sense are those whose primary work is with ideas, the proprietors of knowledge that offers models which are applicable beyond individual situations or has cross-contextual validity and that the society or various groups can use to orient their members, and who are often thereby exempted from the obligation of performing physical labour. For further discussion, see KONRAD, G. and SZELENYI, I. (1979) *The Intellectuals on the Road to Class Power*, Brighton, Harvester Press, pp. 24–35, and SOHN-RETHEL, A. (1978) *Intellectual and Manual Labour: A Critique of Epistemology*, London, Macmillan.

40 For a useful discussion, see THERBORN, G. (1976) 'Working class struggles and theoretical breaks: The social and theoretical formation of historical materialism, in his *Science, Class and Society*, London, New Left Books, pp. 317–413.

41 This point is argued more fully in REY, P. P. (1973) *Les Alliances des Classes*, Paris, Maspero, pp. 171–219.

42 MARX, K. (1894) *Capital, Volume 3. The Process of Capitalist Production as a Whole*, New York, International Publishers, 1967, pp. 791–92.

43 For a straightforward introductory analysis of the capitalist system (and especially the central concept of surplus value) in contemporary terms, see for example JALEE, P. (1977) *How Capitalism Works*, New York, Monthly Review Press, or MANDEL, E. (1973) *An Introduction to Marxist Economic Theory*, New York, Pathfinder Press.

44 For detailed interpretations of these basic contradictory relations of the capitalist mode of production, and particularly of their expression in the current crisis in advanced capitalist societies, see MANDEL, E. (1975) *Late Capitalism*, London, New Left Books; BECKER, J. (1977) *Marxian Political Economy*, Cambridge, Cambridge University Press; GORDON, D. (1980) 'Stages of accumulation and long economic cycles', in HOPKINS, T. and WALLERSTEIN, I. (Eds), *Processes of the World System*, Beverly Hills, Sage; and especially CASTELLS, M. (1980) *The Economic Crisis and American Society*, Princeton, Princeton University Press.

45 BANAJI, J. (1977) 'Modes of production in a materialist conception of history', *Capital and Class* 3, pp. 9–10.

46 For documentation see, for example, SOHN-RETHEL, A. (1978) *op. cit.*, pp. 111–38; ANDERSON, P. (1976) *Considerations on Western Marxism*, London, New Left Books; and BANAJI, J. (1977) *op. cit.*, pp. 1–8 and *passim*.

47 For documentation of current operativeness, see especially BANAJI, J. (1977) *op. cit.*, and the various works cited in footnote 44.

48 MARX, K. (1859) *A Contribution to the Critique of Political Economy*, Moscow, Progress Publishers, 1970, p. 21.

49 SOHN-RETHEL, A. (1978) *op. cit.*, pp. 195–96. The point has been made similarly by LEVIDOW, L. (1978) 'A Marxist critique of the IQ Debate', *Radical Science Journal* 6 7, p. 35: 'We can know nature only by engaging in particular social practices which then determine the form taken by the knowledge produced – which means that we

can never know some exclusively "material" or purely a-social external world.'
50 THERBORN, G. (1976) *op. cit.*, p. 394.
51 For an overview stressing the diversity of such developments see, for example, KOLAKOWSKI L. (1978) *Main Currents of Marxism*, Volumes 2 and 3. London, Oxford University Press.
52 ARONOWITZ, S. (1981) *The Crisis in Historical Materialism: Class, Politics and Culture in Marxist Theory*, New York Praeger, pp. 171, 173–74. (For that matter, as Aronowitz also observes, Marx himself is not immune from this limitation: 'Marx often adopts the discourse of the fetish, that is the systematic form in which capital, presenting itself as the embodiment of nature, circulates ... Thus, Marx does not always allow for the capitalist social relations, of which capital is the material form, to shine through. Except in a few sections, the working class appears in *Capital* as a factor of production, its social existence circumscribed by the logic of accumulation.' (p. 171).) Compare the more strident thesis on proletarian self-valorization and cycles of working class struggles by Toni Negri (1979) 'Capitalist domination and working class sabotage' in NEGRI, T. et al. *Working Class Autonomy and the Crisis: Italian Marxist Texts of the Theory and Practice of a Class Movement: 1964–79*, London, Red Notes and CSE Books, pp. 93–117.
53 The most substantial work to date has been in the development of a feminist vantage point and has included both critiques of the silences and presumptions in classical Marxism regarding the specificity of women's situation and also attempts to apply a Marxist method of inquiry to document and analyze historical forms of patriarchy. As significant recent examples, see BARRETT, M. (1980). *Women's Oppression Today*, London, Verso; O'BRIEN, M. (1981) *The Politics of Reproduction*, London, Routledge and Kegan Paul; and SMITH, D. (1982) *Women, Class and the Family*, Vancouver, New Star Books. With regard to ethnic relations, the British journal *Race and Class* has perhaps offered the most searching critiques of orthodox Marxism and applications of historical materialist methods from a vantage point of racial subordination. There is much attention to the general problems of youth and of ageing, as well as 'passages' through the life cycle, in bourgeois social science. To my knowledge, no work comparable to the critical feminist and ethnic studies cited above but taking an age-based vantage point has yet appeared. Perhaps the fact that ageing is the most universally shared feature of human lives is partly responsible for age categories of subordination being the hardest to perceive and analyze as socially constructed. For useful historical materials in this regard see, for example, ARIÈS P. (1962) *Centuries of Childhood*, New York, Vintage Books.
54 For indicative recent Marxist works on the non-human environment and human biology, see SCHMIDT, A. (1979) *The Concept of Nature in Marx*, London, New Left Books, and TIMPANARO, S. (1975) *On Materialism*, London, New Left Books, respectively. An earlier presentation of the social aspects of this conceptual framework appears in LIVINGSTONE, D. W. (1976) 'On hegemony in corporate capitalist states: Material structures, ideological forms, class consciousness, and hegemonic acts', *Sociological Inquiry*, 46 (3–4) pp. 235–250.
55 A large number of relevant analyses of the workplace have been stimulated by Harry Braverman's *Labour and Monopoly Capital*, New York: Monthly Review Press (1974). Some of the most important subsequent analytical contributions are in the case studies of capitalist labour processes by FRIEDMAN, A. (1977) *Industry and Labour: Class Struggle at Work and Monopoly Capitalism*, London, Macmillan; KUSTERER, K. (1978) *Know How on the Job: The Important Working Knowledge of 'Unskilled' Workers*, Boulder, Westview Press; EDWARDS, R. (1979) *Contested Terrain*, New York, Basic Books; and BURAWOY, M. (1979) *Manufacturing Consent*, Chicago, University of Chicago Press. Other related studies have tried to expand from such a focus on the labour process to link production relations with other institutional aspects of capitalist relations, but with little analysis of the historical

forms of the latter in their own terms. See, for example, AGLIETTA, M. (1979) *A Theory of Capitalist Regulation: The US Experience*, London, New Left Books, and LAZONICK, W. (1979) 'The subjection of labour to capital', *Review of Radical Political Economics*, 10 (1), pp. 1–31. For comparative analyses of historical forms of the state, see especially ANDERSON, P. (1974) *Lineages of the Absolutist State*, London, New Left Books, and THERBORN, G. (1978) *What Does the Ruling Class Do When It Rules?* London, New Left Books. For a similar analysis of household forms, see SECCOMBE, W. (1982) *The Reproduction of Labour Power: A Comparative Study*, PhD dissertation, University of Toronto. Less analytical work has been done on community and marketplace sites, but see KATZNELSON, I. (1979) 'Community, capitalist development and the emergence of class', *Politics and Society*, 9 (2), pp. 203–37 and SOHN-RETHEL, A. (1978) *op. cit.* for suggestive formulations.

56 The systematic empirical study of modes of thought remains very undeveloped in Marxist social inquiry. The theoretical exploration and empirical documentation of modes of cognition in relation to historical modes of production perhaps has been most seriously addressed by the Soviet psychologist A.R. Luria. See his *Cognitive Development: Its Cultural and Social Foundations*, Cambridge, Harvard University Press (1976). Marxist scholars from Lukacs in the 1920s onward, have devoted greater attention to the substantive forms and contents of consciousness, especially in terms of relations between material conditions and ideological domination or 'ruling ideas' in class societies. Gramsci's work on ideological hegemony has stimulated some of the most important recent historical and empirical studies. See, for example, GENOVESE, E. (1974) *Roll, Jordan, Roll: The World the Slaves Made*, New York, Pantheon, and RUDÉ, G. (1980) *Ideology and Popular Protest*, New York Pantheon,.

57 MARX, K. (1932) *The Economic and Philosophic Manuscripts of 1844*, New York, International Publishers, 1964, pp. 137–8. The same conception is reiterated twenty years later in *Grundrisse*: 'The human being is in the literal sense a political animal, not merely a gregarious animal, but an animal which can individuate itself only in the midst of society'. Cited in MESSINGER, E. (1981) 'An introduction to Soviet psychology', *Working Papers on Marxism and Science* (Winter), p. 89.

58 The most fully developed Marxist conception of individual acts to date appears in SÈVE, L. (1974) *Man in Marxist Theory and the Psychology of Personality*, Hassocks, Sussex, Harvester Press, 1978. The following brief account in the text of individual personality differs from Sève's most explicitly in giving greater recognition to natural and biological influences, and in distinguishing between intra and inter-personal relations rather than using the concrete/abstract acts distinction which Sève bases on socially productive labour in capitalism. More generally, while Sève posits his approach to the theory of human personality as merely indicative hypotheses, many of his specific categories and hypotheses are quite directly and formalistically derived from those of Marx's political economy of capitalism rather than interactively with historical or experiential study of individual biographies. In this regard, the following passage is indeed indicative: ' . . . the task of the science of biography, as we understand it, is essentially to grasp the structures, the contradictions, the dialectic of the personal *life* through which the singular personality is formed and transformed and through which activity unfolds: quantitative and qualitative development of the fixed capital of capacities, infrastructures of activity, general P/N [that is, the relation of the product to need] and use-time; superstructures and forms of consciousness; internal necessities of correspondence between capacities and division of time; contradictions with external necessities and forms of individuality; main effects of contradictions at each stage, taking into account the social conjuncture in which the life in question develops, periodic crises of use-time and possible transformations of the general logic of development' (p. 382).

59 JOHNSON, R. (1979) 'Histories of culture/theories of ideology: Notes on an

impasse', in BARRETT, M. CORRIGAN, P., KUHN, A. and WOLFF, J. (Eds), *Ideology and Cultural Production*, London, Croom Helm, p. 74.

60 For elaboration, see SAYER, D. (1979) 'Science as critique: Marx versus Althusser', in MEPHAM, J. and RUBEN, D.-H. (Eds) (1979) *Issues in Marxist Philosophy. Volume 3. Epistemology, Science, Ideology*, Brighton, Sussex, Harvester Press, pp. 27–54.

61 Marx's own most concise summary of his developed method of inquiry appears in the afterword to the Second German Edition of *Capital* (*op. cit.* p. 19): 'The method of inquiry has to appropriate the material in detail, to analyze its different forms of development, to trace out their inner connection. Only after this work is done, can the actual movement be adequately described.' For a brief schematic description of Marx's general method of inquiry essentially in these terms, see MANDEL, E. (1973) *op. cit.*, pp. 13–23. For more detailed discussions, see DELLA VOLPE, G. (1962) *Rousseaue Marx*, Rome, Editori Riuniti; ROSDOLSKY, R. (1968) *The Making of Marx's Capital*, London, Pluto Press 1977; SAYER, D. (1979) *Marx's Method: Ideology, Science and Critique in Capital*, Sussex, Harvester Press; and ZELENY, J. (1980) *The Logic of Marx*, Oxford, Basil Blackwell.

Della Volpe's view of this method has been most succinctly summarized as follow: 'Thus the correct method can be represented as a *circular* movement from the concrete or real to the abstract or ideal and from the latter back to the former. This means precisely a continuous, unavoidable *historical verification of economic abstractions* or categories. These verified categories and abstractions will be specific, determinate concepts. Scientific dialectic, therefore, is but the experimental method itself, always starting from a real, concrete problem, proceeding to a rational (and in this sense 'abstract') hypothesis, and finally coming back to concreteness for the verification.' MONTANO, M. (1972) 'The "Scientific Dialectics" of Galvano Della Volpe', in HOWARD, D. and KLARE, K. (Eds) *The Unknown Dimension: European Marxism Since Lenin*, New York, Basic Books, p. 345.

62 For texts drawing heavily on classical Marxism, see LEVITAS, M. (1974) *Marxist Perspectives in the Sociology of Education*, London, Routlege and Kegan Paul; and SARUP, M. (1978) *Marxism and Education*, London Routledge and Kegan Paul. For representative examples of works placing more emphasis on historical and descriptive accounts of educational issues, see many of the selections in DALE, R. ESLAND, G. and MACDONALD, M. (Eds) (1976) *Schooling and Capitalism*, London, Routledge and Kegan Paul, and DALE; R. and MACDONALD, M., ESLAND, G., FERGUSSON, (Eds) (1981) *Education and the State* 2 Volumes, Lewes, Falmer Press; and, for Canadian examples, MARTEL, G. (Ed) (1974) *The Politics of the Canadian Public School*, Toronto, Lorimer; and NELSON, R. NOCK, D. (Eds) (1978) *Reading, Writing and Riches*, Kitchener, Between-the-Lines.

63 This is not to deny the valuable English work of SIMON, B. (1974) *op. cit.*, as well as of E.P. Thompson and his followers, but merely to register its partial and fragmented character with regard to working class educational practices per se.

64 The most nuanced and insightful of this work has been generated by the Birmingham Cultural Studies Centre, especially WILLIS, P. (1977) *op. cit.*, and the Education Group *op. cit.*

65 Representative studies dealing with these respective options are: (1) CASTELLS, M. (1980) *op. cit.*; (2) ATTALI, (1975) *La parole et l'outil*, Paris, Presses Universitaires de France; and (3) ROWBOTHAM, S. *et al.* (1979) *Beyond the Fragments*, London, Merlin.

66 See, for example, HEAP, S. (1980/81) 'World profitability crisis in the 1970s: Some empirical evidence', *Capital and Class* 12, pp. 66–84.

67 The other major material sites of social relations in advanced capitalist societies, especially the household and the community, and thier very important reciprocal relations with the sphere of production and educational institutions cannot be so succinctly summarized at this point. For an interesting historical study of the

English case, see DAVID, M. (1980) *The State, the Family and Education*, London, Routledge and Kegan Paul.

68 This historical struggle has been most indicatively traced for the English case. See especially SIMON, B. (1974) *op. cit.*

69 Fuller discussion of the relations of cultural ownership and the educational process and of their specific contradictions in capitalist societies appear in chapter 3.

70 For an insightful illustration of such effects with specific reference to US higher education, see BEVERLEY, J. (1978) 'Higher education and capitalist crisis', *Socialist Review* 42, pp. 45–61.

Chapter 2

Class Structure In Advanced Capitalism

The primary purpose of this chapter is to identify structural features of class relations in capitalism and consider empirical profiles of class positions in advanced capitalist societies. This analysis will provide a basic context for proceeding to the systematic examination of current subjective orientations toward educational issues among people in specific objective circumstances. First, the historical basis for the existence of classes is discussed, especially in relation to the development of material production. Then, the advanced capitalist societies are situated within the contemporary world capitalist economy. The main class positions in advanced capitalist production relations are then identified, empirical comparisons are made of the class structures of the major industrial market economies, and the particular development of the Canadian class structure is briefly reviewed. Next, classes are considered more inclusively as social circles which are constituted outside production relations as well, and which involve both core and peripheral positions; data from my Ontario studies are used to illustrate these associations. Finally, the relationship between class position and level of schooling is examined and possible implications for differential support of the established form of schooling are suggested.

Class Existence in Capitalism

Despite some debate about what distinguishes it from other activities, it is an indisputable social fact that work remains the central material activity in most adults' lives in contemporary societies. It is equally indisputable that substantial divisions of labour persist in all modern societies, and that different work experiences are linked both with differences in a number of other material activities and with the ways people tend to think of their work experiences and of themselves in relation to other groups of people. Consider carefully, for example, the accounts of their work by three Americans, a former corporate president, a rank-and-file steelworker, and a mother on welfare:

The excutive is a lonely animal in the jungle who doesn't have a friend
... The corporation is made up of many, many people. I call 'em the
gray people and the black – or white – people. Blacks and whites are
definite colors, solid. Gray isn't. The gray people come there from nine
to five, do their job, aren't particularly ambitious. There's no fear
there, sure. But they're not subject to great demands. They're only
subject to dismissal when business goes bad and they cut off people.
They go from corporation to corporation and get jobs. Then you have
the black – or white – people. The ambitious people, the leaders, the
ones who want to get ahead.

When the individual reaches the vice presidency or he's general
manager, you know he's an ambitious, dedicated guy who wants to get
to the top. He isn't one of the gray people. He's one of the
black-and-white vicious people – the leaders, the ones who stick out in
the crowd.

As he struggles in this jungle, every position he's in, he's terribly
lonely. He can't confide and talk with the guy working under him. He
can't confide and talk to the man he's working for. To give vent to his
feelings, his fears, and his insecurities, he'd expose himself. This goes
all the way up the line until he gets to be president. The president *really*
doesn't have anybody to talk to, because the vice presidents are waiting
for him to die or make a mistake and get knocked off so they can get
his job.

He can't talk to the board of directors, they're cold, they're hard.
They don't have any direct-line responsibilities. They sit in a staff
capacity and they really play God. They're interested in profits.
They're interested in progress. They're interested in keeping a good
face in the community – if it's profitable. You have the tremendous
infighting of man against man for survival and clawing to the top.
Progress.

> *Larry Ross, Ex-president of Conglomerate, Consultant.*[1]

It isn't that the average working guy is dumb. He's tired, that's all ... I
punch in about ten minutes to seven in the morning. I say hello to a
couple of guys I like, I kid around with them.

I put on my hard hat, change into my safety shoes, put on my safety
glasses, go to the bonderizer. It's the thing I work on. They rake the
metal, they wash it, they dip it in a paint solution, and we take it off.
Put it on, take it off, put it on, take it off, put it on, take it off ...

I say hello to everybody but my boss. At seven it starts. My arms get
tired about the first half-hour. After that, they don't get tired any more
until maybe the last half-hour at the end of the day. I work from seven
to three thirty. My arms are tired at seven thirty and they're tired at
three o'clock. I hope to God I never get broke in, because I always
want my arms to be tired at seven thirty and three o'clock. (Laughs)

'Cause that's when I know that there's a beginning and there's an end. That I'm not brainwashed. In between, I don't even try to think.

If I were to put you in front of a dock and I pulled up a skid in front of you with fifty hundred-pound sacks of potatoes and there are fifty more skids just like it, and this is what you're gonna do all day, what would you think about – potatoes? Unless a guy's a nut, he never thinks about work or talks about it. Maybe about baseball or about getting drunk the other night or he got laid or he didn't get laid. I'd say one out of a hundred will actually get excited about work.

Mike Lefevre, Steelworker[2]

I start my day here at five o'clock. I get up and prepare all the children's clothes. If there's shoes to shine I do it in the morning. About seven o'clock I bathe the children . . . I try to make hot food for the kids to eat. In the afternoon it's pretty well on my own. I scrub and clean and cook and do whatever I have to do. Welfare makes you feel like you're nothing. Like you're laying back and not doing anything and it's falling in your lap. But you must understand, mothers, too, work. My house is clean. I've been scrubbing since this morning. You could check my clothes, all washed and ironed. I'm home and I'm working. I am a working mother . . .

Some men work eight hours a day. There are mothers that work eleven, twelve hours a day. We get up at night, a baby vomits, you have to be calling the doctor, you have to be changing the baby. When do you get a break, really? You don't. This is an all-around job, day and night . . .

All I know is what's going on here. I'm an intelligent women up to a certain point, and after that . . . I wish I knew. I guess the big shots decided the war. I don't question it, because I've been busy fighting my own little war for so long.

Jesusita Novarro, Mother on Welfare[3]

Such work-based relationships constitute primary criteria for interpreting social existence generally and, in particular, for speaking of 'social classes' in contemporary society.

The existence of classes has been broadly recognized within human societies for thousands of years. In a wide ranging comparative review of the ways of interpreting social structure in historical societies, Stanislaw Ossowski has noted the occurence of the same general views of class structure from early folklore and ancient philosophy to modern capitalism and socialism. He also observes a striking persistence of fundamentally opposite ways of interpreting class structure, primarily gradational views of class among apologists for the existing social order or relational views among the leading critics of this order.[4] The continuing interplay of these opposed conceptions in popular conscious-ness is suggested by the heterogenous mixtures of gradational and relational abstractions that appear in the response patterns to public surveys of the images of class and class structure in advanced capitalist societies.[5]

Marx's distinctive contribution in this regard was not to identify either the existence of or the opposition between classes, but rather to discover the historical, dialectical character of these relations and to prove '. . . that the *existence of classes* is only bound up with *particular historical phases in the development of production*'.[6] While Marx's work is rich in insights about such class dynamics, he never offered a full systematization of classes within capitalist relations of production.[7] Subsequent historical materialist studies up to the 1970s generally offered little advance in this regard.

The incidence and intensity of class conflicts in advanced capitalist societies have clearly increased since the late 1960s, most notably in Western Europe.[8] There has been a corresponding increase in progressive intellectuals' interest in class analysis.[9] To date, the major thrust of this work has been to specify class positions in terms of major dimensions of production relations in these advanced economies with emphasis on the capitalist labour process, and to identify a number of intermediate or contradictory class positions between the fundamental classes of capitalists and the proletariat or 'working class'.[10] My own research on class structure has had similar starting points with initial attention to production relations.

As noted in Chapter One, the fully developed capitalist mode of production is distinguished by a small group of non-workers both owning and controlling the means of production while the direct producers of goods and services are dispossessed of all active means of production but their labour power. This labour power takes the form of a commodity which they are compelled to sell on the labour market and to incorporate into other commodities through the machinofacture labour process. This labour power serves as the basic source of surplus value of capital. The competitive accumulation of surplus value through the transformation of all possible goods and services into commodities and the exchange of those commodities has become the overarching objective shaping the entire production process. The historical development of the relations between capitalists and workers within the capitalist mode of production can be analyzed in terms of (1) ownership of the means of production, and (2) several aspects of control of the labour process.

Capitalist enterprises have developed by gathering more and more of the available non-human material means of production (land, tools, raw materials) under their ownership, thereby appropriating the products of existing labour processes. Peasants, guild journeymen and wage labourers have all resisted their separation from the means of production. But the early entrepreneurial capitalist of the machinofacture phase succeeded in appropriating most of the material means of production and consolidating their ownership in his own position. With the expanding scale and concentration of capitalist enterprises, partial ownership functions were delegated to hired subordinates and joint stock companies were used to mobilize further sources of capital, but real economic ownership became increasingly centralized in the big stockholders that directed such large corporate enterprises. Today the early struggles over ownership of the immediate means of production are largely forgotten as capitalist enterprises' appropriation has become so extensive. However, the conflict between capital and labour over ownership of means of production persists in many guises within contemporary enterprises. A most indicative example is West Germany's 1978 *Mitbestimmung* law which purported to give trade unions' representatives 'parity' with those of shareholders on the boards of management of the largest industrial enterprises. Once again by conceding some legal claims and detailed ownership functions in the face of an increasingly socialized labour force and immediate capital shortages, capitalists are attempting to retain ultimate control of the investment process by disguising the quintessential contradiction between privatized real ownership and the socialized nature of the production process *per se*. Moreover, the struggle over ownership is not containable within the currently institutionalized forms of actual capitalist production, but rather is most evident where capital is striving to commodify new realms and appropriate the relevant *potential* means of production which all peoples had previously been able to presume as their birthright. One needs only to reflect on the recent corporate merchandising of air cleaners, water purifiers, and video playback recorders to appreciate both the extent of capitalist appropriation and the continually renewed relevance of the struggle over private or genuine public ownership of the means of production.

But capitalists' mere ownership of the various means and products of production has proved a very inadequate way to get more work and surplus value out of contracted labour. Early capitalists' experiences soon taught them that:

> Capital *needs* real control of the labour process precisely because the formal separation of labour from the means of production is cancelled in reality by the material form of labour process in which labour and materials and instruments combine. Capital needs to have control over the form of this combination, because whatever the instruments and materials ... there is always more than one way of affecting the combination and there is always the possibility of the process being informed by some objectives other than that of valorization and potentially in conflict with it (for example, the objectives of healthy and safe working conditions, or of a socially useful product).[11]

Throughout the history of capitalist production, therefore, the labour process itself has increasingly become the major site of the struggle between capital and labour.

Capitalists have consistently tried to bring the *social* relations of production under their own systems of social discipline, from the initial gathering of workers under a single roof so they could be effectively controlled through supervision of the individual capitalist or his foreman, to the recent institutionalization of the hierarchial social power of capital in the form of company 'work criteria'; that is, detailed, formal job descriptions and performance standards that appear to be more impersonal than the will and whim of particular foremen. Such rules serve capital even more reliably and profoundly to allocate and differentiate jobs, enforce speeds and intensities, and generally make capitalist efforts at social control less visible.[12] However, the more that discretion in organizing the way they work is taken away from those who actually do the work, the less conscientious they tend to become in performing a given piece of work. The objective alienation of workers from their products and the concomitant decline in the quality of workmanship generally have been quite tolerable to capitalists whenever they have been able to use increased control of the social relations of production and the threat of the reserve army of the unemployed to command greater productivity from workers, and where capitalist firms and the state can allocate sufficient overhead costs to ensure both minimal product quality and sufficient consumer demand to realize greater surplus value. Increased measures of capitalist discipline have most typically been met by individualistic sabotage and other reactive efforts at 'getting a bit of our own back'. However, the contradiction between self-management and private accumulation begins to emerge in starker structural form in the most advanced industries. In order to try to release the potential productivity that remains locked inside the workers in such capital-intensive industries, capitalists have been driven to experiment with worker self-management schemes. Such experiments have usually led to both higher productivity and substantial difficulties in containing worker initiatives within management systems of norms and rewards. As Richard Edwards notes, 'capitalists themselves are led, even forced, to introduce the very schemes that threaten their grip'.[13]

For just as long, capitalists have tried to gain control over the *technical* relations of production, or workers' relations with the actual operations of production *per se*. They have attempted to centralize knowledge and technical power over the design of production systems, imposing capital's objectives by appropriating the capacity to plan and co-ordinate the physical process of production and relegating many workers to fragmented, routine tasks. In this respect, an increasingly clear division has emerged, as the Brighton Labour Process Group observes:

> ... between those who produce or apply scientific and technological knowledge in the design of production systems and in day to day problem solving involved in the operation of the systems, and those whose relationship with the production system is calculated, standardized and specified in advance by capital in the interests of producing an output which is known with precision in advance.[14]

Nevertheless, the genuine technical requirements of labour in this capitalist form of machinofacture come into contradiction with capital's imperative to gain and reproduce a monopoly over systemic knowledge of the production process in order to impose its accumulation objective. While industrial capitalists 'rent the veil' of the technical mystery and secrecy of earlier conservative labour processes, they cannot reconceal such knowledge without threatening their own existence. As Marx put it:

> By means of machinery, chemical processes and other methods [machinofacture] is continually causing changes not only in the technical basis of production, but also in the functions of the labourer, and in the social combinations of the labour-process. At the same time, it thereby also revolutionizes the division of labour within the society, and incessantly launches masses of capital and of workpeople from one branch of production to another. But if [machinofacture], by its very nature, therefore necessitates variation of labour, fluency of function, universal mobility of the labourer, on the other hand, in its capitalistic form, it reproduces the old division of labour with its ossified particularization.[15]

Thus, while capitalists have continually tried to reduce the mass of labourers to standarized, fragmented tasks and to limit jobs requiring special skills to as few workers as possible (for example, design work, machine setting, maintenance and repair), the continual development of new technologies and new products demands versatile, technically knowledgeable labourers who retain the *collective technical capacity* to plan and co-ordinate the system of production themselves. Capital is compelled to revolutionize the instruments of production to achieve accumulation, but to do so it must encourage both the development of the technical aptitudes of the labourer for such varied work and the inititative and autonomy of some to produce technological innovations.

In this machinofacture process, capitalists also tend to take every feasible opportunity to replace human labour with machinery in the material production process itself. This tendency is also inherently contradictory and, as suggested in Chapter One, intimately associated with economic crises. In the long term, other things being equal, replacing living labour by the dead labour embodied in machinery diminishes the only *productive*, or surplus value creating, element in the production process and generates capital accumulation crises. The introduction of machinery in its capitalist form often threatens workers' immediate interests and is resisted, while the time and energy saving potential of machinery remains ultimately in labour's interest. The labour savings are compelling to individual capitalists, but ultimately disintegrative of any substantial surplus value generating capacity and thus of capital itself. Capitalists can postpone this eventuality by increasing social discipline and introducing new production techniques, and by correspondingly concentrating, centralizing and generally speeding up market relations. But this requires the use of more *non-productive* labour, and such measures can also serve to raise the level of the other contradictory aspects of the capitalist labour process referred to above.

Such struggles over ownership of the means of production and control of the labour process may be expressed in very different and uneven historical tendencies, but they remain the pivotal (though by no means exclusive) basis of class existence and class relations in the capitalist mode of production.

Advanced Capitalist Societies and the World Economy

Uneven development of these tendencies in different capitalist societies should not be confused with the predominance of other modes of production and hence other types of class relations. Capitalism is unique as the first mode of production to have prevailed as a *global* system. The feudal mode of production, for example, prevailed in Europe and Japan while co-existing with other dominant modes in other major regions of the world. In contrast, the unique genesis of the capitalist mode of production in Europe, vitally abetted by often violent appropriation of other regions' production, eventually led to capitalist enterprises subordinating the vast majority of all major pre-capitalist units of production into a world capitalist economy. Today, capitalist enterprises dominate most production activities in societies around the globe, with the notable exception of the transitional socialist states.[16] It is evident that numerous residual units of production remain within the current world system, most notably in the agricultural sector. In addition to machinofacture-based capitalist plantations, there are also numerous commercial haciendas, estates relying largely on migratory labour or share-cropping, and independent simple commodity producers, with the latter types of enterprises often quantitatively more numerous within particular regions.[17] However, such enterprises no longer co-exist with pure capitalist enterprises in the sense of being governed by their own specific laws of motion; rather, internal economic logics and self-sufficiency have been largely disintegrated by the penetration of money lending and merchant capitalist enterprises, so that such production units have become quasi-capitalist enterprises increasingly compelled to try to produce surplus value but on the basis of primitive labour processes. As Marx noted of simple commodity production in nineteenth century 'peasant nations': 'We have here the whole of capitalist production without its advantages, the development of the social forms of labour and the productivity of labour to which they give rise'.[18]

It follows that analyses of particular societies within the current world system cannot properly characterize constituent types of enterprise on the basis of apparent forms of labour. Neither industrial workers in particular nor hired wage labourers in general are any more *identical* with contemporary capitalist enterprises than serfs were with feudal estates. Even when they reached their most fully developed form within medieval western Europe, feudal estates were never the exclusive unit of production, and were themselves sustained not only by serf labour but by a variety of other forms of labour as well, including domestic servant-slaves, day labourers, part-time hired workers and free tenants. Similarly, modern capitalist enterprise requires a variety of forms of labour to sustain it. In addition to industrial wageworkers and other forms of privately-hired labour, self-employed producers, state workers, several forms of peasant labour, and various reserve forms of labour all now function as other *expressions of capitalist production imperatives or tendential laws of motion.*

The development of the current capitalist world economy can be characterized most broadly then in terms of two dialectically related and ultimately contradictory historical tendencies: (1) the privatization of the ownership of the means of production into more concentrated and centralized forms of capital accumulation; and (2) the 'proletarianization' of the labour force and the socialization of the labour process into more collective forms and standardized instruments of work. The extension of capitalist enterprises involves both absolute increases of scale and relative increases in the concentration and centralization of the major enterprises appropriating the products of labour. This extension is signified most obviously by the growing capital assess of the multi-national corporations. 'Proletarianization' refers to increases in abstract labour in two senses: first, the proportion of the labour force that has assumed a proletarian condition to the extent of being both dispossessed of the means of production and 'free' to *seek* alternative work for wages and, secondly, the proportion that has become incorporated into the capitalist machinofacture labour process. As we shall see, not all of these people become full-fledged proletarians or 'working class'.

By the turn of the century the growth of concentrated, centralized capitalist enterprises had become so extensive that, as Lenin and others documented:

> ... the dominance of monopolies and finance capital has established itself; ... the export of capital has acquired pronounced importance; ... the division of the world among the international trusts has begun; and ... the division of all territories of the globe among the biggest capitalist powers has been completed.[19]

At that point, pre-capitalist forms of labour were still prevalent in many societies, but the twentieth century has seen substantial increases in the global level of proletarianization, particularly in the sense of dispossessed surplus populations seeking work for wages. Both of these tendencies have continued up to the present. As a consequence, the class structures of all of the increasingly interdependent societies within this world economy have also tended to become more similar. Albert Syzmanski, for example, concludes in one of the most recent empirical studies that:

> ... the class structures of all the less-developed capitalist regions are tending to become more homogeneous, both among themselves and in relation to the advanced capitalist countries. The tendencies predominant in earlier stages of capitalist imperialism to generate highly diverse class structures among the various colonial regions and to create and/or perpetuate a systematic difference with the advanced countries are no more.... [C]apitalist relations of production are everywhere rapidly displacing feudal and tribal rem-

nants. This is true both in the class structures of societies as a whole and within the declining agricultural sector.[20]

But the development of the world capitalist economy remains *highly* uneven and unequal. The advanced capitalist societies are distinguished as those countries in which the concentration and centralization of capitalist enterprises is sufficient to permit a number of domestic corporations to export capital on a world scale; that is, to invest in productive activity around the globe while maintaining overall control of the enterprise's investment decisions and production process at home. Such sustained levels of capital concentration have been dependent on mobile workers whose labour power can be flexibly applied to initiate and generalize new production activities. In all advanced capitalist societies the vast majority of the potential labour force is now highly proletarianized in this narrow sense. Conversely, in those societies variously termed 'underdeveloped', 'less developed' or 'peripheral', productive activities are generally much less concentrated – with the exception of enclaves controlled by the advanced centres as well as some indigenous enterprises and joint ventures which have become large enough to be capital exporters within their own regions. Both the forms of labour and domestic markets remain much more heterogenous and separated than in the advanced centres. Much of the potential labour force is still unproletarianized, especially the large peasantry that remains tied to the land. One of the leading theorists of unequal development, Samir Amin, has recently offered a very broad empirical estimate of the attendant differences in class structure between the centres and peripheries of the world capitalist system.[21] His results, which are summarized in Table 4, suggest that about ninety per cent of the labour force within the advanced capitalist societies, or more specifically the OECD countries, is linked to the capitalist labour process whereas only about a quarter of the workforce in peripheral capitalist societies, on average, is now so linked. There is currently very great controversy among critical researchers about external and internal dynamics of capitalist development or underdevelopment in the 'Third World.'[22] For our immediate purposes, what is most important to recognize is the general structure of the worldwide capitalist division of labour and the distinctive degree of generalization of capitalist relations of production in the advanced capitalist societies in comparison with the 'less developed' countries that contain three-quarters of the labour force of this dominant mode of production.

Class Positions in Advanced Capitalist Production Relations

The advanced capitalist societies therefore represent the most fully developed form of the capitalist mode of production, and their class structures can be most easily understood in terms of the contradictory historical tendencies of capitalist relations of production outlined in the first section of this chapter. To

Table 4   Class Structure of the World Capitalist System (1975)

	Millions of Persons	World Distribution (%)	Centre & Periphery Distributions (%)
Centres			Centres
Capitalists and middle layers	90	7	24 ⎫
Proletarianized petty bourgeoisie	110	8	29 ⎬ 89
Working class	110	8	29 ⎪
Unemployed	25	2	7 ⎭
Small commodity producers	35	3	11
Total Centres Labour Force	370	27	100
Peripheries			Peripheries
Capitalist and middle layers	20	1	1· ⎫
Proletarianized petty bourgeoisie	80	6	8 ⎬ 19
Working class	50	4	5 ⎪
Urban unemployed	50	4	5 ⎭
Peasantry			
poor and exploited	600	44	61
middle	150	11	15
owners and capitalists	50	4	5
Total Periphery Labour Force	1,000	73	100
Total Capitalist System Labour Force	1,370	100	–

Source: SAMIR AMIN, *Class and Nation, Historically and in the Current Crisis,* New York: Monthly Review Press, 1980, p. 151.

reiterate, these four interdependent aspects are the relations of real ownership of the means of production, and relations within the labour process itself with regard to the social relations of production (this is, supervisory/non-supervisory) and the technical relations of production (that is, intellectual/manual; productive/non-productive). To have real ownership is to have control over the investment and accumulation of capital and allocation of resources. The most essential aspect of the social relations of production is the extent of disciplinary control each position has over the labour power of others in the supervisory hierarchy. Within the technical relations of production, the critical features are the distinctions between labours that conceive or plan production processes and those that routinely execute such processes as specified, and secondly between those labours that serve to create vendible commodities whose sale can achieve surplus value and those engaged rather in the realization or appropriation of such surplus value. Figure 1 summarizes the main types of class positions in the production relations of advanced capitalist societies in these terms. These positions will be outlined in some detail here since they are central to the subsequent analysis of educational issues.[23]

The place of capital is occupied by those who have substantial legal title to property in the means of production. Three objective positions are evident. Most important are the 'corporate capitalists'. These positions, typically corporate directors and top executives, control their enterprises' overall capital

Figure 1 *Main Objective Positions in Advanced Capitalist Production Relations*

General class location	Economic Ownership — Control over investment, resource allocation	Labour Process Relations — Disciplinary control	Labour Process Relations — Technical planning control	Labour Process Relations — Productive labour	Specific class position
Capital	+	+	+	N/A	Corporate capitalists
	+	+	+	±	Small employers
	±	N/A	N/A	N/A	Rentier capitalists
Intermediate elements	+	−	+	±	Petty bourgeoisie
	±	±	±	±	Managers
	−	±	−	±	Supervisors
	−	−	±	±	Non-supervisory professional employees
Dispossessed labours	−	−	−	−	Non-productive proletariat
	−	−	−	+	Productive proletariat
	−	N/A	N/A	N/A	Reserve labours
	−	N/A	N/A	*	Primary domestic labourers

Key:

+ = definite presence of characteristic
− = definite absence
± = intermediate or mixed characteristic
N/A = not applicable
* = reproductive labour

investments and financial allocations process and have superordinate control over labour and production policies. Their policy making efforts are devoted primarily to ensuring capital accumulation and they play no essential role in the actual production of the use values of commodities. Secondly, there are 'small employers' who own their own enterprises and retain overall control of the labour process. However, their number of employees is so small that, if the firm turns out vendible commodities, the owners are likely to do some productive labour themselves, and in any case they must continue to contribute their own surplus labour as well as extracting it from others if the enterprise is to survive. Thirdly, 'rentier capitalists' remain conspicuous even if very indirectly involved in production relations. These are positions with no direct relationship to the capitalist labour process, but whose legal ownership claims on the means of production are substantial enough to provide ample sustenance for their own idleness, and to be collectively considered in corporate capitalists' investment policies. All three positions are unambiguously devoted to maximizing profits, through the greatest feasible exploitation of hired labour.

There are four distinguishable types of objective positions among the intermediate elements within the capitalist production process. Three of these do not have any significant legal ownership claims and their agents must sell their labour power to either large or small capitalist enterprises. These three types of intermediate elements perform both a function of capital (that is, the control and surveillance of the labour process to ensure capital accumulation) and a necessary function of the 'collective worker' (that is, co-ordination and unification of the production process *per se*). These dual roles are often deeply fused in the exercise of daily control and co-ordination of the social and technical relations of machinofacture production. Such elements are both responsible to extract surplus value or surplus labour from other workers and also provide surplus value of labour to capital from their own work. In class terms, such intermediate positions are therefore inherently contradictory. Hence, they are best regarded as a 'pliable ectoplasmic layer' between the positions of capital and the proletariat.[24] 'Managers' are capitalists' closest subordinates within the actual production process and as such they play an essential operational role in decisions upon some of the resource acquisitions and allocations within particular parts of the firm's capital investment process. Even more vital, however, is their exercise of day-to-day control over *both* the social and technical relations of production units. These are positions that are in overall charge of the actual operation of the hierarchy of social discipline and the technical design and planning activities of specific production units, whether such units are themselves primarily concerned with commodities or with technical 'staff' functions. Beneath managers there are two other distinguishable positions, both without any significant ownership claims or role in the capital investment process. 'Supervisors' are positions with immediate disciplinary control over subordinated labour but with no discretionary control over the technical design of the production system. They work under the general control of managers. 'Non-supervisory professional employees' are positions with responsibility for the detailed problem solving involved in the technical design and standardized operation of production systems, but with no assigned supervisory role over other workers. In the social relations of production they may be directly subordinated to either managers or supervisors. In performing essential functions of the collective worker, those in all three objective positions may, if they are involved in firms that create vendible commodities, do productive labour themselves. But again, the social and technical divisions of labour, and of capitalist and collective worker functions, within these intermediate elements is so variegated, both between and within enterprises, that none of the three positions, and certainly not all three together, has much objective economic basis for its own organic solidarity.

There is also one intermediate element within the production process that does not share the common general structural features of these others. The remnants of the 'petty bourgeoisie' retain their old surface form of labour. That is, they maintain real ownership of their *immediate* means of production, while depending exclusively on their own labour and therefore controlling the overall design of their own production systems. However, as already mentioned, such 'self-employed' elements are increasingly dependent on capital in all respects. Their overall ownership is, typically, legally mortgaged to capitalist enterprises, their labour process is reliant on continuing commodity inputs from such enterprises, and whether or not they themselves produce commodities, their activities are tied to the rhythms of the capitalist market.

Among those who are fully dispossessed of any real ownership of the means of production as well as any control of the labour process beyond his/her own immediate position, there are two basic positions within the capitalist labour process. Virtually all employed labourers are now also deprived of any systematic ability to discipline themselves; and, while their ingenuity is often required to deal with local variations in the technical details of their work, design prerogatives have likewise been removed and discretionary acts increasingly circumscribed by standardized procedures. This is the proletarian labour force or 'working class'. The most basic distinction among all these workers is whether they perform productive or non-productive labour. This distinction has been widely misunderstood and the precise balance of productive and non-productive functions in a given objective position within the complex interdependency of the capitalist labour process is often extremely difficult to discern.[25] But it is a critical consideration. As previously noted, the extent of productive labour remains both the pivotal factor in economic crises and, especially through the industrial proletariat employed in extractive, manufacturing, construction and related transportation activities, the ultimate source of all revenues that keep the other activities of the capitalist economy going. Even an approximate sectoral analysis of 'productive and non-productive proletarian workers' is therefore useful for understanding the dynamics of capitalist production relations.

In addition, two other typical types of objective positions of dispossessed labour exist *outside* the capitalist production process *per se* but generally linked to it. 'Reserve labours' are comprised by those who are at least intermittently compelled to sell their labour power on the capitalist labour market but prevented in various ways from doing so with any sustained success. They include: the *temporarily unemployed*, who continue to seek work in given production positions; *students*, whose labour is limited by child labour laws as well as by compulsory and pre-requisite schooling; *pensioners*, whose labour has been terminated by numerous mandatory retirement clauses but who often continue to seek work to ensure their well-being; and most peripherally, the more or less permanently unemployed, or *'lumpen class'*, who comprise a subterranean world primarily engaged in criminal activities and dereliction.[26] The dynamics of all such reserve labour's articulation with the capitalist production process have received very little systematic study to date. All four elements exhibit great variability both in the range of production positions that they respond to and in the regularity with which their agents must seek paid work. However, it appears clear that reserve labours *as a whole* have generally increased with the generalization of the machinofacture phase of capitalist production.

'Primary domestic labour' is labour playing an active reproductive role in the household realm of subsistence. In contrast to reserve labours it has not been compelled to try to sell this labour intermittently for money, but rather to perform the critical daily and inter-generational tasks needed to reproduce all other labour powers without receiving any systematic compensation beyond its own subsistence. Many elements of traditional household tasks – homecrafts such as weaving and knitting, food processing, etc. – have been commodified by capitalist enterprises. This has compelled increasing numbers of the primary household workers, housewives, to seek paid employment to enable purchase of such elements of subsistence. But the many household functions that capital has not yet been able to commodify substantially – such as the bulk of cooking, cleaning, and child rearing tasks, and the daily rejuvenation of labour power – leave domestic labour with a vital role in sustaining the capitalist production process. All unpaid domestic labour therefore has a common *general* structural form, a form that is continually being restructured by capitalist commodification. In advanced capitalist societies, where other labour is 'free', all those whose sole economic function is domestic labour are distinctly oppressed; and those who not only sell their labour power but also continue to perform the primary domestic labour for others, notably 'working wives', are doubly oppressed. However, in concrete terms the specific content, extent and intensity of domestic labour vary immensely according to the combination of objective locations within the capitalist production process and among the reserve labours which it serves.[27]

A simplified graph of the dominant relations between those characteristic positions of advanced capitalist production appears in Figure 2. It is useful to recognize the major differences of this model from that of Erik Olin Wright, since his has been the most specific of the previous theoretical systematizations of economic class locations in such societies, and because many of our specific distinctions appear to be similar.[28] First, Wright continues to view petty bourgeois labour as operating within the small commodity mode of production and to pose several contradictory class locations between the petty bourgeois and capitalist modes of production, namely small employers and 'semi-autonomous wage earners'. While viewing the dimensions of the capitalist labour process somewhat differently than Wright, I also recognize these three objective positions of labour. (The 'semi-autonomous wage earner' and the 'non-supervisory professional employee' positions are roughly analogous). But it should be evident that I consider all three locations to be fully integrated within the capitalist mode of production and their activities determined by its laws of motion. Thus, not only professional employees but also petty bourgeois workers themselves are among the intermediate elements performing contradictory functions within capitalist relations of production. Secondly, while the distinction between productive and non-productive labour positions may make little difference to the identification of intermediate elements where these functions are usually tightly fused, I emphasize the importance of this distinction within the proletariat because of its centrality to economic class struggles, especially in periods of crisis. Wright's formulation, largely in reaction to Hicos Poulantzas' arbitrary exclusion of non-productive, non-manual workers from the proletariat,[29] merely notes the classificatory difficulties caused by interdependent functions. Thirdly, in his most recent formulation Wright speaks briefly of objective locations not directly determined by production relations, and suggests that:

> ... the class location of such positions is determined by their relationship to the fundamental interests of classes defined within the social relations of production.[30]

Such a blunt classificatory rule serves to ignore the facts that the various reserve labours and primary domestic labour all share with the proletariat a complete separation from real ownership of the means of production and that they are not merely appendages of or 'trajectories' into or out of production locations but distinctive locations of labour *in themselves* articulated with the capitalist mode of production. Their material separation from the production process itself gives such labours a lack of internal structural determinacy in objective class terms. Marx made this point in his observations about the fluid, latent and stagnant characteristics of reserve labours and, particularly, the extreme political volatility of the lumpen class.[31] Such observations are applicable to domestic labour to a much lesser degree, given the centrality of such labour in regeneration the labour power of 'breadwinners' often specifically located within the capitalist production process. However, to simply assert as Wright does, for example, that the housewife of a proletarian is *necessarily* part of the working class is to presume away such interdeterminacy and discourage study of the real mechanisms articulating these exterior labours with the production process and actual class struggle.

The foregoing outline of typical objective locations involved in the produc-

Figure 2   Graph of Dominant Relations Between Typical Positions in the Class Structure of Advanced Capitalist Production

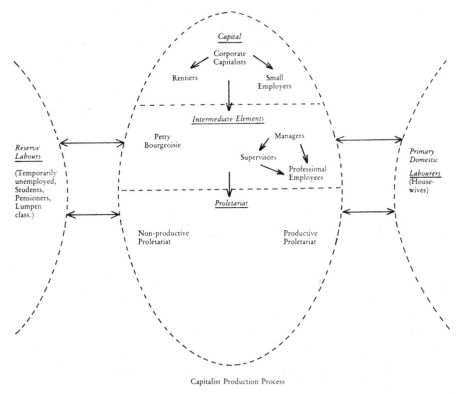

Key: Arrows indicate dominant direction of control in production relations.

tion relations of advanced capitalist societies is simply a beginning for systematic analysis. A full concrete analysis would require sensitivity to a number of important specifications. For example, distinctions between class relations within monopoly and competitive sectors of private enterprise, as well as within private and public sectors, may be highly relevant in considering class influences on many social policy issues.[32]

While there have now been many ethnographic studies of the contemporary capitalist labour process, historical and empirical studies of societal class structures regarded in the above terms have been rare and largely limited to the conventionally defined *occupational* labour force. The most notable comparative study to be published to date is perhaps the work of Val Burris.[33] On the basis of the standardized occupational data provided by the International Labour Office, Burris has estimated the class structures of the active labour force in major industrial market economies. He specifies significant histori-cally-based differences in the current sizes of the traditional petty bourgeoisie of farmers and self-employed workers, documents their continuing decline in all of these countries, and suggests a concomitant shift into other intermediate positions which he, along with many others, calls the 'new middle class'. However, it is inadvisable to attempt any further inferences about class positions in production relations on the basis of these gross occupational categories which mask important distinctions especially in the control of the labour process.[34]

Table 5   Class Structures of Major Industrial Market Economies: Economically Active Male Population

	United States (1970) %	Japan (1970) %	West Germany (1970) %	France (1968) %	Italy (1971) %	United Kingdom (1971) %	Canada (1970) %
Capitalist	1.0	1.0	1.0	1.0	1.0	1.0	1.0
Petty Bourgeoisie	9.6	27.3	13.4	23.5	25.5	9.0	14.2
Agricultural	2.9	13.9	5.2	12.8	10.2	1.7	7.0
Non-agricultural	6.7	13.6	8.2	10.7	15.3	7.3	7.2
New Middle Class	22.2	15.7	15.9	14.4	7.2	18.9	21.6
Managers/Administrators	9.3	9.7	6.5	4.8	3.0	8.0	10.8
Professional/Technical	12.9	6.0	9.4	9.6	4.2	10.0	10.8
Working Class	67.2	56.0	69.7	61.1	66.3	71.2	63.2

Source: Val Burris (1980) 'Class Formation and Transformation in Advanced Capitalism: A Comparative Analysis,' *Social Praxis* 7 (3–4), except for the Canadian distribution which has been calculated in the same manner using Burris' main source, International Labour Office (1971) *Yearbook of Labour Statistics*, Geneva: ILO.

Several more specific empirical estimates of the societal-level class structure of the occupational work force are available, for the United States and Canada respectively. Wright has conducted a secondary analysis of a 1969 US sample survey containing conventional occupational data and some items on the social relations of production,[35] I have done a re-analysis of the more detailed occupational data available in the 1971 Canada Census,[36] and William Johnston and Michael Ornstein[37] have analyzed similar occupational data from a 1977 Canada sample survey. The summary results are presented in Table 6. The most notable difference from Burris' work is that these studies distinguish the supervisory positions (line supervisors, foremen) that Burris' data sources tend to collapse into the working class, especially in the US case.[38] More recently I have conducted interview surveys in Ontario which have specifically asked respondents to locate themselves on each of the four aspects of production relations discussed above. Since Ontario remains Canada's most advanced and largest industrial region, the findings may have considerable relevance for the tendencies of capitalist production relations in other regions of the country and elsewhere. The pertinent results of these surveys, which were done in 1978, 1979 and 1980,[39] are summarized in Table 7 and juxtaposed with 1971 Canada and Ontario census-based analyses. Comparisons must be made cautiously because of methodological and definitional differences, but primarily on the basis of the results in both Tables 6 and 7 several tentative conclusions might be offered:

1   the managerial, supervisory and professional positions, or 'new middle class' appear to constitute a growing proportion of the employed labour force in advanced capitalism;

2   the proletariat or working class positions appear to have been declining recently as a proportion of the employed labour force; and

3   while petty bourgeois positions have clearly exhibited a long-term decline[40] – with the predominant shifts appearing to have been first into working class positions and more recently into 'new middle class' ones – such positions have also been replaced by small employers, who in spite of concentrating tendencies still represent major employers of hired labour and constitute the majority of capitalists.

Several of the comparative features of the class structures of the US and Canada suggested by Table 6 are also worthy of note here. Both societies have large 'new middle class' elements in relation to working class positions; this may be indicative of both their high levels of generalization of machinofacture production processes and their positions as powerful industrial economies

Table 6   Estimates of the Class Structure of the United States and Canada: Economically Active Population

	United States (1969) %	Canada (1971) %	Canada (1977) %
Corporate Capitalists	1–2	.7	1.1
Small Employers	6.7	2–3.5	13.8
Petty Bourgeoisie	4.5	7.5–9.5	6.4
Managers	12	5.9	11.0
Supervisors	35–46 { 18–23	29.4 { 11.9	31.0 { 11.0
Professional Employees	5–11	11.6	14.6
Non-productive Proletariat		28–30	
Productive Proletariat	41–54	58–62 { 30–32	53.2

Sources: For the U.S., WRIGHT, E.O. (1978) *Class, Crisis and the State*, London, New Left Books p. 86.
For Canada 1971, LIVINGSTONE, D.W. *Class and Class Consciousness in Advanced Capitalism* (to be published); and for 1977, JOHNSTON, W. and ORNSTEIN M. (1980) 'Measuring social class: A comparison of Marxist and Conventional approaches', paper circulated by the Red Feather Institute for Advanced Studies in Sociology, January.

Table 7   Class Structures of Ontario: Economically Active Population

	Canada (1971 Census) %	Ontario (1971 Census) %	Ontario (1978–1980 Surveys) %
Corporate Capitalists	.7	1.0	1
Small Employers	2.35	2–3.5	6–7
Rentier Capitalists	–	–	1–2
Petty Bourgeoisie	7.5–9.5	6–7.5	7–9
Managers	5.9	6.5	8–10
Supervisors	29.4 { 11.9	30.6 { 12.6	33–41 { 14–18
Professional Employees	11.6	11.5	11–13
Non-productive Proletariat	58–62 { 28–30	58–62 { 29–31	45–50 { 23–25
Productive Proletariat	30–32	29–31	22–25

Source: LIVINGSTONE, D.W. *Class and Class Consciousness in Advanced Capitalism* (to be published) and LIVINGSTONE, D.W. and HART, D.J. (1981) *Public Attitudes Toward Education in Ontario 1980*, Toronto, OISE Press, Appendix 1.

within the world capitalist system. Canada has a larger petty bourgeoisie and possibly a smaller proportion of small employers; this perhaps reflects the earlier and more autonomous transition of the US from small commodity production into the capitalist mode. But the most significant difference would seem to be the relatively larger size of the US 'new middle class', especially the managerial elements; such differences may be primarily associated with the distinctive roles of the US and Canada within the world economy. Throughout most of this century, the US, along with Japan, (West) Germany, France, and – at least until the 1970s – the UK, have constituted the 'major imperialist formations'. That is, their enterprise aggregates have been sufficiently large and concentrated and their systems of production sufficiently autocentric for them to be significant net exporters of capital. Canada, along with the other white Dominions of Australia and New Zealand, and Italy, along with the other countries of western Europe have been 'secondary imperialist formations'. While such societies have had sufficiently concentrated capitalist enterprises to be significant gross exporters of capital on a world scale, their enterprises have not generally been of large enough scale either to compete equally with the major imperialists' enterprises or to prevent the extensive penetration of their own domestic domains by such enterprises when production and/or market opportunities have become attractive. Secondary imperialists' investments abroad have typically occurred where they are either complementary or non-competitive with the major imperialists' enterprises. Hence, in spite of their highly generalized capitalist labour processes, countries like Canada have tended to operate as net importers of capital, as indicated both by substantial levels of foreign corporate investment and technological dependence. The larger managerial sector of the US is therefore consistent with its position as the leading major imperialist power.[41]

Recognition of Canada's global position as a secondary imperialist social formation is critical to understanding the historical development of the Canadian class structure. Already in the early years of the century, Canada had many highly concentrated capitalist enterprises, especially in the banking, commercial and resource extracting sectors with the aid of British portfolio investment. The Royal Commission on Corporate Concentration has martial-led the available evidence to suggest that industrial concentration generally increased during two early merger waves in the 1910s and 1920s, that it increased substantially from the late 1940s to the early 1950s and that it was apparently fairly stable from the mid 1950s to the early 1970s. The Commission also noted that while Canadian industries are generally more concentrated than enterprises in other advanced capitalist formations, the average size of our dominant corporations is generally much smaller than those of major imperial-ist formations.[42] These tendencies are partially explained by Canada's excep-tional *accessibility* to capital export from the major imperialist formations, most emphatically the United States in its emergence to global dominance in this century. This condition is reflected in the level of foreign control of Canadian capital which rose from less than fifteen per cent before World War I to over thirty per cent by the mid-1950s, and has since fluctuated between twenty-eight and thirty-seven per cent with much higher levels of control in the most concentrated productive sectors of the economy.[43] The recent implementation of a National Energy Policy (NEP) to increase Canadian ownership in this economic sphere, a spate of highly visible US investments largely by Canadian real estate-based companies, and the apparent toughening of the criteria used by the Foreign Investment Review Agency (FIRA) represent marginal changes that have not yet had any discerniable effect on the general secondary imperialist character of the Canadian enterprise structure.

This pattern òf concentration of capital, as well as an increasing centraliza-tion of economic control in such large conglomerate enterprises, is evidenced by the composition of the corporate capitalist elite. As Wallace Clement, following John Porter, has tried to document for the 1951–1972 period, Canada's small corporate elite was becoming more concentrated, harder to enter from the lower classes, and increasingly dominated by compradors and absentee directors.[44]

The second fundamental historical tendency of capitalist development, the socialization of the labour process, also has had a distinctive trajectory in Canada. It should be emphasized that in the early nineteenth century, Upper Canada was, to use Amin's term, a young central formation based on the predominance of the independent commodity form of production, courtesy of mass European settlement.[45] By 1900, Canada therefore possessed a capacity for independent achievement of a fully developed capitalist mode of produc-tion, even though established relations with major imperialists, the UK and increasingly the US, necessitated interdependent achievement with a heavy emphasis on commercial capital. By the turn of the centrury, at least a bare majority of the workforce were wage earners and industrialization had been expanding rapidly for more than a decade. As Leo Johnson has observed in his survey of the development of class in Canada in the twentieth century up to the 1960s:

'As capitalism has grown and developed in Canada, the composition of the labour force has changed in two distinct ways. First, a larger and larger proportion were drawn from pre-capitalist and pre-industrial occupations, such as agriculture and menial labour, into the capitalist labour market and machine-related production, and second within the capitalist sector itself, changes in composition have occurred. Related to these changes has been the gradual decline of the status and independence of client groups such as the professional occupations.[46]

The most pronounced change has been the absorption of the petty bourgeoisie. The decline of these small commodity producers, primarily farmers but including independent craftsmen and shopkeepers, has seen them drop from 47.5 per cent of the workforce in 1901 to 9.3 per cent in 1967.[47] Conversely, wage earners have increased from 52.5 per cent to 88.9 per cent of the labour force over the same period. The industrial proletariat, 'blue collar' production workers, made up 47.6 per cent of the hired work force by 1901. While capitalist enterprises have been increasingly generalized ever since then, by 1921 production workers had declined to 37.5 per cent of the total hired work force, whereas 'white collar' workers had grown proportionately from 29.0 per cent to 43.6 per cent.[48] These proportions remained fairly constant up to the 1950s, after which time there has been some further decline of the proportion of production workers and expansion of the proportions of white collar and service workers. Johnson's analysis is again informative. As he notes:

High immigration and large scale capital formation drastically transformed the Canadian economy from small-scale craft production to large-scale machine production based upon readily available cheap labour during the era of Macdonald's National Policy. This expansion of capital and transformation to a capitalist mode of production accelerated rapidly during the 1890–1910 period. Despite the rapid expansion of production, the enormous immigration of the 1896–1911 period ... created a huge surplus of low-skilled labourers which effectively halted the transformation toward capital intensity ... High levels of immigration encouraged a shift toward the use of menial labour ... By 1920, while large scale manufacturing and capitalist production had almost entirely eliminated crafts production, still it had not created modern capitalist-intensive production. Rather a large and increasing proportion of the work force was engaged in essentially pre-industrial (and thereby, essentially pre-capitalist) forms of menial labour. In other words, while capitalist social labour relations had been established, capitalist industrial modes of production, [that is, capitalist machinofacture] in many regions and occupations, had not. On the other hand, the expansion of capitalist production and particularly the creation of large manufacturing units necessitated the creation of a large white collar apparatus to manage it.[49]

The next two decades of great capital expansion and great depression saw the industrial proletariat consolidate its economic position while the wage position of menial labourers declined. The Second World War and federal government initiatives facilitated the incorporation of most of the Canadian labour force into advanced modes of industrial production, involving large shifts of the non-capitalist work force to urban industrial centres and leaving only a few marginalized pools of rural non-farm menial labour beyond the capitalist production process. The incorporation since the 1940s has also involved the increasing proletarianization from unpaid domestic labour of married women, and the creation of a growing labour reserve composed variously but including urban unskilled workers, sponsored immigrants, rural menials, students, semi-retired and housewives, all ready to sell their free labour in a capitalist market. By 1961, as Johnson summarizes:

> ... the capitalist economic system was virtually all encompassing in Canada, taking in the vast majority of the work force and employing them in both capitalist social relations and in capital-oriented modes of production. The growth and development of capitalism, however, had not followed a regular pattern of growth and transformation. Rather it had been subjected to large and dramatic convulsions in the relationship of capital and labour, each of which created a period of unrest and heightened labour consciousness.[50]

Unfortunately, there are no available studies more specifically documenting societal class structures in terms of positions in production relations prior to the 1970s, and no systematic empirical assessments of the extent of articulation of those outside the official labour force with the capitalist production process. My own survey research for Ontario in the late 1970s has, as noted, examined the class structure within the capitalist production process explicitly in terms of specific positions in production relations. This research has also begun to document the intermittent articulation of the labour power of reserve labours and housewives with capitalist labour markets; while the *direct* role of their occasional labour power may be quite marginal, consideration of the existence and extent of these positions is very important for an adequate understanding of the complete class structure of advanced capitalist societies. Adam Przeworski has suggested that the growth of such 'surplus populations' has been *the* most substantial change in the overall class structure of advanced capitalist societies in the present century.[51] A summary profile of the general class structure of Ontario in the late 1970s, based on these surveys, is presented in

Figure 3. In particular, it should be observed that the surplus populations dependent on capitalist production now comprise over forty per cent of the adult population.

Figure 3   General Class Structure of the 18+ Ontario Population, 1978–1980

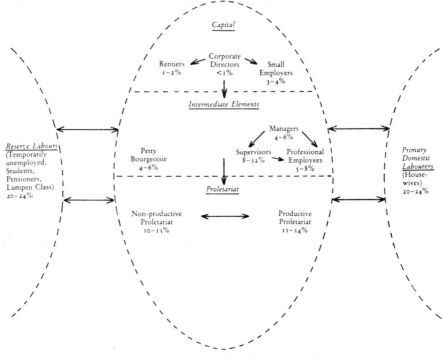

Capitalist Production Process.

Key: Arrows indicate dominant direction of control in production relations.

Class Circles: Cores and Peripheries

The increasing size and visibility of these 'surplus populations', serves to underline the fact that classes are constituted at several material sites beyond the capitalist production process. Recent historiographic and ethnographic studies are painstakingly documenting the historical forms of the material sites of class relations and the interconnections between these workplaces and other sites, most notably households and cultural communities.[52] There are now numerous case studies of distinctive working class and capitalist class communities within advanced capitalist societies. Most of these studies have focused on the cores of the polar class positions in production relations, groups which have often tended to live within relatively homogenous and easily identified residential and cultural class communities. There have been very few community studies of people in more peripheral capitalist positions (that is, small employers, rentiers) and working class positions (that is, 'white collar' or non-productive proletariat). Indeed, there has been a prevalent tendency to collapse these peripheries of both capitalist and working class social circles into those amorphous residues called the 'middle class'. At least with regard to these class peripheries, the inclination of traditional intellectuals to generalize selected aspects of the life situations within 'middle class' residues into universal ways of life in advanced capitalism has been accepted quite uncritically by most Marxist scholars.

More generally, there has been very little systematic analysis of class circles and their cores and peripheries in advanced capitalism.[53] *Class circles* refer primarily to those who share similar class positions in production or, if not directly engaged in the production process, are intimately linked to such positions as reserve labours or domestic labourers through shared household and communal relations. In general, then, capitalist, working class, and intermediate strata circles should be distinguishable, as well as several more mixed forms (for example, capitalist-intermediate, working class-intermediate), and also marginalized people without intimate social contact with those in the capitalist production process. My Ontario surveys suggest that capitalist circles now constitute about two per cent of the adult population, working class circles about forty per cent, intermediate strata circles around one-third, and other mixed circles and marginalized people about one-quarter.[54]

The *cores* of both the capitalist and working classes are based in the most concentrated enterprises of the economy. The capitalist core are the 'corporate capitalists', the owners and directors of the largest and most powerful enterprises. Whatever criteria have been used to distinguish this core (for example, firm capital assets over five million dollars, firm size over one thousand employees), they and their intimates number less than one per cent of the population in all advanced capitalist societies. The working class core is the 'industrial proletariat', those dispossessed workers employed as manual labour in the extractive, manufacturing, construction and related transportation industries of the economy. In Ontario, I estimate that the core of the working class now constitutes between five and twenty per cent of the population, depending on whether only the largest (that is, 1,000 + employees) or all industrial firms are included, and whether those economically dependent on these productive proletarians are considered.[55]

With particular reference to contemporary working class community studies, Brook and Finn recognize that:

> As it is, 'reading back' from community studies is an uncertain exercise. We are dealing with a peculiarly untheorized, naturalized, impacted problematic which methodologically conceals its own tracks.[56]

Such cautions are all the more in order for any aggregate-level effort to characterize class circles.

My purpose here is to examine empirical connections between the class positions in production identified in the preceding section with a number of other objective social characteristics relevant to establishing more concrete profiles of class circles. Again my Ontario surveys provide the main data source.[57] Limited assessments will be made of the extent to which class positions in production constitute distinct class circles in terms of communal and household relations. Any substantial differences between the corporate elite or industrial proletariat core positions and the peripheral capitalist or working class positions respectively, will also be noted. The specific characteristics on which data are readily available for these assessments are: age, sex and ethnicity, as well as inter-generational class mobility, inter-class marriage rates and trade union membership.

We can look first at the association between class positions in production and other irreducible social attributes of all individuals, namely age, sex and ethnicity. The data are presented in Tables 8, 9 and 10. With regard to age, aside from the highly predictable finding of young students and old pensioners, the most notable differences shown in Table 8 are that rentiers are generally old and corporate capitalists and managers are most likely to be middle-aged. The patriarchal dominance of capitalist production is clearly indicated in Table 9 by the finding that around three-quarters of all direct proprietary and supervisory positions are held by males. Moreover, while nearly all corporate capitalists are males, over ninety per cent of the productive proletariat is also male. This is in marked contrast to the predominance of females in the non-productive proletariat. Finally, as Table 10 indicates, corporate capitalists and rentiers are

Table 8   Class Position by Age, Ontario 1978–80

	18–24 %	25–34 %	35–54 %	55 + %
Corporate Capitalists	–	2	60	38
Small Employers	5	35	60	10
Rentiers	–	–	10	90
Petty Bourgeoisie	10	23	45	22
Managers	7	22	58	13
Supervisors	20	22	45	13
Professional Employees	10	42	38	10
Non-Productive Proletariat	33	22	32	13
Productive Proletariat	18	29	41	12
Housewives	12	30	39	19
Temporarily unemployed	44	33	18	5
Pensioners	–	2	3	95
Students	90	7	3	
Total 18+ Population	20	22	33	25

Table 9   Class Position By Sex, Ontario 1978–80

	% Male
Corporate Capitalists	96
Small Employers	75
Rentiers	55
Petty Bourgeoisie	76
Managers	80
Supervisors	72
Professional Employees	55
Non-Productive Proletariat	42
Productive Proletariat	92
Housewives	2
Temporarily Unemployed	67
Pensioners	50
Students	55
Total 18+ Population	50

Table 10   Class Position By Ethnicity, Ontario 1978–80

	British %	*French %*	*Other European %*	*Non-European %*	*Unspecified %*
Corporate Capitalists	84	2	10	1	3
Small Employers	61	2	36	1	1
Rentiers	84	–	13	3	–
Petty Bourgeoisie	53	7	35	3	2
Managers	67	5	20	5	3
Supervisors	53	8	28	6	5
Professional Employees	57	6	31	3	3
Non-Productive Proletariat	50	12	29	6	3
Productive Proletariat	49	8	34	5	5
Housewives	54	11	28	5	2
Temporarily Unemployed	47	15	30	4	4
Pensioners	60	11	25	1	3
Students	43	6	33	11	7
Total 18+ Population	54	8	30	4	4

very largely of British ethnic origins while most other class positions and especially the proletariat are of more diverse ethnicities. This is a particularly notable finding in light of Canada's status as the most ethno-linguistically 'fractionalized' of all the advanced capitalist societies.[58] Both the middle-aged, British, male character of corporate capitalists in Ontario, and the ethnically diverse and sexually divided nature of the proletariat should be kept in mind as important contextuating factors for the subsequent analysis of education.

Studies of inter-generational class mobility documenting substantial upward mobility have been very popular among traditional social scientists in the post-War expansionary period; in contrast, the topic has been an anathema to many Marxist critics who have preferred to puncture the illusory quantifications of stratification research and assert working class solidarity. The reverse intellectual postures may well come to characterize the current period of economic stagnation. In any case, little of the previous empirical mobility research relying on conventional occupational categories is directly comparable with a study based on relations of production criteria. One of the most recent and extensive of these studies, the 1972 British survey by the Oxford Social Mobility Group, does offer some observations that are directly relevant to the mobility and stability of the industrial proletariat. John Goldthorpe concludes that:

> ... the British working class should be recognized as being rather distinctive. To judge from the data of other national mobility studies relating to the 1960s or early 1970s, it would seem very doubtful if the industrial labour force of any other society is second-generation to the same extent. For example, as compared with the three-quarters who may be reckoned second-generation blue-collar in the British case, the corresponding proportion for the industrial working classes of the United States and of Sweden would appear to be only a little over a half and for the French working class, somewhat under a half. The major source of the difference here is that in these latter countries there is a sizeable minority of industrial workers who ... are the sons of, and who have often themselves for some time been farmers, smallholders or peasants, or agricultural workers.[59]

Clearly Britain, as the oldest industrial capitalist society, has had a diminished petty bourgeoisie for some time, whereas in the other advanced capitalist societies the petty bourgeoisie made up around a quarter or more of the labour force until the World War II period. However, as Burris' data in Table 5 indicates, the petty bourgeoisie has *continued* to be a much more significant factor in the case of France (and of Italy and Japan) than in North America where it had been reduced by the early 1970s to about the same overall size as in Britain. In short, the greater upward mobility of the industrial proletariat in North America than in Britain has also been a consequence of the considerably greater post-War expansion of the North American economy. Indeed, the recent empirical research conclusion has been that the majority of occupational transitions between fathers and sons in post-War North America have been a necessary outcome of the changing composition of the labour force associated with such expansion.[60]

It would appear to follow that as expansion lags and opportunities for upward mobility diminish, the inter-generational mobility rates of industrial workers would more closely approximate British levels of the early 1970s. In any case, as Table 11 indicates, nearly two-thirds of the industrial proletariat in Canada's most advanced industrial region in the late 1970s was second-generational. The majority of non-productive proletarian workers, as well as housewives and the temporarily unemployed were also of proletarian family origins. The marginal distributions in this table suggest the major post-War transformations of the Ontario class structure. While the petty bourgeoisie still tends to reproduce itself internally, its proportions have been markedly reduced, and the offspring of petty bourgeoisie fathers make up significant proportions of all other current class positions. Furthermore, while rentiers have generally inherited their proprietorship from their fathers, other capitalist positions appear to have been very open to upward mobility, especially from intermediate strata origins. In the post-War expansion, corporate capitalists were only able to reproduce fast enough to fill about one-quarter of the available positions, with one-third of the new generation being drawn from managerial family origins and the rest from more subordinate class origins including the proletariat. Such openness may have been quite typical historically as capitalist enterprises and the machinofacture process have become more generalized. However, as Porter and Clement's longitudinal Canadian data suggest at least for the corporate elite,[61] the structural limits of this openness may now have been reached.

The tendencies for class circles to reproduce themselves are more immediately indicated by class marriage patterns. The exceptional efforts of leading families to ensure that 'money marries money' have long been readily apparent.[62] While working class youths may often have had even more compelling material incentives for attempting to 'marry upward', case studies have typically found quite high intra-class marriage rates in working class communities, as well as significantly greater tendencies than among the intermediate strata to depend generally on kinship relations.[63] Table 12 presents the relevant results of the Ontario survey. While the data are limited to marriage partners' own *current* class positions, two striking findings do emerge. Corporate capitalist wives, along with rentiers, are extremely unlikely to be directly involved in the production process or therefore to have many necessary sustained contacts with subordinate classes. Their role in reproducing the 'high society' of bourgeois culture always remains ostentatiously visible. Conversely, the wives of productive proletarians may be regularly forced into wage labour, and when they are the chances are extremely high that it will be into a proletarian position. The data suggest that the productive proletariat, and perhaps the temporarily unemployed (the majority of whom

Table 11 Class Position by Father's Main Class Position, Ontario 1978

Respondent's Current Class Position	Father's Main Class Position (%)						
	Capitalist	Manager	Supervisor	Professional Employee	Petty Bourgeoisie	Proletariat	Row Totals
Corporate Capitalists	23	31	8	6	14	18	<1%
Small Employers	12	18	3	5	26	36	4%
Rentiers	65	5	5	5	20	—	1%
Petty Bourgeoisie	1	7	7	4	51	30	5%
Managers	3	19	6	9	20	40	4%
Supervisors	1	9	17	4	23	46	9%
Professional Employees	2	25	5	11	23	34	7%
Non-Productive Proletariat	3	11	5	8	14	59	13%
Productive Proletariat	3	3	3	5	22	64	12%
Housewives	5	7	7	3	24	54	22%
Temporarily Unemployed	4	3	8	8	28	50	8%
Pensioners	1	5	4	9	44	37	9%
Students	6	13	11	11	30	29	5%
Total 18+ Population	4%	9%	6%	6%	25%	48%	100%

Table 12 *Class Position by Spouse's Class Position, Ontario 1978*

	Capitalist	'New Middle Class'	Petty Bourgeoisie	Proletariat	Housewife	Reserve Labour	No Spouse
				Spouse's Class Position (%)			
Corporate Capitalists	1	11	2	2	81	1	2
Small Employers	15	14	20	12	31	3	5
Rentiers	–	–	–	–	31	69	–
Petty Bourgeoisie	–	21	5	20	35	–	19
Managers	–	21	6	19	42	–	12
Supervisors	–	10	3	30	27	1	29
Professional Employees	–	27	2	20	28	5	18
Non-Productive Proletariat	1	18	6	27	13	6	29
Productive Proletariat	–	9	1	34	34	5	16
Housewives	5	27	11	41	–	8	8
Temporarily Unemployed	1	6	1	30	27	5	30
Pensioners	–	7	3	14	29	12	35
Students	–	5	–	–	2	9	84
Total 18+ Population	1	16	5	26	20	7	25

have productive proletarian occupations), are very likely to live in homogenous working class households.

Finally, we can briefly consider the extent to which those in different class positions have developed political vehicles for expressing their own social interests. In addition to the pervasive advertising activities of their enterprises, capitalists can convey their points of view through an integrated network of business associations, commissions, advisory boards, clubs, lobby groups, etc. This network, much more than their direct political participation has facilitated the corporate elite's hegemonic influence over major political parties' programs and government policy making in many areas, including education.[64] Intermediate elements have now created a variegated array of formal associations and, more recently, some professional unions. Among the proletariat, trade unions have historically represented the most genuine sustained expression of the interests of working people.[65] There have been many limitations on such expression in Canada as elsewhere,[66] but the unions remain today the major organized vehicle for conveying working class political concerns both internally and to other sectors of society. Table 13 indicates the extent to which different class positions in Ontario are currently associated with trade union membership. About two-thirds of the productive proletariat are union members. Their industrial unions, the largest and most powerful in the country, are often dominated by the monopoly sector productive proletariat, over three-quarters of whom are unionized. Only about one quarter of the non-productive proletariat is now unionized along with similar proportions of professional employees and supervisors; unionization has increased signifi-

Table 13   Class Position by Trade Union Membership, Ontario 1978–80

	% Trade Union Members
Corporate Capitalists	–
Small Employers	3
Rentiers	–
Petty Bourgeoisie	4
Managers	5
Supervisors	20
Supervisors	20
Professional Employees	25
Non-Productive Proletariat	25
Productive Proletariat	67
Housewives	1
Temporarily Unemployed	20
Pensioners	10
Students	2
Total 18+ Population	20

cantly in all three groups over the past decade, especially in the state sector, and all three are often members of the same union.

This array of associated attributes by no means provides an adequate account of the material structures of class circles or their influential cores in this particular advanced capitalist region. It should, however, offer a richer context than production relations alone for appreciating the analysis of class-based educational practices which comprises the remainder of the book.

Class Position and Schooling

Assessing the equality of educational opportunities in relation to parental socio-economic status has been perhaps the major preoccupation of sociologists of education over the past generation. Study after study throughout the advanced capitalist countries has documented substantial differences between those from upper and lower status family backgrounds in levels of cognitive achievement, educational aspirations, levels of schooling attained, and consequent adult economic success.[67] The weight of evidence has made it difficult for any researcher to deny that 'a large proportion of individual differences in educational attainments are consistently accounted for by non-scholastic factors'.[68] In the past decade, there are discernible tendencies for empirical research on educational equality issues to become more polarized according to researchers' general political sympathies. More progressive scholars have focused on documenting ways in which schooling simply transmits or reproduces the inequities of family economic status, while more traditional researchers have scrutinized the specific effects that schools can have in facilitating individual development on more meritocratic criteria.[69] In any event, the usefulness of this massive body of data is vitiated for our purposes by two factors: (1) a general denial of the contextual effects of the changing structure of production relations on individual educational and economic opportunities; and (2) the almost universal reliance on occupational status gradations rather than class positions as the basis for assessing the extent of inequality.

The major structural modifications of most advanced capitalist societies' production relations after World War II have had considerable implications for educational equality. Most obviously, the traditional self-employed occupations (such as independent farmers, artisans and shopkeepers) which had relatively little need for formal education, rapidly diminished as a proportion of the labour force, to be replaced by occupations more fully integrated within the capitalist machinofacture process and with greater formal requirements. The extension of capitalist enterprises, the technological advancement of machinofacture and post-War population growth meant that the pyramidal occupational structure of the capitalist economy came to have more jobs at the upper levels than could possibly have been filled by any inheritance mechanisms. Even more significantly, the pyramid itself broadened in the middle to include a growing proportion of intermediate level jobs involved in co-ordinating and supervising a more capital-intensive production process. These jobs especially required a wide array of formal technical skills and associated social skills.

The expansion of the educational system therefore has been intimately related to these structural changes in production, with increasing equalization of opportunities for primary and secondary level participation for students from all class backgrounds and diminishing effects of class origins on such participation. As Table 1 suggests, such class-based differences in general *participation* rates as now occur among young people must be located at the end of secondary school and in entry to and completion of post-secondary level schooling. Even the post-secondary level is far from the elite preserve it tended to be in the pre-war era. This is not to deny the occurence of differential *treatment* of students related to social class distinctions, for example, in informal grouping at the primary level, in formal streaming into secondary school programmes, and in differential access to various university and college programmes. It is rather to recognize explicitly the necessarily broadening structure of participation in which such differential treatments may occur.

A number of writers have noted such a distinction between 'equality of condition' and 'equality of opportunity',[70] that is, the existing structure of social positions and the chances various individuals have to obtain any given position. However, even the most sophisticated, longitudinally-based empirical research still tends toward an individualistic fallacy, in observing trends toward decreasing direct effects of father's occupational status on educational attainment without making any reference to this *changing* structural context.[71]

Secondly, even Marxist scholars such as Bowles and Gintis, whose work has been based theoretically on the structure of capitalist production and its influence on education, have depended on occupational hierarchies for their assessments of class influences on educational attainment.[72] Such a procedure not only confounds a Marxist model of class relations with a gradational stratification model but also, as noted previously, can give quite misleading empirical indications of the positions that many people occupy in the structure of production relations.[73]

The most relevant of previously published empirical research on class and educational attainments is probably the work of J.K. Lindsey. Using a Marxist model of class relations, which at least with regard to the polar capitalist and productive proletariat positions is roughly comparable to the class distinctions identified in the present study, Lindsey has conducted a secondary analysis of the International Education Association's 1964 survey of student achievement.[74] He analyses the relations in seven advanced capitalist societies between parental class position and thirteen year old students' school programmes (vocational, general, academic), mathematics test scores and further education desired. He notes especially the domination of the capitalist class over others and the contrast between this class and the working class. More specifically, for the major industrial economies included in his study he concludes:

In both England and Scotland, we find a sharp dominance of the capitalists over the working class for all three variables ... In [West Germany], we again find the strong contrast between capitalists and the working class, but here the difference is much less for mathematics score than for program and education desired ... In France, the strong difference between the capitalist and working classes appears for program and for education desired, but not for mathematics scores ... In the USA, where the 'controllable' variable, school program, reflects a more egalitarian system than in the European countries, except Sweden, social class differences in mathematics score are much greater than in any other country studied. The mechanism by which these class divisions are so strongly maintained requires further study, but must be closely linked with 'academic ability' and hence with family social class background. As in all countries, social class differences in education desired are marked in the USA.[75]

While Lindsey's findings suggest several important specifications of the class reproduction thesis within the schooling process itself, this work has not yet been followed up by more contemporary large-scale research or linked with current ethnographic studies.

Table 14 provides an estimate of the influence of father's main class position on the level of schooling attained by the current adult population of Ontario. Clearly the offspring of managers and professional employees have been much more likely than most others to complete post-secondary schooling, whereas nearly two-thirds of those from productive proletarian backgrounds have dropped out by the end of secondary school. The relatively low rates of completion of secondary schooling among the children of the petty bourgeoisie and small employers are probably indicative of the lack of internal formal education incentives that has characterized small commodity forms of production. Corporate capitalist and rentier fathers appear in the samples in numbers too small to give reliable results, but there are many indications that corporate capitalist families use educational institutions to maintain their dominant positions. For example, Clement documents that in 1972, two-thirds of the Canadian corporate elite in family firms had attended private schools and notes that university attendance has been the norm among the elite as a whole.[76] Indeed, the completion of university remains most starkly inequitable in terms of class background. As the bracketed percentage figures in Table 14 indicate, those from managerial and professional employee families have also had a much better chance than others to become university graduates. Moreover, the best quantitative estimates of pre-War and current university attendance trends in advanced capitalist societies suggest that although the participation rates of those from manual working class families have at least tripled, their chances of attendance, relative to those from more dominant class backgrounds, have hardly changed.[77]

Table 14 Father's Main Class Position by Respondent's Educational Attainment, Ontario 1978

Father's Main Class Position	Elementary Only %	Secondary Incomplete %	Secondary Complete %	Post-Secondary Incomplete %	Post-Secondary Complete %	(University Completion)
Small Employers	30	20	11	24	15	(12)
Petty Bourgeoisie	31	23	18	8	20	(8)
Managers	–	15	19	12	54	(34)
Supervisors	–	33	29	17	21	(10)
Professional Employees	7	20	20	15	38	(28)
Non-Productive Proletariat	14	32	25	13	16	(8)
Productive Proletariat	24	38	15	9	14	(6)
Total 18+ Population	21	28	17	14	20	(11)

However, particularly in view of the post-War structural changes in production, the clearest indication of the relationship between class and education is provided by the educational attainments of those currently occupying different class positions. Wright's empirical modelling of income determination for the US case, for example, suggests that level of schooling now plays a crucial mediating role in determining class position.[78] Table 15 summarizes the survey findings on educational attainments by class position for the present adult population of Ontario. Corporate capitalists clearly tend to have the most schooling. Indeed, university attendance appears to have become 'almost compulsory' not only for the corporate elite, as Clement observed,[79] but for the entire corporate capitalist class. Small employers and rentiers, on the other hand, have tended to have quite unexceptional educational attainments. Managers and professional employees remain much more highly schooled than the other class positions, with the majority in both cases having completed post-secondary education. The finding that about two-thirds of professional employees now have acquired a post-secondary certificate is in part indicative of the post-war expansion of such technical design and planning positions in the labour process, and most notably in the state sector. At the other extreme, while productive proletarians now have significantly more years of schooling than their fathers, about two-thirds still have not completed secondary school. As I have previously documented, general educational attainments have increased dramatically during the post-war years. But the fact that the attainments of the productive proletariat as a whole and of the sons and daughters of the productive proletarians in particular are not very distinguishable from those of old-age pensioners is indicative of a very substantial class bias against the core of the working class in contemporary schools.

The educational interests of different classes will be considered more fully in later chapters. But these findings do suggest that corporate capitalists, along with managers and professional employees, may have the most vested general interest in maintaining the established forms and contents of current educational programmes. This inference is further supported by the evaluations that respondents in different class positions offer regarding the value of their own education for their work. As Table 16 shows, over two-thirds of corporate capitalists, managers and professional employees in Ontario consider that their schooling has been quite a lot of use for their work. At the other extreme again are productive proletarians with less than one-quarter expressing such positive views. Comparable assessments are offered by rentiers, who quite simply do not work, and by housewives, who have obtained little training relevant to domestic labour in the schools and who are also constrained from applying what they have learned in the active labour force. These general results are also very consistent with Lindsey's previously cited finding that the strongest class-based differences among thirteen year olds are in their desires for further schooling.

But the persistent accumulation crisis makes major reorganization of established forms of schooling increasingly imperative. It would seem that the

Table 15   Class Position by Educational Attainment, Ontario 1978–80

	Elementary Only %	Secondary Incomplete %	Secondary Complete %	Post-Secondary Incomplete %	Post-Secondary Complete %	(University Completion)
Corporate Capitalists	–	3	8	11	78	(70)
Small Employers	18	21	16	11	34	(21)
Rentiers	20	25	15	15	25	(16)
Petty Bourgeoisie	23	28	19	9	20	(11)
Managers	4	10	20	11	55	(40)
Supervisors	13	26	23	11	27	(12)
Professional Employees	–	10	14	14	62	(43)
Non-Productive Proletariat	15	29	30	14	12	(3)
Productive Proletariat	28	36	20	8	8	(2)
Housewives	12	32	28	9	19	(6)
Temporarily Unemployed	26	24	22	19	9	(7)
Pensioners	36	32	18	5	8	(7)
Students	–	26	22	49	3	(7)
Total 18+ Population	18	26	22	14	20	(11)

*Table 16 Class Position by Assessed Usefulness of Own Formal Education for Work,
Ontario 1978*

	'Great Deal' or 'Quite a Lot' of Use in Work %
Corporate Capitalists	6̲8̲
Small Employers	31
Rentiers	18
Petty Bourgeoisie	31
Managers	7̲4̲
Supervisors	45
Professional Employees	7̲2̲
Non-Productive Proletariat	39
Productive Proletariat	23
Housewives	19
Temporarily Unemployed	28
Pensioners	37
Students	37
Total 18+ Population	34

classes that benefit most from such institutions either must find a more cost-efficient form for reproducing their educational dominance while subtly diminishing the opportunities of other groups, or else risk losing some educational initiative to popular movements for more open educational alternatives. The core of the working class would appear to have little to lose in supporting such alternatives.

The above concluding observations should serve to remind the reader that classes themselves can never be reduced to either material sites alone or to sets of static attributes. The noted English historiographer, E.P. Thompson has quite aptly observed that ' . . . class itself is not a thing, it is a happening'.[80] More exactly, as the model of social totalities outlined in Chapter One suggests, social classes are always constituted as lived associations at several material sites permeated by class-based modes of thought, through the consciousness and practical activities of particular individual subjects. The remainder of this book will focus first on the material site of schooling, then more broadly on class-based educational ideologies, and then public attitudes toward educational issues, in order to begin to understand what is now 'happening', especially outside the schools, to social class relations in education.

Notes

1 Studs Terkel (1974) *Working: People Talk About What They Do All Day and How They Feel About What They Do*, New York, Pantheon, pp. 407–8.
2 *Ibid.*, p. xxxiv.
3 *Ibid.*, pp. 303–5.
4 OSSOWSKI, S. (1957) *Class Structure in the Social Consciousness*, London, Routledge and Kegan Paul, 1963.
5 For representative studies of this genre, see for example LOPREATO, J. and HAZELRIGG, L. (1972) *Class, Conflict and Mobility: Theories and Studies of Class Structure*, San Francisco, Chandler, HILLER, P. (1975) 'The nature and social location of everyday conceptions of class', *Sociology* 9 (1) (January), pp. 1–28; and BULMER, M. (Ed) (1975) *Working Class Images of Society*, London, Routledge and Kegan Paul. Significantly, the most recent studies have begun to pay closer attention to the influences of social relations outside the workplace on class imagery; see CURRAN, J. (1981) 'Class imagery, work environment and community', *British Journal of Sociology* 32 (1) (March), pp. 111–26.
6 Letter from Marx to Weydemeyer (1852), cited in MCLELLAN, D. (1971) *The Thought of Karl Marx*, New York, Harper and Row, p. 164.
7 The only explicit attempt in *Capital* is a short fragment printed posthumously in Volume 3, MARX, K. (1894) pp. 885–86. Some of Marx's historical case studies do offer quite detailed accounts of political relations among class groupings, especially *The Class Struggles in France: 1848 to 1850* and *The Eighteenth Brumaire of Louis Bonaparte*. For the most extensive recuperation of Marx's works on class, see DRAPER, H. (1978) *Karl Marx's Theory of Revolution, Volume II: The Politics of Social Classes*, New York, Monthly Review Press.
8 For documentation see especially CROUCH, C. and PIZZORNO, A. (Eds) (1978) *The Resurgence of Class Conflict in Western Europe Since 1968* 2 Volumes. Toronto, Macmillan.
9 Among the major contributions are GORZ, A. (Ed) (1976) *The Division of Labour: The Labour Process and Class Struggle in Modern Capitalism*, Atlantic Highlands, NJ, Humanities Press, POULANTZAS, N. (1975) *Classes in Contemporary Capitalism*, London, New Left Books, CARCHEDI, G. (1977) *On the Economic Identification of Social Classes*, London, Routledge and Kegan Paul, WRIGHT, E.O. (1978) *Class, Crisis and the State*, London, New Left Books, and WALKER, P. (Ed) (1978) *Between Capital and Labour*, Montreal, Black Rose Books.
10 Whatever resonance this formal theorizing of class structures has with social reality owes much to the more historically and empirically grounded studies of Harry Braverman and his successors as referred to in footnote 55 of Chapter One. For a recent assessment by one of the major exponents, see WRIGHT, E.O. (1980) 'Varieties of Marxist conceptions of class structure', *Politics and Society* 9 (3), pp. 323–69. It should be noted that Wright is currently overseeing a series of large-scale sample surveys focused primarily on dimensions of class relations within production. The results of these surveys in the United States, Great Britain, Italy, Sweden, Australia and several other countries will allow detailed comparisons of the economic class structures of advanced capitalist societies for the first time on the basis of empirical data pertaining directly to Marxist categories.
11 Brighton Labour Process Group (1977) 'The capitalist labour process', *Capital and Class* 4 (Spring), p. 5.
12 See especially EDWARDS, R. (1979) *Contested Terrain*, New York, Basic Books.
13 EDWARDS, R. (1978) 'The social relations of production at the point of production', *Insurgent Sociologist* 8 (2–3) (Fall), p. 123.
14 Brighton Labour Process Group (1977) *op. cit.*, p. 17.

15 MARX K. (1867) *Capital. Volume 1*, New York, International Publishers, 1967, pp. 486–87. For current documentation see especially KUSTERER, K. (1978) *Know-How on the Job: The Important Working Knowledge of 'Unskilled' Workers*, Boulder, Westview Press.

16 Any meaningful discussion of 'actually existing' socialism is beyond the scope of this book. Consistent with the argument developed in the text, it may be noted that, if the socialist mode of production is to succeed the capitalist mode, it is also likely to take over the existing labour process of machinofacture as it finds it, complete with residual capitalist features of intellectual/manual division, hierarchical discipline, and fragmentation of tasks. But socialist enterprises, governed by the objective of providing for social needs, immediately begin to transform the extant forms of labour to make them respond to a wider range of needs and aspirations than capital accumulation. At the moment, with the capitalist mode of production in its fully developed form and retaining global influence, and with all transitional socialist economies still associated with this capitalist world economy, it is extremely difficult for analysts to concretize abstract socialist relations of production in a determinate way. Analysts of such avowedly socialist formations as the USSR, China and Cuba should beware, even more than analysts of historical modes of produciton, of deducing the existence or non-existence of transitional socialist enterprises from the appearance or non-appearance of particular 'adequate' forms of labour. For one of the most insightful discussions to date, see BAHRO, R. (1978) *The Alternative in Eastern Europe*, London, New Left Books.

17 A detailed formal discussion of such agricultural enterprises as well as several insightful case studies appear in PAIGE, J. (1975) *Agrarian Revolution*, New York, Free Press.

18 MARX, K. (1962) *Theories of Surplus Value, Part 3*, Moscow, Progress Books, 1971, p. 487.

19 LENIN, V. (1917) *Imperialism, The Highest Stage of Capitalism*, Peking, Foreign Language Press, 1965, p. 106.

20 SYZMANSKI, A. (1981) *The Logic of Imperialism*, New York, Praeger, p. 442.

21 AMIN, S. (1980) *Class and Nation, Historically and in the Current Crisis*, New York, Monthly Review Press.

22 At the most fundamental level this is a theoretical controversy over the specific character of the dominating mode of production within Third World economies. For overviews, see especially BANAJI, J. (1977) 'Modes of production in a materialist conception of history', *Capital and Class* 3, pp. 1–44; FOSTER–CARTER, A. (1978) 'The modes of production controversy', *New Left Review* 107 (January-February), pp. 47–77; and AGH, A. (1980) *Labyrinth of the Mode of Production Controversy*, Budapest, Institute for World Economy of the Hungarian Academy of Sciences. At a more immediate level it is a bitter polemical dispute over negative and positive aspects of capitalist penetration. For polar positions, see FRANK, A.G. (1979) *Dependent Accumulation and Underdevelopment*, New York, Monthly Review Press, and WARREN, B. (1980) *Imperialism: Pioneer of Capitalism*, London, New Left Books and Verso Editions, respectively.

23 The following discussion of class positions is more fully documented in LIVINGSTONE, D.W. *Class and Class Consciousness in Advanced Capitalism* (to be published).

24 Carchedi's (*op. cit.*) recent analysis of the functional aspects of capitalist production relations has focused especially on delineating the dual functions of such positions, but his portrayal of them as the 'new middle class' is as misleading as the many journalistic accounts. (For a British example, see MILLAR, R. (1966) *The New Classes*, London, Longmans.) As Hal Draper (1978) has aptly stated (New York, Monthly Review Press, 1978), in his valuable recent recuperation of all Marx's specific class analyses: 'It is one thing to recognize the existence of increasing

numbers of new intermediate elements of various sorts, as Marx did; it is another thing to construct out of these elements an organic class that is meaningful enough to seriously affect social and political life. This requires a cohesiveness, a fund of common interests, an objective basis for solidarity and social unity, such as do not exist among the disparate elements of this ectoplasmic class construct [that is, the 'new middle class'] . . . As the polar classes tense apart, there no longer is a compact class like the old petty bourgeoisie in the living space between them.' (pp. 626–27). It should immediately be added, as Carchedi also generally recognizes, that as the capitalist labour process has developed there has been a continual tendency to subordinate and standardize *previous* intermediate element functions into proletarian positions whenever possible.

25 For sophisticated neo-Marxist analyses see GOUGH, I. (1972) 'Marx's theory of productive and unproductive labour', *New Left Review* 76, pp. 49–72; CARCHEDI, G. (1977) *op. cit.*, and O'CONNOR, J. (1975). 'Productive and unproductive labour', *Politics and Society* 5 (3).

26 The 'lumpen class' has been perhaps the most misapprehended and surely the least studied of all Marxist economic class distinctions. As DRAPER, H. (1978) *op. cit.*, p. 478 summarizes: ' . . . the lumpen-class is the catch-all for those who fall out, or drop out, of the existing structure so that they are no longer functionally an integral part of the society. To survive at all, in the interstices of the society, they may have to adopt a parasitic mode of existence. The tendency toward illegality, criminality, and so on simply arises from the scarcity of other choices.'

27 The 'domestic labour debate' has recently been one of the most vigorous among Marxist theorists and has begun to lead to systematic empirical research on such historical and positional variations within capitalism. See, for example, FOX, B. (Ed) (1980) *Hidden in the Household: Women's Domestic Labour Under Capitalism*, Toronto, Women's Press.

28 See WRIGHT, E.O. (1978) *op. cit.*, pp. 61–87, and especially Table 2.9 on p. 77.

29 POULANTZAS, N. (1978) *op. cit.*

30 WRIGHT, E.O. (1978) *op. cit.*, p. 91.

31 See DRAPER, H. (1978) *op. cit.*, pp. 453–78.

32 For suggestive examples, see O'CONNOR, J. (1981) 'The Fiscal Crisis of the State revisited: Economic crisis and Reagan's budget policy,' 'Kapitalistate 9, pp. 41–61.

33 BURRIS, V. (1980) 'Class formation and transformation in advanced capitalism: A comparative analysis', *Social Praxis* 7, (3–4), pp. 147–79.

34 See WRIGHT, E.O. (1980) 'Class and occupation', *Theory and Society* 9 (1) (January), pp. 177–214.

35 WRIGHT, E.O. (1978) *op. cit.*

36 LIVINGSTONE, D.W. *op. cit.*

37 JOHNSTON, W. and ORNSTEIN, M. (1980) 'Measuring Social Class: A Comparison of Marxist and Conventional Approches', paper circulated by the Red Feather Institute for Advanced Studies in Sociology, January.

38 It should be noted that for the US only, Burris used data directly from the national census rather than from the ILO standardized classification.

39 All three of these surveys involved random samples of the 18+ population of Ontario (N = 1025, 1084, and 1108 respondents respectively) as well as special supplementary samples of corporate capitalists. The research designs and sample characteristics are presented in detail in LIVINGSTONE, D.W. (1979) *Public Attitudes Toward Education in Ontario 1978*, Toronto, OISE Press, LIVINGSTONE, D.W. and HART, D.J. (1980) *Public Attitudes Toward Education in Ontario 1979*, Toronto, OISE Press; and LIVINGSTONE, D.W., and HART, D.J. (1981) *Public Attitudes Toward Education in Ontario 1980*, Toronto, OISE Press.

40 See for example, BURRIS, V. (1980) *op. cit.*, p. 155.

41 For further discussion of distinctions between social formations in the contemporary

world system and of implications for educational practices, see LIVINGSTONE, D.W. (1979) 'The world capitalist economy and the limits of educational reform', *Canadian and International Education* 8 (1), pp. 5–26.

42 *Report of the Royal Commission on Corporate Concentration*, Ottawa, Minister of Supply and Services (1978) pp. 11–42 and *passim*. On the origins and early sectoral development of capitalist enterprises in Canada, see especially the historical analyses of RYERSON, S. (1973) *Unequal Union: Roots of Crisis in the Canadas, 1815–1873*, Toronto, Progress Books, and NAYLOR, T. (1975) *The History of Canadian Business, 1867–1914*, 2 volumes. Toronto, Lorimer. An excellent critical overview of such works appears in McNALLY, D. (1981) 'Staple theory as commodity fetishism: Marx, Innis and Canadian political economy', *Studies in Political Economy* 6 (Autumn), pp. 35–63.

43 The basic data source for these figures is Statistics Canada, *Canada's International Investment Position* Catalogue 67–202 (annual).

44 See CLEMENT, W. (1975) *The Canadian Corporate Elite*, Toronto, McClelland and Stewart, pp. 172–223.

45 AMIN, S. (1976) *Unequal Development: An Essay on the Social Formations of Peripheral Capitalism*, New York, Monthly Review Press, p. 222. The early development of the capitalist labour process is outlined in PENTLAND, H.C. (1981) *Labour and Capital in Canada 1650–1860*, Toronto, Lorimer.
The Quebec economy's distinct origins in a seigneural system of production have been an important factor in many continuing differences with English Canada.

46 JOHNSON, L. (1972) 'The development of class in Canada in the twentieth century', in TEEPLE, G. (Ed) *Capitalism and the National Question in Canada*, Toronto, University of Toronto Press, p. 163. The remainder of this historical account relies heavily on Johnson's work. It should be noted that his estimates of class size are based exclusively on census occupational categories, with the typical limitations.

47 JOHNSON, L. (1972) *op. cit.*, pp. 148–53, 163. Compare my own estimates in Tables 6 and 7.

48 *Ibid.*, pp. 163–64.

49 *Ibid.*, pp. 169–70.

50 *Ibid.*, pp. 171–72. For a very brief update of this analysis, see JOHNSON, L. (1979) 'The capitalist labour market and income inequality in Canada', in FRY, J. (Ed) *Economy, Class and Social Reality: Issues in Contemporary Canadian Society*, Toronto, Butterworth, pp. 153–68. On specific struggles between capitalists and workers, see, for example, the various issues of *Labour/Le Travailleur*; JAMIESON, S. (1968) *Times of Trouble: Labour Unrest and Industrial Conflict in Canada 1900–1966*, Ottawa, Queen's Printer, and WOLFE, D. (1977) 'The state and economic policy in Canada, 1968–1975', in PANITCH, L. (Ed), *The Canadian State: Political Economy and Political Power*, Toronto, University of Toronto Press.

51 PRZEWORSKI, A. (1977) 'Proletariat into a class: The process of class struggle from Karl Kautsky's *The Class Struggle* to recent controversies', *Politics and Society* 7 (4).

52 The leading sections of the capitalist class have seldom suffered from a dearth of recorders. See, for example, BALTZELL, E.D. (1958) *Philadelphia Gentlemen: The Making of a National Upper Class*, New York, Free Press, and CLEMENT, W. (1975) *op. cit.* Working class historiographies have been a much more episodic matter. English historians have done the most original research on working class communities, see especially THOMPSON E.P. (1963) *The Making of the English Working Class*, Harmondsworth, Penguin Books, and SAMUEL, R. (Ed) (1981) *People's History and Socialist Theory*, London, Routledge and Kegan Paul. One of the most insightful US examples is CUMBLER, J. (1979) *Working-Class Community in Industrial America: Work, Leisure and Struggle in Two Industrial Cities, 1880–1930*, Westport, Greenwood Press. For Canadian case studies, see especially VAISEY, G.D. (1980) (compiler) *The Labour Companion: A Bibliography of Canadian Labour History*,

Halifax, Committee on Canadian Labour History. One of the most detailed ethnographic studies of working class household relations to date is LUXTON M. (1980) *More than a Labour of Love: Three Generations of Women's Work in the Home*, Toronto, Women's Press. For a useful overview of class and household formation, see RAPP, R. (1978) 'Family and class in contemporary America', *Science and Society* 42 (Fall), pp. 278–301.

53 For one of the most suggestive schematic discussions, see DRAPER, H. (1978) *op. cit.*, p. 35 ff.

54 LIVINGSTONE, D.W. *Class and Class Consciousness. op. cit.*

55 *Ibid.*

56 BROOK, E. and FINN, D. (1977) 'Working class images of society and community studies', *Working Papers on Cultural Studies* 10, p. 133.

57 LIVINGSTONE, D.W. (1979) *op. cit.* and LIVINGSTONE, D.W. and HART, D.J. (1980) *op. cit.*
Traditional social scientists from Pitirim Sorokin to Seymour Lipset have been disposed to assert that there is a long-term tendency for the 'permanent core' of the working class to decline in importance relative to a growing fluid periphery. It is very relevant to our later assessment of the political capacity of the industrial proletariat to note here the contrasting empirically-based argument for the 'matura-tion' of the working class offered by GOLDTHORPE, J. (1980) *Social Mobility and Class Structure in Modern Britain*, London, Oxford University Press, p.262: 'In its demographic aspects, this argument would claim two things: first, that as under conditions of advanced industrialism the working class, in the sense of the body of manual wage-workers, tends proportionately at least to contract, it becomes at the same time increasingly second generation in its composition, owing in part to a decline in downward mobility and in part to a decline in the inflow of labour from the now insubstantial agricultural sector; and secondly, that decisive mobility from the working class, while probably increasing in volume, tends to be achieved at a relatively early age, with the result that the bulk of the industrial working class, as it exists at any one point in time, is made up of men whose mobility opportunities are in fact relatively few and limited.'

58 The class character of this ethnic diversity is analyzed in more detail in LIVINGSTONE, D.W. (1978) 'Class Structure, Ethnicity and Immigration in the Development of twentieth Century Canadian Capitalism', paper presented at the Annual Confer-ence of the Canadian Association for South Asian Studies, London, Ontario, May.

59 GOLDTHORPE, J. (1980) *op. cit.*, p. 260. This volume also contains valuable documentation of the communal relations of occupational classes.

60 The most relevant of such occupation-based mobility analyses for the current study is ORNSTEIN, M.D. (1981) 'The occupational mobility of men in Ontario', *Canadian Review of Sociology and Anthropology* 18 (2) (May), pp. 183–215.

61 CLEMENT, W. (1975) *op. cit.*, pp. 172–223.

62 See, for example, John Foster's documentation of the extraordinarily high incidence of intra-group marriage among the big employers of three early industrial capitalist English towns, in *Class Struggle and the Industrial Revolutin*, London, Methuen (1974), pp. 260–69.

63 See, for example, FOSTER, J. (1974) *op. cit.* and for contemporary kinship relations, GOLDTHORPE, J. (1980) *op. cit.*, 147–74.

64 The structure and processes of this influence network have been most fully documented for the United States, especially by G.W. Domhoff. For his most recent work, see DOMHOFF, G.W. (1979) *The Powers that Be: Processes of Ruling Class Domination in America*, New York, Vintage Books. For Ontario, extensive historical evidence is provided by NELLES, H.V. (1974) *The Politics of Development: Forests, Mines and Hydro-Electric Power in Ontario, 1849–1941*, Toronto, Mac-millan.

65 Marx's nuanced assessment of the revolutionary potential and reformist constraints inherent in the trade unions of the nineteenth century deserve critical review today. See especially DRAPER, H. (1978) *op. cit.*, pp. 81–46.

66 For accounts of the development of Canadian trade unions, see LIPTON, C. (1973) *The Trade Union Movement of Canada 1827–1959*, Toronto, NC Press, and LAXER, R. (1976) *Canada's Unions*, Toronto, Lorimer.

67 Among the most notable of these were the Coleman Report in the US and the Plowden Report in England. See COLEMAN, J.S. CAMBELL, E.Q., HOBSON, C.J., McPARTLAND, J. MOOD, A., WEINFELD, F.D. and YORK, R.L. (1966) *Equality of Educational Opportunity*, Washington, DC, US Department of Health, Education and Welfare, Office of Education, and HMSO (1967) *Children and Their Primary Schools*, A Report of the Central Advisory Council for Education. II: Research and Surveys, London, Her Majesty's Stationery Office. For a good critical review of the relevant empirical research in Canada, see HARP, J. (1980) 'Social inequalities and the transmission of knowledge: The case against the schools', in HARP, J. and HOFLEY, J. (Eds), *Structured Inequality in Canada*, Scarborough, Prentice-Hall, pp. 219–46.

68 HUSEN, T. (1979) *The School in Question: A Comparative Study of the School and its Future in Western Societies*, London, Oxford University Press, p. 88.

69 For pessimistic examples of the 'reproduction thesis' see JENCKS, C. SMITH, M., ACLAND, H., BANE, M.J., COHEN, D.K., GINTIS, H., HENYNS, B. and MICHELSON, S. et al. (1972) *Inequality: A Reassessment of the Effect of Family and Schooling in America*, New York, Basic Books, BOWLES, S. and GINTIS, H. (1976) *Schooling in Capitalist America*, New York, Basic Books, JENCKS, C. (1979) *Who Gets Ahead? The Determinants of Economic Success in America*, New York, Basic Books, and APPLE, M. (1979) *Ideology and Curriculum*, Boston, Routledge and Kegan Paul. For optimistic examples of the human capital and genetically-based variants of the meritocracy thesis see JUSTER, T. (Ed) (1975) *Education, Income and Human Behavior*, New York, McGraw-Hill, and HERNSTEIN, R. (1973) *I.Q. in the Meritocracy*, Boston, Little, Brown, respectively; see also RUTTER, M. MAUGHAN, B., MORTIMORE, P. and OUSTON, J. (1979) *Fifteen Thousand Hours*, Cambridge, Harvard University Press.

70 See, for example, PARKIN, F. (1971) *Class, Inequality and Political Order*, London, Paladin, pp. 13–47.

71 See, for example, OLNECK, M. and CROUSE, J. (1979) 'The I.Q. meritocracy reconsidered: Cognitive skill and adult success in the United States', *American Journal of Education* 88 (November), pp. 1–31. As noted earlier, some of the recent empirical research on mobility, such as that of ORNSTEIN, M.D. (1981) *op. cit.*, does express a sensitivity to the changing occupational structure but this work is not primarily concerned with educational attainments.

72 For a critique of Bowles and Gintis in this regard, see GORELICK, S. (1977) 'Undermining hierarchy: Problems of schooling in capitalist America,' *Monthly Review* 29 (5) (October), pp. 20–36. Bowles and Gintis' reply appears in *Monthly Review* 30 (6) (November 1978), pp. 59–4.

73 See WRIGHT, E.O. (1980) *op. cit.* For an empirical illustration of this lack of identity, see WRIGHT E.O. and PERRONE, L. (1977) 'Marxist class categories and income inequality', *American Sociological Review* 42 (1), pp. 32–55.

74 LINDSEY, J.K. (1981) 'Social class and the educational system: An international comparison', *Canadian Review of Sociology and Anthropology* 18 (3) (August), pp. 299–320. This schema is based on two dichotomous variables: production/non-production, and control function in society/direct involvement in the economic process (p. 301). In addition to 'capitalists' and 'production working class', the schema generates four other categories: 'ideological class', 'white collar workers', 'small independent producers' and 'small shopkeepers'. While the last two categories, containing self-employed proprietors, may be distinguishable on production

criteria (and politically important in countries still containing a substantial petty bourgeoisie, such as France), Lindsey's application of both dichotomies is quite insensitive to more complex interdependencies among those fully incorporated into the capitalist labour process. Thus, the fact that *some* intermediate elements serve *productive* co-ordinating and unifying functions in the collective worker is ignored. The forced dichotomy between 'ideological' and 'white collar' workers denies marked degrees of variation in control and surveillance functions – hence, technicians must be regarded as part of a controlling ideological class while accountants must be workers (p. 302). While Lindsey's identification of 'capitalists' and 'production working class' positions appears to be fairly similar to the current corporate capitalist and productive proletarian distinctions (aside from the minor problem of including non-productive sector manual workers in the latter), this typical conflation of occupation with production relations further vitiates any comparisons with his other class categories. Lindsey's class schema is discussed in greater conceptual detail in 'The conceptualization of social class', *Studies in Political Economy* 3 (Spring), 1980 pp. 17–36.

75 LINDSEY, J.K. (1981) *op. cit.*, pp. 309, 313.
76 CLEMENT W. (1975) *op. cit.*, p. 338.
77 See, for example, HALSEY, A.H. HEATH, A and RIDGE, J.M. (1980) *Origins and Destinations: Family, Class and Education in Modern Britain*, London, Oxford University Press, p. 188.
78 WRIGHT, E.O. (1979) *Class Structure and Income Determination*, New York, Academic Press, pp. 97–106, 113–81. Compare JENCKS, C. (1978) *op cit.*, and ORNSTEIN M.D. (1981) *op. cit.*
79 CLEMENT, W. (1975) *op. cit.*
80 THOMPSON, E.P. (1965) 'The peculiarities of the English', in MILIBAND, R. and SAVILLE, J. (Eds) *The Socialist Register*, London, Merlin Books, p. 357.

Chapter Three

State Schooling And Class-Based Educational Ideologies

Ideologies are organized sets of conceptions that are articulated by spokes-persons as ideational expressions of the interests of social groupings. As such, they are both consequences of and frames for much intellectual work. When intellectuals can generally treat the values and ideas of powerful groups as disembodied realities, and either ignore the distinctive concerns of subordinate groups or regard them merely as 'deviant' from such dominant values, we are in a condition of pronounced ideological domination. This condition diminishes when the existence of alternative standpoints and world views is apparent and the role of human agency in creating, maintaining and changing such views as well as in disseminating some more widely than others is recognized. Neo-Marxist scholars have recently devoted growing attention to conditions of ideological domination both in advanced capitalist societies generally[1] and in the public schools in particular.[2] There is also now a rich body of ethnographic research documenting ways in which subordinate group cultures create their own sub-cultural codes, symbols and styles.[3] Such subcultures are of widely varying distinctiveness and persistence, and they generally contain elements of both accommodation and resistance to dominant cultures. These sub-cultures, which are expressed in many sites including schools, may be regarded as 'hot houses' for the generation of new ideological interpretations of social reality, some of which may find sustained articulation and take root in the larger subordinate parent cultures. There have also been some very important critical efforts to identify major features of and changes in the prevailing contemporary educational ideology, primarily through analysis of state policy documents.[4] However, at least in liberal democratic states, such official ideologies are always mediated expressions, never simply the unilaterally imposed views of dominant groups. Post-War Marxist studies of the state have tended to emphasize either its structural compatability with capitalist interests or institutional networks linking state agents with powerful corporate groups, and consequently to impute quite a monolithic, capitalist-dominated character to state systems.[5] But some more recent critical empirical studies find the state to be ' ... in many ways a rather fragile structure of alliances, one that is shot through with contradictions. The elite contains within it various classes and ethnic categories in an unstable alliance.'[6] In any case, the actual process of ideological mediation at the societal level remains very poorly understood, at least with regard to educational policy making.[7] In particular, there has been little systematic research as yet on class-based educational ideologies *per se*. Among the most evident ingredients are the public discourses of organic intellectuals of dominant and subordinate class circles. To begin a critical analysis of such educational ideologies is the main purpose of this chapter.

First, ideologies are situated generally as aspects of social reality, and distinguished from both lived cultures and ideological hegemony. Next, the history of class conflict over education in capitalism is very briefly noted and primary dimensions of educational relations in advanced capitalism are identified. With reference to these underlying dimensions of everyday educational practices, the educational interests of capitalist and working classes are then compared. The remainder of the chapter is an attempt to characterize explicit expressions of themes related to such underlying dimensions of educational practices in current class-based educational ideologies. This empirical analysis relies on the public discourse of spokespersons for the most organized cores of the capitalist and working classes in English Canada.

Cultures, Ideologies and Hegemony

The historical materialist approach used in this study assumes that material and ideational aspects are *always* combined and have reciprocal effects in concrete social relations, but that material social existence pre-conditions individual comprehension in the particular sense that contradictions in the modes of production and reproduction of material life ultimately determine the transformation of material existence and lead to most major changes in the ideational forms through which we become conscious of society.[8] Therefore, to gain a fundamental understanding of ideational phenomena one must examine them in connection with the contradictions of material life. As noted previously, the major contradiction of material production in class societies has been between increasingly socialized, capable forces of production and increasingly restricted private ownership and control of the production process. The approach then will be to rely on the fundamental contradictory relations of the capitalist mode of production,[9] as they apply to educational institutions in particular, as a preliminary basis for conducting a thematic analysis of current educational ideologies.

This procedure is only intended to ensure consideration of the ideological themes most directly relevant to fundamental dimensions of material educational practices. It is not intended to collapse or reduce *ideational aspects* of social relations into discrete *material sites* or to suggest that mental relations are determined in the same way as material relations. As Richard Johnson notes:

The characteristic feature of the ideological-cultural instance is the production of forms of consciousness – ideas, feelings, desires, moral preferences, forms of subjectivity ... [T]here is no separate institutional area of social life in which forms of consciousness arise: mentalities and subjectivities are formed and expressed in every sphere of existence.[10]

In this regard, it is crucial to recognize that cultures and ideologies are by no means identical. Gramsci was the first to realize that the dynamics of ideological domination are impossible to fathom without such a distinction. As Johnson summarizes in another important essay:

Gramsci employs three key terms of cultural/ideological analysis (where culturalism and structuralism employ only one): 'common sense' which refers, concretely, to the *lived culture* of a particular class or social group; 'philosophy' (or sometimes *'ideology'*) which refers to an organized set of conceptions with a more or less transformative relation to lived culture; and *'hegemony'* which describes the state of play, as it were, between the whole complex of 'educative' institutions and ideologies on the one hand, and lived culture on the other: the extent to which common sense is made to conform both to 'the necessities of production' and to the construction of consent and a political order.[11]

When established ideologies become palpably inconsistent with social existence, then common sense also becomes problematic and open to ideological reconstruction.

Just as historical materialism has focused on class relations in the sphere of production as a pivotal factor to explain changes in material relations, so class-based ideologies may be seen as central factors for understanding ideational changes in social relations. The least ideological ideas are perhaps some of those dealing with the observable non-human environment *per se*. But most recurring views pertaining to social relations reflect the interests of the material social grouping from which they originate. In any class society, the ideologies of materially powerful social groups tend to be promulgated as universal or natural truths. In Marx's initial formulation:

The ideas of the ruling class are in every epoch the ruling ideas, that is, the class which is the ruling *material* force of society, is at the same time its ruling intellectual force. The class which has the means of material production at its disposal, has control at the same time over the means of mental production, so that thereby, generally speaking, the ideas of those who lack the means of mental production are subject to it. The ruling ideas are nothing more than the ideal expression of the dominant material relationships, the dominant material relationships grasped as ideas; hence of the relationships which make the one class the ruling one, therefore, the ideas of its dominance.[12]

Marx emphasized in his mature economic studies that appearances origina-
ting from the essential character of the capitalist mode of production, and in
particular from the commodity form of the product of labour and the value
form of that commodity, lead to forms of consciousness that hide the most
basic features of that mode and provide the basis of capitalist legal and political
ideology. But he also continued to believe that the proletariat would be
compelled to develop revolutionary consciousness with relative ease as the
material contradictions inherent in the capitalist mode of production unfolded
and, hence, never elaborated his views on the effects that fetishized appearances
can have on political consciousness.[13] Thus Marx's own treatment of ideology,
both in terms of the pervasiveness of capitalist ideology and the relatively easy
emergence of proletarian consciousness, tended to obscure the fact that class
ideologies and cultures are generated and reproduced in often complex
struggles and negotiations between dominant and subordinate classes.

At the most general level, just as material aspects of social relations in any
epoch may be seen to contain both recurring patterns of activities and creative
acts by individuals and groups, so the ideational aspects involve recurring ways
and means of thought and unique thoughts. To paraphrase Marx, we create
both our own material and intellectual history, but not just as we choose. More
specifically, ideological forms are not transformed entirely and abruptly any
more than are modes of production and reproduction. Every historical period
has seen the co-existence of, as well as latent and manifest conflicts between,
numerous particular currents and systems of ideological thought, and even the
most dominant ideological world-views have usually contained many ideas
from prior eras and other cultures.

Several levels of ideational phenomena and of ideological domination can be
distinguished within any historical mode of thought, including forms of
signification, explicit cognitions, implicit assumptions and subliminal suggestions. The emphasis here will be on the most easily documentable cognitive
level.

The historical materialist premise that fundamental dimensions of ideological
forms are intimately grounded in basic aspects of human material existence is
supported by historical and anthropological studies which have found: (1) that
the general patterns of recorded thought in all civilizations have been recur-
ringly concerned with the following basic issues: issues of human relations with
the animate and inanimate environment; issues of relationships between
humans (including the bases of superiority and subordination, the relative
significance of the individual and the collectivity, and territorial relations
between peoples); issues of innate dispositions of humans (including the
rational or instinctual character of human nature, and the importance of mind
versus matter); and issues of human destiny or purposes and the location of
such purposes in time;[14] and (2) that distinct historical modes of thought, in
terms of widely assumed positions on these issues, are associated with different
epochs of production. In particular, the development of the capitalist mode of
production in western European societies from the sixteenth century to the late

1880s was associated with an increasingly dominant pattern of thought characterized by possessive individualism, nationalism, mastery over nature, rationalism, materialism, and secular progress.[15]

The dominant western mode of ideological thought, along with the capitalist mode of production, has experienced substantial attacks and modifications since the 1880s. But it is important to recognize that this mode of thought and most of its domain assumptions still serve, as well as the capitalist material modes of production and reproduction, to shape and constrain the more concrete 'ruling ideas' and most specific ideologies and issues in advanced capitalist societies,[16] including most of the aspects of educational ideologies we will discuss here.

In terms of the general features of ideological forms cited above, my attention will be limited to a very particular focus within the issue domain of relationships between humans; that is, limited to what current capitalist and working class educational ideologies have to say about central underlying dimensions of class relations in the educational institutions of advanced capitalist societies. It is at this level of explicitly organized conceptions that the relations between dominant and subordinate class cultures always remain most volatile. As John Clarke *et al* observe in a passage that deserves to be quoted at length to end this section:

> So hegemony cannot be taken for granted – either by the state and the dominant classes, or, for that matter, by the analyst. The current use of the term, to suggest the unending and unproblematic exercise of class power by·every ruling class, and its opposite – the permanent and finished incorporation of the subordinate class – is quite false to Gramsci's usage. It limits the historical specificity of the concept. To make that point concrete: we would argue that, though the dominant classes remained massively in command during the 1930s, it is difficult to define them as 'hegemonic'. Economic crisis and unemployment disciplined, rather than 'led', the working classes into subordination in this period. The defeats suffered by the labour movement in the 1920s powerfully contributed to the coercive sway of the former over the latter. By contrast, the 1950s seem to us a period of true 'hegemonic domination', it being precisely the role of 'affluence', as an ideology, to dismantle working-class resistance and deliver the 'spontaneous consent' of the class to the authority of the dominant classes. Increasingly, in the 1960s, and more openly in the 1970s, this 'leadership' has again been undermined. The society has polarized, conflict has reappeared on many levels. The dominant classes retain power, but their 'repertoire' of control is progressively challenged, weakened, exhausted. One of the most striking features of this later period is the shift in the exercise of control from the mechanisms of consent to those of coercion (for example, the use of the law, the courts, the police and the army, of legal repression, conspiracy charges and of force to contain an

escalating threat to the state and to 'law and order'). This marks a *crisis* in the hegemony of the ruling class. Hegemony, then is not universal and 'given' to the continuing rule of a particular class. It has to be *won*, worked for, reproduced, sustained. Hegemony is, as Gramsci said, a 'moving equilibrium', containing 'relations of forces favourable or unfavourable to this or that tendency'. It is a matter of the nature of the balance struck between contending classes: the compromises made to sustain it; the relations of force; the solutions adopted. Its character and content can only be established by looking at concrete situations, at concrete historical moments. The idea of 'permanent class hegemony' or of 'permanent incorporation' must be ditched.[17]

Class Conflict and the Structure of Educational Relations in Advanced Capitalism

In the transitional period that preceded the development of state-run systems of elementary schooling in most capitalist societies in the middle part of the nineteenth century, the educational practices of different social classes were often quite distinct.[18] But as labour became incorporated within capitalist machinofacture,[19] it was more and more difficult for subordinate classes to sustain autonomous educational networks, and vital for capitalists to ensure that workers were properly trained, especially morally, for the 'double freedom' of wage labour. Lazonick notes, with reference to the English case, that by the 1870s:

> The mass schooling system was certainly not a primary mechanism in *subjecting* labour to the domination of capital. That had been done more by modes of repression (both within the workplace and elsewhere), than by modes of indoctrination. But once all anti-capitalist movements had been repressed, the mass schooling system was to function as a prime ideological mechanism in the attempt by the capitalist class, through the medium of the state, to continually *reproduce* a labour force which would passively accept that subjection. At the same time, it had set up a public institution which could potentially be used by the working class for just the contrary purpose.[20]

With the extension of industrial machinofacture, school systems also grew rapidly. For example, in the US between 1880 and 1910 the number of high schools increased more than twelve fold.[21] However, even in this most advanced case, the incorporation of young people in the schools was then far from complete; in 1911, only 11 per cent of Americans of high school age and considerably smaller proportions of working class youths were in school.[22] Particularly in the early part of the century, several movements for *independent* working class education, especially for adults and older youths, did continue to experience at least brief success in some countries.[23] But over the past century, working class demands for more equal access to state-provided schooling facilities have very largely replaced efforts to maintain any substantial alternative form of working class educational network. Indeed, while workers (as well as small commodity producers) initially opposed business-initiated compulsory school attendance laws, trade unions and even such revolutionary organizations as the First International came to support state-run school systems as workers' demands for literacy and other social knowledge mounted. As Barry Rubin notes with regard to the late nineteenth century in the US:

> Workers and their organizations supported government-supported public education for two reasons. First, they desired education for themselves and their children as a means of personal advancement. This was in part a response to the new structure of the economy which began to demand formal education as a means to social mobility. Second, an educated people, it was believed, was a prerequisite for democracy ... The combination of the capitalists' need for mass education and the workers' demand for education as a means to equality became a powerful force leading to the creation of the American school system.[24]

Serious contradictions in this arrangement have led to continuing class conflicts of varying intensity and visibility over both the control and content of public programmes as well as the unequal extent of educational provisions.[25] Such contradictions became most evident as the last major economic crisis wore on in the 1930s, and were recognized by many writers on the left, Marxists and reconstructionists alike. One of the clearest expressions, offered by Richard Frank in 1937, is summarized as follows:

> The bourgeois state was forced, by popular pressure as well as by the needs of industry, directly to undertake the education of its people. [There were] two contradictions in this process which made it possible for education to be part of a left-wing movement. The first is the contradiction between the rulers' need to fool the people and keep them docile as opposed to the bourgeoisie's need to provide some education to workers and others which would accurately depict various realities about the existing system. The second contradiction is that between the bourgeoisie's need to control education and the popular demand (and need) for a measure of control over public schools.[26]

Such insights appear to have been promptly forgotten again in the post-War period of affluence and considerable working class quiescence.

The works of both the revisionist educational historians and the radical deschoolers of the past decade or so have provided useful descriptive accounts of the generally dominant form of schooling in advanced capitalism. A sharp division has been created between children and adults as learners. The more generic phenomenon of education becomes regarded as identical with formal schooling. Attendance at lower levels is compulsory. There is centralized administrative control of the structure of activities. Intellectual/manual divisions (academic/vocational) are pronounced, especially at the secondary level. Moreover, at post-primary levels, the curriculum is generated by experts. Teachers dominate the classroom interaction and individualistic achievement is emphasized, through such means as competitive grading. The main emphasis is on providing basic literacy in technical and social skills, whereas political education or even civic literacy are little encouraged.[27] One cannot fail to observe how comparable many of these features are with those of the capitalist form of machinofacture. As in the capitalist production process, both working class and some middle class people as well as students have frequently resisted the extension of this dominant form of schooling and sometimes struggled for alternative forms. In this manner, they have contributed to the uneven development of this dominant form in the public educational institutions of all advanced capitalist societies.

In a somewhat idealized fashion, H. Svi Shapiro has described the major categories of educational thought of the radical working class movement in the US between 1900 and 1925 as displaying:

> ... concern for the democratic management of educational institutions; the integration of theoretical and practical activity; an emphasis on the development of social consciousness; a notion of education committed to broad humanistic goals; a concept of non-hierarchical teacher-student relationship; a collective approach to the production and assessment of educational work; and a change in the structure and organization of knowledge towards the interrelating of disciplines and perspectives, and the development of curricula that are grounded in daily life and common experience.[28]

He further argues that such educational concerns – relating as they do to issues of authority structures, the division of labour and social hierarchy, limited definitions of culture and unequal resource distribution – are responses to the conditions of our social existence and merge in working class movements during periods of social upheaval.[29] However common or rare such tendencies may have been in past periods of social instability in advanced capitalism, they do together represent a systematic working class-based alternative mode of education to the dominant form of schooling. Such tendencies have persisted, sometimes quite visibly as in the Freinet movement centred in France.[30] The extent of support for these competing dominant and radical modes of education expressed in class-based educational ideologies and in public attitudes may be indicative of the potentials for both reactionary and genuinely progressive educational change in the current period of educational crisis.

During the relatively quietist generation of economic and educational expansion following World War II, educational researchers interested in contemporary social class differences generally preoccupied themselves with documenting working class 'deviations' from dominant value aspirations and, latterly, with pragmatically assessing the effectiveness of compensatory reforms to give working class kids equal opportunities.[31] As suggested above, with the intensification of collective class conflicts since the mid-1960s, more attention has been devoted to analyzing the modes of inculcating capitalist ideology into working class youths as well as to identifying distinctive features of working class and other student cultures. Such research began first in France and Italy – where working class ideologies had remained most evident, particularly through the communist parties and trade unions – and in Britain, where cultural barriers between classes remained more deeply entrenched than in other parts of the English-speaking world.[32]

Particularly in Britain, some of the recent historiographic and ethnographic work taking a subordinate group standpoint on educational practices has become quite sensitive to the distinction between lived cultures and ideological representations, and to the different methods of study they require. As Richard Johnson notes:

Cultural analysis concerns those shared and lived principles of life, characteristic of particular classes, social groups and social milieu. It is always particular, located, observational. It attempts to grasp forms of consciousness as ensembles of lived beliefs and their modes of expression. It has always to concern particular groups of persons ... Commonsense, or culture, is intimate with practical activity. It suffices, for most of the time, to manage the world of practical action. Since this world itself is problematic, culture must perforce take heterogeneous and sometimes contradictory forms. The analysis of ideologies (or all forms of the analysis of systems of signification or representation) takes a different, but related, object: conceptions of the world, of the self or of nature in a different moment of their circulation. The *possibility* of this form of analysis rests upon particular conditions: that thought and evaluation may be concretized in 'texts' or objects and may be there analyzed in another more abstracted way. In particular the possibility of this arises wherever 'conception' is separated from other activities and becomes thereby the province of 'intellectuals'. This particular division of labour has, in modern societies, acquired immensely elaborated institutional forms, especially in the educational curricula and in the whole range of the media. Conceptions are carried in the minds of social individuals but are also written down, communicated, inscribed and coded in different ways. This real abstraction allows us to take ideologies or ideological fields as a definite object of critical study though it provides no warrant to forget their actual connection with wider processes, or indeed to vacate the other 'cultural' ground. It is only in combination, indeed, that cultural and ideological analysis approaches a more complete account of the ways in which specific forms of consciousness are produced.[33]

It must be stressed that the current study is limited to a partial reading of class-based ideological discourse and some subsequent assessment of ideological effects on consciousness. It says very little about lived cultures *per se*. For such an inquiry to be of lasting value it will have to be more carefully combined with particular cultural analyses, and with educational practice, than has been possible to date. However, if one accepts the model of social totalities suggested in Chapter One, both ideological and cultural analyses must also begin to take more explicit account of connections with the structural context of historically established material forms of educational practice. In this regard, even the most recent research on ideology and school cultures remains prone to Bill Williamson's critique of the 'new sociology of education', that:

> . . . they want to understand the ideology of education without having first worked out its political economy. It is not sufficient to be aware only of the fact that the principles governing the selection of transmittable knowledge reflect structures of power. It is essential to move beyond such suspicions to work out the precise connections.[34]

The recent growth of grounded Marxist studies of political economy is beginning to provide this necessary basis. Most relevant is the work on the labour process, as discussed in Chapter Two, which has served to clarify the material dimensions of the contemporary struggle between capital and labour in capitalist production. While a Marxist political economy of education is still in its infancy, there have been significant recent efforts to identify some of the basic dimensions of social class relations within the capitalist schooling process and their connection with the labour process and social relations generally in advanced capitalism.[35] The identification of primary dimensions of educational relations in advanced capitalism which is offered below attempts to build on these preliminary efforts, as well as on some of the critical insights of the radical educators of the 1930s.

A clarifying comment is probably in order here about the nature of the correspondence between education and material production. First, the suggestion of a general correspondence between material *forms* of production relations and educational relations in capitalism is based on historical, empirical studies within each institutional sphere.[36] In my view, it has been adequately established that institutions of mass schooling emerged initially as a response to the needs of the capitalist labour process. Moreover, as this labour process has become more generalized, mass schooling has also become more pervasive and taken on increasingly analogous surface forms. Also, empirical studies such as the works cited above have established that class conflicts have played an active role in shaping not only capitalist production but also educational practices. However, such observations are not sufficient to establish any unilateral relationship of economic determination of education.[37] While initiatives for educational reform, for example, may often be provoked by immediate economic conditions – such as the educational cutbacks and reorganization proposals stimulated by the current accumulation crisis – educational reforms have sometimes anticipated apparent changes in the economy.[38] Perhaps even more frequently, school systems have maintained established institutional features in spite of continual changes in the capitalist production process. Educational relations then are at least relatively autonomous. From a structuralist perspective, Michael Carter has suggested, with regard to the capitalist labour process and schooling, that:

> [A] concrete understanding of correspondence is necessary in order to understand the subordinate set of structures, and an understanding of the incipient contradictions in the dominant set of structures is necessary to understand correspondence. Precisely because the subordinate set of structures by assumption constitute a separate set of structures, however, they possess a relative autonomy from the dominant set of structures which permits them to develop internal contradictions, and even to develop contradictions to the dominant structures.[39]

It must immediately be added that it is not abstract categories of political economy that constitute the structural relations between production and education. It is the lived associations of particular historical subjects that have generated and continue to reproduce *and* transform such internal contradictions in both spheres. With this in mind, we can attempt to identify major internal contradictions of educational systems in advanced capitalism. Until such educational contradictions are carefully specified, the 'correspondence principle' is likely to continue either to be reduced to a matter of analogous surface structures of schooling serving ultimately to reproduce capitalist production structures or, alternately, to be rejected as an overly determinist and economistic account of actual educational practice.

The central contradiction in the educational relations of advanced capitalism is between the private appropriation of ownership of major means of production and distribution of information (for example, magazines, newspapers, television and radio, publishing companies) by dominant classes, and the growing experiential requirements of more fully socialized access to accurate information and knowledge in order for all people to operate productively and live meaningfully in a complex machinofacture-based society. More specifically, class relations in capitalist forms of education may be regarded in terms of the ownership of major means of cultural production and control of social and technical aspects of relations within the schooling process itself.[40]

Relations of ownership in education refer to the possession of major means of cultural production. As part of the continual historical tendency of capitalist enterprises to appropriate and turn into commodities all potential means of production, capitalists have appropriated many of the instruments for producting and conveying information on a wide scale and attempted to dispossess subordinate classes of alternative cultural sources and organizations for interpreting their own social reality for themselves. The extension and increasingly concentrated ownership of the mass media and the generalization of state-run mass systems of schooling have been the most evident instruments of this cultural dispossession. Of course, state schooling institutions are not fully 'owned' by capitalist enterprise; they have been established as formally separate, staffed out of public funds rather than private profits, and have thereby acquired their own logic of development. Nevertheless, ownership control of the means of such state schooling, most manifest in the governing bodies with power to make official policies about both the form and extent of schooling provisions and the curricular content, has been from the outset largely out of the hands of workers, especially at post-primary levels.[41] Moreover, direct dominant class control of cultural institutions has been made less necessary through the increasing commodification of culture into forms reflecting dominant class viewpoints and the relatively greater appropriation of cultural 'wealth' by the dominant classes that this has facilitated.[42] Corporate capitalists' heavy reliance on the use of private schools and university access are evident elements of this extensive appropriation. But subordinate class resistance to such cultural dispossession has continued in both direct and indirect ways. There have been continuing spasmodic efforts by working class communities to gain control over their local schools, as well as attempts to construct and disseminate working class curricular materials. Moreover, the pervasiveness of dominant class cultural possession suggested by the absence of working class content in the formal curriculum, as well as by the reified treatment of 'cultural capital' and ideological dominance in much of the recent research in educational sociology, is belied by the studies that have closely observed working class youths' cultural practices in schools and discovered persistent sources of contradictory world views.[43]

The relations within the schooling process itself are increasingly comparable in form with those of the labour process in capitalist enterprises in both their social and technical aspects.[44] The *social* relations of the schooling process are interpersonal aspects of the activities of those actually involved in the everyday conduct of schooling, especially authority relations. Somewhat as the social relations of capitalist production have become characterized by extensive supervisory hierarchies and impersonal rules in the attempt to control wage labourers and better extract their labour, the school system has taken on a similar social organization in order to control and select students and to accomplish its own social division of labour. There have been clear tendencies, just as in industry, toward greater administrative centralization and for the direct personal command of classroom interaction by teachers to be buttressed by more aspects of the direction of students being submerged in detailed sets of work criteria.[45] Once more it should be noted that such correspondence of forms cannot be reduced to an economistic determination. As Douglas Holly has commented:

> In the process of education, learning is systematized, given a social
> organization which reflects epistemologically the social relations of the
> general society, but it is also made subject to specific, personalized
> social relations. The social organization represents the social relations

of education. Under capitalism these are exploitative, appropriating the mental activity of the many to the purposes of the few. The specific, reflexive relations are those generic to learning: they are the definitive social relations in education. These are related to the general social relations obviously, but they are not necessarily determined by them. Under certain circumstances ... the dominant purposes of capital are deflected, and conflicting purposes incorporated into social relations within the education process. Such an analysis is presumably necessary to explain the fact of historical development itself. Learning – which is always social learning – either reproduces existing social relations or projects new ones. Its systematic organization as education contains always the possibility of conflicting versions of the world, the success of one or other of which rests upon the dialectical interaction between specific learning relations and general social ones.[46]

Holly also identifies two organizing principles and styles of social control-coercive authority and moral 'academic' rationality – with the former being most relevant to the education of routine workers and the latter to the education of managerial/technological workers; he notes the irreconcilable, confused existence of both styles of control within British comprehensive schools.[47]

More generally, as self-motivation and self-management remain even more critical ingredients to the success of the schooling process than to the capitalist labour process and while labour market relations remain the principal mechanism of consummating the social division of labour, even indirect coercive measures of social control and selection face distinct systemic limits in schools. The uneasy post-War solution has been to respond to popular educational and occupational aspirations by increasing the accessibility of advanced schooling to an extent which, while indeterminately beneath the populace's collective intellectual capacities, is increasingly beyond the capitalist-organized production system's capacity to utilize.[48]

The *technical* relations of the schooling process concern the relations of the people involved with the actual work process of learning itself. Not only does the continual revolutionizing of production techniques to enhance capital accumulation require a versatile, technically knowledgeable labour force but, more specifically, advanced capitalist machinofacture needs both a general labour force with the basic cognitive skills to follow abstract rules and perform shifting, operational detail tasks, and also a smaller proportion of workers who attain sufficient general scientific knowledge in specialized fields to conduct the technical adaptation, redesign and repair of various machinofacture production systems. These are the most fundamental *economic* factors underlying the twentieth century expansion of state schooling.

The overall technical form and content of school curricula and teaching methods have become increasingly standardized and segmented for most students just as the tendential development of capitalist machinofacture has relegated a growing proportion of the *potential* work force to contend for routinized, operative jobs. Holistic, critical perspectives are often prescribed even in advanced training for the most demanding specializations. An indicative case is provided by Eckhard Kanzow's description of the polytechnical engineering colleges of West Germany. These college programmes have involved up to forty hours of compulsory tuition a week plus extremely heavy homework assignments in studies that:

> ... actually consist of a mish-mash of heterogeneous kinds of training quite unconnected with each other. No coherent program has ever been developed. It is almost entirely a matter of learning facts and formulae by heart, and of learning how to assimilate fragmentary and disconnected bits of information rapidly. The result of all this is that students cannot gain any understanding beyond the scope of their special subjects; cannot develop the ability to learn for themselves; complete lack of any critical perspective on their subjects; lack of independence in making decisions, or in developing for themselves their own concepts or ways of thinking within their subjects.[49]

Even the pace of learning is increasingly being engineered into curriculum packages at most levels.[50]

In the elite university institutions preparing managerial personnel and advanced scientific researchers there is an evident tendency for teachers and students to have significant discretion in organizing the technical form of their learning process.[51] But lower level curricula must also attempt to remain flexible enough to encourage versatility as well as acceptance of routine by the general student and potential proletarian worker, and to encourage development of expert planning and co-ordination skills as well as acceptance of the prospect of highly restricted specialties by many potential intellectual workers. Otherwise, the technical aptitudes of the work force are unlikely to remain adequate to revolutionize and operate the instruments of capitalist production. Within the capitalist form of schooling generally, as Bowles and Gintis have suggested:

> The imperative of enhancing labour power consistent with the evolving forces of production often ... clashes with the objective of reproducing the social, political and economic conditions for the perpetuation of capitalism as a system.[52]

The tendency to try to resolve these contradictory social and technical demands on the schooling process through differential treatment of students from different class origins has seldom been more graphically documented than in the recent classroom ethnographies of Jean Anyon.[53] Working with a conception of social class similar to Erik Olin Wright's, she identified quite homogenous working class, middle class, affluent professional and executive elite communities and observed the schooling process in grade five state school classrooms in each community during the 1978–79 school year. Her accounts of classroom practices in the working class and executive elite communities provide striking contrasts:

> *The Working Class Schools.* In the two working class schools, work is following the steps of a procedure. The procedure is usually mechanical, involving rule behaviour and very little decision making or choice. The teachers rarely explain why the work is being assigned, how it might connect to other assignments, or what the idea is that lies behind the procedure or gives it coherence and perhaps meaning or significance. Available textbooks are not always used, and the teachers often prepare their own dittoes or put work examples on the board. Most of the rules regarding work are designations of what the children are to do; the rules are steps to follow. These steps are told to the children by the teachers and often written on the board. The children are usually told to copy the steps as notes. These notes are to be studied. Work is often evaluated not according to whether it is right or wrong, but according to whether the children followed the right steps. ... The control that the teachers have is less than they would like. It is a result of constant struggle with the children. The children continually resist the teachers' orders and the work itself. They do not directly challenge the teachers' authority or legitimacy, but they make indirect attempts to sabotage and resist the flow of assignments ... The children are successful enough in their struggle against work that there are long periods where they are not asked to *do* any work, but just to sit and be quiet. Very often the work that the teachers assign is 'easy', that is, not demanding, and thus receives less resistance. Sometimes a compromise is reached where, although the teachers insist that the children continue to work, there is a constant murmur of talk ... Sometimes the teachers themselves join in the conversation because, as one teacher explained to me, 'It's a relief from the routine' ...

> *Executive Elite School.* In the executive elite school, work is developing one's analytical intellectual powers. Children are continually asked to reason through a problem, to produce intellectual products that are both logically sound and of top academic quality. A primary goal of thought is to conceptualize rules by which elements may fit together in systems, and then to apply these rules in solving a problem. School work helps one to achieve, to excel, to prepare for life ... While strict attention to the lesson at hand is required, the teachers make relatively little attempt to regulate the movement of the children at other times ... [T]he children could get materials when they needed them and took what they needed from closets and from the teacher's desk. They were in charge of the office at lunchtime. During class they did not have to sign out or ask permission to leave the room; they just

got up and left. Because of the pressure to get work done, however, they did not leave the room very often. The teachers were very polite to the children, and the investigator heard no sarcasm, no nasty remarks, and few direct orders.[54]

Now, admittedly, these are extremely homogenous capitalist and working class communities and schools, and a more heterogenous blend of contradictory relations would undoubtedly be found within the typical comprehensive school classroom which includes numerous children from intermediate social class groups. But the prevalent tendencies in the material experience of schooling by children from the polar class circles of advanced capitalism is probably quite accurately expressed by the above descriptions.

All of these contradictory aspects of the capitalist form of education, in relations of cultural ownership and in social and technical aspects of relations within the schooling process, can be further specified in relation to the extent of dominance of the capitalist mode of production and forms of machinofacture in different times and places.[55] The empirical focus in the subsequent analysis will be on the specific case of English Canada. To go beyond this preliminary analysis of current class-based educational ideologies it would be necessary to take more specific account of the particular historical origins and development of state schooling in Canada's regions.[56] However, it will be assumed that the basic contradictions outlined here do serve as a material basis for many of the educational formulations by different class ideologues in all advanced capitalist societies.

In sum then, capitalist forms of education, having first offered free and equal educational opportunities in order to culturally dispossess and socially incorporate the population and to provide augmenting basic technical skills, must then severely restrict such opportunities – in terms of both the scope of the curricula and the numbers who are permitted to achieve their educational aspirations. If capitalist production relations are to be reproduced effectively, the capitalist schooling process must continue to play these contradictory roles while maintaining a relative autonomy from capitalist enterprises, and without drastically upsetting such popular aspirations. In this context, as lower level opportunities have expanded it has been extremely difficult to limit aspirations for and access to higher levels of schooling. This situation has led to especially profound experience of educational contradictions by students in post-secondary, non-university settings. As an extreme example, consider the case of the predominantly working class students of the aforementioned West German engineering colleges who at the end of the 1960s reacted against the highly restrictive social and technical relations of their schools by rebelling in more profound ways than the widely-noted university student protests of the day. Their efforts involved indefinite strikes, from classes, boycott of exams, occupation of public buildings, collective attempts to design new training methods and programmes, expulsion of a bureaucratic leadership, organization of 'anti-schools', and also the penetration into factories. The depth of this threat to capitalist reproduction resulted in withdrawl of grants from those on strike, strikers being called up for military service, attempts to blacklist the strikers from future employment, police brutality and other repressive measures.[57] The basic contradictions of capitalist education have seldom been expressed in a clearer way. The pertinent question in the absence of such direct political manifestations is whether these materially-based contradictions are directly reflected, obscured or opposed in the current educational ideologies of different social classes.

Class Interests and Educational Concerns

Human relations are not *a priori* antagonistic because of any innate division of diverse interests. Rather, as Sartre states:

> ... it is divisions between men, resulting from the mode of produc-
> tion, which make interest (particular or general, individual or class)
> appear as a real moment of the relations between men ... It is not
> diversity of interests which gives rise to conflicts, but conflicts which
> produce interests.[58]

It follows that class interests are historically specific, social relational phenomena. In class modes of production the extraction of uncompensated surplus labour from direct producers by non-producers establishes some fundamentally opposed interests between such groups. Within the capitalist mode of production, the relations between capitalists and proletarians (as discussed in Chapter Two) have given rise to distinctly opposed general interests. Most fundamentally, in terms of the ownership of the means of production, it is in the interest of capitalists continually to secure and fortify their acquired status by appropriating more private property. Conversely, proletarians with no real ownership of the means of production can only become collective 'masters' of the productive forces of society by negating the existing mode of appropriation, breaking down previous securities for individual private property in the means of production. Secondly, in terms of the control of the labour process, it is in the interest of the capitalist class incessantly to seek further ways to exploit the majority's labour power, while it is in the interest of the proletariat to take control of work into the hands of the majority themselves to be governed by their own historical social needs.[59]

On the basis of the discussion in the preceding section, I would suggest that fundamentally opposed interests of capitalists and proletarians within the capitalist mode of education may be similarly distinguished. With regard to cultural ownership, it is in the interest of capitalists to appropriate as much private property as possible in the major means of cultural production, whereas it is in the interest of the proletariat to abolish private appropriation and assert communal ownership of educational resources. It is in capitalists' fundamental interest to establish hierarchical authority in the social relations of schooling, while it is in the proletariat's interest to fight for collective co-ordination and shared decision-making in educational work. As for the technical relations of schooling, it is in capitalists' fundamental interest to centralize advanced technical design and planning knowledge in exclusive schools as much as possible, and in the proletariat's to make all technical knowledge freely accessible.

To state such fundamentally opposed interests is by no means to presume that the class-based ideologies that animate class struggle are ever unambiguously expressed in such terms. As Michael Burawoy observes:

> ... interests are shaped and organized in the political arena as well as in the material world of production through ideological processes ... [M]ost obviously, class interests are shaped in opposition to other classes, opposition encountered in the political arena as well as the economic arena, opposition that acts as a force of constraint as well as a pressure group organized within institutional channels.[60]

Moreover, the economic and/or political interests of particular fractions of the capitalist or proletarian classes may be at odds with each other or with the fundamental interests of their respective classes as a whole. The reconciliation of such fractional interests is a central factor in the estabishment of ruling class hegemony, as well as in the assertion of counter-hegemony by subordinate classes. It is important here to recognize the difference between *fundamental* class interests (which concern the structure of social relations itself and call into question the mode of production or mode of education) and *immediate* class interests (which, in the present instance, take the capitalist mode of schooling as a given and concern day to day existence within it).[61] Capitalist ideology, like all minority ruling class ideologies, is successful to the extent that it is able to represent its own fundamental interests as the unquestioned universal interests of society, and to preoccupy the populace with issues pertaining to their own immediate interests. For example, the doctrine of the 'rights of private property' still serves capitalists' fundamental interest in appropriating the means of production, and the doctrine of 'technological rationality' increasingly serves capitalists' fundamental interest in control of the labour process in advanced capitalism.[62] While both of these ideological beliefs are in rather uneasy tension with the political doctrine of 'liberal democracy', they do appear to be very widely held both within the capitalist class and outside it. While a considerable diversity of interests on more immediate concerns may be demonstrable both within capitalist fractions and among subordinate groups, such diversity is therefore not a sufficient basis to conclude that ' ... there is no well marked dominant ideology in the later phases of capitalism ... [T]he dominant ideology ceases to be crucial for the coherence of the dominant class.'[63]

Immediate proletarian interests may often be diametrically opposed to immediate capitalist interests but still be accommodated. For any substantial proletarian ideology to speak explicitly of the proletariat's fundamental interests and to link these with the immediate interests of various subordinate class fractions would be to indicate the emergence of the working class as a revolutionary class.

Even if such a simple two-class system were fully constitutive of advanced capitalist societies, the contradictory and dynamic character of the material relations of the capitalist mode of production would impel capitalist and proletarian ideologues frequently to shift their thematic focus from fundamental to immediate concerns in order to attempt to reflect material existence plausibly and thereby either reproduce capitalist ideological dominance or build proletarian oppositional consciousness, respectively. But as the analysis in Chapter Two indicates, class relations in actual capitalist social formations are far more complex than suggested by the above abstract discussion of capitalist and proletarian interests. Capitalist domination has typically involved alliances with prior ruling classes or other intermediate class elements, with associated effects on the character of the dominant ideology.[64] Of particular pertinence in advanced capitalist formations are the new, non-propertied intermediate elements that are directly involved in shaping, diffusing, repairing, regulating and executing symbolic control of the cultural field. As we have seen in Chapter Two, they often have a very strong immediate interest in supporting some variant of the prevailing form of schooling.[65] But it should also be recognized that such 'ectoplasmic layers' do not have fundamental class interests in the same distinctive sense as the polar classes of the capitalist mode of production.

In the following case study of educational ideologies in English Canada, attention is largely restricted to spokespersons for the most organized cores of the two polar classes. Such a limited focus is justified not merely because this is a preliminary study but also by the fact that these spokespersons formally represent the leading vehicles through which the primary class struggle of capitalism is now actually being fought. It should also be clearly understood that we are not dealing here with educational ideologies as they actually exist in the social relations of class cultures – as lived conceptions intimately tied into practical activity – but only with the explicit public rhetorics of certain class ideologues. Such public rhetorics seldom involve detailed analyses or descriptions, but rather *selective* statements drawn from more nuanced understandings and critiques of schooling to suit specific events and audiences. However, it can be argued that such discourse does serve to isolate the most serious contradictions perceived between class interests and the actual operation of educational institutions. The basic purpose of the following discourse analysis is to discern the logics and thematic emphases such ideologues are currently using to attempt to influence lived conceptions of education.

Current Class-Based Educational Ideologies in English Canada*

Over twenty years ago, in attempting to analyze the historical development of the content of English education, Raymond Williams distinguished four sets of educational ideologies which rationalize different emphases in curricular content, related these to the social positions of those holding such views, and suggested that curricular changes over the past century have reflected the relative power of these classes and groups.[66] In the early 1970s, Michael Young offered a tabular summary of Williams' thesis (see Figure 4), and noted the lack of any systematic research to follow up these largely schematic speculations.[67] There have been numerous historical studies documenting the educational ideologies expressed by different class-based movements in the pre-World War II period in several advanced capitalist societies.[68] However, there has been very little historical research on the interplay between the educational ideologies of major classes,[69] and virtually no study of the educational ideologies associated with contemporary social classes. The excellent recent work of the Birmingham Education Group on post-War English educational settlements[70] focuses very insightfully on the changing contours of Labour and Conservative Party policies, as well as the contributions of associated intellectuals (particularly sociologists). But they make only passing reference to the educational views of business and labour spokespersons. The focus here will be on such class-based educational views, which may be regarded as providing the effective ideological boundaries for the mediated expressions of educational policies by both the political parties and the state in contemporary English Canada.

While the aforementioned fundamentally contradictory tendencies of the relations between capital and labour have long characterized advanced capitalist societies, it should be recognized that the dominant form of production

Figure 4   Historical Class-Based Educational Ideologies in England

Social Position	General Ideology	Educational Policies
Aristocracy/Gentry	Liberal/Conservative	Non-vocational; the 'educated' man; an emphasis on character.
Merchant and Professional Classes	Bougeois	Higher professional and vocational courses: education as access to desired positions.
Radical Reformers	Democratic	Expansionist: 'education for all'.
Working Classes/ Subordinate Groups	Populist/Proletarian	Student relevance, choice, participation.

Source: Adapted from Michael Young (1973) 'Curricula and the Social Organization of Knowledge', in Brown, R. (Ed), *Knowledge, Education and Cultural Change*, London: Tavistock, p. 347.

* with the assistance of Doug Hart.

relations is now quite different from the earlier classical period of capitalist development. The much greater concentration of capital and to a lesser extent of labour, the growth and systematic intervention of the state in the economy, and increasing reliance on scientific knowledge-based forces of production have become associated with a variety of institutionalized *co-operative* practices (for example, consortiums, joint private-public ventures, collective bargaining), quite unfamiliar to the earlier more openly competitive phase. There appear to have been some concomitant *general* shifts in the dominant thematic emphases of the ideological forms in advanced capitalist societies, most evidently on the individualism-collectivism dimension. As Mellos has observed in one of the few systematic empirical studies of current capitalist ideologies in Canada:

> The opposing class interests of a capitalist society, based on the contradiction between capital and labour, are concealed in the ideology where the society is depicted as a unitary harmonious organism of interdependent parts engaged in the solution of common problems. The economic institution and the state are assigned the role of satisfying in collaborative, co-ordinated fashion, the common societal interest. Whereas the harmony of societal interests in liberal capitalism was a function of the competitively pursued individual interests, the harmony of interest now is portrayed as the unity of interests collectively pursued in universal co-operation ... The perpetuation of claims to universality by the neo-liberal ideology is facilitated precisely because co-operation, universal participation and collaboration are categories which can be more easily promoted as related to the common good than the classical liberal structures of competitive individualism. This is so in that the link between co-operative material structures of action and the communal good is direct whereas in the conditions of classical capitalism the action/communal good link was mediated by the individual.[71]

In the Canadian case, nascent expressions of collaborationist themes can be seen as early as the 1880s,[72] although they may not have become prevalent until several generations later.[73] Mellos' analysis illustrates how pervasive such general themes have now become in the public rhetoric of current corporate spokespersons.[74] Comparable studies of the thematic concerns of labour spokespersons in English Canada remain to be done, but there are substantial indications that expressions of anti-capitalist political ideologies by labour spokespersons have diminished in recent decades.[75] A growing acceptance of the institutions of collective bargaining has led to numerous labour leaders promulgating a corporatist ideology, even after the onset of the current economic crisis.[76]

Recent public statements on educational issues by spokespersons for corporate business and organized labour in English Canada will be analyzed here. For the most part, the review is restricted to the most prominent and accessible public statements made since the visible onset of economic crisis in 1973–74. In the case of corporate business, positions advanced by officials of business associations, and editorials and articles appearing in the major business publications of English Canada have been reviewed. These organizations and journals are countrywide in scope; however, their membership and readerships are concentrated in central Canada. For labour, editorials and articles appearing in union publications, together with the reports of proceedings at conventions of the Canadian Labour Congress and the Ontario Federation of Labour have provided major sources.[77]

This analysis is informed by the essential asymmetry in the relationship between fundamental and immediate class interests which distinguishes the respective positions of capital and labour in the current social order. The critique of educational institutions advanced by spokespersons for corporate business is contextuated by the continuing contribution of these institutions to the reproduction of social relations preserving the dominance of corporate capital. There are, as noted earlier, contradictory aspects within the requirements of production met by educational institutions which may be expected to find expression in ideology. There are conflicts between the specific interests of individual firms and industries and the general interests of corporate capital as a whole which, it may be anticipated, will similarly become objects of ideological discourse. Finally, there is no reason to presuppose that the ideological perspectives of individual corporate spokespersons will necessarily neatly correspond to the optimal strategy or outcomes for corporate capital as a whole (or that history has ceased to operate behind the backs of capitalists with the attendent costs of learning by the experience of unintended consequences). The above are grounds for anticipating that the corporate 'business creed' on education will not be entirely coherent or prescient. At the same time, there is no implication of necessary contradiction between fundamental and various immediate capitalist class interests.

In the case of labour spokespersons, ideological discourse may be expected to reflect a diversity of immediate interests, some of which may appear to correspond with the immediate interests of corporate capital. Indeed, in spite of the increasing incidence of class conflict over immediate issues in the current protracted economic crisis, both labour spokespersons and rank and file workers currently remain embedded within a continuing structure of educational and social institutions that presume the predominance of interests antithetical to the fundamental interests of the working class. Nevertheless, in order to ascertain the actual relative emphases on themes dealing with fundamental and immediate class interests in any given period, empirical assessments of the public discourse of class spokespersons are required.

The presentation of this analysis is organized in terms of the three primary dimensions of class relations in the capitalist form of education identified above: relations of cultural ownership, and social and technical aspects of relations within the schooling process.

Cultural Ownership of the Schools

Corporate business and cultural ownership

There is a spectre haunting the business community – the spectre of the intentions of youth ... What we are talking about here is the biggest threat currently facing free-enterprise business (and democratic government) in the history of the Western world. Our youth turns to Mao, Lenin and Trotsky. It thinks in terms of communes rather than individual virtues and achievement. It wants blood warmth and reassurance. We offer it computer capability and the vision of a world which will harness the stars to our purposes. It is not enough. We do not offer youth the challenge it wants. And we are leaving it open to ideological contamination – contamination by creeds that are alien to individual good and individual dignity. We offer slogans with an ideological base – that of free enterprise: what individual and corporate effort can do for the world and its peoples. But the young do not hear. We are headed for failure for reasons of our own making: the free-enterprise-oriented business community has made neither its intentions, its achievements nor its principles clear.[78]

Executive Editorial, 1969.

The war of ideologies – between our society and the new left – will be won as we reach out to the millions of open-minded students searching for answers to today's social problems. First we have to take our ideas to the youngsters where they are – at school, at work or on vacation. Most of our students are not getting complete answers in school about how our economic system works.[79]

J. W. Popkin, Sun Life economist, 1968.

... the economic base of Canada's liberal democracy is sadly in need of repair ... it is wholly appropriate that the Canadian Chamber of Commerce should draw attention to the need for cutting the educational coat according to the job market cloth.[80]

K. MacDonald, Business Writer, 1975.

Every businessman has a self-interest in finding ways to achieve a harmonizing of educational objectives with those of the business community which is the ultimate user of its end product.[81]

George Temple, Senior Corporate Executive, 1976.

The foundation of the positions on education advanced by spokespersons for corporate capital is the identification of the public interest with the self-interest of businessmen. The first two quotes indicate how sensitive corporate business has been to any visible questioning of this identity in the recent past. In the current view, the stated needs of corporate capital must be met because such demands entail a functional re-adjustment of schooling to the requirements for renewed economic growth. Growth is taken as both the over-riding common goal of the community and the specific domain of business enterprise. Thus corporate spokespersons argue that it is in the public interest that policy-makers give priority to 'harmonizing' educational outputs with business needs.

As Mellos and others have noted,[82] corporate spokespersons now advance the identification of the public good with the interests of large business within a corporatist ideological framework. The functional interdependence of institutions and individual role performances within the economy are taken as cause for concerted, conscious, purposeful co-operation based upon directions established by the needs of corporate business. Even though corporations themselves must necessarily compete in the marketplace, the competition of 'egotistical' actors is no longer seen as the basis of the economic order and the mechanism which defines the common good. The weight of competing, narrow interests becomes, in fact, a source of disruption. There is some criticism on occasion of the behaviour of individual firms as contrary to the common interest. Overwhelmingly, however, the current weakness of the economy and of the educational system is ascribed to the free play of egotistical orientations among the 'people' in various guises. Inflation, welfare costs, unemployment – all are laid at the feet of a populace unrestrained in pursuit of personal interest, and unwilling to adapt to economic realities. What is preserved from classical liberalism is the insistence that profit and the autonomy of corporate capital to pursue it remain the essential bases of a workable and prosperous economic order.

The significance of these themes for education is to be understood in relation to a perceived failure by business to maintain adequate control of the content of schooling through control of employment. It is taken for granted by spokespersons for corporate capital that the primary function of the education system is to supply appropriately skilled and motivated labour for the business community. In line with the 'corporatist' perspective outlined above, the job market is presented less as a field of opportunities for individuals (although appeals to individual initiative and to self-interest appropriately circumscribed by the 'realities' of the situation are not precluded) than as a roster of employers' requirements. Educational services are not for the most part directly purchased by business. Rather, business buys the labour of the 'end product' of the education system. It is the student or 'product', rather than the employing firm, who has been the client of the system. In this three-way transaction, students are seen as unprepared and unwilling to make rational assessments of the services they receive based on market value. The public educational system is thus not adequately constrained by the demands of employers as transmitted by students in search of marketable skills. Remote control of schooling through ownership of the means of production and employment is thus regarded as seriously flawed.

In recent years there has been some movement toward a re-privatization of education in the areas of advanced, technical job skills. This has taken the form both of private educational enterprises and employer-sponsored training in which the firm essentially sells to the government the training provided to its own workers. It is the latter form of direct ownership which receives some explicit support from business spokespersons.[83] In general, however, business spokespersons display more interest in a strengthening of the remote control of the market through political and ideological initiatives than in reprivatization of education.

The emphasis upon corporatist themes rather than those of individualistic competition can be partially understood in terms of a perceived failure of the labour market to produce a shaping of students' attitudes and choices as a self-interested response to future conditions of employment. This ideological initiative is, however, equally directed against pluralistic ideology and practice. The legitimacy and influence accorded to excessively diverse interests is held responsible for widening the gap between schooling and labour market requrements and for blocking a political remedy to the failure of remote control by employers:

> Education is too serious a matter to be left to educators alone. There has never been a time in history when ethics and purposes have been under greater attack by government, communities, interest groups and individuals. There has never been a time when it was so necessary for businessmen to assist the educator to turn out a product more economically, and more capable of taking a productive place in an increasingly competitive world.[84]

There is not only a disillusionment with the pluralist model of decision-making, but an absence of explicit support for that version of corporatism which recognizes several 'functional' groupings – notably including organized labour – whose interests are harmonized within public or quasi-public planning agencies. Organized labour is largely ignored in education statements by spokespersons for corporate capital. The notable exception concerns a demand that the unions relinquish what influence they hold over skills training through the system of apprenticeships and licensed trades. Labour is the 'human energy', 'fueling the economic engines', but without any identifiable role in defining the public good.

In essence, spokespersons for corporate capital now demand the curtailment of competition with business interests in the sphere of educational policy-making and, as detailed in a later section, of contending interests represented in the curricula and working practices within the schools as well. The nature of the improvements spokespersons for corporate capital seek in the 'outputs' of the school system are better delineated in relation to the social and technical relations of schooling which are to produce them than as a dimension of cultural ownership in itself. What should be noted here is that the corporate ideology which legitimates this educational reformation is to enter into the curriculum itself as a category of knowledge and a dimension of the morality of good citizenship. On occasion, this interest is expressed directly in terms of shaping student attitudes toward business to approximate more closely those held by the business community itself. More often, however, this is conveyed as a need for 'economic literacy':

> Many job seekers show little understanding about the Canadian business system, the economic principles through which it operates. Yet I believe a knowledge of fundamental economic principles is, today, as essential as math or grammer ... Unfortunately, many of our students make no effort to understand the basic relationships between economic productivity and our national prosperity.[85]

More specifically, misconceptions about the role of profits must be redressed:

> Students, in particular, tend to ask questions like ... 'What about big profits?' They perceive us as dull, and business jobs as boring. They believe business is big, and that big is bad. Business has a social mission in this country – to produce goods and services of an economic nature. Its mission is to satisfy customers ... Business has been able to marshall the talent and ingenuity that make the 'good life' possible for so many people in Canada. Profits – and the role they play in our lives – is one of the most misunderstood features of the capitalistic system. After all, they are simply a measure of business income surplus over expenses.[86]

Such calls for greater understanding of purportedly immutable objective conditions both contain a legitimation of corporate capital and imply a deeper moral imperative upon individuals to prepare to be productive. This is to be the motivational foundation of a new work ethic in education.

The claims by spokespersons for corporate business are rooted in the currently secure assumptions that the educational system must act as a service industry for corporate business, and that the 'products' of that system must find places within a labour market largely constituted by private employers. Business spokespersons are concerned with up-grading a pragmatic acceptance of the 'business system' among job seekers to an active commitment with lower expectations. Clearly, the schools are increasingly regarded as central vehicles for re-invigorating the popular legitimacy of corporate business. In contrast to the clarion calls of the late 1960s,[87] there is presently little apparent concern among corporate spokespersons in Canada that the educational system might be capable of nuturing forces offering a serious challenge to the 'business system' as a whole.

Organized labour and cultural ownership

> I work in schools, and some of the people handling these kids have such an inbred hatred of the Movement that we belong to, that they're painting a completely distorted picture of what we do and what we are. These kids are so confused ... they graduate with a feeling that the Union Movement is the result of some kind of an unholy alliance between Karl Marx and Al Capone. I'm serious. They are as confused

as this. The only answer to it is to find some way to get our own speakers into the schools to talk to these kids, and the kids today, we may find a lot of faults with them, but they're by no means stupid ... they'll soon know who is giving them the true picture.[88]

L. Dobbin, Canadian Union of Public Employees Delegate, 1971.

The trade union Movement, of all movements in this province, has to begin to realize and put forth that education, complete and full education for all people, and all working people in this province is a right, and is a right like other rights that has to be won ... and it has to be fought for. We all have the right to learn and a profession by which we can make a decent living. We all have the right to understand the history of our country, the factors that have made it what it is and the problems that we have. We all have the right to understand our culture, to participate in it, to appreciate it. We all have the right to understand the ideas that have made this world what it is and that are and will be, including the ideas of the Trade Union Movement as socialism. These questions and these programs have to be fought for ... in every school board, in every school district, and there are forces which the Trade Union Movement can link up with, which are fighting for some of these issues and in very concrete ways.[89]

C. Guettel, Toronto Newspaper Guild Delegate, 1974.

What do our children learn about the dignity of labour? What kinds of attitudes are absorbed about blue-collar work? What do they learn about the significance of the labour movement – particularly its prominence in struggles for social benefits ... ? Precious little.[90]

Barry Fleming, Executive Assistant,
Public Service Alliance of Canada, 1979.

Let's talk a bit about democracy ... [T]he facts are that almost all our institutions are monopolies controlled by a privileged few who rape our resources, shape our minds, heap economic misery and social injustice upon us. They tap our phones, open our mail, infiltrate our organizations, and they manipulate us at every turn ... Should we not insist on something more than just the privilege of casting a vote every four or five years? ... What about involving institutions of people and giving *them* something to say in the economic planning and development of this country? ... What about social democracy: the right to decent standards of housing, adequate educational facilities and opportunities, access to universal health delivery systems? ... We have literally thousands, perhaps hundreds of thousands, of on-the-job representatives, stewards, committee members, local union activists that hold positions and command respect in the work place, that have a trust relationship with the workers we are privileged to represent. We are going to put this communications system to work ... every

communications media at our disposal, in schools and seminars, or any
time when two or three are gathered together.[91]
Denis McDermott, President, Canadian Labour Congress, 1980.

Union spokespersons tend to regard the current educational system as a
serious threat to working class identity and solidarity, and to the legitimacy and
renewal of working class organizations. There are specific charges that some
sites within the school system – particularly those preparing students directly
for employment – are essentially willing or oblivious captives of business
interests, inculcating anti-union attitudes and building identifications with
business owners. More broadly the schools are seen as transmitting a version of
the current social order and its history which favours business interests. The
educational system is seen to operate against working class identification and
solidarity in serving to perpetuate the status distinctions between mental and
manual labour, between professional and 'labouring' occupations, and by
ignoring or misrepresenting the role and history of working class institutions.
Union spokespersons are concerned with the implications for recruitment and
for the popular support of unions, of a new generation of students who are
ignorant of the benefits achieved by organized labour.[92] Finally, union
spokespersons view the schools' antipathy to validating working class identity
and solidarity as an integral aspect of a social system which denies material
opportunities to working class children in the service of meeting the labour
requirements of employers and preserving class inequalities. The schools are
regarded as streaming children from working class families into the types of
jobs which the dominant culture has already taught them to devalue. The
schools are thus seen to legitimate the pattern of unequal rewards between
manual and 'professional' work while inculcating beliefs and attitudes hostile to
working class organizations opposing such inequities.[93]

The central educational demands of union spokespersons are for balanced
treatment of different interests and distributive justice in the allocation of
symbolic and material rewards. These demands are advanced on the basis of
the functional contribution of labour to the public good as direct producers
of goods and services, and on the basis of the rights of citizenship and
numerical predominance of the working class. The latter argument in particular
is extended to include other politically and economically disadvantaged
groups:

> Most key decisions on education are made by people far removed from
> the classroom. Their priorities are to train young people to recreate
> society as it is today – a society in which a few control the system in
> which the rest of us work, live and play. [W]e want this changed.[94]

Spokespersons for organized labour deny the equation of the public interest
with the interests of corporate capital, and advance their own interests as those
of the majority of citizens. Yet despite the claim that control of both economic
and educational institutions resides with elites at best insensitive and at worst

actively opposed to working class interests, union spokespersons typically have advocated electoral and lobbying strategies focused on incremental reform of established institutional forms. In regard to educational programmes in which organized labour has an immediate interest, notably in the areas of skills training and work experiences, leading trade unionists have supported participation in essentially corporatist, tripartite bodies.[95]

Support for these initiatives within central policy-making bodies co-exists with a widespread pessimism regarding the potential of these efforts in isolation from on-going local struggle to secure an immediate and enduring presence within the schools. Thus, there is frequent internal division within the union movement over formal participation in tripartite programmes, based upon assessments concerning the real possibilities of effective union influence. In effect, such initiatives – be they centres for labour studies in community colleges or skills training programmes at the secondary or post-secondary level – become the object of debate regarding the likelihood that the programme will become a further site of anti-labour activity:

> We in our industry [typographical] have had some very sharp experiences in this matter of programmes at the post-secondary colleges that are supposed to be devoted to apprenticeship training, being manipulated and used by management-type teachers to spread anti-union propaganda in the middle of the teaching programme, which is related to the technology in our industry, keyboard operators and so on. We have protested that and fought a vigorous fight on that. However, this fight in my opinion has to be a continuing one because these colleges, using our taxes are developing indeed propaganda against the Union Movement. All you have to do is pick a brochure in our trade ... and you'll be shocked, because most courses deal with management instruction ... Now this attempt by graduates from these courses to go out into the field of Labour to undermine our organizational activity must be fought whole-heartedly.[96]

The experienced weakness of union influence within the schools brings labour's immediate interest in gaining access to the resources of the public educational system into conflict with equally immediate concerns for the preservation of the organizational integrity of the unions themselves. Distrust of in-school programmes leads to an emphasis upon training in settings where union influence is more securely established (for example, on the extension of licenced trades with apprenticeships served primarily in the work place).[97] The conflict is most intense where the training of union cadres is at issue. Spokespersons for corporate business in the 1960s expressed some concern that management training programmes within the universities were failing to attract sufficient numbers of the better students.[98] There was, however, little or no sense that those in such programmes (or programmes for the technical professions) might suffer a critical change in allegiance away from corporate business. Within organized labour, however, the belated establishment of post-secondary programmes relevant to the training of union cadres has been approached with serious reservations:

> I think we have to be careful about this [community college centres for labour studies] because as you know, about fifty per cent of the people we educate, management takes them; and they're the ones that start giving us warnings. So I say if we're going to educate our people and management is going to take them ... why should we pay to support this with our tax dollars in order to educate the people, and they end up by being the worst bunch of bastards that you ever run across.[99]

There has been a long felt need within the union movement to narrow the gap between the education of union cadres and that of the management representatives they deal with.[100] Yet it is clear from even a cursory reading of labour journals that it is the unions' own resources for leadership training rather than vastly greater but 'untrustworthy' resources of the public educational system that labour spokespersons are intent on relying on for political education in the foreseeable future.[101]

There are further contradictions within the educational demands of organized labour, similarly rooted in the dispossession of labour from control over the state school system, but reflecting a division between immediate and fundamental class interests rather than a clash of immediate interests. While the mark of these more basic conflicts can be found in current labour statements, they were most clearly evident in the reaction of union spokespersons to liberalizing education policy initiatives of the late 1960s, most notably the Hall-Dennis Commission Report in Ontario.[102] The distance between immediate and fundamental working class interests remains clearly visible in the on-going defence by union spokespersons of such liberal reforms.

Organized labour embraced such recommendations for the same reasons that these became anathema to spokespersons for corporate business – they appeared to advance the needs and interests of the individual against those of the current social order. From their different vantage points, both corporate capital and organized labour spokespersons interpreted such proposed liberal reforms as Hall-Dennis in terms of a challenge to 'labour discipline'. As we have seen, spokespersons for corporate capital have viewed liberal educational reforms as sponsoring a parasitic, self-indulgent individualism over a socially responsible work ethic. Nevertheless, the individualistic and therapeutic focus of these child-centred policy initiatives generally failed to locate such educational reforms in the broader societal context of different and contending interest groups, and thereby remained effectively compatible with capitalists' fundamental interests. Such limitations are evident in positions developed by union spokespersons which attempted to move beyond the immediate interests of the labour movement.

Labour spokespersons had little difficulty in assimilating the child-centred approach into an-on-going critique of the subservience of the schools to business interests. It was argued that reforms in the direction of child-centred learning could result in an approach to work-related training described as follows by one labour spokesperson with experience in educational consultative bodies:

> Their approach was how do we turn out little robots for our factories. How do we develop an attitude on the part of our youth which says they aren't interested in pensions, they aren't interested in anything but coming to the factory with the only perspective being: How much can I offer this employer who has been good enough to give me a job?[103]

In reaching beyond immediate interests, however, an idealized relationship between education and individual abilities and aspirations was set out by labour spokespersons without reference to the transformation of the structural relations needed to realize such an objective. The concept was advanced of a 'free educational system', a system which would be based on:

> ... the idea of the individual, not being an appendage of this or that economic structure that turns out so many people for so many factories, but a person who has talents in many, many directions, that should be given the full scope of his ability...[104]

The same ideal is echoed in a recent electoral programme advanced by the Metro New Democrats and Labour Council of Metropolitan Toronto:

> Schools maintain a class bias that makes it difficult for working class students to succeed. The notion that academic programs are more socially valuable than manual or technical classes encourages the labelling of technical and commercial students as inferior and is used to justify massive wage gaps between work of this kind and 'professional' jobs. On the contrary, we need students and workers who are well rounded and who develop their capacities in academic, technical and manual work.[105]

The depiction of societal and particularly labour force needs as congruent with the fullest development of individual abilities is clearly at odds with the current organization of the labour process – in particular with the existing divisions between mental and manual labour, and tendencies toward job fragmentation and de-skilling which union spokespersons themselves have explicitly recognized and opposed in regard to the skilled trades.[106] Interests around job content must call into question the current organization of work or else devolve into localized concerns for ensuring equality of opportunity with regard to higher level occupations. The contradiction between 'child-centred' learning and the 'products' required by employers is not directly confronted in the critique of education offered by spokespersons for organized labour. Rather, equality of opportunity with regard to access to post-secondary education is also demanded, entailing in part the expansion of the number of places available in post-secondary institutions. In effect, demands for opportunities for individual mobility push up against the barriers of the labour market in terms of the scarcity of higher level positions, without directly addressing issues of the nature and bases of these limits. This interest in opportunities of individual mobility co-exists with demands for according dignity and greater material rewards to manual labour and furthering students' identification with those who perform it. Aspirations for mobility are, however, a source of opposition to demands by corporate spokespersons that many students be led to reduce their expectations and undertake programmes leading to manual work. Contradictions between class solidarity and individual mobility remain obscure insofar as such demands have been merely aggregated. However, the educational interests of corporate spokespersons are frequently seen to encompass a direct challenge to the attempts of working class families to secure a better life for their children through occupational mobility.[107]

Social Relations in the Schooling Process: School Discipline

Corporate business and school discipline

For some, the 'reality' of the workplace, and the accompanying work-oriented discipline, means a harsh adjustment from the 'anything goes' atmosphere of high school. Let me hasten to add that schools, or teachers, are only one of many influences on the 'citizens' we are producing. I realize that negative or hostile attitudes are spawned in the atmosphere of the home. And that once ingrained these attitudes are hard to eradicate. But I also recognize that in some classrooms these attitudes are reinforced by a lack of discipline and a feeling that quite a number of these students are unmanageable. The end result, in some cases, is student indifference. Again let me pose the question: has the pendulum moved too far? Are we allowing too much freedom in the classroom?[108]

> H.E. Wyatt, Chairman, Canadian Chamber of Commerce
> and Vice-Chairman, Royal Bank of Canada, 1980.

For corporate spokespersons the social relations of the schooling process are now most critically a matter of controlling the patterns of everyday conduct within the schools. At the centre of their critique of educational practices are issues of student discipline. There is a reciprocal equation of school discipline with labour discipline. Proper school discipline is stressed as essential to students' subsequent acceptance of labour discipline, while the fundamentals of labour discipline are presented as the attitudinal and behavioural requirements of the learning process. In both instances, the emphasis is upon acceptance of external constraint. Most obviously, this means regular attendance and consistent compliance with management rules and directions in both school and work settings. The goal, however, is much more ambitious, namely to shape a personality more appropriate to the 'social responsibilities' of work and citizenship. Thus the schools are to produce young workers having:

schools produce young workers —

... a tolerance of delayed gratification, a certain measure of respect for authority, and a willingness to accommodate one's individual desires to the interest of group cohesion and purpose.[109]

What is notably absent here is an emphasis upon competition. To a degree this theme is implicit in other demands – notably for the narrowing of the curriculum such that students cannot escape into purportedly undemanding programmes, and for a *demonstrable* raising of standards in those subject areas representing work-related basic skills. The idealization of competition has, however, in many instances been overshadowed by corporate themes of co-operation and adaptation. This appears to reflect circumstances in which the primary concern is with up-grading and re-directing the mass of students rather than the 'best', in a situation where the expectations of the 'average' student for rewards in the job market are already deemed excessive:

Admittedly, many jobs can be boring and repetitive, but too many young people ... find it hard to accept or even to grasp that you do not become a foreman, a work supervisor, a manager, or an executive, within the first six months or so. Even those displaying potential are unaware that experience is an important ingredient in business success. They want instant gratification – they also want to be entertained.[110]

In the face of perceived resistance to routinized work, corporate ideology urges accommodation; a moderation of 'egotistical' strivings which will result in rewards to the individual as an outcome of national economic recovery.

The stress upon accommodation, particularly to routinized work, should not be mis-read as an intention to produce 'cheerful robots'. Spokespersons for corporate capital are concerned that the 'indulgence' and 'permissiveness' of the schools have undermined acceptance of 'work discipline' in the very basic sense encountered above. However, they are also critical of a passivity among students as incompatible with the internalized self-discipline and self-direction required in some degree of most workers in modern industry. The demand is essentially that the schools instil a toleration of externally directed, routinized work while concurrently developing capacities for self-motivation and self-management beyond routine:

The irony [of permissiveness] is that the high school graduates who enter the post-secondary stage are called upon, in planning and executing university and community college work, to exercise the very self-discipline to which they are strangers. There is an almost complete lack of initiative in trying to learn something new without specific instructions.[111]

The corporate interest in having the schools promulgate self-disciplined engagement in routine work is nicely captured in the following impassioned plea:

It is not a simple matter, as theorists maintain, of responding to stimuli and using pocket calculators. It is a matter of being able to read an instrument manual, of being able to interpret the effect of physical and mechanical conditions on delicate machinery, and of being able to conduct a comprehensible conversation on technical and commercial topics. How long does it take to learn the nuances of expression and differences in meaning? Experience is a wonderful teacher, but at what cost must those starting on careers struggle to learn from scratch what might have been instilled years before? At what cost will those raised in permissive atmospheres discover that the self-discipline their teachers decried is an indispensible ingredient of success in any field of endeavour?[112]

Spokespersons for corporate business do not explicitly identify or address the apparent contradiction between instilling a toleration of routine and a capacity for independent judgement and initiative. Least of all is there any suggestion as to how working practices within the schools might be restructured to meet both objectives simultaneously.

Corporate spokespersons are, however, unremittingly hostile to the kind of 'engagement' produced by liberalized educational structures and 'child-centred' learning. Such liberalization initiatives are now portrayed exclusively in terms of the replacement of work by 'amusement'. The main critique is of the limited usefulness of learning which is fun, in light of the transition which must be made to work. At one level the corporate preference is for passive acceptance of routine work over passive enjoyment of entertainment. Amusement, however, also appears to represent the broader threat of active engagement in learning on the basis of individual interest rather than acceptance of externally imposed objectives. Spokespersons for corporate business, when characterizing the nature of the work in the abstract, speak of challenges and opportunities for self-fulfillment:

> Challenge, fulfillment, satisfaction – all these are a by-product of productive work, apart form the more tangible rewards such as financial gain. And let us not forget the important role that creation of wealth plays in Canadian society. Without it, we wouldn't have our education system in the first place.[113]

It is clear, however, that individual 'self-actualization' is to emerge as a by-product of an active commitment to assigned tasks (the better part of which will, in most circumstances, entail routinized work). It is the absence of explicit commitment to this structure of authority in liberalized education which appears to have led spokespersons for corporate capital to a growing condemnation. Capacities for self-management in state schools appear valuable only to the extent that they are taught in the context of the acceptance of external direction.

Organized labour and school discipline
Are we producing clock numbers for industry and business in our

educational system, or are we going to develop human beings who will not accept everything that the establishment gives them; who will be curious, who will challenge, who will question?[114]

M. Fenwick, Vice President, Ontario Federation of Labour, 1968.

There is much discussion in the Ontario school system today about the need for a compulsory core curriculum program in the schools. We feel that the return to a rigid compulsory curriculum is neither desirable nor justified ... The slogan 'back to the basics' implies a serious restriction in subject choices available to students, as well as a return to row-seating, drills, memory-work and regurgitation tests, and teacher-centred learning (in those schools where this type of approach has changed in practice as well as in theory) ... We cannot agree with the regressive and misleading calls for a return to what was in the past. The failure of the school system to equip all students with the necessary skills is a real one, but it predates the liberalization of the curriculum.[115]

Metro New Democrats – Labour Council
of Metropolitan Toronto, 1980.

If labour spokespersons have understandably refrained from supporting the use of the schools to instil work discipline, they are even farther from elaborating a model of social relations within the school congruent with their own class interests than spokespersons for corporate capital. Labour spokespersons generally support liberalized social relations within the schools. Such support is, however, not predicated upon a perceived increase in congruence between 'child-centred' education and labour interests. Class-based streaming is seen to have continued in spite of liberal reforms. The presence of organized labour within the schools is not perceived to be significantly greater than previously. Liberalized social relations are supported because the 'back to the basics' and discipline-oriented movements are identified with business interests in reducing what is taught to exclude other than work-related skills, and in limiting the resources available to education. The current system offers at least a rhetorical basis for labour demands. These, in large part, focus on the technical relations rather than the social relations of schooling – notably the breadth and organization of the curriculum and of knowledge, and the resource requirements for its transmission. What is notably absent in the education statements of most union spokespersons is any reference to the relationship between liberalized social relations of schooling and those of the unionized workplace or the union hall. There is little or no counterpart to the kind of correspondence argument developed by spokespersons for corporate capital, wherein school discipline is to parallel work discipline. At the height of campus rebellion in the late 1960s, there were frequent rhetorical statements of support for greater student roles in educational decision-making:

> In our society today it's not only sufficient that our children have access to education. I think it depends largely on the type of education ... Our children today have to be equipped to go out into society and to be able to play a constructive role and also feel that they are living a purposeful life. Most of our children today ... feel alienated because of the fact that they have very little say into what our educational system will be ... [T]hese people must and they should have a say in the formulation of education and to what type of education is needed, if they are to go out into society and play a role and try to do something to correct the ills and bring about the just society ...[116]

More recently there are some suggestions in the statements of labour spokespersons that allowing students to be critical of the 'authoritative' statements of teachers will encourage a critical attitude to the authority of management when they enter the work force. But union spokespersons do not appear to have looked seriously to the social relations of schooling as a source of new attitudes and organizational skills regarding collective responsibility and collective action in the interest of the working class.

Technical Relations in the Learning Process: Skill Requirements

Corporate business and skill requirements

> After twelve or thirteen years in the system, the basic skills which come most easily to the young have not been acquired. The significance of this deterioration to the business community is grave indeed – nothing less than a failure of the education system to fill the vacancies caused by natural wastage. Even if changes were made in the system now, many years must elapse before any improvement can be expected.[117]
>
> George Temple, Senior Corporate Executive, 1976.

> There appear to be three major areas where young graduates entering the work force are deficient: One is basic skills. The second is an inability to communicate adequately, and the third area is an apparent lack of personal philosophy or work ethic ... Obviously we have missed a vital area. To my mind we must readjust the value system of our society, including the parents, the pupils – and the educators. We must gear more of our thinking toward encouraging skills training.[118]
>
> H.E. Wyatt, Chairman, Canadian Chamber of Commerce and Vice-Chairman, Royal Bank of Canada, 1980.

We are turning out a large group of highly educated people we don't need. If Canada does not significantly increase its output of technical workers in the next five to ten years, we will be forced to sell off our resources and buy the manufactured goods of other countries. Canada would become a kind of 'slave state' to more highly developed countries. We must realize it is no disgrace to work with our hands.[119]

Rene Martinet, Corporate Training Services Manager,
Dominion Bridge Company, 1980.

Corporate spokespersons' concern with the technical relations of the actual learning process is now focused on 'rationalization' and increasing productivity, primarily through simplification and standardization of the tasks for both students and teachers. The curriculum is to be re-structured to concentrate course offerings in areas of general work-related skills. Within this are included not only 'basics', but the 'economic literacy' which is seen as a key element in rejuvenating the 'work ethic'. Teachers are still granted the central role in this reduced and concentrated curriculum but increasingly to be augmented by educational technology:

> Since the beginning of time, education has been the result of inter-action between two human beings, and all educative processes need this interaction. If modern teaching aids can augment and enrich this relationship then they are contributing to the quality of education. If, however, they are just frills brought in to relieve the demands on the teacher, or to climb aboard the multi-media bandwagon – then I would seriously question their efficacy. Perhaps the key question here is are they enhancing or detracting from the students' ability to absorb the education basics?[120]

Some new educational technologies, particularly micro-computers, have been advertised by computer industry representatives as extending the scope for child-centred, individualized instruction. Corporate spokespersons typically, however, support teacher-centred learning, particularly in the sense that they continue to look to teacher-student interactions as the basis for creating in the student a sense of 'engagement' while simultaneously accepting external direction. At the same time, they tend to see reforms in classroom management, including improved discipline and curtailment of 'unproductive' activities and 'frills', as the major sources of improved learning efficiency – and teacher redundancies.

The demand that the 'education coat be cut' according to the 'job market cloth' does not mean a tight matching of primary and secondary level programme content to job content. Rather, it entails instruction in general work-related skills which are open-ended and can be built upon or refined in a range of different work settings – in other words, the creation of labour force entrants who will be increasingly technically adaptable and capable of mobility among work settings in response to changing conditions.

Flexibility is sought in the case of advanced skills as well. There is criticism of rigidities introduced by the trades and even the professions as inhibiting students' movement into the labour force as well as interchangeability of labour and the development of combinations of skills in response to the requirements of the labour process. Business schools themselves are not exempted from the charge that in following the model of professional training they have lost touch with the actual conditions of work.[121]

Corporate statements offer little support for extensive training of skilled labour where they do not have a preponderant influence over programme content. But corporate spokespersons acknowledge that conflicts of interest among firms and between individual firms and industries as a whole have impeded the responsiveness of training programmes to actual and changing demands. The flexibility and adaptability of training which is in the interests of industries as a whole is compromised as individual firms seek a quick return, through training restricted to their immediate needs or the 'pirating' of trainees from other firms. Condemned as even more short-sighted by leading corporate spokespersons is the failure to train at all, or to use trainees merely as cheap labour.[122]

Organized labour and skill requirements

... [T]he government is continually breaking [apprenticeship] down and saying you don't have an apprenticeship, you've got a man that can do one thing, and one thing only, and therefore he doesn't need an apprenticeship. The auto industry has been broken down now so that no one hires an auto mechanic, they hire a muffler specialist, a transmission specialist and any other type of a specialist, but never a mechanic ... I'd like to see them bolstering the apprenticeship and keep the lines as they are now, and not let them separate the apprenticeships into lower and lower paid jobs.[123]

Bill Signal, Plumbers and Steamfitters Delegate, 1977.

There's the problem of the education system turning more and more to just turn out students to be docile and good little workers and not to be really educated people, and we want to turn that around as well ...[124]

Cathy Beeman, Canadian Union
of Public Employees Delegate, 1977.

We think that a 'core skill program' in which all students have a real opportunity to develop essential life skills, should be introduced ... The program would not emphasize ... drills or rote learning, but would emphasize learning through much practice ... Class sizes would have to be small so as to maximize individual attention. Specialized teachers would have to be trained and assigned to this work outside the present staffing levels, so that other class sizes do not increase.[125]

Metro New Democrats – Labour Council
of Metropolitan Toronto, 1980.

The public discourse of union spokespersons about education is now most frequently concerned with the skill content of the learning process itself, and quite clearly opposes corporate statements at three key points. First there is resistance to any rationalization through reducing the range of the curriculum and emphasizing 'basics'. In opposing a return to 'basics' in favour of incorporating basic skills training with the teaching of 'essential life skills', labour spokespersons reject a narrowing of the curriculum to what can be commodified in labour-power. Basic skills are to be taught in a way which reflects the total needs and interests of individuals. This includes demands for more sensitive guidelines for skill development and cognitive abilities of different ages of students instead of emphasis on standardized curriculum and content *per se*.[126]

The second point of conflict represents a specification of this concern with 'really educated people', in calls for curricular content which recognizes that the experiential interests of students reflect social location – primarily class membership, but also ethnic community and sex. While corporate spokespersons seek the production of 'economic literacy' in the form of mastery of a general body of 'objective' knowledge organized in standard form, labour spokespersons seek to incorporate the particular history of the labour movement and the skills and knowledge required by labour organizations within the curriculum:

> While a majority of the students in our schools are from working class families, the history of the labour movement, issues of collective bargaining, workers' rights and the role of labour in our society have been virtually omitted from most present curricula. This must change.[127]

Opposition to anti-labour bias is regarded as most critical in the area of work experience programmes for secondary level students. Here, the distinction between 'life skills' and a technocratic concept of 'job skills' represents an opposition which is immediately political:

> In normal working situations, job-oriented activities include the total complex of actions in which the employee is involved during the working day. For example, in many plants arrangements are made through collective bargaining for trade union activity. Similarly, work experience must make provision for the familiarization of the student with trade union activities as an integral part of working life.[128]

While labour spokespersons have not, as noted earlier, commonly considered the social relations of schooling in terms of a correspondence with union practices, there is an insistence that students in the workplace become engaged in union activities as a part of their training. In a sense, the social relations of the unionized workplace are presented as a dimension of the technical relations of work.

The third point of conflict with immediate corporate interests similarly concerns job-related training but focuses upon the 'use-value' of training to individuals. Labour spokespersons express great interest in an organization of skills training which could provide continuity of employment and a cushioning of shocks due to changing economic conditions. Corporate spokespersons are interested precisely in making labour adaptable to such changes. This issue has been defined most clearly in relation to the preservation and extension of the licensed trades model for the organization of skills and allocation of work. For business spokespersons the trades model represents a 'rigidity' to be attacked increasingly. In contrast, the apprenticeship system remains the focus of labour leaders' calls for expanded skills training, and the tradesperson remains the idealization of the skilled worker. Spokespersons for organized labour condemn the fragmentation of trades through specialization, as well as the impoverishment of apprenticeship training through the use of trainees as cheap unskilled labour. It is urged that current work experience programmes in the state schools be designed to facilitate continuation into apprenticeship – and into secure jobs:

> More and more these days, governments and industry, parents and students are looking to apprenticeship training as a means of providing jobs for our young people and there is no doubt that careers in the skilled trades area have much to recommend them. However, we must not fall into the trap of believing that training apprentices creates jobs. Job creation must come first ... We believe that the government policies should create more jobs in the skilled trades area and that the required apprenticeship training programs for these jobs should have considerable input and involvement from the labour movement, public and post-secondary schools and the general public.[129]

What is problematic in statements of union spokespersons on skills training is how the commitment to an extension of the trades model of skilled work is to be reconciled with the tacit acceptance of the existing shape of the labour market. Union demands regarding the level of organization of skills training assume the evolution of the labour market in the direction of an increasing proportion of highly skilled positions. Yet even in union leaders' own statements about current deskilling it is evident that this assumption is hardly secure. The trades organization of skills is at risk in large part because it has come into increasing conflict with the actual structure of the labour process. While criticisms of trends toward deskilling, routinization and job fragmentation are voiced, the focus of resistance has tended to be on the packaging and certification of skills of those who will hold available jobs, not the changing structure and content of the jobs themselves.

Union spokespersons, as noted above, oppose programmes seen to sacrifice opportunities for advanced training in favour of supplying business with 'adaptable' semi-skilled labour. Yet their own concern that programmes match real employment prospects comes into conflict with the objective of well-rounded, skilled workers and, in some instances, with the trades system itself.[130] If adaptation to rather than challenge to the current and evolving organization of work creates conflicts at this level, the contradictions are yet sharper in the case of more general statements by union spokespersons regarding a well-roundedness which would dissolve the distinctions between mental and manual labour and give full scope to human potential.

Thus, labour spokespersons are clearly opposed to the kind of rationalization of the learning process proposed by representatives of corporate capital, and to the implication that greater productivity is achievable with reduced educational resources. Labour leaders are increasingly advancing alternate demands for *added* curricular content and *extensions* of school services. Any decline in productivity as measured in terms of performance in basic subjects is ascribed by union spokespersons primarily to inadequate educational funding and resources to meet the special needs of a more diverse and disadvantaged school population. Opposition to corporate interests regarding the technical relations of schooling is, however, limited insofar as it does not extend to encompass demands with explicit implications for the technical relations of work.

Summary Remarks

The recent statements of corporate and union spokespersons in English Canada exist as rival claims to represent the public interest in education and incompatible demands regarding the reorganization of social and technical relations of schooling. The ideological discourse of corporate spokespersons offers an equation of the interests of corporate business with the common good and a schedule of demands for reform of school organization which virtually ignore the existence of rival claims by spokespersons for organized labour. In contrast, the legitimacy and the substance of educational demands by union spokespersons are founded upon a direct if limited characterization of the school system as an arena of class struggle. Union spokespersons advance demands congruent with immediate working class interests against the interests of capital, but fail to make demands explicitly calling into question the structure of capitalist production relations. The hidden dimension in the discourse of corporate spokespersons is the class struggle over the relationships between schooling and labour market. Union spokespersons are, conversely, silent about the extent of acceptance of and accommodation to the rights of employers encompassed in the definition of immediate educational demands.

There is a distinct ideological advantage gained in portraying corporate interests as arrayed against irresponsible, inefficient, 'egotistical' individuals rather than acknowledging any rival claimant to the representation of the public good. This attempt at mystification by corporate spokespersons does not hinder their formulation of concrete demands for the more complete subordination of working class interests in the process of schooling. It is clear that the substantive demands of corporate spokespersons – for essentially 'moral' education in a new work ethic, for a reform of classroom management to emulate labour discipline and increase 'efficiency', and for a rationalization of curriculum to contribute similarly to ideological domination and cost-effectiveness – are congruent with both their immediate and fundamental class interests. Where corporate spokespersons advance apparently conflicting demands – in particular, for an organization of the social relations of schooling which habituates students to routinized work and rule-governed behaviour while instilling capacities for self-management and individual initiative in mastering the technical relations of the work process – these demands reflect contradictory requirements of the labour process itself as currently organized.

The situation is otherwise for union spokespersons. Insofar as demands are presented in terms of the rights of citizenship, and equality of access and opportunity within the educational system, the oppositional ideology of union spokespersons does not fundamentally challenge the ideological domination of the schools by corporate capital. This ideological hegemony is clearly evident in the shape of labour spokesperson's demands. While spokespersons for corporate capital champion 'economic literacy' as the inculcation of objective knowledge divorced from any but the common interest, labour spokespersons urge the teaching of labour history as a legitimate but 'partisan' interest of a particular group. Where spokespersons for corporate capital offer a definition of work-related skills lodged within the 'objective' technical requirements of labour processes, union spokespersons advance a concept of 'essential life skills' in the workplace centred on knowledge of union activities, which again appears as a reflection of partisan interests rather than the objective nature of work relations. The demands of corporate spokespersons for a revival of the 'work ethic', if not partaking of the same trappings of objectivity, yet make appeal to a 'moral imperative' of the workplace that is of broader currency than class or union solidarity (essentially, a symbol of the old universalism of classical liberalism is transposed to a corporatist context).

Union spokespersons often tend to see those in control of the educational system as agents of the ideological domination of corporate business. Yet, despite the designation of the schools as overwhelmingly the ally of business in the class struggle, the demands of union spokespersons fall considerably short of appropriation of the means of schooling, even in the area of work-related training. We have seen that there is ambivalence over union participation in state education precisely because the kind of direct control foresworn as a goal by leading spokespersons is seen by many cadres as necessary in view of the pervasive anti-labour bias within the schools.

A significant expression of the encapsulation of the demands of union spokespersons is the treatment of the social relations of schooling. Corporate spokespersons operate with an explicit, if internally contradictory, correspondence theory of school and labour 'discipline'. Union spokespersons resist 'teacher-centred' education as a strategy for reducing the resources devoted to education. Child-centred learning is seen to open possibilities for incorporating content critical of the dominant ideology and reflective of working class experience into the curriculum. There is, however, no sense of employing the social relations of schooling to instil fundamentally different attitudes and practices regarding collective action. There is no general link made between the social relations of schooling and those of union practices.

The focus of demands by union spokespersons is upon the technical rather than the social relations of schooling. As noted above, this represents resistance to an organization of knowledge (that is, 'back to the basics') which would exclude curricular content dealing with working class experience and trade unionism. The most important site for inclusion of such content is in work-related training where political education of potential new members is seen as necessary to the renewal of the unions themselves. The opposition of union spokespersons to anti-labour bias in programmes which teach job skills is clear and unequivocal. What is striking is the extent to which union demands regarding the technical content of job skills programmes are incomplete, implicitly conflicting, and superficially similar to those of corporate spokespersons. (That labour demands at this level have not been a target for co-optation by corporate spokespersons is likely due to conflicts over socialization into union activities and over the 'rigidities' of the trades model of training.) The demands of labour spokespersons do not, for the most part, extend beyond the organization of skills to the organization of work. In essence, individual rights to advanced training are asserted against the 'objective' criteria of labour force needs proposed by corporate business. Similarly, union spokespersons find themselves in superficial agreement with spokespersons for corporate capital on the need to upgrade the status and attractiveness of manual labour and increase recruitment to manual skills training programmes. Yet, at the same time, they see the need to resist the streaming of working class children in the schools which forecloses upon individual occupational mobility into semi-professional and professional work. Here the dilemmas of advancing the rights of the individual against unquestioned labour market structure are made more complex by the implications for working class solidarity.

In this chapter, on the basis of an outline of primary materially-based dimensions of the capitalist mode of education, partial sketches of the current surface logics of corporate capitalist and organized labour educational ideologies in English Canada have been presented. Very little of the actual texture of these class-based educational ideologies has been conveyed, to say nothing of the dynamic relations of such conceptions with lived class experience of the material contradictions of the capitalist mode of production. The intent of such a preliminary exploration is to begin to identify and concretize the determinate abstractions[131] of the capitalist mode of education underlying and animating the apparent class relations involved in the everyday reproduction of and contestation of this dominant institutional form.

With regard to cultural ownership in education, the analysis indicates that labour ideologues do not significantly question capitalist appropriation at this point, and are only expressly concerned to infuse more working class curricular content within this dominant form of schooling. Within the schooling process itself, just as in the labour process generally within advanced capitalism, the material contradictions between capitalist and proletarian interests remain more direct. The immediate interests of the capitalist and working classes are now frequently expressed as real oppositions on specific schooling process issues, especially such technical aspects as skill training requirements and provisions. It is on these dimensions of the schooling process that ideological class struggle appears to have increased most in the current crisis.

The themes and emphases of current class-based educational ideologies may differ substantially in other advanced capitalist societies. In particular, working class educational ideologies may express considerably more strident views in countries such as Italy, France and England with more sustained working class political cultures and more powerful political organizations. Furthermore, in all such societies, capitalist and working class ideologies develop not only in relation to each other but through the mediation of intermediate class elements who may develop various distinct ideological perspectives having varied affinities with capitalist and working class interests. Within the present context of widespread capitalist ownership of the major means of cultural production, it has been the extensive participation of articulate 'middle class' and petty bourgeois elements in the major policy making organs of the state that has generated much of the ideological diversity of immediate educational interests[132] as well as the appearance of pluralism in advanced capitalism. Nevertheless, wherever the capitalist mode of production prevails, such intermediate ideological perspectives remain effectively constrained by the fundamental class interests and historical lived cultures of the capitalist and working classes – however obscurely these may be expressed through organized political and ideological vehicles.

Recent neo-Marxist research on the process of ideological domination within the school, and even more recently on working class school cultures of resistance, offer valuable insights into the construction of everyday working class culture. However, in order to go fruitfully beyond such studies it is necessary to identify clearly the extent to which, and the ways in which larger class forces outside the schools impinge on these processes of reproduction and contestation within the schools. Ideological discourse analyses systematically based on historical materialist premises may be – when much more fully developed and confirmed in working class experience – of some considerable aid to working class forces in continuing efforts to mobilize themselves against capitalist domination and for a broadly-based socialist transformation of education and society.

Notes

1 For indicative works, see ENZENSBERGER, H. (1974) *The Consciousness Industry: On Literature, Politics and the Media*, New York, Seabury Press; BAUDRILLARD, J. (1973) *The Mirror of Production*, St. Louis: Telos Press, 1975; EWEN, S. (1976)

Captains of Consciousness: Advertising and the Social Roots of the Consumer Culture, New York, McGraw-Hill, GOULDNER, A. (1976) *The Dialectic of Ideology and Technology: The Origins, Grammar, and Future of Ideology*, New York, Seabury Press; WOLFE, A. (1977) *The Limits of Legitimacy: Political Contradictions of Contemporary Capitalism*, New York, Free Press; and THERBORN, G. (1980) *The Ideology of Power and the Power of Ideology*, London, Verso Editions. Perhaps most significant is the burgeoning 'Gramsci industry', one of the most recent examples of which is BUCI-GLUCKSMANN, C. (1981) *Gramsci and the State*, London, Lawrence and Wishart.

2 For major examples, which display the rapid recent growth of an activist component in such analyses, see APPLE, M. (1979) *Ideology and Curriculum*, Boston, Routledge and Kegan Paul; SHARPE, R. (1980) *Knowledge, Ideology and the Politics of Schooling: Towards a Marxist Analysis of Education*, London, Routledge and Kegan Paul; and GIROUX, H. (1981) *Ideology, Culture and the Process of Schooling*, Philadelphia and Lewes, Temple University Press and Falmer Press. A useful overview is offered in ARNOT, M. and WHITTY, G. (1981) 'From Reproduction to Transformation: A British View of Recent American Work on the Sociology of the Curriculum'. Revised version of a paper delivered at the British Sociological Association Sociology of Education Study Group, London School of Economics, May.

3 The work of the Centre for Contemporary Cultural Studies at the University of Birmingham has been central in this regard. See especially HALL, S. and JEFFERSON, T. (Eds) (1976) *Resistance Through Rituals: Youth Subcultures in Post-War Britain*, London, Hutchison, and on school-related subcultures, WILLIS, P. (1977) *Learning to Labour: How Working Class Kids Get Working Class Jobs*, Westmead, Saxon House.

4 The best examples are FINN, D. GRANT, N. and JOHNSON, R. (1977) 'Social democracy, education and the crisis', *Working Papers in Cultural Studies* 10, pp. 147–98; DONALD, J. (1979) 'Green Paper: Noise of crisis', *Screen Education* 30 (Spring, pp. 13–49; and especially Education Group (1981) (including FINN, D. *et al.*) Centre for Contemporary Cultural Studies, *Unpopular Education: Schooling and Social Democracy in England Since 1944*, London, Hutchinson.

5 The seminal works exhibiting these tendencies are POULANTZAS, N. (1968) *Political Power and Social Classes*, London, New Left Books and Sheed and Ward, 1973, and MILIBAND, R. (1969) *The State in Capitalist Society: The Analysis of the System of Power*, London, Weidenfeld and Nicholson, respectively.

6 OLSON, D. (1980) *The State Elite*, Toronto, McClelland and Stewart, p. 125. The work of James O'Connor has been most important in developing this perspective empirically. See, for example, (1981) '*The Fiscal Crisis of the State* Revisited: Economic crisis and Reagan's budget policy', *Kapitalistate* 9, pp. 41–61.

7 It may be of interest to note here that one of the major contemporary studies of educational policy making by a traditional British social scientist, KOGAN, M. (1975) *Educational Policy Making: A Study of Interest Groups and Parliament*, Hamden, Linnet Books, concludes that:
'Any single policy takes on multiple guises and is viewed differently at many points of a complex system: pupils, teachers, the head, the chief education officer and his administrative and advisory staffs, councillors, the local electorate, the national electorate, Parliament, the DES, researchers, journalists, teacher educators, the churches, employers and the trade unions. In this book we have taken on a fragment of social concern and are yet still uncertain as to how so vast and complex a structure interacts, creates new policies and somehow moves forward. That uncertainty is, we believe, widely shared and should be a matter of concern for those who feel that education should be under democratic control. The only certainty is that the DES (Department of Education and Science) wields determi-

nant authority and great power. Democratic and pluralistic ideas demand more than that ...' (p. 238).

8 The classic statement of this approach appears in MARX K. (1859) *A Contribution to the Critique of Political Economy*, Moscow, Progress Publishers, 1970, expecially pp. 20–22 of the preface. A more detailed presentation of all of the concepts used in this analysis appears in LIVINGSTONE, D.W. *Class and Class Consciousness in Advanced Capitalism* (to be published).

9 Modes of reproduction and particular patriarchal forms of social relations are also vital considerations in an adequate historical materialist analysis of the fundamental determinants of material existence in class societies. Only very recently has systematic historical materialist theorizing of this sphere in relation to modes of production begun. See KUHN A. and WOLPE, A. (Eds) (1978) *Feminism and Materialism: Women and Modes of Production*, Boston, Routledge and Kegan Paul, and especially SECCOMBE, W. (1982) *The Reproduction of Labour Power: A Comparative Study*, Ph.D. Dissertation, University of Toronto.

10 JOHNSON, R. (1979) 'Three problematics: Elements of a theory of working class culture' in CLARKE, J. CRITCHER, C. and JOHNSON, R. (Eds), *Working Class Culture*, London, Hutchinson, p. 232.

11 JOHNSON, R. (1979) 'Histories of culture/theories of ideology: Notes on an impasse', in BARRETT, M. CORRIGAN, P., KUHN, A. and WOLFF, J. (Eds), *Ideology and Cultural Production*, London, Croom Helm, p. 73.

12 MARX, K. and ENGELS, F. (1846) *The German Ideology*, New York, International Publishers, 1970, p. 64.

13 For a fuller discussion, see JOHNSON, C. (1980) 'The problem of reformism and Marx's theory of fetishism', *New Left Review* 119 (January-February), p. 70–96. There are, to be sure, many 'hints' toward such a relational view in *Capital* and other works such as *The Eighteenth Brumaire*; see especially HALL, S. (1977) 'Re-thinking the base-superstructure metaphor', in BLOOMFIELD, J. (Ed), *Class, Hegemony and Party*, London, Lawrence and Wishart, pp. 43–72.

14 For a functionalist elaboration of these dimensions see, for example, KLUCKHOHN, C. (1953) 'Universal categories of culture' in his *Anthropology Today: An Encyclopedic Inventory*, Chicago, University of Chicago Press, pp. 507–23. A particularly relevant case study is SEELEY, J.R. SIM, R.A. and LOOSELEY, E.W. (1956), *Crestwood Heights: A Study of the Culture of Suburban Life*, New York, Basic Books.

15 For documentation, see especially McNEILL, W. (1963) *The Rise of the West*, Chicago, University of Chicago Press, and CAMERON, K. (1977) *Humanity and Society: A World History*, New York, Monthly Review Press. For a more specific example, see THOMPSON, E.P. (1967) 'Time, work-discipline, and industrial capitalism', *Past and Present* 38, pp. 56–97.

16 See LIVINGSTONE, D.W. (1976) 'On hegemony in corporate capitalist states', *Sociological Inquiry* 46(3–4), pp. 235–50.

17 CLARKE, J.R. HALL, S., JEFFERSON, T. and ROBERTS, B. (1976) 'Subcultures, cultures and class: A theoretical over-view', in HALL, S. and JEFFERSON, T. (Eds) *op. cit.*, pp. 40–41.

18 Such class differences have been most fully documented for the English case. For an overview see JOHNSON, R. (1979) 'Really useful knowledge: Radical education and working class culture, 1790–1848' in CLARKE J. CRITCHER, C. and JOHNSON, R. (Eds) *Working Class Culture* London, Hutchinson, pp. 75–102.

19 Marx's treatment remains the seminal work for understanding this process of the real subordination of labour, especially part IV of Volume I of *Capital* New York, International Publishers, 1967 (1867).

20 LAZONICK, W. (1979) 'The subjection of labour to capital: The rise of the capitalist system', *Review of Radical Political Economics*, 10 (1), p. 14.

21 Cited in RUBIN, B. (1972) 'Marxism and education – Radical thought and educational theory in the 1930s', *Science ι ιd Society* 36 (2), p. 172.

22 BOGGS, G. (1970) 'Education, the great obsession', *Monthly Review* 22 (4) (September), pp. 20–23.

23 Among the most substantial of these movements were those instigated by the Plebs League in England around the period of the First World War, and by the Socialist Party, Workers' Educational Bureau, trade unions and other groups in the same period in the U.S. For accounts, see PHILLIPS, A. and PUTNAM, T. (1980) 'Education for emancipation: The movement for independent working class education 1908–1929', *Capital and Class* 10 (Spring), p. 18–42, and SHAPIRO, H.S. (1979) 'Radical movements, ideology, and the sociology of educational ideas', *Social Praxis* 6, (3–4), pp. 193–215. An indicative recent example is the workers' right to study movement initiated in Italy in the late 1960s; see TALIANI, E. (1977) 'The right to study: Workers' demands for an alternative educational strategy', in KLOSKOWSKA, A. and MARTINOTTI, G. (Eds) *Education in a Changing Society*, London, Sage, pp. 177–205

24 RUBIN, B. (1972) *op. cit.*, pp.173–74.

25 For historical overviews that are relatively sensitive to working class opposition, see SIMON,B. (1974) *Studies in the History of Education*, 3 volumes, London, Lawrence and Wishart, on Britain; as well as NASAW, D. (1979) *Schooled to Order: A Social History of Public Schooling in the United States*, New York, Oxford University Press, and SCHECTER, S. (1977) 'Capitalism, class and educational reforms in Canada', in PANITCH, L. (Ed) *The Canadian State*, Toronto, University of Toronto Press, pp. 373–416.

26 Cited in RUBIN, B. (1972) *op. cit.*, pp. 199–200.

27 For documentation see, for example, KATZ, M. (1971) *Class, Bureaucracy and Schools: The Illusion of Educational Change in America*, New York, Praeger, and REMIER, E. (1971) *School is Dead: Alternatives in Education*, Garden City, Doubleday.

28 SHAPIRO, H.I. (1979) *op. cit.*, p. 212.

29 *Ibid.*, p. 213. Compare JONES, D. and DUNN, T. (1980) '–"All of Us Common People" and education in the depression', *Canadian Journal of Education* 5 (4), pp. 41–56.

30 For discussion, see CASTLES, S. and WUSTENBERG, W. (1979) *The Education of the Future: An Introduction to the Theory and Practice of Socialist Education*, London, Pluto, pp. 182–89.

31 Classic examples are HYMAN, H. (1953) 'The value systems of different classes: A social psychological contribution to the analysis of stratification' in BENDIX, R. and LIPSET S.M. (Eds) *Class, Status and Power* Glencoe, Ill, Free Press, pp. 426–42, and COLEMAN, J.S. CAMPBELL, E.Q., HOBSON, C.J., McPARTLAND, J., MOOD, A., WEINFELD, F.D. and YORK, R.L. *Equality of Educational Opportunity* Washington, D.C., US Department of Health, Education and Welfare.

32 See, for example, BOURDIEU, P. and PASSERON, J-Cl. (1970) *Reproduction in Education, Society and Culture* London, Sage, 1977 and BERNSTEIN, B. (1975) *Class, Codes and Control* Vol. 3 London, Routledge and Kegan Paul.

33 JOHNSON, R. (1980) 'Cultural studies and educational practice', *Screen Education* 34, p. 13.

34 WILLIAMSON, B. (1974) 'Continuities and discontinuities in the sociology of Education' in FLUDE, M. and AHIER, J. (Eds) *Educability, Schools and Ideology* London, Croom Helm., p. 10.

35 The seminal work is, of course, BOWLES, S. and GINTIS, H. (1976) *Schooling in Capitalist America*, New York, Basic Books. Their argument relies substantially on Braveman's perspective on the capitalist labour process and has been subjected to similar charges of mechanistic and economistic biases, especially with reference to

their application of a 'correspondence principle' to explain the form of schooling in different economic periods; see for example the critique by GORELICK, S. (1977) 'Undermining hierarchy: Problems of schooling in capitalist America', *Monthly Review* 29 (5) (October), pp. 20–36, and Bowles and Gintis' reply in *Monthly Review* 30 (6) (November 1978), pp. 59–64. For somewhat more nuanced efforts to specify the relations of the schooling process *per se* with general reference to capitalist social relations and the labour process, see especially HOLLY, D. (1977) 'Education and the social relations of a capitalist society' in YOUNG, M. and WHITTY, G. (Eds) *Society, State and Schooling*, Barcombe, Falmer Press, pp. 172–91, and the recent work of APPLE, M.W. especially (1980) 'The other side of the hidden curriculum: Correspondence theories and the labour process', *Journal of Education* 62 (1), pp. 47–66; 'Analysing determinations: Understanding and evaluating the production of social outcomes in schools', *Curriculum Inquiry* 10 (Spring), pp. 55–76; and (1981) 'Curricular form and the logic of technical control: Building the possessive individual' in BARTON, L. MEIGHAN, R. and WALKER, S. (Eds), *Schooling, Ideology and the Curriculum*, Lewes, Falmer Press.

36 With regard to the organization of production, prime sources are the works of Braverman and others as cited in Chapter One, footnote 55. Concerning the development of educational organizations in capitalism, some of the major comparative historical sources used are ARCHER, M. (1979) *Social Origins of Educational Systems*, London, Sage; WILLIAMSON, B. (1979) *Education, Social Structure and Development: A Comparative Analysis*, New York, Holmes and Meier, and LIVINGSTONE, D.W. *Economies, States and Education* (in process).

37 Longitudinal comparative research has by now clearly demonstrated how erroneous were earlier prevailing assumptions of one-way linear relations between even the most apparent indicators of economic and educational development. See, for example, GALTUNG, J. (1972) 'On the relationships between human resources and development: Theory, methods and data', *Journal of Development Studies* 8 (3) (April), pp. 137–53.

38 SCHECTER, S. (1977) *op. cit.* discusses some clear instances in Canadian education, especially the reforms initiated by Egerton Ryerson in the mid nineteenth century.

39 CARTER, M. (1976) 'Contradictions and correspondence: Analysis of the relation of schooling to work' in CARNOY, M. and LEVIN, H. (Eds) *The Limits of Educational Reform*, New York, McKay, pp. 59–60.

40 An earlier, more fully illustrated discussion of these aspects of class relations in capitalist forms of schooling appeared in LIVINGSTONE, D.W. (1979) 'The world capitalist economy and the limits of educational reform', *Canadian and International Education* 8 (1), pp. 5–26.

41 For documentation of the domination of such governing bodies by business and professional groups see, for example, NEARING, S. (1971) 'Who's who on our boards of education', *School and Society* 5 (108) (January); BOWLES, S. and GINTIS H. (1976) *op. cit.*, pp. 186–91; THOMPSON, E.P. (1968) *Education and Experience* Leeds, Leeds University Press; and SMITH, D.N. (1974) *Who Rules the Universities? An Essay in Class Analysis*, New York: Monthly Review Press. For illustrations of the consequent domination of formal curricular content, see for example, ANYON, J. (1978) 'Elementary social studies textbooks and legitimating knowledge', *Theory and Research in Social Education* 6, pp. 40–55; and JEGLUM, A. (1978) 'Ideological bias in the curriculum: How we teach working class students to deny their own reality', *Working Teacher* 1 (3) (Winter), pp. 23–7.

42 It is in this restricted sense of commodified cultural products rather than in the larger sense of lived cultures that Pierre Bourdieu's formulation of the appropriation of 'cultural capital' may be seen to apply. In his terms: ' … the inheritance of cultural wealth which has been accumulated and bequeathed by previous generations only really belongs to those endowed with the means of appropriating it for

themselves. In view of the fact that the apprehension and possession of cultural goods as symbolic goods ... are possible only for those who hold the code making it possible to decipher them, in other words, that the appropriation of symbolic goods presupposes the possessions of the instruments of appropriation, it is sufficient to give free play to the laws of cultural transmission for cultural capital to be added to cultural capital and for the structure of the distribution of cultural capital between classes to be thereby reproduced ... An [educational] institution officially entrusted with the transmission of the instruments of appropriation of the dominant culture which neglects methodically to transmit the instruments indispensable to the success of its undertaking is bound to become the monopoly of those social classes capable of transmitting by their own means, that is to say, by that diffuse and implicit continuous educational action which operates within cultured families ... the instruments necessary for the reception of its message, and thereby to confirm their monopoly of the instruments of appropriation of the dominant culture and thus their monopoly of that culture'. See BOURDIEU, P. (1977) 'Cultural reproduction and social reproduction' in KARABEL, J. and HALSEY, A.H. (Eds), *Power and Ideology in Education*, New York, Oxford University Press, pp. 488, 494.

43 See especially WILLIS, P. (1977) *op. cit.* Similar observations can probably be made about the subordinated viewpoints of girls and ethnic minority students; see for example McROBBIE, A. *Young Women and Leisure: How Working Class Girls Get Working Class Husbands* (forthcoming).

44 The social and technical aspects of relations within the schooling process are, of course, only analytically separable at most times. As Douglas Barnes, for example, observed in a detailed analysis of language use in the classroom: 'From the point of view of the teacher, everything he says has for him a sociocultural function, in supporting his roles as a teacher and as a teacher of [a subject], and ... could also be placed on a scale for its conceptual function, according to how far it is also being used to organize the subject matter of the lesson'. BARNES, D. BRITTON, J. and ROSEN, H. (1971) *Language, the Learner and the School*, London, Penguin Press. (Cited in WARWICK, D. (1974) 'Ideologies, integration and conflicts of meaning' in FLUDE, M. and AHIER, J. (Eds) *Educability, Schools and Ideology*, London, Halstead Press p. 106.)

45 On the changing forms of social control in classrooms, see, for example, ELSHTAIN, J. 'The social relations of the classroom: A moral and political perspective', *Telos* 27 (Spring), pp. 97–110; WHITTY, G. and YOUNG, M. (1976) *Explorations in the Politics of School Knowledge*, Driffield, Nafferton Books; and GRACE, G. (1978) *Teachers, Ideology and Control: A Study in Urban Education*, London, Routledge and Kegan Paul.

46 HOLLY, D. (1977) *op. cit.*, pp. 181–2.

47 *Ibid.*, pp. 182–7.

48 See, for example, LOCKHART, A. (1975) 'Future failure: The unanticipated consequences of educational planning' in PIKE, R. and ZUREIK, E. (Eds) *Socialization and Values in Canadian Society*, Volume II, Toronto, McClelland and Stewart, pp. 182–208.

49 ROTH, K.H. and KANZOW, E. (1970) *Unwissen als Ohnmacht*, Berlin, Voltaire, p. 224. (Cited in GORZ, A. (Ed) (1976) *The Division of Labour: The Labour Process and Class Struggle in Modern Capitalism*, Atlantic Highlands, Harvester Press.) Compare the curricula of the British Mechanics Institute over a hundred years earlier, as discussed in SHAPIN, S. and BARNES, B. (1976) 'Science, nature and control: Interpreting Mechanics Institutes' in DALE, R. ESLAND, G. and MACDONALD, M. (Eds) *Schooling and Capitalism*, London, Routledge and Kegan Paul, 1976, pp. 55–65.

50 See, for example, APPLE, M. (1981) *op. cit.*

51 Such autonomy is, however, discernibly limited even in the most elite university settings. See, for example, LIVINGSTONE D.W. and MASON, R.V. (1978) 'Ecological crisis and the autonomy of science in capitalist society: A Canadian case study', *Alternatives* 8 (1) (Winter, pp. 3–10, 33.

52 BOWLES, S. and GINTIS, H. (1976) *op. cit.*, p. 279.

53 ANYON, J. (1980) 'Social class and the hidden curriculum of work', *Journal of Education* 162, pp. 67–92.

54 *Ibid.*, pp. 73, 76, 83, 87. For comparable accounts of the schooling process in quite homogenous social class settings, see LITT, E. (1963) 'Civic education, community norms, and political indoctrination', *American Sociological Review* 28 (1), pp. 69–75; CONNELL, R.W., 'Class and gender dynamics in a ruling class school', *Interchange*, 12, 2–3, pp. 102–17; MARTELL, G. (Ed) (1974) *The Politics of the Canadian Public School*, Toronto, Lorimer, Parts One and Two; and LIND, L. (1975) *The Learning Machine*, Toronto, Anansi.

55 For a schematic outline of such forms of production and education, see CASTLES, S. and Wustenberg, W. (1979) 'The relationship between form of production, division of labour, social conditions of workers, skill level and education' in CASTLES, S. and USTENBERG, W. *op. cit.*, pp. 195–201.

56 For reviews of the origins and development of state schooling in English Canada, see, for example, PRENTICE, A. (1979) *The School Promotors*, Toronto, McClelland and Stewart; SCHECTER, S. (1977) *op. cit.*, and BLEASDALE, G. (1978) 'Towards a political economy of capitalist education values' in NELSON, R. and NOCK, D. (Eds), *Reading, Writing and Riches*, Kitchener, Between-the-Lines, pp. 11–39. On situating Canadian capitalist production and education systems in a global context, see LIVINGSTONE, D.W. (1979) *op. cit.*

57 See GORZ, A. (1976) *op. cit.*, pp. 188–9.

58 SARTRE, J.P. (1976) *Critique of Dialectical Reason I. Theory of Practical Ensembles*, London, New Left Books, pp. 216, 218–9.

59 See especially MARX, K. and ENGELS, F. (1848) *The Communist Manifesto*, New York, Appleton-Century-Crofts, 1955, p. 21, and the discussion in DRAPER, H. (1978) *Karl Marx's Theory of Revolutin, Vol. II. The Politics of Social Classes*, New York, Monthly Review Press, pp. 17–48. Study of the historical relations between class interests and human needs remains a large gap in Marxist inquiries. For formal exploratory efforts, see HELLER, A. (1976) *The Theory of Need in Marx*, London, Allison and Busby; SCHNEIDER, M. (1975) *Neurosis and Civilization: A Marxist/Freudian Synthesis*, New York, Seabury Press; and SÈVE, L. (1978) *Man in Marxist Theory and the Psychology of Personality*, Atlantic Highlands, Humanities Press.

60 BURAWOY, M. (1981) 'State and social revolution in South Africa,' *Kapitalistate* 9 (1981), p. 102.

61 Compare WRIGHT, E.O. (1978) *Class, Crisis and the State*, London, New Left Books, pp. 88–91. For a more nuanced treatment of types of class interests see WESOLOWSKI, W. (1979) *Classes, State and Power*, London, Routledge and Kegan Paul. On the relation between objective and subjective interests in Marxist theory, see BALBUS, I. (1971) 'The concept of interest in pluralist and Marxian analysis', *Politics and Society* 1 (1) (February), pp. 151–77.

62 The classic studies of the development of these two quintessential strands of capitalist ideology are MACPHERSON, C.B. (1962) *The Political Theory of Possessive Individualism*, London, Oxford University Press; and MARCUSE, H. (1964) *One-Dimensional Man: Studies in the Ideology of Advanced Industrial Society*, Boston, Beacon Press.

63 ABERCROMBIE, B. and TURNER, B. (1978) 'The dominant ideology thesis', *British Journal of Sociology* 29 (2) (June), p. 149.

64 See, for example, GRAY, R. 'Bourgeois hegemony in Victorian Britain' in BLOOMFIELD, J.J. (1977) *op. cit.*, pp. 73–93.

65 The critical role of such intermediate class elements in reproducing the dominant schooling structure and ideology has been stressed both by BERNSTEIN, B. (1977) 'Classes and pedagogies: Visible and invisible' in KARABEL, J. and HALSEY, A.H. (Eds) *op. cit.*, pp. 511–34, and by BOURDIEU, P. and PASSERON, J-C. (1979) *The Inheritors*, Chicago, University of Chicago Press.

66 WILLIAMS, R. (1961) *The Long Revolution*, London, Chatto and Windus.

67 YOUNG, M.F.D. (1973) 'Curricula and the social organization of knowledge' in BROWN, R. (Ed), *Knowledge, Education, and Cultural Change*, London, Tavistock, pp. 346–48. Compare HOLLY, D. (1977) *op. cit.*, pp. 96–7.

68 Most impressive is the historiographic work on English working class cultural politics and popular education movements. See especially SIMON, B. (1974) *op. cit.*, DOBB, A.E. (1919) *Education and Social Movements, 1700–1850*, London, Longmans; HARRISON, J. (1961) *Learning and Living 1790–1960*, London, Routledge and Kegan Paul; and MILLAR, J.P. (1979) *The Labour College Movement*, London, National Council of Labour Colleges. A good overview is provided by Education Group, Centre for Contemporary Cultural Studies, (1981) *op. cit.*, pp. 33–46.

69 The work of American radical revisionist historians of education deserves mention in this regard. The studies of Michael Katz (KATZ, M. (1971)) *op. cit.* and others have documented the ideological conflicts between business and professional interest groups that were involved in the consolidation and later elaboration of the US mass schooling system. However, the lack of attention in such research to the less fully recorded educational concerns and ideologies of working class groups and their interaction with dominant groups has only recently begun to be overcome through careful local case studies. See, for example, WRIGLEY, J. (1980) 'Class politics and school reform in Chicago' in ZEITLIN, M. (Ed), *Classes, Class Conflict, and the State*, Cambridge, Winthrop, pp. 153–71, and HOGAN, D. (1978) 'Education and the making of the Chicago working class, 1880–1930', *History of Education Quarterly* 18 (3), pp. 227–70.

70 Education Group, C.C.C.C. (1981) *op. cit.*, pp. 47 ff.

71 MELLOS, K. (1978) 'Developments in advanced capitalist ideology', *Canadian Journal of Political Science*, 11, (4) (December), pp. 829–861.

72 See, for example, Royal Commission on Relations of Capital and Labour (1973) *Canada Investigates Industrialism: The Royal Commission On The Relations of Labour and Capitalism, 1889* (abridged). Edited with an introduction by G. Kealy, Toronto, University of Toronto Press.

73 William Lyon Mackenzie King was a central figure in this ideological emergence. See especially his (1918) *Industry and Humanity: A Study in the Principles Underlying Industrial Reconstruction*, Toronto, University of Toronto Press, 1973, and the recent critical interpretation by CRAVEN, P. (1980) *The Impartial Umpire: Industrial Relations and the Canadian State, 1900–1911*, Toronto, University of Toronto Press. For accounts of the related development of dominant ideological themes in Quebec, see DUMONT, F. et al. (1974) *Ideologies au Canada Francais, 1900–1929*, Quebec, Les Presses de l'Universite Laval, and MONIERE, D. (1981) *Ideologies in Quebec: The Historical Development*, Toronto, University of Toronto Press.

74 MELLOS, K. (1978) *op. cit.*

75 For a very general historical overview of capital and labour-based ideological discourse in Canadian electoral politics, see BRODIE, M.J. and JENSON, J. (1980) *Crisis, Challenge and Change: Party and Class in Canada*, Toronto, Methuen. For more specific documentation of labour-based ideologies see ROBIN, M. (1968) *Radical Politics and Canadian Labour, 1880–1930*, Kingston, Queen's University Centre for Industrial Relations, MILLER, R. and ISBESTER, F. (Eds) (1971) *Canadian Labour in Transition*, Scarborough, Prentice-Hall of Canada, and PENNER, N. (1977) *The Canadian Left: A Critical Analysis*, Scarborough, Prentice-Hall. The

Quebec labour movement has provided the most important recent exceptions; see DRACHE, D. (Ed) (1972) *Quebec – Only the Beginning: The Manifestoes of the Common Front*, Toronto, New Press.

76 The central statement in this regard was formulated by Joe Morris and other Canadian Labour Congress leaders as *Labour Manifesto for Canada,* Ottawa: CLC, 1976. For critical analyses of the widespread expression of corporatist political structures in Canada, see PANITCH, L. (1979) 'Corporatism in Canada?' in SCHULTZ R. et al (Eds), *The Canadian Political Process,* Toronto, Holt, Rinehart and Winston, pp. 53–72, and GONICK, C. et al. (1980) "Corporatism and the Body Politic' *Canadian Dimension* 15 (3) (December), pp. 29–44.

77 Major sources used for corporate business views include *Canadian Banker and ICB Review* (journal of the Canadian Bankers' Association), *Canadian Business* (journal of the Canadian Chamber of Commerce), and *Executive*. Extensive use has also been made of an address by H.E. Wyatt (Chairman, Canadian Chamber of Commerce), 'Walking the Educational Tightrope', a speech presented to the Third Congress of the Canadian School Trustees' Association, June 1980. Major sources of labour views include *Canadian Labour* (journal of the Canadian Labour Congress), *Ontario Labour* (journal of the Ontario Labour Federation), and *Steelabour* (journal of the United Steelworkers), as well as the *Proceedings of Conventions* of The Canadian Labour Congress and the Ontario Federation of Labour, and the Metro (Toronto) New Democrats-Labour Council of Metropolitan Toronto, *Municipal and Education Program*, 1980.

78 *Executive* Editorial, 'Apathy? Complacency? Death? *Executive* 11 (2) (December 1969) p. 17.

79 Quoted in 'Business and Student: Chasm or Challenge?' *Canadian Business* (November 1968), p. 90.

80 MACDONALD, K. (1975) 'Let's get rid of the free-lunch philosophy', *Canadian Banker and ICB Review* (November-December) p. 53.

81 TEMPLE, G. (1976) 'What business can do about education', *Canadian Business* (June), p. 48.

82 See MELLOS, K. (1978) *op. cit.*

83 See LITCHFIELD, R. (1978) 'Coming soon: A labour shortage,' *Canadian Business* (July) p. 49; also MACDONALD, K. *op. cit.*, p. 55.

84 TEMPLE, G. (1976) *op. cit.*, p. 46 f.

85 WYATT, H.E. (1980) *op. cit.*, p. 12.

86 HAINEY, A. (1979) 'Business and education', *Forum* 5 (4) (October), pp. 161–2.

87 In addition to the articles quoted at the head of this section, see, for example, the editorial, 'Take a stand or be run over', in *Executive* (June 1969), p. 21.

88 DOBBIN, L. (1971) Debate on Education Resolutions 5, 6 and 9, *Ontario Federation of Labour (OFL) Convention Proceedings, 1971,* p. 8.

89 GUETTEL, C. (1974) Debate on Education Resolution S-3 (covering resolutions 24, 25, 28, 29 and 30), *OFL Convention Proceedings 1974,* p. 62.

90 FLEMING, D.B. (1979) 'The child as learner and worker', *Canadian Labour* (September 7), p. 14.

91 MCDERMOTT, D. (1980) Address of the President. *Canadian Labour Congress Thirteenth Constitutional Convention,* Winnipeg, May 5, p. 4. Thus, the electoral rhetoric of the central union bureaucracy in English Canada begins to reflect the same appropriation concerns as the more radical leaders who only a few years earlier, in the enthusiasm for business-government-labour tripartism, had been isolated as 'commies' and 'crazies'. Compare, for example, the earlier views of the president of the Canadian Union of Postal Workers: 'As long as a society is controlled by private interests, production will be carried out in order to make profits. Research, technology, the courts, the police, and the media all may become weapons to be used against us in our struggle for decent wages and working

conditions ... [A]s long as this situation exists, we will be on the defensive.'
PARROT, J-Cl. 'Militancy, not co-operation', *Canadian Dimension* 12 (4–5)
September, p. 14.)

92 See especially Metro New Democrats-Labour Council of Metropolitan Toronto,
op. cit. p. 29 and resolutions 17 and 18, *OFL Convention Proceedings, 1979*, pp. 17,
87.

93 See especially Metro New Democrats-Labour of Metropolitan Toronto, *op. cit.*, p.
26, and OFL Convention Proceedings 1977, p. 76 ff.

94 Metro New Democrats-Labour Council of Metropolitan Toronto, *op. cit.*, p. 26.

95 See resolution 21, *OFL Convention Proceedings 1979*, p. 87; WAGG, L. (1976)
'Labour Education' (editorial), *Canadian Labour* (December); resolution 13, *OFL
Convention Proceedings 1976*, p. 3; resolution 6, *OFL Convention Proceedings
1972*, p. 5.

96 Delegate *OFL Convention Proceedings 1976*, p. 3.

97 See Metro New Democrats-Labour Council of Metropolitan Toronto, *op. cit.*, p.
32; resolution 49 *OFL Convention Proceedings 1977*, pp. 76, 77; resolution 1, *OFL
Convention Proceedings 1972*. p. 4.

98 See, for example, SINCLAIR, S. (1968) 'How does business stack up on campus?'
Canadian Business (May), pp. 32–38.

99 Delegate *OFL Convention Proceedings 1976*, p. 3.

100 See WAGG, L. (1976) *op. cit.*

101 See, for example, D'AMOUR, P. (1979) 'Port Elgin – a school for leaders', *Canadian
Labour* (August 24), pp. 8, 12; 'Back to the Locals', *Steelabour* (January 1979), p. 6.

102 HALL, E.M., DENNIS, L.A. *et al* (1968) *Living and Learning. The Report of the
Provincial Committee on the Aims and Objectives of Education in the Schools of
Ontario*, Toronto, Queen's Printer. While state education commissions *per se* are
not directly treated in the current analysis, it should be noted that such bodies are
typically dominated by intermediate class elements who are 'insiders' in the current
educational system and therefore have little affinity with fundamental working class
interests. For critical assessments of recent state education commission reports in
Canada, see especially MARTELL, G. (1974) 'The schools the state and the corporations' in MARTEL, G. (Ed) *The Politics of the Canadian Public School*, Toronto,
Lorimer, pp. 3–36; LOCKHART, A. 'Educational policy development in Canada' in
CARLTON, R. et al. (Eds.) *Education, Change, and Society*, Toronto, Gage pp.
76–88; BULLOCK, C. (1978) ('The "Futility of Changeless Change": The Worth
Report, Progressivism and Canadian Education' in NELSON, R. and NOCK, D.
(Eds), *op. cit.*, pp. 307–18; and VAN DER VELDON, J.H. 'Child centred ideology as
social reproduction: Hall-Dennis and the Ontario schooling crisis' (to be pub-
lished).

103 Delegate *OFL Convention Proceedings 1968*, p. 7.

104 *Ibid.*

105 Metro New Democrats-Labour Council of Metropolitan Toronto, *op. cit.*, p. 26.

106 See, for example, FLEMING, D.B. (1979) *op. cit.* p. 15; also discussion on resolution
49, *OFL Convention Proceedings 1977*, p. 76–7.

107 See, for example, the discussion of basic skills training and work experience
programs in Metro New Democrats-Labour Council of Metropolitan Toronto, *op.
cit.*, pp. 27, 29, 30–81.

108 WYATT, H.E. (1980) *op. cit.*, p. 13.

109 *Ibid.*, p. 15.

110 *Ibid.*, p. 14.

111 MACDONALD, K. (1975) *op. cit.*, p. 52.

112 TEMPLE, G. (1976) *op. cit.*, p. 46.

113 WYATT, H.E. (1980) *op. cit.*, p. 5.

114 FENWICK, M. (1968) Debate on Hall-Dennis Report, *OFL Convention Proceedings*

1968, p. 7. Mr. Fenwick was labour representative on the Hall-Dennis Committee.
115 Metro New Democrats-Labour Council of Metropolitan Toronto, *op. cit.*, pp. 27–28.
116 Delegate, *OFL Convention Proceedings 1968*, p. 8.
117 TEMPLE, G. (1976) *op. cit.*, p. 46.
118 WYATT, H.E. (1980) *op. cit.*, pp. 6, 9.
119 MARTINET, R. (1980) Speech to Conference on Technological Training, Toronto, January, 1980, Quoted in Toronto *Globe and Mail*, January 29, 1980.
120 WYATT, H.E. (1980) *op. cit.*, pp. 11.
121 See MAXWELL, S. (1975) 'Do business schools fit business practice?' *Canadian Banker and ICB Review* (January-February), pp. 43–45.
122 See, for example, LITCHFIELD, R. (1978) *op. cit.*, p. 48.
123 SIGNAL, B. (1977) Debate on Education Resolution 49, *OFL Convention Proceedings 1977*, p. 76.
124 BEEMAN, C. (1977) Debate on Education Resolution 45, *OFL Convention Proceedings 1977*, p. 75.
125 Metro New Democrats-Labour Council of Metropolitan Toronto, *op. cit.*, pp. 27–28.
126 *Ibid.*, p. 28.
127 *Ibid.*, p. 27.
128 *Ibid.*, p. 32.
129 *Ibid.*, p. 32.
130 See, for example, BRADFORD, R. (1979) 'Labourers' training and rehabilitation centre', *Canadian Labour* (August 10), p. 13.
131 The centrality in historical materialist theorizing of determinate abstractions which are derived from simple abstractions of everyday life, as well as the widespread misunderstanding involved in Western Marxism's heavy theoretical reliance on formalistic abstraction, are most graphically outlined in BANAJI, J. 'Modes of production in a materialist conception of history', *Capital and Class* 3 (Fall), pp. 1–44. See also the discussion in Chapter One.
132 See, for example, TAPPER, T. and SALTER, B. (1978) 'Elite ideologies in conflict: The case of higher education' in their *Education and the Political Order: Changing Patterns of Class Control*, London, Macmillan, pp. 142–74.

Chapter Four

Mass Opinion in Educational Crisis: A Class Analysis

Mass opinion consists of a set of private responses to the exigencies of social life unmediated by group discourse or by common interests. Rather than being mediated by group interests *qua* group, mass opinion is mediated by personal interests and, as advertising expands the universe of private wants in proportion to human needs, mass opinion comes to reproduce the needs of advanced corporate capitalism to dispose of high technology, high energy, high profit goods produced by capital intensive modes ... Mass opinion is not public opinion in that it bears no special, necessary relation to the constitution of public policy. A *public sphere* is constituted by the process of publics taking active, effective, unreserved participation in creating public policy. A set of words which may or may not find its way into the public policy process is not public opinion, that is, it does not necessarily result in overt behaviour compatible to the message embodied by those words. More likely, mass opinion is collected and used aganst the interests of the public in that it is used to manage and mold opinion of the masses after, long after, policy has been produced.

T. R. Young, Red Feather Institute[1]

In advanced capitalist societies, the public sphere is both atrophied and localized. Few social groups have access to sustained means for producing and widely distributing information and opinion, and hence to effective participation in public policy making. As Young observes:

The growth of the state, the biased access of monopoly capital to the policy process through its 'think' tanks; the use of the electronics capacity of the society for advertising and for entertainment; the conflation between public opinion and mass opinion as well as the systematic exclusion of radical theory in the media and the university all diminish the public sphere.[2]

In the absence of an open public sphere, subordinate social groups have often had little direct political recourse for their frustrations except *ad hoc* mobilizations and street demonstrations. Since the late 1960s, most advanced capitalist societies have seen protest movements by blacks and other ethnic minorities, women, students, old people, 'peaceniks', gay people and others. Typically such movements have been dismantled, co-opted, or reverted ·to invisibility. Recently the trade union movement with its firmly established organizational basis has become increasingly politicized; in the wake of rising unemployment and inflation, the last year or so has seen the biggest ever labour marches in several countries.

The extent to which trade unions and other subordinate group organizations are now able to play a full role in the development of public policy is likely to depend on how sensitive their leaders are to the genuine interests of their members. Such organizations have tended to take on hierarchical structures similar to those inherent in capitalist enterprise; it is only through facilitating open public discourse both within and between subordinate group organizations that corporate media influences can be effectively combated, different group interests clearly identified, and responsive policy alternatives generated and acted upon. In any society, however, collective group interests and individual private interests are always reciprocally related. The degree to which the private interests of subordinate group individuals have become ideologically captive to corporate capitalist domination has been somewhat exaggerated by some critical theorists.[3] Many of the recent spontaneous mobilizations attest to the sources in immediate material conditions and lived cultures of subordinate individuals that can lead directly to political struggles resisting and rejecting the widely promulgated corporate capitalist 'way of life'. More generally, there are many indications that, even in the post-war expansionary era, those in subordinate positions have more commonly been pragmatic acceptors of their material condition than true believers in capitalist values.[4] In all of these respects, then, accurate readings of the current private dispositions of individuals within subordinate groups, as well as those in other social locations, to accept the *status quo* or to support various social alternatives, should be of relevance for efforts at clarifying and developing genuine collective interests and effective political programmes in subordinate group organizations.

However accurate textual readings such as those in Chapter Three may be in analyzing the logics and themes of the educational ideologies articulated by corporate and labour leaders, it is quite another matter to infer the connections of such ideological discourses with the lived conceptions and practices of their class circles as a whole, to say nothing of any wider effects. Some contextual differences are fairly clear. The internal structures of business associations and trade unions differ considerably, with the political power of trade unions being founded on the effectiveness of their collective organizations, whereas the power of capitalists remains based on control of the means of production and is *not* transferred to business associations by individual firms.[5] Secondly, union bureaucracies have become demonstrably more responsive to the most immediate demands of rank-and-file members in the current protracted economic crisis of capitalism.[6] But research documenting the extent to which the public discourses of corporate and labour leaders correspond with the dispositions of their own class circles and others on fundamental policy issues has been almost completely lacking. The purpose of this chapter is to provide some empirical indicators of the current subjective dispositions of those in different class positions regarding acceptance of or support for changing current educational provisions. The primary means of this assessment will be mass opinion surveys on educational issues in Ontario.

First, the general purpose and design of the surveys will be outlined. Next, the limitations of mass opinion surveys will be specified. Then, the immediate historical context of the most recent survey will be briefly described. The remainder of the chapter presents the survey findings on the most relevant issues according to class position. Attitudes concerning financial support for education will first be analyzed. Then, expressed preferences on aspects of the form and content of education based on the primary dimensions of cultural ownership and social and technical relations of the schooling process will be considered.

Purpose and Design of the Opinion Surveys

The Ontario Survey of Educational Issues has been conducted in 1978, 1979 and 1980.[7] The intent of the surveys has been to provide representative readings of the general public's dispositions on basic educational issues; readings that could be of some aid to ordinary citizens and social group leaders: (1) to situate accurately their own general views in relation to others; (2) to gauge the levels of and trends in support and opposition concerning alternative general educational policy directions; and (3) for leaders and potential leaders especially, to develop their own specific policy proposals and efforts to mobilize public support on the basis of balanced judgements of the limits acceptable to the majority of their own social groups and the citizenry as a whole, rather than in response to the loudest voices or conventional presumptions about group interests. Such opinion surveys can be a useful instrument for such purposes, *but* only if they emphasize basic questions of educational form and content rather than diffuse sentiments and topical fads, are widely and undistortedly publicized, and are treated as a basis for *furthering* informed dialogue and broadening the public sphere. Most prior opinion surveys, certainly in education, have been of irregular, *ad hoc*, superficial character with little interest in organizational alternatives or discerning trends in policy preferences.[8] The current survey project has attempted to offer ongoing profiles of mass attitudes on some of the major issues of possible educational change. We have disseminated the results widely, not only through the mass media, but also by distributing complimentary copies of the reports to major interest groups and by making the report available for purchase at minimum cost. In general, both the discrepancies discerned between currently announced state policy directions and popular attitudes on some educational issues, and also the substantial expressed opposition of views within the citizenry on other issues, surely support the necessity of widening public dialogue and continuing to generate alternative policy options.

Each survey has involved representative samples of the entire adult (that is, persons eighteen years and over) population of Ontario, excluding those residing in institutions, and in the far north. Each sample has included over one thousand respondents. In addition, special supplementary samples of corporate directors have been selected in each survey because of their very small numbers in the population as a whole. Our approach has been to begin by regarding education most generally, including all types and levels of educational activities, and to attempt to identify and order commonly expressed themes and issues of various social groups. The identification of major perceived issues has benefited from participant observation in various educational sites, extended dialogues and workshops with various community groups, and reviews of education statements of spokespersons for major social groups (including the corporate and labour views presented in Chapter Three). The specific items to be used in the interview surveys have been discussed with an advisory committee containing representatives from a cross-section of Ontario groups, including corporate and small business, organized labour and reserve labour (for example, Anti-Poverty Alliance), and several intermediate groups. These items have also been refined through preliminary open-ended interviewing and pilot testing. The resulting questionnaire and descriptive report for the most recent survey contain sections on the following: overall assessment of education, financial priorities, curricular goals, equal educational opportunities, school organization, schooling and work, and the politics of education.

General Limitations of Opinion Surveys

It is little known that in 1880 Marx prepared one of the earliest mass opinion questionnaires.[9] It was intended to draw descriptions of actual social conditions from French workers and to encourage critical reflection on these conditions. The survey faced numerous obstacles – including its length and workers' very limited spare time for such a new undertaking, workers' limited literacy, and the depressed state of the French labour movement following the Paris Commune – and was never published. More recently, large-scale opinion surveys based on random population samples have become notorious in Marxist circles. Young offers one of the most trenchant critiques:

> The public sphere is reduced . . . by confusing mass opinion for public opinion. Public opinion must be the product of interacting persons in free and undistorted demystified discourse . . . And samples, polls, and surveys do not constitute a public sphere. In the first instance, they represent only mental images; in the second, they are politically

anchored in their selection, timing, phrasing, and especially in their deployment. Finally, surveys, polls, and samples are mediated by private psychological impulses rather than by discourse of a solidarity in democratic assembly.[10]

While such observations may be generally true, they do not deny the *potential* usefulness of opinion surveys which are intended to facilitate public discourse. Of course, the extent of ideological domination is an essential consideration; I have tried to convey something of the current ideological character of Canadian society through the analysis of explicit corporate and labour ideologies in Chapter Three. But there are several other limitations which remain inherent in opinion surveys whatever the ideological climate and which users should clearly recognize.

The major limitations involve the imputation of subjective meanings, the generalizability of findings, specific contextual effects on attitudes, atomistic bias, and the influence of researchers' own values. First, there may be considerable variation in the actual subjective meanings different respondents attach to a given question or response option, as well as restrictions to the range of subjective responses because of the form in which the researcher puts the question. With sensitive pilot studies, one can become relatively confident in interpreting general tendencies in the distribution of attitudes on a given public issue, but should remain more cautious about imputing precise meanings to specific substantive response options. Secondly, the findings of a region-wide survey such as the present one cannot simply be assumed to be generalizable to all local communities. Local surveys in some communities might find substantial variations from province-wide summary patterns, variations that should be taken into account in local policy making. Thirdly, expressed attitudes are, in comparison with institutional structures, ideological traditions and routine individual activities, typically the most transitory aspect of social reality. Current events may provoke rapid shifts in attitudes. By ignoring the social events occurring in the period in which their surveys are conducted, pollsters tend to suggest that their results represent rather more enduring, universal features of social reality than is actually the case. In the following section I will note prominent events that may have influenced some responses to the most recent survey. Fourthly, and most importantly, it indeed should be recognized that mass opinion research atomizes people's expressions of opinion, whereas attitudes are actually embedded in ongoing social relations between people. Collective expressions of attitudes may differ considerably from individual interview responses. Nevertheless, such summaries of individual dispositions at a given point can serve both to situate current collective expressions and to identify generalized individual pre-dispositions toward future collective expressions in a given policy area. Finally, the influence of the researchers' own values cannot be eliminated entirely from any phase of social research, and particularly from the interpretations of findings presented in research reports. Even in reports that emphasize descriptive accounts of largely quantitative data, the most effective safeguard against the possibility of undue influence of researchers' values is to provide both the measurement instrument and the decision-making criteria used, so that readers remain free to make their own interpretations.[11]

From critics of varied political persuasions, the most sustained objection to *any* use of opinion surveys as an element in the policy process have typically been based either on claims of widespread public ignorance or on the observance of disparities between survey respondents' expressed attitudes and the general public's actual behaviour.[12] The Ontario public definitely lacks highly detailed information on many aspects of the school system. However, our analyses suggest that differences in specific policy-related technical knowledge very rarely make any significant difference in expressed attitudes on general educational policy issues. Moreover, whatever 'false consciousness', exists appears to be highly variable between issues. In any case, there is no substantiated basis in the general citizenry's differential technical knowledge for not taking careful regular readings of views on major educational issues and attempting to use the results fully and openly in the policy making process.

Expressed attitude – practical activity disparities represent a more serious objection. In particular, the material limits on subordinate individuals' verbal conservatism should not be underestimated. As Martin Glaberman, a former autoworker, has observed:

> It is true that many workers have very reactionary views on a whole range of subjects, like race, sex, age, skills, and so on. Workers are not the noble savage, all pure and honest and forthright and revolutionary. But reality, which is a thirty-six second job for the rest of your life, reality which is sabotage recorded every single day in the Chrysler plants in Windsor, Ontario, is a reality which forces workers to behave in contradiction to their own stated beliefs ... The reality forces workers to fight. If the resistance reaches a certain point, workers walk out. If attacked by the police, they fight back. Suddenly they see that they have shut down half an industry. They see people in other plants are coming out. The reality of struggle frees them to think about a new society – in the process of struggle for it.[13]

Gramsci has made a similar point in more theoretical terms:

> The active man-in-the-mass has a practical activity, but has no clear theoretical consciousness in his practical activity, which nonetheless involves understanding the world insofar as it transforms it. His theoretical consciousness can indeed be historically in opposition to his activity. One might almost say that he has two theoretical consciousnesses (or one contradictory consciousness); one which is implicit in his activity and which in reality unites him with all his fellow workers in the practical transformation of the real world, and

one superficially explicit or verbal which he has inherited from the past and uncritically absorbed.[14]

However, contradictory consciousness is not only a function of ideological hegemony. Expressed attitude-practical activity disparities are common to corporate elites, policy experts and ordinary citizens alike for a variety of very practical reasons. But there is considerable evidence that expressed attitudes on mass opinion surveys about social issues are not merely unreflective clichés or gratuitous utterances; rather, such views do change in relation to the changing material environment in which respondents live.[15] As long as the general limitations of such surveys are understood, they may be used to assess the extent to which expressed attitudes reflect or contradict the fundamental class interests inherent in practical activity in capitalist society, both for the 'man-in-the-mass' and the dominant class.

Immediate Historical Context of the 1980 Survey

The public events occurring in any particular period are likely to have some immediate influence on many people's interpretation of and attitudes toward related general public policy issues. In this section, I will list the major events that were widely reported in Ontario during the first two weeks of September, 1980, a period including a week prior to our most recent survey as well as the week during which it was actually administered. The listing is based largely on reviews of major Ontario newspapers, especially the *Toronto Globe and Mail* and the *Toronto Star*.

Educational concerns are usually quite prominent in the media at the beginning of the school year, but no more so than usual this year. There were four substantial issues that received some recurring press coverage during this period: private schools, student discipline, French instruction, and teacher strikes. The rapid growth of enrolments in Catholic, Hebrew and other religiously-affiliated private schools was frequently noted, usually with observations about the emphasis of most of these schools on student discipline. Discipline issues in the state schools also received considerable attention, most notably through a controversy in Halton county over the use of a 'penalty box' to confine emotionally disturbed and disruptive children. French instruction issues were mentioned primarily in connection with discussions at the First Mininsters' Conference on the Constitution about the federal governments' human rights charter provisions for education in either English or French across Canada wherever the numbers warrant. A much disputed French high school in Penetanguishene also opened at this time amid continuing controversy. Concerns about a strike by Calgary state school teachers, that had begun in May, intensified with the opening of the new school year and there were frequent reports in the Ontario press about this strike.

Other educational matters that received brief attention in this period were the continuing 'over-enrolment' of students in faculties of education, the Toronto-Dominion Bank's decision to cut down its provision of Canada Student Loans because of their unprofitability, the Ontario Teachers' Federation's intention to request self-governing status, and several special education issues, especially reaction to the Ontario government's proposed bill to facilitate creation of special education programmes throughout the province. It should also be noted that schooling and work issues which had received recurring media attention over the past year (such as the shortage of training for skilled tradespersons, critiques of the relevance of the school curriculum for the workplace, and the decline of education as a job ticket) were scarcely mentioned in the press during this period.

With regard to other social events, there were three subjects that received a great deal of attention in the press. The First Ministers' conference on the Constitution corresponded exactly with the week that this survey was administered and ferderal-provincial jurisdictional disputes over issues ranging from natural resources to education were a major preoccupation of the media. The first large-scale walkout by federal government clerks also occurred that week, with the picketing of major postal centres and a growing likelihood of a national strike. Thirdly, the termination of Terry Fox's cross-Canada run, by lung cancer, stimulated a variety of fund-raising activities for cancer research. Controversy over the public provision of social services also attracted considerable press coverage, primarily in terms of reaction to the publication of the Hall report on Canada' health care system (specifically to its recommendation to scrap health insurance premiums in Ontario and to restrict doctors' fees), as well as in terms of reports on shortages of such services as daycare and hospital beds, and the criticisms by the Minister of Community and Social Services of an excessive involvement of social work professionals in Ontario families. Environmental problems also received recurring mention, especially in terms of waste disposal issues in Hamilton and Kitchener, radiation hazards in Toronto, and Inco smelter stack emission standards in Sudbury. The issue of corporate concentration in the mass media was also raised with the announcement of several federal government inquiries.

In somewhat narrower economic terms, plant closings continued to be a prominent issue, most notably through Labour Day protests and a sit-in by workers at a Brampton automotive parts plant for better severance pay. Safety problems in mining were also frequently cited, primarily in relation to the opening of hearings by the royal commission on working conditions in Ontario mines. The efforts of Massey-Ferguson, the ailing multi-national farm equipment company, to get government financial assistance were often mentioned. September began with statistical reports of the Canadian economy's worst quarterly performance in eighteen years.

On the world scene, some attention was given to Iranian politics, particularly the continuing US hostages affair, to the peaceful transfer of political power in China, and to the US presidential election campaign. But the international issue of overwhelming media interest was the strike of Polish workers for free trade unions and the aftermath of this strike.

Of course, this listing is hardly inclusive of all events that may have had an impact on Ontarians during this period, and even its accuracy is highly dependent on capitalist media reporting. Moreover, our main sources are Toronto-centred and therefore not likely to be sensitive to all important events in other Ontario regions. In any case, regardless of how prominent or distinctive any of the above events may have been, both the Ontario public and our respondents in particular were undoubtedly aware of them to differing degrees. This listing merely goes a small step beyond typical opinion surveys in attempting to convey some of the immediate historical conditions in which responses were offered.

Class and Current Educational Attitudes

These surveys have asked a wide variety of questions about current educational programmes. Attention here will be largely restricted to major aspects of educational provisions implicated in any major reorganization initiative. In view of the various limitations on attributing meaning to expressed attitudes on such surveys, the main interest will be in general tendencies rather than specific policy options. The findings will be treated under four headings: financial priorities, and the preferred form and content of education with regard to the three primary dimensions of educational relations (that is, cultural ownership, and social and technical relations of the schooling process). The survey results were analyzed in terms of the influences of a number of social background variables: class position, age, sex, and ethnicity, as well as contact with schools, educational attainment, religion, mother tongue, family income, provincial region and community size. Several variables were found to have some significant effects on such educational attitudes. Most notably, younger people and those most involved with schools are generally most supportive of ensuring or extending existing levels of educational services. But class position was found to be the most persistent differentiating factor on these financial and organizational issues, and it is these class effects that will be the focus of the following analysis.[16]

Financial Priorities for Education

The major response to date by government decision makers to the current accumulation crisis has been to cut back real educational expenditures with a consequent overall reduction in the extent of educational services. The current levels of and trends in expressed support by major class groups for educational expenditures may be a key indicator of the extent to which such a simple response can continue to be used. The specific financial issues of most relevance here are: the fiscal priority for education in relation to other possible areas of public expenditure; the desired rate of growth of total educational expenditure *per se*; and the preferred level of utilization of available education resources, especially teachers.

With regard to general fiscal priorities, Table 17 displays the rankings that Ontario respondents have given to education in relation to a number of other public policy areas over this three year period. In 1980, education ranked second only to health and medical care. Over this period, education and job training have shown clearer tendencies to increasing priority than any other cited areas. The priorities for most policy areas appear to have remained quite stable, and in particular there has certainly been no discernible increase in general public support for subsidies to private enterprise.

There are a number of significant class differences in fiscal priorities as suggested by Table 18. Health care is highly ranked within all class positions, but capitalists and especially corporate capitalists express greater concern for maintaining public order and aiding capital investment than do proletarians and other dispossessed people, and a lesser concern for most other social services. These differences increased over the three years period. With specific regard to corporate directors and the productive proletariat, the most powerful cores of the polar classes, the biggest differences concern job training and job creation – areas of declining interest for corporate capitalists in the current crisis and of rapidly growing concern for most workers. The strongest priority for general public education is expressed among non-supervisory professional

Table 17 '*Which of the Following Should Have the Strongest Claim on Tax Money?*' (*1978–80*)

Public policy area	% ranking as strongest claim		
	1978* (N=1032)	1979 (N=1084)	1980 (N=1108)
Health and medical care	28	36	28
Public education	8	12	15
Job creation	22	12	14
Job training	6	10	12
Conservation of natural resources and pollution control	7	6	7
Development and use of energy sources	**	8	6
Retirement benefits	5	4	6
Maintaining public order	4	3	4
Incentives to private industry	6	3	3
Research for industrial development	2	2	2
Welfare and public housing	5	2	2
Consumer protection	1	2	1

* Several other policy areas were included in the 1978 survey, so the relevant items have been weighted slightly to make them more comparable with the later surveys.
** Not asked in the 1978 survey.

Table 18 Strongest Claim on Tax Money, 1980

	Public order %	Capital* investment %	Health care %	Public education %	Job training and creation %	Other social services** %	N
Corporate Capitalists	19	24	23	17	13	5	(138)+
Small Employers	7	22	23	15	25	7	39
Rentiers	–	15	50	10	10	15	20
Petty Boiurgeoisie	–	16	27	14	25	9	50
Managers	7	15	25	19	27	7	56
Supervisors	3	18	27	15	22	13	127
Professional Employees	4	16	24	25	22	9	69
Non-Productive Proletariat	5	10	24	19	24	19	134
Productive Proletariat	3	7	27	5	39	19	108
Housewives	3	8	28	15	29	15	234
Temporarily Unemployed	5	5	21	12	35	22	38
Pensioners	4	7	34	11	20	20	143
Students	–	6	34	24	21	14	72
Total 18 + Population	4	11	28	15	26	16	1108

* (Incentives to private industry + Research for industrial development + Development and use of energy resources.)

** (Retirement benefits + Welfare and public housing + Conservation and pollution control + Consumer protection.)

\+ Respondents to special survey of corporate executives.

employees, whose jobs are typically most dependent on advanced educational qualifications, and by those who are currently students themselves, rather than by either capitalists or proletarians. While a diversity of policy priorities still finds strong support within most class groups, the recent trends do suggest the potential emergence of more pronounced conflicts between the most powerful polar class cores, especially over the allocation of public expenditures to effective job training programmes.

However, the public's relative fiscal priorities are not direct indicators of the desired *scale* of state expenditure on education or other policy areas. We have therefore asked respondents what they would like to see happen to public spending for education in the next budget year. As Table 19 shows, the overwhelming majority of the general public are now in favour of either maintaining or increasing real educational expenditures. This is the case for all levels from elementary schools to universities. Moreover, there has been a significant increase in support for increased real spending on education over the past five years,[17] as well as a more recent decline in the small core of support for definite decreases in educational spending. The most striking finding is that there is strong majority support in *all* class positions for at least ensuring the current scale of real educational expenditure. While capitalists tend to give the least support to increased spending, in accord with an immediate class interest in reprivatizing the economy and holding down state expenditures generally, they also express a diminishing disposition for real decreases; apparently there

Table 19   Desired Level of Public Spending for Education in the Next Budget Year,
1980.

	Increase %	Keep up with inflation %	Decrease %	Not stated %
Corporate Capitalists	36	53	19	8
Small Employers	30	43	14	13
Rentiers	11	60	29	–
Petty Bourgeoisie	35	45	15	5
Managers	43	47	5	5
Supervisors	37	49	12	2
Professional Employees	46	43	10	1
Non-Productive Proletariat	35	53	7	5
Productive Proletariat	34	53	12	2
Housewives	38	51	7	4
Temporarily Unemployed	38	50	12	–
Pensioners	21	59	16	4
Students	48	34	5	3
Total 18 + Population	36	50	10	4

is a growing perception among capitalists in Ontario that the blunt tactic of simply cutting back education funds has diminishing marginal economic and political returns. The strongest support for increased spending is found, not surprisingly, among managers, professional employees, and students – whose jobs and job prospects are most dependent on educational certification. But some of the negative consequences of cutbacks had become so evident by early 1981 (for example, closure of neighbourhood schools) and the sentiments opposing further cuts so prevalent, that the provincial government felt compelled at that moment to bring in an education budget that almost matched inflation.

But the growing opposition to further substantial cuts in general education expenditure is generally outweighed by the deepening fiscal crisis of the state, and by the competitive business pressures that continue to prevent capitalist enterprises from contributing a greater proportion of their declining average profits for state social service budgets, except under the pressure of more widespread mass political mobilization. State policy makers' attention, therefore, has become increasingly focused on the question of educational reorganization, to make 'better' use of available resources and eliminate 'redundant' programmes. While arrays of specific models are being considered by various public commissions, the central factor underlying the development of all such alternatives remains the use of teachers, who, for the foreseeable future, continue to represent both the dominant financial expenditure and the primary educational resource at all major levels. Accordingly, we have asked survey respondents whether, in the current context of declining elementary and high school enrolments in Ontario, teachers should be laid off or redeployed to provide more special services for disadvantaged children and smaller classes. As Table 20 indicates, a strong majority of the general public are now in favour of retaining 'surplus' teachers to provide more personal service. The level of support for retaining teachers has recently been increasing. The only major opposition to retaining 'surplus' teachers is in the dominant core of the capitalist class, with corporate capitalists strongly in favour of lay-offs.

This is in line with the commonly expressed current theme among corporate spokespersons to rationalize the curriculum. Proletarians are, along with those in most other class positions, very supportive of retaining teachers. This is similarly in line with many union leaders' education statements and resolutions. The clearly opposed sentiments expressed within the two most powerful class cores over the use of teachers could animate serious conflicts over the specific alternative forms of educational reorganization that will be proposed in the 1980s. But as the discourse analyses of Chapter Three should suggest, corporate leaders have been sufficiently sensitive to the widespread support for retaining teachers to couch their rationalization proposals in more indirect and curriculum-centred terms.

Preferred Form and Content of Education

While specific proposals for reform were at best embryonic at the point of our most recent survey, primary dimensions of class relations in education will unavoidably be implicated in any major initiative to reorganize the current educational system. As discussed in Chapter Three, these include: (1) cultural

Table 20   Views on the Use of 'Surplus' Teachers, 1980

	Retain teachers %	Lay off teachers %	Not stated %
Corporate Capitalists	18	76	6
Small Employers	66	31	3
Rentiers	42	52	6
Petty Bourgeoisie	61	37	2
Managers	62	28	10
Supervisors	68	29	3
Professional Employees	76	21	3
Non-Productive Proletariat	74	24	2
Productive – Proletariat	73	25	2
Housewives	74	24	2
Temporarily Unemployed	75	25	–
Pensioners	63	31	6
Students	74	25	1
Total 18 + Population	70	26	4

ownership – the extent of possession and control of the major means of cultural production residing with different classes, in terms both of the direct appropriation of educational resources and of the emphasis on their class interests and viewpoints in curricular content; (2) social relations – the patterns of social organization of authority within educational institutions; and (3) technical relations – the kinds of learning objectives to be emphasized within the educational process itself, with particular regard to linkage with the sphere of production. The current dispositions among respective class positions with regard to these primary dimensions should provide some indication of the levels of immediate support that different types of reform initiatives may be likely to receive. Only a few of the survey items dealing with these cultural ownership, social organization, and learning process dimensions of educational relations can be dealt with briefly here.

Attitudes About Cultural Ownership In recent years corporate leaders have become increasingly insistent on the legitimacy of their interests in public education, based on their tax contributions and their need for 'quality' educated people to aid in their continued creation of a wealthy society. As Hal Wyatt, corporate banker, puts it:

> [Businessmen] need a continuing supply of qualified potential employees who are able to function well in the working environment – people who accept the role of work as a necessary part of our economy, and of our society ... Canada's future rests in the perception young people have of the role business and industry play in our everyday lives, and their understanding of how this country of ours functions.[18]

Conversely, union leaders have expressed growing concern about corporate media domination and the absence of labour viewpoints in education that could provide young people with an adequate understanding of the Canadian economy and society. Our survey data permit some assessment of the current attitudes of those in different class positions concerning the extent of direct class control of the organizational development of schools, the perceived degree of equality of educational opportunity for different classes, and the emphasis on different class viewpoints in the curriculum.

According to sociologists such as Bourdieu and Bernstein, dominant class cultural control in advanced capitalist societies has become very much a matter of the language codes and symbols that prevail in different family and communal settings, on the one hand, and formal schooling, on the other, and the differential appropriation of cultural wealth by different classes that is facilitated. As noted in Chapter Two, our surveys have consistently found strong *individual* perceptions of this process, with corporate capitalists, managers and professional employees seeing much greater usefulness of their own formal school knowledge than do proletarians (See Table 16). The issue of concern here, however, is mass awareness of differential *class* appropriation of education, with regard first to influence over organizational policy making and, secondly, to equality of educational opportunity.

The most recently developed major institutions of schooling in Ontario, as in most other advanced capitalist settings, are the community colleges.[19] Our respondents were asked to assess the extent to which the interests of large business, small business, professionals and their associations, and wageworkers and their labour unions are represented in the development of community college programmes. The results are summarized in Table 21. There are several discernible tendencies. Consistent with other attitudinal research on class consciousness, corporate capitalists express the clearest support for political pluralism and moderate representation of different interests.[20] There is a general disposition among those in most class positions to perceive greater influence by large business and professionals than by wageworkers and small business. But the perceived differences in the extent of corporate and labour influence are larger among the intermediate elements than within the proletariat itself. In general, there appears to be a quite widespread acceptance of an image of pluralistic class control of the community colleges with no class group being clearly regarded as dominant. It should be noted, however, that productive proletarians and students, as well as managers, are more likely than most others to express the differential influence between workers and the managerial and professional intermediate class elements who in fact have directly controlled much educational policy making in recent times.

We have asked a variety of questions about the perceived equality of

Table 21   Perceived Representation of Class Interests in the Development of Community Colleges, 1980

| | Proportion Perceiving Strong Interest of: | | | |
	Large Business %	Small Business %	Professionals %	Workers %
Corporate Capitalists	21	22	25	13
Small Employers	31	11	36	16
Rentiers	7	12	19	6
Petty Bourgeoisie	39	16	32	17
Managers	38	13	45	17
Supervisors	40	14	39	20
Professional Employees	40	21	35	23
Non-Productive Proletariat	34	17	31	26
Productive Proletariat	41	11	50	27
Housewives	32	13	32	21
Temporarily Unemployed	47	13	52	45
Pensioners	22	13	28	18
Students	46	15	42	15
Total 18 + Population	35	14	36	21

educational opportunity in terms of occupational class, sex, and ethnic differences. Small majorities in most class positions have expressed support for a meritocratic model of educational achievement within school programmes.[21] More mixed views have been found concerning equality of outcomes, with all capitalist positions as well as managers clearly expressing a belief in meritocratic selection, while proletarians and most others are quite divided with nearly equal proportions supporting meritocracy and the view that schools serve to direct students to the same general levels in the labour force as their parents.[22] Most relevant perhaps is the issue of equality of opportunity for post-secondary education. Our findings are summarized in Table 22. Strong majority support is expressed in nearly all class positions, and certainly within the productive proletariat, for the notion of equal opportunity of those from all family class backgrounds to obtain a higher education. The broad equality of opportunity rhetoric of dominant class spokespersons in the still expansionist 1960s has now been largely replaced by narrower meritocratic arguments concerning student selection. But neither the broader nor the narrower versions of the dominant ideology of educational equality have found much sustained opposition in explicit critiques of selection biases by labour leaders, in spite of the stark reality of class inequality documented in Chapter Two (See Table 14) and strongly suggested by numerous earlier studies showing similar differences by family occupational background.[23]

With regard to the emphasis on different class viewpoints in curricular content, labour education statements now do strongly and consistently stress

Table 22 *'Students from Families of All Occupational Backgrounds (Such as Managerial, Professional, Clerical, and Blue Collar Levels) Have an Equal Chance of Getting a Higher Education in Ontario Today.' (1979)*

	Agree %	Disagree %	Don't know %	N
Corporate Capitalists	62	28	10	(148)*
Small Employers	71	26	3	35
Rentiers	70	20	10	20
Petty Bourgeoisie	74	23	3	54
Managers	72	25	3	61
Supervisors	71	23	6	91
Professional Employees	54	41	5	78
Non-Productive Proletariat	72	21	7	121
Productive Proletariat	77	20	3	151
Housewives	78	16	6	262
Temporarily Unemployed	73	21	6	54
Pensioners	82	14	4	116
Students	71	22	7	41
Total 18 + Population	75	21	4	1084

* Respondents to special survey of corporate executives.

the need to get working class viewpoints into the schools. We have asked respondents to what extent, if any, they think there is a class bias against students from working class families in Ontario schools. The results appear in Table 23. The respondents as a whole are quite equally divided on this issue, with slightly more expressing the view that such a bias exists than denying its existence. Most class positions, including the proletariat, are also highly divided on this issue. While capitalists are less inclined than most others to express an opinion on the issue, corporate capitalists in particular are least likely to say that such a class bias exists. Students themselves, professional employees, and especially the unemployed are more likely than corporate capitalists to recognize discriminatory treatment of working class students.

Secondly, with a more explicit focus on curriculum content *per se*, we have asked respondents whether Ontario schools should give more emphasis than they do now to teaching students about: (a) business and property rights in the free enterprise system; and (b) the labour movement and workers' rights. As Table 24 shows, the majority of proletarians support more emphasis on workers' rights while the majority of corporate directors are opposed. However, proletarians are even more strongly in favour of increasing emphasis on business and property rights, as are overwhelming majorities in *all* other class locations. These findings indicate relatively consistent expressed views of their class interests among both corporate capitalists and small employers.

Those in the productive proletariat, the most organized core of the working class, express a largely unquestioned support for business property rights and a prevalence of contradictory class consciousness even at this most evident content level of cultural approporiation.

Table 23   Extent of Perceived Bias Against Working Class Students, 1980

	Great or some extent %	None – schools neutral or sensitive %	Not stated %
Corporate Capitalists	35	41	24
Small Employers	50	34	16
Rentiers	50	25	25
Petty Bourgeoisie	53	38	9
Managers	46	47	7
Supervisors	50	43	7
Professional Employees	60	39	1
Non-Productive Proletariat	51	44	5
Productive Proletariat	45	50	5
Housewives	45	44	11
Temporarily Unemployed	70	25	5
Pensioners	43	40	17
Students	58	38	4
Total 18 + Population	49	42	9

Table 24 Support for Greater Emphasis on Business Rights and Workers' Rights in Ontario Schools, 1980

	More emphasis on business and property rights			More emphasis on workers' rights		
	Agree %	Disagree %	Not stated %	Agree %	Disagree %	Not stated %
Corporate Capitalists	77	10	13	24	52	24
Small Employers	88	2	10	31	50	19
Rentiers	80	–	20	45	40	15
Petty Bourgeoisie	79	6	15	36	43	21
Managers	73	11	16	42	38	20
Supervisors	77	9	14	40	37	23
Professional Employees	76	8	16	45	23	32
Non-Productive Proletariat	75	9	16	55	20	22
Productive Proletariat	76	6	18	57	20	23
Housewives	73	7	20	43	30	27
Temporarily Unemployed	82	5	13	58	20	22
Pensioners	71	6	23	45	29	26
Students	76	7	17	48	23	29
Total 18 + Population	75	7	18	46	30	24

In summary, we have found little expression of concern to change existing mechanisms of dominant class appropriation of the schools as means of cultural production. The prevailing tendency for capitalists and proletarians alike is to accept current forms of schooling as 'natural' and to be preoccupied with the interplay of their more immediate class interests in terms of much narrower issues of curricular content and some of the programme orientation matters to be dealt with in the following sections. While awareness of personal possession or dispossession of the instruments for appropriating school knowledge does reflect capitalists' cultural dominance over the school, there is greater reluctance of not only capitalists but also proletarians to recognize the existence of unequal opportunities for educational advancement and a general class bias against working-class children in the schools. It is only when issues of cultural ownership are dealt with in the more discrete terms of curricular content that clearly divergent class interests are widely recognized between the class cores. In this respect corporate capitalists tend to express a coherent awareness of their immediate class interests in both opposing workers' rights and defending business and property rights. Productive proletarians, in their desire for more emphasis on workers' rights in the school curriculum, are most clearly opposed to capitalists. But the great extent to which such industrial workers are currently ideologically dominated is indicated by the finding that this immediate proletarian interest remains encapsulated within a largely unquestioned acceptance of business property rights, much as are the educational ideologies expressed by most labour leaders. Capitalist cultural appropriation of the schools would appear to be ideologically quite secure at the moments of our readings of mass opinion.

Attitudes About the Social Organization of Schools Discussions about the social relations in the educational process, or, more narrowly, the social organization of schools, invariably revolve around the themes of freedom and authority. The major authority issues on which we have assessed mass opinion are the adequacy of current student discipline measures, the preferred general form of school authority structure, and the preferred degree of administrative centralization of the school system. The major freedom issues are the amount of freedom of curricular choice allowed to students and the right of teachers to strike.

Inadequacy in the exercise of authority over students has been the most widely perceived problem throughout the past decade in Ontario and elsewhere.[24] As Table 25 indicates, the majority of those in all class positions except students themselves tend to think of the current treatment of discipline in the high schools as too permissive. This is particularly true of the 'proprietary classes', capitalists and the petty bourgeoisie, whereas there are somewhat smaller majorities in most other class positions. It is also notable that even among students there is very little perception that current school discipline is too restrictive. The heightening of this ethos of anti-permissiveness in recent times may be understood partly in terms of a stagnant economic context in which the schools are increasingly unable to provide expected

Table 25   Orientations to High School Discipline, 1979

	Too permissive %	About right %	Too restrictive %	Don't know %
Corporate Capitalists	<u>86</u>	7	6	1
Small Employers	<u>74</u>	19	–	7
Rentiers	<u>75</u>	15	–	10
Petty Bourgeoisie	<u>79</u>	10	3	8
Managers	62	23	5	10
Supervisors	59	24	5	12
Professional Employees	67	19	3	11
Non-Productive Proletariat	56	28	6	10
Productive Proletariat	55	29	7	9
Housewives	59	27	3	11
Temporarily Unemployed	64	23	7	6
Pensioners	70	13	2	15
Students	<u>44</u>	44	6	6
Total 18 + Population	62	23	4	11

educational and career direction to growing numbers of students, and of a partially consequent youth culture increasingly expressing frustration and aimlessness.

Such general sentiments, however, tell very little about the types of organizational solutions of discipline problems that the public would support. Our surveys have asked a variety of questions about perceived and preferred patterns of social organization of authority within the schools, and responses generally express the view that adequate resolution of the discipline issue should be sought at the school level rather than within student-teacher classroom relations. One of the most relevant items focuses on high school authority structures and asks respondents to choose between current decision making structures and two alternative models, one with a clearer chain of command and more authority for school principals, and the other with the local social community more involved and exercising more decision making authority. As Table 26 summarizes, there is very little support for the current sort of authority structure, a result consistent with the generalized dissatisfaction about student discipline. However, the respondents as a whole offer substantial support for both alternative models. Similar divided preferences appear within most class positions. The most notable exceptions are again the proprietary classes, capitalists and the petty bourgeoisie, who express majority support for more centralized, principal-centred authority. Corporate capitalists especially are almost unanimously opposed to any devolution of authority to local communities. While, the proletariat remains divided, there has been a

Table 26   Preferred High School Authority Structure, 1980

	More authority for principal %	As now %	More authority for local communities %	Not stated %
Corporate Capitalists	55	17	9	19
Small Employers	51	14	28	7
Rentiers	51	6	24	19
Petty Bourgeoisie	55	12	30	4
Managers	45	18	28	9
Supervisors	40	14	40	6
Professional Employees	46	14	35	5
Non-Productive Proletariat	37	18	36	9
Productive Proletariat	37	20	39	4
Housewives	42	19	26	13
Temporarily Unemployed	32	27	41	–
Pensioners	48	19	24	9
Students	29	29	38	4
Total 18 + Population	42	18	32	8

recent trend to increasing support for community-based school authority structures.

Expressed attitude differences between class positions on several other authority issues pertaining to preferences for centralized or local administration of educational activities are somewhat more pronounced. Table 27 summarizes findings regarding the preferred level of responsibility for determining suitable tests for high school course completion and graduation. The majority tend to support local control, with about a third wanting to combine this with some central authority and very little support for exclusive central control. In distinction from all other class positions, corporate capitalists would prefer to have such administrative control fully centralized. Along with managers, their closest subordinates in the corporate structure, they are also much less likely than most others to express any support for local control. Proletarian preferences for local control are similar to those in most other class positions. In any case, in light of the widely perceived inadequacy of current authority structures and the substantial subordinate class support for more open, participatory decision making, recent ostensibly objective recommendations to reduce the general public's role in educational decision making to a more 'selective consultation', on the basis of observed low levels of participation in these current structures[25] should be regarded with considerable scepticism.

As noted in Chapter Three, there was a great deal of emphasis on a child-centred model of schooling in the state policy initiatives in Ontario in the

Table 27   Preferred Locus of Control of High School Testing, 1980

	Local authorities %	Local and central authorities %	Central authorities %	Don't know %
Corporate Capitalists	11	36	50	3
Small Employers	35	46	19	–
Rentiers	64	23	13	–
Petty Bourgeoisie	54	33	9	3
Managers	27	48	23	2
Supervisors	43	40	16	1
Professional Employees	47	37	15	1
Non-Productive Proletarians	54	31	12	3
Productive Proletarians	52	31	13	4
Housewives	56	28	14	2
Temporarily Unemployed	53	38	9	–
Pensioners	59	19	13	9
Students	55	29	14	2
Total 18+ Population	51	32	14	3

late 1960s. The 'new middle class' elements that sponsored such liberalizing reforms laid particular stress on students' freedom of choice in learning. The resulting system of elective courses in high schools was castigated by many business interests from the outset. In the wake of the current economic crisis and the extraordinary difficulty of providing adequate career guidance for many students, the electives system has become increasingly vulnerable to corporate and other conservative critics. State education policy in this regard appears about to be reversed in Ontario.[26] Opinion surveys early in the decade indicated wide popular support for increasing students' freedom of choice.[27] The current pattern that emerges from questions on the preferred form of students' selection of courses appears quite different, as Table 28 indicates. Less than a quarter of the respondents now favour giving students the discretion to set their own programmes of study; on the other hand, there is also very little support for completely required programmes of study. Over two-thirds of all respondents favour a high school course structure in which students retain some choice of optional courses but are required to take not only language and maths but mandatory courses preparing them for further education or employment. While majority support is expressed in all class positions for such a compulsory core curriculum it is notable that corporate capitalists are clearly the strongest supporters.

Finally, the right to strike won by teachers' struggles in the early 1970s has remained a controversial issue. While teachers' right to strike has been legally established in Ontario since 1975, vocal reactions of some groups to recent strikes led to a public commission to review the collective bargaining process. Table 29 summarizes the most recent views. There has been little discernible

Table 28 Preferred Freedom of Student Choice in High School Course Selection, 1980

	Great deal of choice, set own programmes	Much choice, required Language/ Math courses	Some choice, required Language/ Math and Career courses	No choice, required Language/ Math courses and set Career programmes
	%	%	%	%
Corporate Capitalists	–	5	89	5
Small Employers	3	19	72	6
Rentiers	–	25	75	–
Petty Bourgeoisie	8	17	57	15
Managers	3	12	73	9
Supervisors	2	12	77	9
Professional Employees	2	19	71	8
Non-Productive Proletariat	10	14	68	6
Productive Proletariat	13	14	64	9
Housewives	9	12	71	6
Temporarily Unemployed	5	13	68	9
Pensioners	9	13	60	13
Students	8	22	67	3
Total 18+ Population	8	14	68	8

change over the 1978–80 period in the distribution of opinions on this issue. A small majority have continued to express opposition to teachers' right to strike. Corporate capitalists and the petty bourgeoisie have consistently expressed greater resistance to this right than most other class groups, while productive proletarians remain alone in expressing majority support for teachers' legal right. Students and professional employees are quite evenly split on the question.[28] On several occasions the Ontario labour movement has effectively mobilized itself to help teachers defend their collective interests on this issue. It remains one of the most definite points on which a more sustained teacher-worker alliance might be built.

If one considers the continuing contradictions in the actual social relations of the schooling process and the concomitant limits on capitalist ideological discourse – particularly in terms of the simultaneous need to encourage individual intitiative as well as acceptance of subordination and imposed social discipline – the strong degree of support for an anti-permissive ethos among the productive proletariat may appear somewhat surprising. It should be noted here that industrial workers express even more compliant views on the development of vocational students' attitudes (for example, 'punctuality', 'industriousness').[29] However, such questions on permissiveness and punctuality refer to the most diffuse of social values. Numerous attitude studies have found similarly high consensus at this level of abstraction and attributed it in part to the widely varied interpretations of meaning such concepts allow, their irrelevance to practice, or easy pragmatic acceptance.[30] While much of the emphasis in corporate ideological discourse in the current period is, as illustrated in Chapter Three, focused on subordination themes of social

Table 29   Views on Teachers' Right to Strike, 1980

	Agree %	Disagree %	Not stated %
Corporate Capitalists	12	82	6
Small Employers	29	64	7
Rentiers	26	68	6
Petty Bourgeoisie	21	77	2
Managers	42	56	2
Supervisors	34	58	8
Professional Employees	42	41	17
Non-Productive Proletariat	33	60	7
Productive Proletariat	54	38	8
Housewives	34	57	9
Temporarily Unemployed	25	55	20
Pensioners	23	64	13
Students	47	39	14
Total 18+ Population	35	56	9

discipline, the compliant verbal attitudes of workers are undoubtedly based to some extent on both narrower immediate concerns with continuing employability and job security, as well as uncritical absorption of dominant ideological conceptions. But it is particularly relevant here to recall Glaberman's comments regarding the material limits on the verbal passivity of Windsor auto workers.[31] Indeed, at the time this survey was being conducted and both monopoly and competitive sectors of the production proletariat were individually expressing such compliant views on student work habits, they were also beginning the largest mobilization of Ontario labour in recent years in protest against plant closing in places such as Windsor. In any case, attitude differences between the capitalist and proletarian class cores on some of the more concrete aspects of the social organization of schooling cited above are considerably greater. Some of these differences appear to have increased over the past few years. The clearest and strongest tendency is corporate capitalists' sensibility to keeping influence on the school authority process largely out of the hands of local communities, while the working class, along with several potential allies, has expressed a slowly growing conscious interest in community-oriented forms of the social organization of schools.

Attitudes About Learning Process Objectives Raymond Williams' provocative historical sketch of class-based educational ideologies in England[32] suggests that the most pronounced class differences in educational attitudes may centre on preferences with regard to the learning process *per se*, and more particularly on the desired aims and objectives of this process. As the central practical activity of educational institutions that is most directly and fully experienced by most people, the learning process might well be expected to be the prime focus of distinct educational views related to different groups' material conditions. In any case, the major preoccupation in most discussions of the objectives of the learning process in advanced capitalist settings has been on skill requirements, as the discourse analysis in Chapter Three illustrates. Our surveys have probed mass opinions on several aspects of the learning process generally related to skill requirements; the general form of organization of the learning process in the elementary grades, priorities for different learning objectives in secondary and post-secondary schooling, as well as the levels of technical skill regarded as necessary for most of the current workforce and the issue of how closely the learning process providing such skills should be linked with job opportunities.

We have first asked respondents whether they would prefer to have the learning process in elementary schools organized in terms of standard courses that are structured by educational specialists or, alternatively, in terms of courses which may vary from community to community, shaped by local teachers on the basis of the actual experiences of particular groups of children. The results appear in Table 30. A small majority of all respondents favour standard courses at the elementary level. However, the fact that over a third opt for courses based on children's actual experience while very few are unwilling to choose between the two approaches suggests some substantial division in current popular philosophies of learning. The most notable class difference is that corporate capitalists are more strongly opposed to an experiential approach than all others. As well as being the strongest supporters of standard courses. Only among students and the unemployed is there majority support for an experientially-based learning process.

Table 30   *Preferred Organization of the Elementary School Learning Process, 1980*

	Standard courses in all schools %	Courses based on children's actual experience %	not stated %
Corporate Capitalists	74	16	10
Small Employers	53	47	–
Rentiers	40	50	10
Petty Bourgeoisie	67	30	3
Managers	58	36	6
Supervisors	66	30	4
Professional Employees	47	45	8
Non-Productive Proletariat	55	34	11
Productive Proletariat	57	36	7
Housewives	53	39	8
Temporarily Unemployed	42	58	–
Pensioners	54	27	19
Students	43	54	3
Tatal 18+ Population	54	37	9

As we have seen in Chapter Three, labour spokespersons have based their education proposals largely on the need to *add* working class, women's and minority ethnic viewpoints onto the existing curricula; they have placed little stress on learning needs based on the distinctiveness of working class cultures, apart from very general comments about the need for more language and maths skills. Also, at least on this issue, the liberal philosophy of child-centred education now receives only minority support, even among the intermediate elements where it originated. Corporate rhetoric about the purported excesses of such 'progressive' educational philosophies in practice may also have helped to dissuade the proletariat from more concern to link pedagogical practice to working-class experience. But it is also clear that, while working class circles want greater local community influence over the social organization of schools, they apparently are now not a great deal more likely than corporate capitalists to regard relativist learning processes as being in their interests.

In contrast to the apparent inter-class consensus on increasing standardization of the general structure of the learning process, there are substantial class differences in preferences for specific types of learning objectives, especially at the secondary and post-secondary levels. Our survey respondents have been asked to express their preferences among a wide variety of possible educational objectives for different levels of education. At the secondary school level, a growing priority for job training has been expressed through the past decade, and more recently for basic reading, writing, and number skills. The development of creativity and critical thinking skills has also retained a relatively high priority, but most possible objectives that are less directly relatable to the sphere of production (for example, moral education, physical fitness, Canadian history, political education, art and cultural studies) have generally been regarded as much less central.[33] Table 31 summarizes the basic patterns of secondary school priorities expressed in the most recent survey by those in different class positions. Opposed tendencies are quite evident between capitalists and proletarians, especially corporate capitalists and the productive proletariat. The majority of corporate capitalists give top priority to basic skills or creativity and very little importance to job training in secondary school, while productive proletarians display almost exactly the reverse tendencies. These patterns correspond closely with the same groups' fiscal priorities for tax dollars.

Table 31   Highest Priority Educational Objective for Secondary Schools, 1980

	Basic skills/ creativity %	Job training %	Other objectives %
Corporate Capitalists	57	13	28
Small Employers	41	33	23
Rentiers	41	20	39
Petty Bourgeoisie	35	28	34
Managers	39	24	37
Supervisors	22	47	29
Professional Employees	30	33	37
Non-Productive Proletariat	19	52	27
Productive Proletariat	15	55	30
Housewives	28	40	31
Temporarily Unemployed	36	51	13
Pensioners	24	32	42
Students	23	49	27
Total 18+ Population	26	41	32

With regard to the universities, we have asked a related question about whether more emphasis should be placed on broad arts and science education, the current balance between general and professional job-oriented programmes maintained, or more emphasis placed on job-oriented programmes. The results appear in Table 32. Not surprisingly, in this period of rising unemployment, the majority in most class positions would like to see the universities place more emphasis on job-related programmes. Certainly, university students in most advanced capitalist societies have dramatically reversed their priorities in recent years; the majority of the best students are now opting for professional programmes whenever possible, in spite of dire warnings from university administrators about the consequent 'decline of civilization'.[34] Corporate capitalists are again quite strikingly different in their attitudinal tendencies from most others, offering strong support for either maintaining the *status quo* or placing more emphasis on broad arts and science education. Aside from corporate capitalists, only among professional employees is there less than majority support for expanding professional programmes. However, professional employees are considerably more divided in their sentiments. The inherent contradiction here is that although they are most likely to appreciate the value of professional education – since their own positions are most fully dependent on such forms of education – they are currently unlikely to want to encourage more potential competition in their own fields.

Table 32   Preferred Curricular Emphasis in University Programmes, 1980

	More broad education in arts and science %	Current emphases should be maintained %	More job-oriented programmes %
Corporate Capitalists	20	51	29
Small Employers	5	28	62
Rentiers	5	35	60
Petty Bourgeoisie	2	32	60
Managers	10	30	57
Supervisors	4	35	59
Professional Employees	16	41	41
Non-Productive Proletariat	4	31	59
Productive Proletariat	6	27	59
Housewives	3	31	61
Temporarily Unemployed	3	39	58
Pensioners	4	26	61
Students	4	44	52
Total 18+ Population	5	32	58

General expressions of support for job-related training do not in themselves convey any notion of the levels of technical skills that respondents think should be provided in such programmes. We have therefore asked a series of questions about skill requirements needed for current jobs. First, we were interested in views as to whether the current labour process involves more or less skill and independent judgement than in the past. As noted in Chapter Three, corporate educational ideology stresses the growing need for versatile skill workers to meet global competition. Some trade union statements are quite compatible, in the sense that they emphasize the importance of skilled trades and advanced technical skills training; but other labour voices express concern about routinization, fragmentation and de-skilling in many trades. The results of our main question on this issue are summarized in Table 33. The results are remarkably uniform with a clear majority in all class positions perceiving an increasing need for technical skill and independent judgement in most jobs. Indeed, more detailed analyses confirm that this view is at least as prevalent among the monopoly sector productive proletariat who have the most routinized jobs as it is anywhere else.

Table 33 'Compared to Twenty Years Ago, Do You Think the Work Most of the Canadian Labour Force Does Now Involves More or Less Skill and Independent Judgement?' (1980)

	More %	About the same %	Less %	Don't know %
Corporate Capitalists	57	23	14	6
Small Employers	60	12	26	2
Rentiers	60	20	20	–
Petty Bourgeoisie	59	15	24	2
Managers	59	14	25	2
Supervisors	63	17	13	7
Professional Employees	58	11	23	8
Non-Productive Proletariat	59	15	20	6
Productive Proletariat	66	16	13	5
Housewives	54	14	24	8
Temporarily Unemployed	57	10	28	5
Pensioners	59	16	22	3
Students	55	17	18	10
Total 18+ Population	58	15	21	6

It may appear from such readings that acceptance of 'technological rationality' has become as secure a basis of capitalist ideological domination as dispositions toward possessive individualism have long been.[35] However, the capitalist labour process remains a much more contradictory reality than either the corporate view of scientific-technical progress or the routinization and de-skilling thesis[36] of some critics can adequately capture. This is reflected in attitudes regarding more specific aspects of skill requirements for current jobs. In short, workers' perceptions of increasing skill requirements are a partially accurate recognition of the collective technical knowledge needed to work in advanced machinofacture, however 'ossified' its capitalist social form may be. Moreover, proletarians do not express preoccupation with narrow or highly specific skills for immediate employment. In our surveys, the majority of proletarians, just as the majority of corporate capitalists and most others, want emphasis in education placed on *general* technical skills and knowledge.[37] The central class opposition is over how such school-based skills acquisition should be linked to the world of work.

The different interests of most hired labour and corporate capitalists on this issue do find expression in popular sentiments. As Table 34 indicates, in 1978, proletarians and most other workers gave strong majority support to the regulation of the educational system, and of skill training provisions in particular, to match job opportunities. A small majority of students were opposed, perhaps reflecting an immediate interest in not placing restrictions on their own perceived educational opportunities; there might be less opposition in today's even sterner employment conditions. Professional employees were again clearly divided. On the one hand they have exceptional sensitivity to restrictions on access to advanced education since it was their own primary road to occupational success; on the other hand they may also be exceptionally insecure about uncontrolled flows of trained people into their own fields. Corporate capitalists express just as deep a division. However, their division reflects a more fundamental contradiction of the capitalist form of schooling.

As the previous discussion of the basic contradictory relationships of the fully developed capitalist mode of production should suggest, however much capitalists may wish to centralize technical design and planning knowledge to enhance their real appropriation of the labour process, it remains imperative to overproduce workers in a wide variety of skill areas and have them compete in highly segmented labour markets, in order to ensure both the continual revolutionizing of production techniques and the disciplining of the labour force. Our data suggest that, at least in their expressed attitudes, corporate

Table 34   Regulation of the Educational System to Match Job Opportunities, 1978

	Agree %	Disagree %	Not stated %	N
Corporate Capitalists	37	42	21	(114)*
Small Employers	50	24	26	39
Rentiers	**	**	**	–
Petty Bourgeoisie	61	24	15	61
Managers	62	32	6	42
Supervisors	62	27	11	83
Professional Employees	43	38	19	60
Non-Productive Proletariat	65	20	15	139
Productive Proletariat	67	18	15	125
Housewives	62	24	14	226
Temporarily Unemployed	68	14	18	81
Pensioners	71	16	13	93
Students	34	52	14	31
Total 18+ Population	61	23	16	1025

* Respondents to special survey of corporate executives.
** Rentiers not separable from pensioners in this survey.

capitalists now tend to be of mixed minds about subordinating their interest in centralizing technical knowledge within a very highly trained elite to this continuing need for a versatile and fully mobile skilled labour force with no prior guarantees. In contrast, the clearly expressed preference of many proletarians for early job training, and for close association between the sorts of vocational skills to be mastered and the general fields of economically required occupations, is at odds with both fundamental and immediate capitalist interests. The finding that the expressions of this class opposition over learning objectives are most pronounced regarding the secondary school level is consistent with the likelihood that it is at this level that the frustrations of the capitalist schooling process in relation to life chances have been most deeply experienced by most working class people.[38]

Concluding Remarks

While the current accumulation crisis continues to exert unrelenting pressure on state budgetary allocations, these surveys of mass opinion suggest that there is little conscious support even in the capitalist class for pursuing simple cutback tactics in Ontario education to aid in resolving this crisis.[38] With regard to the matter of the general sorts of reorganization of the school system that are likely to be widely supported, there is currently neither much expressed disposition to question capitalist appropriation of major means of cultural production nor even much opposition to the prevalence of capitalist ideological codes and viewpoints in the schools. Little satisfaction is expressed with current school authority structures, but there is a fairly balanced division of general support for more centralized or more participatory alternatives. While there may be some continuing controversy in this area, the imminent prospect appears to be some further administrative centralization at capitalist forces' initiative; the retention of current forms of school authority on top of a precarious balance of forces is a somewhat less probable option. The most likely area of class conflict over school reorganization, suggested by mass opinion, involves the specific objectives of the learning process in relation to the workplace. Proletarians want to tighten this link; capitalists must keep it loose. A concrete animating issue could be proposed future uses of teachers, with more sensitive linkage requiring relatively more teachers and a looser linkage being compatible with reduced numbers. This prospect appears quite plausible in view of the finding that the expressed opinions of corporate capitalists and proletarians are already most opposed on the general issue of use of 'surplus' teachers. While the corporate-based educational rhetoric of rationalization and standardization clearly now commands the heights of state policy making,[39] a teacher-labour movement alliance has already been weakly established. Such an alliance *could* mobilize much of the expressed popular support for retaining teachers as the impact of 'rationalized restructuring' is more widely felt.

It is relevant to note here that the numerous job training programmes established by state agencies in recent years to mediate this structural contradiction between capitalist and worker educational interests have so far, with few localized exceptions, proved quite ineffectual.[40] However much state officials may wish to provide an orderly induction of young workers into production, these programmes have tended to become reduced to attempts to induce orderliness into unemployed youth. To tailor such training programmes to capitalists' job market cloth today is to stress the basic technical skills (that is, literacy and numeracy) and 'generic' social skills (for example, responsibility, flexibility) required for rapid changes of technical competence in accumulation-driven machinofacture. Conversely, to address workers' aspirations, job training programmes must 'be for specific jobs that have specific requirements',[41] preferably with a sufficiently comprehensive array of advanced technical skills to ensure some economic security. The irresolvability of this contradiction in advanced capitalist market economies, and its deepening in periods of economic crisis, are quite clearly reflected in the opposed opinions on secondary school learning objectives offered here by corporate capitalists and proletarians, as well as by continual dispute about the adequacy of such employment training programmes.

Overall, these survey readings do not suggest pervasive ideological domination. Indeed, they indicate the existence of considerable divisions of opinion within the capitalist class on various immediate interests, as well as the isolation of corporate capitalists' attitudes on a number of educational issues, and some common sentiments among proletarians and intermediate elements that are clearly being denied in the current educational restructuring. In a supplementary analysis of the 'inner cores' of the major class circles, namely the corporate elite and unionized monopoly sector industrial workers, the patterns of expressed opinion about educational issues, and particularly the points of opposition, are found to be very similar to those of the remainder of corporate capitalists and productive proletarians, respectively.[42] Of course, expressed attitudes and, certainly, mass opinion surveys are most ephemeral aspects of social reality. At best, they can point to private sentiments that can serve as one of the bases of social practice. The specific social consciousness expressed within different class positions is constantly vulnerable to ideological struggle by organized agencies of opposed class forces. The mass opinions about educational issues that are analyzed here obviously continue to be mediated by such ideological struggle. But the analyses do suggest that the active support of some intermediate class elements is likely, because of their relative size and their currently intermediate attitudes on many vital educational issues, to be decisive in any initiatives of either leading capitalist or proletarian forces to resolve the current crisis in their own favour.

Only the likelihood of a deepening material crisis of accumulation and the continuation of the fundamentally contradictory class relations of the capitalist mode of production throughout this crisis can be asserted with any assurance here. The potential significance of these survey findings for political practice is particularly difficult to assess because mass opinion surveys are largely a post-World War II phenomenon. We have no such surveys in earlier protracted capitalist crises to tell us about comparative levels of expressed mass opinion, or their relations with the practical actions of the major class forces. Indeed, there are very few other current opinion surveys of educational or social issues available in any of the advanced capitalist societies that permit a class analysis of their results; there are a great many that serve to obscure the existence of class-based attitude differences. Gender, ethnicity, and age-based relations, as well as various other particular social locational factors, have their own influences on social consciousness, and can also serve to specify some of the class-based educational attitude differences presented here. But to recognize these influences should not be to deny or obscure general class influences, especially when, as in the present instance, class position shows the most pronounced and persistent relations with such educational attitudes.[43]

Ideological hegemony is increasingly being recognized by progressive intellectuals as a complex and subtle process, not merely the widespread acceptance of dominant class values and viewpoints. Our surveys provide indications, for example, that some of the essential ideological precepts of ownership classes' continuing appropriation in advanced capitalism (most notably the twin ethos of possessive individualism and technological rationality) remain widely taken for granted. But many more specific capitalist beliefs about education are regarded with uncertainty or rejected. As Bob Jessop has noted in a general review of research on political cultures:

> Various studies have shown that schools and the mass media, for example, have only a limited impact in efforts to inculcate dominant values. This suggests that affirmation of dominant values is less important than the absence of concepts and values for structural criticism.[44]

In the following chapter, I will review briefly some of the alternative conceptions of the educational and societal future that are currently available to aid in such critical reflection and widened public discourse. But, surely, the analyses of class-based educational ideologies and expressed attitudes presented here suggest the conclusion that more critical working class-based organizations, and more extensive work by aligned radical intellectuals, are needed for either the social democratic or socialist options for resolving the current crisis to have much chance of success. However, history read from the vantage point of subordinate classes shows graphically that the practical reality of liberatory action has frequently occurred before aligned intellectuals' theoretical awareness that it might. This has also been the case in the emergence, however briefly to date, of socialist governments (that is, workers' councils of direct class rule) in advanced industrial societies.[45]

Notes

1 YOUNG, T.R. (1980) 'The Public Sphere and the State in Capitalist Society' Paper presented at the Annual meeting of The American Sociological Association, New York, August, pp. 13–14. (Emphasis added).

2 *Ibid.* p. 35.

3 Most notably MARCUSE, H. (1964) *One-Dimensional Man* Boston, Beacon Press.

4 For a useful overview, see MANN, M. (1970) 'The social cohesion of liberal democracy' *American Sociological Review* 35, pp. 423–39. For a somewhat more recent and more nuanced opinion survey-based analysis of the extent to which class location and other structural characteristics – as well as presumed differential exposure to ideological mediations – influence acceptance of dominant values, see JESSOP, B. (1974) *Traditionalism, Conservatism and British Political Culture* London, Allen and Unwin. In a more speculative vein, the fact that only small minorities of the populace have usually been fully involved as fighters against or defenders of the established order in prior periods of profound social unrest suggests another possible reason for considering mass opinion. That is, it seems that the largely private dispositions of the majority to support change or the *status quo* have often been of decisive import. See, for example, RUDÉ, G. (1980) *Ideology and Popular Protest* New York, Pantheon.

5 See OFFE, C. and WIESENTHAL, H. (1979) 'Two logics of collective action' *Political Power and Social Theory* 1, pp. 67–115.

6 See MARTIN, R. (1978) 'The effects of recent changes in industrial conflict on the internal politics of trade unions: Britain and Germany'; and DEPPE, R. (1978) et al. 'The relationship between trade union action and political parties', both in CROUCH, C. and PIZZORNO, A. (Eds) *The Resurgence of Class Conflict in Western Europe Since 1968*, Volume 2, London, Macmillan.

7 The summary descriptive reports of these surveys are all available in published form: LIVINGSTONE, D.W. (1979) *Public Attitudes Toward Education in Ontario 1978* Toronto, OISE Press, LIVINGSTONE, D.W. and HART, D.J. (1980) *Public Attitudes Toward Education in Ontario 1979* Toronto, OISE Press, and LIVINGSTONE, D.W. and HART, D.J. (1981) *Public Attitudes Toward Education in Ontario 1980* Toronto, OISE Press. These reports also contain appendices with details of the research design, sample composition and sampling tolerances, as well as copies of the interview schedules. The reports may be purchased from Publication Sales, The Ontario Institute for Studies in Education, 252 Bloor Street West, Toronto, Ontario M5S 1V6.

8 The prior Canadian surveys have been critically reviewed in LIVINGSTONE, D.W. (1979) *op. cit.* pp. 1–3. Recent surveys have continued to display similar features, but with some increasing interest in issues of school re-organization. See, for example, WARREN, P.J. (1978) *Public Attitudes Towards Education in Newfoundland and Labrador* St. John's, Memorial University, CEA Task Force (1979) *Results of a Gallup Poll of Public Opinion in Canada about Public Involvement in Educational Decisions* Toronto, Canadian Education Association, Ministry of Education (1979) *Attitudes of the Public Towards Schools in Ontario* Toronto, The Ministry, HUGHES, A.S. (1979) *Public Attitudes Toward Post Secondary Education in the Maritime Provinces* Halifax, Atlantic Institute of Education, KIELTY, F. et al. (Eds) (1980) *Canadians Speak Out: The Canadian Gallup Polls 1980 Edition* Toronto, McNamara Press; and Opinion Research Index (1981) *Public Attitudes Towards Alberta Universities* Calgary, University of Calgary.

9 Both the questionnaire and a brief account appear in WEISS, H. (1973) 'Karl Marx's "Enquète Ouvrière"' in BOTTOMORE, T. (Ed) *Karl Marx* Englewood Cliffs, Prentice-Hall, pp. 172–84.

10 YOUNG, T.R. (1980) *op. cit.* p. 19. Compare Education Group, Centre for Contemporary Cultural Studies (1981) *Unpopular Education* London, Hutchinson, pp. 208–10.

11 This information is presented in the Appendices of the published reports as indicated in note 7. False precision has been an endemic problem in research quantifying expressed social attitudes. Only attitude patterns that are both substantively relevant to the theoretical perspective developed in earlier chapters as well as statistically significant at the .05 confidence level will be discussed in this text. For assessments of the uses and limitations of statistical criteria of significance see IRVINE, J. et al. (1979) *Demystifying Social Statistics* London, Pluto.

12 These objections have been dealt with in more concrete detail in LIVINGSTONE, D.W. and HART, D.J. (1980) *op. cit.*

13 GLABERMAN, M. (1975) *The Working Class and Social Change* Toronto, New Hogtown Press, pp. 14–16.

14 GRAMSCI, A. (1971) *Selections from the Prison Notebooks* London: Lawrence and Wishart, p. 333.

15 See, for example FLETCHER, F. and DRUMMOND, R. (1979) *Canadian Attitude Trends 1960–1978* Montreal, Institute for Research on Public Policy.

16 All significant attitudinal differences associated with each of these social background variables are presented and discussed in the summary reports.

17 This conclusion is based not only on our own findings, but also on comparisons with a 1975 survey by AULD, D. (1979) 'Public sector awareness and preferences in Ontario' *Canadian Tax Journal* 27, (2), pp. 172–82.

18 WYATT, H.E. (1980) 'Walking the Education Tightrope' Speech delivered at Third Congress on Education, Canadian School Trustees Association, Montreal, June 1, p. 6.

19 For an insightful general account of the economic and political factors involved in this development, see CAMERON, D. (1972) *Schools for Ontario: Policy Making, Administration and Finance in the 1960s* Toronto, University of Toronto Press.

20 Compare, for example, HUBER, J. and FORM, W. (1973) *Income and ideology: An Analysis of the American Political Formula* New York, Free Press, and RINEHART, J. and OKRAKU, I. (1974) 'A study of class consciousness' *Canadian Review of Sociology and Anthropology* 11 (August), pp. 197–213.

21 LIVINGSTONE, D.W. (1979) *op. cit.* pp. 10–11.

22 *Ibid.*

23 For a useful overview see HARP, J. (1980) 'Social inequalities and the transmission of knowledge' in HARP, J. and HOFLEY, J. (Eds) *Structural Inequality in Canada* Scarborough, Prentice-Hall, pp. 219–46. But labour leaders have not needed to be dependent on traditional social scientists' research in this regard. More serious is their general failure to make effective use of the documentations produced by working class community activists themselves; see, for example, Park School Community Council (1974) 'Downtown kids aren't dumb: They need a better program' in MARTEL, G. (Ed) *The Politics of the Canadian Public School* Toronto, Lorimer, pp. 39–64.

24 For Ontario, see LIVINGSTONE, D.W. and HART, D.J. (1981) *Public Attitudes 1980 op. cit.* pp. 6–9 and ADAMS, M. et al (1976) *Educational Perspectives: A Survey of 10,000 Ontario Students, Teachers, and Parents* Toronto, Ministry of Education, pp. 79–80. Compare ELAM, S. (Ed) (1978) *A Decade of Gallup Polls of Attitudes Toward Education, 1969–1978* Bloomington, Phi Delta Kappan.

25 See CEA Task Force (1979) *op. cit.*

26 The benchmark policy documents in this regard are Provincial Committee on Aims and Objectives of Education in the Schools of Ontario (1968) *Living and Learning* Toronto, Newton Publishing Company for the Ontario Department of Education; and Ministry of Education (1981) *Secondary Education Review Project Report* Toronto, The Ministry.

27 See, for example, ADAMS, M. (1972) *Quality Education in Ontario* Toronto, Environics Research Group, pp. 73–76.

28 It should be noted that most teachers are located in the professional employee position. By our estimates, about sixty per cent of the Ontario teaching force support their own right to strike. It follows that the attitudes of other professional employees are less supportive.

29 LIVINGSTONE, D.W. and HART, D.J. (1980) 'Educational Ideologies and Public Attitudes in Advanced Capitalism' Paper presented at Symposium on the Production of Social Distinctions in Classrooms: Beyond Passive Analysis, Ontario Institute for Studies in Education, Toronto, November, pp. 49–52.

30 See, for example, M. ADAMS, et al. (1976) *op cit.*, pp. 39–47, regarding expressed views of abstract and concrete aspects of Ontario education. Compare MANN, M. (1970) *op. cit.*

31 GLABERMAN, M. (1975) *op. cit.*

32 WILLIAMS, R. (1961) *The Long Revolution* London, Chatto and Windus. See the summary in Figure 4.

33 Further details are provided in LIVINGSTONE, D.W. and HART, D.J. (1981) *op. cit.*, pp. 15–18.

34 See, for example, SANOFF, A. (1982) 'Hard times come to graduate schools' *U.S. News and World Report*, January 25, pp. 46–47.

35 QUINNEY, R. (1974) *Critique of Legal Order* Boston, Little and Brown, pp. 12–13, argues that: 'The modern institutional order finds its legitimation in an ideology that stresses the rationality of science and technology. A generalized belief in the importance of controlled scientific-technical progress gives legitimacy to a particular class – the one that utilizes science and technology. The extent to which this ideology pervades the whole culture limits the possibility of emancipation, limits even the perception of the need for liberation'.

36 For the most fully developed version of this thesis, see BRAVERMAN, H. (1974) *Labor and Monopoly Capital* New York: Monthly Review Press. This comment is by no means intended to deny the central contribution of Braverman's work to Marxist studies of the capitalist labour process.

37 See LIVINGSTONE, D.W. and HART, D.J. (1981) *op. cit.*, p. 29.

38 There appears to be less current reluctance to pursue such blunt tactics in the other major state social service sectors, as indicated by the recent crushing of a strike by Ontario hospital workers. See especially Ontario Public Service Employees' Union (1980) *Ontario's Mental Health Care Breakdown* Toronto: OPSEU.

39 See, for example, MATAS, R. (1982) 'Dramatic schooling changes in the works' *Toronto Globe and Mail* January 6, pp. 1–2.

40 As Lloyd Axworthy, Canadian Employment Minister, noted recently in announcing yet another attempt, 'There has been a vacuum in our training approach. Not only does industry have to modernize – so do training programs.' See MONTGOMERY, C. (1982) 'Federal training blitz aimed at skilled jobs' *Toronto Globe and Mail* January 7, p. 1. See also Employment and Immigration Canada (1981) *Labour Market Development in the 1980s* Ottawa, Minister of Supply and Services. An insightful analysis of the English experience, and most particularly of the Manpower Services Commission, is provided by Education Group, Centre for Contemporary Cultural Studies (1981) *Unpopular Education* London, Hutchinson, pp. 228–40.

41 Ontario Ministry of Education official cited in MATAS, R. (1982) *op. cit.*, p. 1.

42 The corporate elite have been defined here as members of the boards of directors of corporations having sufficient assets to be ranked within the biggest three hundred capitalist enterprises in Canada. The inner core of the working class is regarded as unionized proletarian workers in firms with over one thousand employees in the primary resource industries, manufacturing, construction, and related transportation sectors of the economy. Further details appear in LIVINGSTONE, D.W. *Class and Class Consciousness in Advanced Capitalism* (to be published).

43 See, for example, LIVINGSTONE, D.W. and HART, D.J. (1981) *op. cit.*, pp. 5–8 and passim. Of course, Marxist analysts must also be wary of the opposite problem of class reductionism.

44 JESSOP, B. (1974) *op. cit.*, p. 266.

45 For illustrations see LOMAX, B. (1976) *Hungary 1956* London, Allison and Busby; MAILER, P. (1977) *Portugal: The Impossible Revolution* London, Solidarity; and HOYLES, A. (1973) *Imagination in Power: The Occupation of Factories in France in 1968* London, Spokesman Books.

Chapter Five

Intellectual and Popular Images of the Educational and Social Future

Three essential ingredients can be distinguished in any effort to restructure current social reality: understanding of the existing society, a vision of the future, and a strategy for getting there. However elaborate it may be, an image of a desirable future that is not based on a critical understanding of contemporary social forces and strategically linked with social practice is merely a suggestive fantasy. Conversely, when normatively-based envisioning of possible futures is truncated or deferred – as it typically has been within twentieth century forms of thought – approaches to the future are likely to consist of either ameliorative or apocalyptic extrapolations from historical conditions, and largely expedient political tactics. In previous chapters, I have offered a critical if incomplete understanding of the character of current advanced capitalist societies and especially of educational conditions, in terms of general analyses of class relations. In the following chapter, I will make a few more general remarks about strategies for creating educational and social futures. What is presented here is basically a critical inventory of alternative images of the future that might be considered by subordinate group activists in educational and social change initiatives. First, the sorts of visions of the future that have been articulated by bourgeois and traditional intellectuals and by socialist intellectuals, respectively, are reviewed. Then some empirical assessments are offered of the images of the future held by ordinary citizens and particularly by 'rank and file' members of different class positions. Popular sentiments about the future have been largely ignored by visionary intellectuals and policy makers, bourgeois and socialist alike.

Intellectual Traditions and the Future[1]

Throughout this century, it has been commonplace for shapers of mass opinion in advanced industrial societies to dismiss as merely 'utopian' anyone who puts forward a vision of desirable future society, and to get on with more 'realistic' pursuits. In the judgment of one social analyst, this tendency has become so pronounced that ' . . . for the first time in the three thousand years of Western civilization, there has been a massive loss of capacity or even will, for renewal of images of the future . . . constructive images . . . generally accepted idealistic images'.[2] Of course, it should also be recognized that one person's 'realism' has often been another's 'utopia' and that anti-utopian attacks also often imply a rival moral view of what general principles should determine the life and structure of society.[3]

The major contending intellectual traditions of our epoch may be broadly distinguished as bourgeois and socialist.[4] Socialists have been explicitly committed to an egalitarian restructuring of society, identifying foremost with those who are materially disadvantaged and exploited, while the more predominant bourgeois and traditional intellectuals have characteristically viewed the continuation of most social inequalities as inherently unavoidable and presumed to be speaking to and for universalistic interests. But twentieth century socialists have, generally, been at least equally scornful of 'utopians' as bourgeois thinkers have been. Despite these concerted attacks, some visionary thinkers have continued, within both bourgeois and socialist traditions, to put forward images of preferred futures.[5] The critical social analyses and/or strategies of most of the idealistic visionaries to be considered here have been woefully inadequate, but their images of preferred futures do deserve serious consideration in humane efforts to shape the future.

As noted in Chapter Three, the system of dominant beliefs that emerged with the Industrial Revolution and the Renaissance is clearly distinguishable from the world view of the Middle Ages by its emphasis on individualism, nationalism, mastery over nature, rationalism, materialism, and secular progress.[6] The twentieth century has seen substantial, if segmented, intellectual questioning of each of these precepts as articles of faith. Massive collectivist restructuring has also occurred in some societies. We are, perhaps, living in a period of epochal transition. But while the several varieties of socialist intellectuals have been a most visible contending force against established structural inequalities, they have continued to overlap significantly in their mode of thought with those bourgeois intellectuals most deliberately concerned with legitimating current social relations. Of course, this is merely to observe again that historical ideological forms can no more be abruptly overturned than material structures can. The images of preferred futures drawn by some visionaries do, however, suggest dimensions of quite comprehensive transformations of existing societies.

My purpose here is to provide a brief indicative summary of bourgeois and socialist attempts to construct images of the future. In this space, I can only cite from among the Western bourgeois and socialist visions and make reference to Canadian examples where available.

Bourgeois Intellectual Visions of the Future

A tenacious adherence to the value of individual liberty *per se* remains a constant distinguishing tenet of contemporary bourgeois ideology. However, as the discourse analysis of Chapter Three illustrates, the conception of *laissez faire* competition and individual entrepreneurial initiative promulgated by political philosophers from Hobbes to Mill has been largely displaced by consumerist-oriented versions of possessive individualism more appropriate to the highly concentrated and centralized capitalist enterprises of today. Similarly, the straightforward nineteenth century belief in the immutability of social progress has given way to a more complex and generalized notion of the power of science and the inevitability of technological rationalization, which has become just as central as possessive individualism in the dominant contemporary bourgeois world view. The prevailing bourgeois approach to the future is best exemplified by efforts at 'value-free' technological forecasting. Using a variety of 'objective' techniques, such studies end up making ameliorative extrapolations of existing social conditions. But, virtually all such works, even those scientific extrapolations that have recently perceived nature's limits to material progress, may be seen as ambiguous attempts to reconcile such de-personified technological rationality with a modicum of individual consumer rights.

Herman Kahn's 'basic, long-term multifold trend' is a representative and influential example. He posits increasing accumulation and diffusion of scientific and technological knowledge, growing literacy and education, worldwide industrialization and modernization, as well as increasingly bourgeois, bureaucratic, meritocratic elites, and an increasingly 'sensate' (utilitarian, hedonistic) culture and increasing affluence and leisure.[7] The closely related 'post-industrial society' image promulgated by such authors as Daniel Bell anticipates continuing technological growth and innovation (particularly in the area of intellectual technologies for decision-making), the growing centrality of theoretical knowledge, continuing expansion of tertiary-level occupations and the increasing eminence of a professional and technical class.[8] Marshall McLuhan's probes and postulations on the extension of technocratic media to the 'global village' are perhaps the most widely-known Canadian example of this dominant approach to thinking about the future.[9] To the technological forecaster – typically a consultant to corporations or state agencies – creating the social future apparently means discovering trends and then using further technical ingenuity to either mute or facilitate them. However sophisticated they become, such approaches are based on a presumption that the future really depends on forces that are beyond human capacity to control in any significant way. The enduring image of the future left by all such writings is one of irreversible technocratic trends remote from whatever social and political capacities ordinary people might retain.

As this technological mode of thought was applied to conceiving educational futures by traditional intellectuals in the period of liberal reforms that persisted into the early 1970s, it usually resulted in the anticipation of continuing trends toward more open learning systems. The 'basic long-term, multifold trend in education' was seen to involve such items as child-centred learning as enjoyment, a broad and changing curriculum responding to individual needs and interests, with development of the whole individual, lifelong learning, and plenty of compensatory education.[10] As the current economic crisis has become more evident, educational forecasters along with the rest have tended to concentrate somewhat more on technological rationalization *per se*; the most recent educational forecasts are preoccupied with such matters as adapting education to 'tomorrow's electronic world', and how to teach faster by engaging both body and mind in the learning process.[11] The basic assumption that continues to underlie such technological forecasting, whatever references are made to specific policy choices within educational or other societal institutions, is that such institutions must adapt to a future 'post-industrial' society whose basic structure is inevitable.[12]

This is by no means to suggest that all bourgeois and traditional intellectuals are easily accepting of such 'value-free', 'surprise-free', extrapolationist conceptions. When one examines the efforts of such intellectuals to set out more morally-explicit images of preferred futures, there is no such underlying consensus to be found. In this respect, I can agree with Warren Wagar's judgment that the central spiritual fact of the last hundred years of Western intellectual thought has been an ever-accelerating disintegration. 'Everything fragments. A steadily rising number of educated people are engaged in producing a steadily rising number of competing and essentially private systems of belief or escape from belief.'[13] Any attempt to categorize this cacophony of proposals must be incomplete. Relying largely on Michael Marien's bibliographic surveys of the general English language literature[14] and Hugh Stevenson's similar efforts in Canada,[15] I will simply outline some of the most prominent recent forms of bourgeois thinking about preferred futures. These may be identified respectively as *cosmic evolutionist, reconstructed individualist, ecological limits, decentralist, world order models* and *piecemeal change* perspectives. It should be noted that the social form of education is often not singled out for detailed treatment in these normative images of the future. But its character is strongly implied in the general delineation of desired social forms and, almost invariably, education is appealed to as the critical strategic process for realizing the preferred future.

Cosmic evolutionism is the highly abstracted, optimistic view that humanity is generally being transformed to a more desirable stage, travelling irrepressibly through any number of idealized levels of spiritual existence and consciousness. Teilhard de Chardin's writings on the development of an Ultra-Humanity, with its thinking sphere (that is, 'noosphere') becoming increasingly unified, probably offer the most elaborate schema of this type.[16]

Reconstructed individualism begins with a much less lofty focus on human needs and interests and tries to sketch out new social forms that could fulfil such individual needs better than the present society. Pitirim Sorokin's *The*

Reconstruction of Humanity is a comprehensive blueprint of this type, while B.F. Skinner's advocacy of a technology of behaviour that can shape environment for a better society provides a more controversial example. The quasi-political pronouncements of some recent socio-biologists, while even more shrouded in scientism than Skinner's, are just as controversial among intellectuals; but, socio-biology could provide more comprehensive technical rationales than Skinner's mechanical behaviourism for normative social policies that purport to be scaling down social institutions in order to give vent to creative individual instincts.[17]

The recent concern with *ecological limits to growth* has given rise to essentially the reverse approach. That is, population growth, resource scarcities, rampant technology and pollution threats may be perceived as requiring substantial changes in individual interests and habits, as well as some governmental reform. The British *Blueprint for Survival* and Ferkiss' discussion of 'ecological humanism' spell out their various desired changes in individual and social ethos most clearly.[18]

Decentralist thinkers represent a more long-standing reaction against the general dehumanizing effects of big business and big government. In direct contrast to technological extrapolationists such as Kahn, they have advocated small-scale communities and technologies, modest comfort rather than affluence, and a do-it-yourself philosophy. Ralph Barsodi has proposed the most elaborate decentralist future, and Schumacher and Illich are among the most imaginative recent proponents.[19]

The desire for peace is even more long-standing and has become of heightened concern in a world of big powers and resource scarcities. The *World Order Models Project* represents the most ambitious effort yet to envision preferred social futures on a global scale. In one of these studies, Richard Falk[20] has developed a model of preferred global institutions based specifically on the values of peace, social and economic well-being, fundamental human rights, and protection of environmental quality. He has done this in the context of a detailed analysis of historical trends and patterns in world society and has tried to outline a transition strategy.

Distinct from and more numerous than all of the above currents of morally-explicit bourgeois thought that at least suggest some fundamental restructuring of established social relations, *piecemeal change thinkers* manage to propose desirable futures without questioning any of the dominant social structures. Such thinkers generally have differed from technological extrapolators only in their lack of pretense to scientific neutrality. One indicative example of such a vision of piecemeal change is the 'humanistic capitalism' image, promulgated by John D. Rockefeller and others,[21] which argues that business and social policy should be more closely integrated, with the growth and consumption ethic being balanced by ecological and self-realization ethics. In substance it differs little from *Industry and Humanity*,[22] published by McKenzie King in 1918 while he was working for the Rockefellers, and before becoming Canada's Prime Minister.

As the current crisis has persisted, inadequacies of extrapolative economic forecasting based on technological optimism have become more obvious. Conversely, the more pessimistic technological projections in recent years have won corporations and governments few supporters. Dominant groups have been moved to rely more directly on the possessive individualism strands of the dominant ideology, and on those conservative intellectuals who most convincingly espouse them. In these views, the stress on consumer affluence is de-emphasized in favour of 'supply side' economic individualism and an insistence on the importance of human creativity (which is at least vaguely to recognize the centrality of productive labour to any capitalist revitalization). However destructive neo-conservative economic and social policies may prove to be of established institutional forms, they remain steadfastly focused on market criteria and therefore involve inherently piecemeal visions of the future. Particularly in American variants, such views often reflect an ingenious interweaving of normative appeals to acquisitive individualism with ostensibly scientific analyses – the essential feature of modern capitalist ideological dominance.[23]

The extent of ideological dependence on the United States is generally overwhelming in Canadian bourgeois policy literature. As Stevenson's bibliography shows, this writing is predominantly within the piecemeal change mode. It has characteristically been reflective of American themes, but with cycles of reactionary nationalist sentiment. Very little of this work has been of a positive visionary nature. The most notable recent exception is probably Herschel Hardin's *A Nation Unaware*,[24] which sees in the Canadian economic foundations of public enterprise and interregional distribution, the distinct roots of a new, ideologically vigorous, world culture.

Technological forecasters of educational futures have sometimes offered quite detailed visions. This has not been an especially demanding task, since such models invariably take the persistence of many of the established structural features of state-run, mass-based school systems in advanced capitalism for granted and proceed to speculate about details of more open or closed curricula.[25] However, more normatively-based alternative images of the future among bourgeois and traditional intellectuals tend to offer only vague suggestions about how education should be provided. In such images, the open-closed continuum of the learning process is expanded beyond the range permitted by established school structures. At one extreme is the ultimate in closed learning systems, Skinner's box. At the other, are various decentralist approaches emphasizing educational pluralism and self-determination.[26]

Among the latter, the deschooling view developed by Ivan Illich and Everett Reimer has been the most substantial.[27] As noted earlier, the deschoolers' critique systematically identifies and attacks most of the dominant internal structures of schools, including features that had been taken for granted even by most contemporary socialist intellectuals. They also propose an array of alternative forms of education including skills exchanges, peer matching, and a related educational voucher system. There are richly provocative materials here

for humane efforts to create educational futures. However, it is when traditional intellectuals offer their most radical critiques of and alternatives to the
established order that the limitations of their visionary approaches become
most apparent. Illich and Reimer offer no specific analysis of the social forces
involved in maintaining current educational institutions nor any substantial
awareness of the pervasive effects of labour markets in shaping the immediate
educational interests of learners.[28] Hence they are surprised when their widely
heard populist appeals have little impact on the dominant structure of
schooling. Illich's proposals have probably been considered more seriously in
Ontario than anywhere else in the advanced capitalist societies. But when a
post-secondary education commission put forward his only proposals that
would have any direct impact on the array of social forces and the character of
labour markets (that is, a moderate voucher financing system, and a very
limited de-linking of certain kinds of certification and jobs), these were rejected
out of hand. Illich, the classic traditional intellectual, himself begins to be
drawn toward socialist conclusions:

> In fact, a technological society that provides conditions for men to
> recuperate personally (and not institutionally) the sense of potency to
> learn and to produce, which gives meaning to life, depends on
> restrictions that must be imposed on the technocrat who now controls
> both services and manufacture.[29]

Overall, such twentieth century intellectual visions of desirable alternative
futures appear to have served the hegemonic interests of dominant groups in
Western capitalist societies just as well as do the much more extensive
'objective' efforts of most bourgeois and traditional intellectuals to document
existing social relations as the enduring reality. Even in the most radical
alternative visions, the critiques of current conditions and the proposals put
forward generally either ignore existing wealth and power inequities, or
criticize apparent inequities whilst remaining oblivious to the material relations
of domination and exploitation that serve to reproduce them, and assume that
populist appeals or localized community actions will be sufficient to overcome
obstacles. Even the most fervent decentralists have been content to make
populist appeals, which at best have inspired some isolated new community
experiments. Very rarely is the preferred image linked to a detailed analysis of
society or strategic considerations. Even where this is the case, as in the most
sophisticated world order models, there is no theoretical effort to discern the
relations among social forces underlying observable trends, or to connect
suggested strategies with identifiable social groups. The fundamental understanding, visions, and strategies of active bourgeois social forces remain largely
unaffected by such disengaged visionaries. At the heart of each of these
bourgeois or traditional intellectual efforts at developing an image of a desired
alternative future is a definite one-sidedness. What lies at the basis of
contemporary bourgeois thought is an inability to go beyond the appearances
of the form of corporate capitalism to the reality of the ensemble of social

relations. No adequate intellectual conception of a desired alternative future is possible until the totality of corporate capitalist social relations begins to be grasped and strategic agents based on such analysis are identified.

Socialist Intellectual Visions of the Future

The early socialists, without exception, were 'utopian'. Thinkers such as Fournier, Weitling, Saint-Simon, Owen and Cobbett were all moved by their revolutionary distaste for the capitalist disorder to attempt to develop precise pictures of how the world ought to be.[30] While recognizing a debt to these founders of socialism, Marx and Engels, in the light of their own scientific socialism, vigorously dismissed utopian socialists' visions as pure fantasies.[31]

Marx and Engels were generally reluctant not only to delineate detailed and abstract notions of the future, but also to develop even the broadest systematic theory of the dynamics of socialism. But, within their writings, especially the early writings, there is an image of a world-scale future society which would be non-alienating, based on production for need, and where full social and political democracy would flourish. There are fragments of discussions of the future society in such later works as *Critique of the Gotha Programme* (Which Lenin's *State and Revolution* does little more than echo) and in Engels' *The Origin of the Family, Private Property and the State*.

The basic features of Marx's notion of a desirable form of education for a socialist society, as well as for the proletariat in advanced industrial capitalism, are quite discernible in his writings. However, education is never treated, as it commonly is in dominant bourgeois conceptions, as an isolated institutionalized phenomenon. Rather, it is regarded as an integral living part of the social totality, with dialectical relations with material production and social consciousness. Educational conditions are taken into account, for example, in Marx's early development of a theory of personality, the theory of technology in *Capital*, as well as in analyses of child labour and consideration of political strategies of the labour movement.[32] As Castles and Wustenberg summarize:

> The core of Marxist theory is the idea of the development of a new type of human being: 'the totally developed individual' who is capable of controlling a rational process of production and distribution within a new form of society – an association of free men' ... Linking education with productive work is a basic element of the Marxist theory of education. Indeed, in some Eastern European countries there has been a tendency to reduce Marxist education theory to this principle. Polytechnic education really means much more than this. Its aim is to produce 'fully developed human beings', which means people who are capable not only of doing productive work but also of controlling production and running society. Every person must be capable of mastering the aims, technology and concrete methods of

production processes, and understanding their relationship with society in general. This does not mean that specialization can be completely avoided, but rather that everybody must possess sufficient basic knowledge and capabilities to be able to learn any occupation as needed. The preconditions for this are:

- a high level of education for everybody;
- overcoming the division between manual and mental work: polytechnic education is pointless if one person spends a lifetime doing purely mental work, another only manual labour; all workers must have the chance of doing both;
- removal of the distinction between working and learning, between school and work; every child should take part in socially necessary production from an early age; every adult should have the chance to go on learning, both at work and elsewhere;
- everybody must participate in planning and decision-making; once polytechnic education has given everybody an understanding of social aims and technological problems, there can be no justification for excluding anybody from the organs of planning and decision-making: a society with polytechnic education cannot but be a democratic society.[33]

More specifically, in the Geneva Resolution of 1866 Marx called on the labour movement to struggle within capitalism for a type of formal education which would combine the learning of basic cultural capabilities (reading, writing, basic science grounding), development of bodily capacity (gymnastics, sports), and technological training which 'imparts the general principles of all processes of production and simultaneously initiates the child and young person in the practical use and handling of the elementary instruments of all trades'.[34] Marx clearly perceived that the generic nature of machinofacture would compel capitalists to encourage the development of basic skills, and that the essential educational conflict would be over the extent to which workers could be turned into insecure and malleable specialists or, conversely, expand their versatility and general understanding of both the production process and the structure of society.[35] As we have seen in previous chapters, in spite of a massive degree of segmentation of labour markets and fragmentation of the social division of labour in production, this conflict remains central to capitalist forms of schooling today.

The official inheritors of Marx and Engels – in the form of Kautsky and the Second International, and Stalin and the Third International – dismissed all discussions of a preferred future as reactionary, utopian and a general heresy. The lack of a conception of a desirable socialist society has been a serious shortcoming of Marxist praxis. To take the example of the Russian Revolution, the Bolsheviks simply did not have a conception of what was to be done after the Kerensky government had been overthrown. It would appear that the Bolsheviks attempted to find theoretical guidelines in a haphazard fashion in various footnotes of Marx and Engels, without ever aiming to develop a theory based on the specificity of their situation and the inherent possibilities contained within that period. The theoretical confusion and fierce debates on exactly what was developing and should be developing in the immediate years after the revolution is a reflection of the lack of clear goals and a general theory of socialist society. Debate and confusion were ended once the monolithic state under Stalin was erected and a new theory was imposed. Those who dared to question were eliminated.[36]

The promising initial efforts, led by Krupskaya and others, to develop a polytechnical educational system in the first socialist country, as well as the subsequent educational bureaucratization and replication of many of the structural features of capitalist forms of schooling in both the Soviet Union and other transitional socialist countries, are usefully outlined by Castles and Wustenberg. As they conclude with regard to the German Democratic Republic (GDR), which has the most quantitatively developed school system in the Soviet bloc:

> The SED [the ruling Socialist Unity Party] has taken the marxist concept of polytechnic education and robbed it of its real content. Instead of 'totally developed individuals' capable of creatively transforming society, the aim is the well-trained, hard-working, conformist wage workers. This leads to a double contradiction. First, by stifling originality and creativity from the earliest age the SED may well defeat its own aim of the rapid development of the forces of production. Scientific creativity is the result of the free development of children's curiosity and search for knowledge ... Second, even in the emasculated form in which it is practised in the GDR, polytechnic education does raise questions about the political and social implications of the production process. The SED does all it can to keep the population of the GDR ignorant of the real problems of society, and treats them as if they were politically infantile ... The contradiction between constantly telling [highly educated] working people that they are the rulers of society, and in reality excluding them from any form of control will not remain latent forever.[37]

The post-war intellectual and worker opposition movements opposing existing party structures in such countries, most notably Yugoslavia, Hungary, Czechoslovakia, and Poland, offer increasingly graphic confirmation of this view. It is through the practical efforts to obtain economic and political self-government in such transitional societies, with major enterprises no longer based on capital accumulation and with advanced forms of machinofacture production, that the most concrete outlines of a possible future socialist society have begun to emerge.[38] Similar grounded efforts have been reciprocally related with some of the most specific intellectual conceptions of economic democracy and socialist education to emerge in advanced capitalist societies.[39]

However, the dominant tendency among Marxist intellectuals in advanced capitalism over the past several generations has been to ignore such efforts both at home and abroad. With the bureaucratization and isolation of the Soviet State and the failure of other proletarian revolutions in Europe, major thinkers of Western Marxism became increasingly secluded in universities and/or bureaucratized Russian Communist parties. Thus they came much more into contact with idealist and official systems of thought than with working-class practice.[40] Just like the major bourgeois spokesmen, these professional Marxist philosophers came to rely heavily on formalistic scientific methods while tending to diminish generic sensuous elements of social life. Under these conditions, they generally lapsed into pessimism about the future. As Perry Anderson observes:

> ... between 1920 and 1960, Marxism slowly changed colors in the West. The confidence and optimism of the founders of historical materialism, and of their successors, progressively disappeared. Virtually every one of the significant new themes in the intellectual muster of this epoch reveals the same diminution of hope and loss of certainty.[41]

The most substantial exception at a philosophical level has been the work of Ernst Bloch.[42] He has attempted to re-evaluate utopian views and hopes of humanity from within a Marxist perspective. He argues, for instance, that:

> ... [U]topian possibilities are established in the concreteness and openness of the material of history: indeed of the material of nature itself. This is the objective-real possibility which surrounds existing actuality with tremendous latency, and affords the potency of *human* hope its link with the *potentiality within the world*. Concrete utopia is bound up with dialectical materialism, and prevents it from defaulting – prevents it from discarding its visions of a goal ahead.[43]

But Bloch's work has been largely ignored to date.[44]

On a more practical level, therefore, it is not surprising that most of the concrete socialist visions of preferred futures in this century have been generated by non-orthodox socialists, mainly by people engaged in either anarchist, syndicalist or religious socialist movements. Following in the tradition of Proudhon,[45] a number of twentieth century anarchists have tried to animate their preferred futures by publishing fairly concrete sketches. Kropotkin's turn of the century outline of non-hierarchical organization in *Fields, Factories and Workshops* remains the most detailed vision.[46] Contemporary anarchists such as Paul Goodman, Murray Bookchin and Colin Ward have offered more partial pictures of decentralized social forms in response to current problems of alienation and technological change.[47] The Paris Commune, the Spanish collectives, and the university student movements of the 1960s may all be seen in part as testaments to the appeal of the anarchist mode of the thought.

Starting with the Christian Socialists of the nineteenth century, there have been attempts by religious intellectuals to respond to the social problems of unregulated capitalism by combining the social gospel with socialist politics. Visions suggesting spiritual regeneration in co-operative communes appeared quite frequently in the aftermath of World War I, and there are still prominent religious leaders engaged in reformulating and struggling for the same moral vision.[48] Religious socialist visions have inspired some of the most enduring confederated communes, such as the Israeli *kibbutzim* movement. While remaining a very small part of the population of Israel, these co-operatives have been among the most effective communities in breaking down unnecessary social division of labour and encouraging combined development of education with work on an advanced technological basis.[49] There have also been attempts, particularly in France, to create a Christian Marxist vision of the future.[50]

Canadian socialist thought has always depended heavily on British and American influences, and in no way has it surpassed their visionary accomplishment. The most elaborate Canadian socialist visions were largely inspired by the social gospel movements in the 1920s. But the new co-operative commonwealths proposed by Salem Bland and Edward Partridge were soon forgotten.[51] The founding of the Co-operative Commonwealth Federation (the predecessor of the current New Democratic Party) in the early 1930s provided a major vehicle for the development of socialist thought, but the polygot composition including religious socialist, trade unionist and agrarian protest tendencies, as well as the British Fabian-inspired intellectuals of the League for Social Reconstruction, led to the dominance of pragmatic politics and the muting of visionary inclinations.[52] The small Canadian Communist parties have typically adhered to external proscriptions on preferred futures thinking, and the anarchist tradition has been quite negligible in Canada. However, confrontation with anarchist formulations has begun to stimulate some possibility of original thinking about desirable political futures among mainstream English Canadian socialists.[53] In Quebec, Jacques Grand'Maison's prolific writings on alternative social forms are the prominent example of visionary religious socialist thought.[54] The recent electoral success of the Parti Quebecois is probably provoking more serious reflection in this period about desirable alternative futures than has occurred since Confederation. But this is only to say that, to date, Canadian socialist thought has been just as devoid of intelligible, indigenously developed images of preferred futures as Canadian bourgeois thought has been.

One of the very few socialist movements in this century in an advanced capitalist society that has systematically attempted to develop a new theory and model of the desired future in conjunction with its specific social conditions has been *guild socialism*.[55] I will therefore outline it in some detail. Guild socialism was a British middle class intellectual movement which existed in a coherent shape from approximately 1912 to 1921.[56] The guild socialist critique of capitalism was that its democracy was a mere sham based on an assumption that people were politicaly free and had the right to vote. This democracy amounted to one minute each election, the time it took to cast a ballot, so that in a lifetime a person would have achieved an hour of democracy at best. There was no freedom and no equality as long as the fundamentally irrational wage system existed. According to guild theorists, the wage system was based on the autocracy of capitalism and was the basic problem with the capitalist order. Due to the wage system, a class struggle existed which could only end when the autocracy of capital was replaced by the self-government of workers.[57] In short, wage slavery perverted the latent potentiality of humanity.

The transition to a new society based on the ideas embraced by guild socialism was already underway. The guild theorists argued that in Britain workers were beginning to fight for control of the factories; new forms of rank and file organization to fight for union democracy and for a militant political platform were emerging.[58] Central to the entire guild movement was the view that unions had to be transformed into a small number of industrial unions that were organized on an industry-wide basis. As G.D.H. Cole, the leading spokesperson, argued:

> If industry is to be nationalized, only strong trade unions can prevent bureaucracy ...; if industry is to be syndicalized, only strong trade unions will be capable of running it. On either showing, trade unionism should be the first concern of labour.[59]

Existing in a period of international revolution and upsurge in worker militancy, the guildsmen learned a great deal from the experiences of socialists elsewhere. They became part of the movement that rejected reform for revolution as the only possible road to socialism. Cole was very clear, writing in 1920, that the State was a ruling class institution, a bureaucratic complex created for the master class and of no use to the workers. Given the nature of the State, the two possibilities for social revolutions, according to Cole, were either some industrial action like a general strike where the state crumbled, or civil war. Although difficulties existed with either alternative, Cole was extremely sceptical about the possibility of armed civil war, as the British workers were unarmed and the army was stable.[60]

Central to the transition from capitalism to guild socialism therefore was the process of education. Education was used in two senses. One was the informal sense in which workers learned from their own concrete practice. For example, Cole and Mellor suggested that:

> Step by step they will gain a foothold in control, and their experience will serve as an education alike to the leader and to the rank and file, till at length they find that they are quite able to dispense with the capitalist, and to carry on production themselves for the common benefit.[61]

The second sense was that of a formal education in workers' institutions like trade unions or the Central Labour College. In the struggle for socialism, 'even if education is not everything, it is at least a very great deal'.[62] In all of this intellectual outpouring about preferable organizational forms for a future socialist society, very little more specific was said about the form of education.

What, then, was the guild socialist preferred image of the future? For nearly all the movement's theorists, 'guild' implied voluntary organization and democratic management. The guild notion of socialism was a positive synthesis of the two dominant trends of the workers' movement at the time, namely syndicalism and the state socialist reformism of the Fabian socialists and Labour Party. It was argued that although the syndicalists were fundamentally correct in believing that there should be self-government in industry, their concern for producers was one-sided as there was more in society than producers and production. Whereas the Labour Party was concerned only with distribution of income and advocated nationalization as a universal panacea, the guild socialists perceived such state socialism as no more than state capitalism because nationalization *per se* produces no fundamental change in capitalism.[63]

In summary, the guild socialists would have a series of national industrial guilds which would be productive and which would control democratically all branches of manufacturing and resource extraction. All workers in an industry would be in a guild and their trades or specialities might be separately organized within this guild. As well, there would be a civic guild that would organize all state employees. National guilds would emerge from the transformation of industrial unions in the new society. All the guilds would be united in a central body; the guilds on a local basis would control production, and the national guild would serve the role of settling general problems and dealing with national issues in an industry. The Congress of Guilds would co-ordinate production and mediate differences that might emerge between guilds. The consumers would be represented via their own organization, and the consumers and producers would be organized on a local basis into communes. At the local level, coordination of problems and disputes would be settled in negotiation between local guild and consumer representatives. On a national level the consumer and guild organizations would also negotiate and settle disputes. The major bodies would be made up half by producers and half by consummers. Cole felt that voting and representation should be based on function, so citizens would often get more than one or two votes on the basis of their function as an individual or group, irrespective of the size of the group.[64]

The above description only hints at the great detail of the guild socialist image of future society. The guild socialists themselves were not consistent about whether this future society was considered a utopia or not, although at one point it was referred to as a 'scientific utopia'.[65] Certainly it was not an image developed out of concerns with the dynamic social relations of a future socialist society, but a more or less precise and schematically detailed model overly concerned with form.[66] But it was qualitatively different from most other twentieth century intellectual thinking about preferred futures in advanced capitalist societies. That is, it attempted to base itself on a real medium that, at that period, appeared to offer the potentiality for the guild socialist society, namely a militant working class that was moving in the direction of control of the factories.[67] To attempt to realize its preferred future it developed a conception of industrial unions that could be transformed into guilds.

In the final analysis, guild socialism remained a middle class intellectual movement throughout its existence. It was limited to a very specific period and all of its members and major theorists abandoned it within a short time. It was a reflection, nonetheless, of a social idealism that gripped both the intellectual and the worker. Its failure lay in its obsession with the form of the new society and in not developing a general theory of real social relations which would have helped it to exist beyond this limited period of revolutionary unrest from 1912 to 1921. Guild socialism did, however, provide a real contribution in its concern for industrial democracy and general social organization that went beyond reformism and syndicalism. In the broadest sense, the guild theorists stood for self-government based on decentralized producer and consumer organizations. The challenge remains to develop a liberating theory of the dynamics of the transition to socialism that takes into account such conceptions as those of the guild socialist intellectuals.

Explicit images of preferred futures among twentieth century Western socialist intellectuals have been even rarer than in bourgeois thought. When they have appeared it has typically been not as the formulation of a fluid theory of a desired socialist society, but as static schema unrelated in any dynamic way with the development of historical understanding or strategic considerations. The current international capitalist crisis represents a new period of great 'potentiality within the world', to use Bloch's term. There have recently been major advances in theoretical understanding of the historical dynamics of the economic and political bases of modern capitalism.[68] There is also a growing theoretical and strategic understanding of the nature of ideological hegemony, as indicated by the recuperation of Gramsci's work.[69] There is even some evidence of wider socialist interest in formulating visions of the future than at any time in this century.[70] But, for the moment, Western socialist intellectual visions of preferred futures remain less developed than those of the guild socialists and quite unconnected with the gains in historical understanding and strategic capacity. This is at once the failure and the promise of contemporary Western socialist thought.

Popular Images of the Future[71]

Over the past generation, in most advanced capitalist societies, professional futurists and other intellectuals, as well as many expert-dominated public and private commissions, have engaged in a wide variety of such more-or-less systematic efforts to envision probable or preferable societal futures.[72] Whether extrapolating present societal trends or stating a moral position on a particular sort of future, such efforts to construct long-term social policies have generally either ignored or presumed the actual orientations to the future existing among the general public. The common if generally tacit justification for this exclusion in advanced capitalism – as in the technologically rational societies of the Soviet bloc – is the general public's limited technical and academic knowledge. But inability to recall specific mathematical principles and historical details[73] is not a sufficient basis for inferring a similar incapacity to respond to social issues affecting everyday life. As Walter Hardwick, director of an intensive survey of the attitudes of Greater Vancouver citizens on urban issues concluded:

> There is really a high level of understanding of the nature and complexity of the major problems which have to be faced . . . to ensure a livable environment. The so-called experts don't appear to be any more knowledgeable than the public-at-large. The language of the public may be less sophisticated, but its depth of understanding is equal to that of the decision-makers' . . . In fact, when it comes to making policies for the future, I'm prepared to believe that almost any group of fifty citizens could do just as well as a group of experts in the fields of pollution, transportation and housing. After all, the citizen lives with these issues every day.[74]

In the realm of state schooling (as within all the major institutions of advanced capitalist society) policy making is done largely within a mileau of experts, under highly technical criteria of ways and means; and, while there may be shifts in the dominant educational philosophy of the associated intelligentsia, there is little disposition to comprehend public preferences that do not speak directly to such criteria. The numerous mass opinion surveys on current education have seldom been concerned with anything but reactions to institutionalized activities and school structures.[75] Hence, as in other areas of social policy making, the lay public is given a dependent reactive position. The few survey researchers who have asked have begun to discover significant differences in issues and preferences expressed by educational leadership and expressed by the general public.[76] But little effort has been made to determine whether such differences encompass any elements of alternative views of desirable future policies.

Some studies that have compared the attitudes on *current* issues of policy makers and the upper economic groups with those of the general public have recognized that the purported ignorance of social issues among the mass public is a misconception, much of the 'ignorance' that does exist being attributable to the avoidance of major issues and use of distracting themes by policy makers themselves; moreover, in spite of such obstacles, the mass public has been found to be both more liberal than political leaders and the upper economic groups and quite cogent on many issues.[77]

In view of these facts, the conducting and undistorted dissemination of sensitive studies of mass opinion toward the societal future may be seen as one small step toward increasing the lay public's collective self-awareness in large advanced industrial societies. Awareness of their own views of the future is, in any case, *one* of the minimal conditions required for all subordinate groups to begin to play an authentic role in long-term social policy making in all such societies.

A very small amount of scholarly research on ordinary people's images of the future has been conducted. This scattering of largely 'exploratory' studies over the past generation has dealt mainly with very diffuse and abstract orientations to the future and, partly for this reason, has been very easy for policy makers and the public alike to ignore. The general importance of images of the future as mediating factors in social action has been postulated by several contemporary traditional and socialist scholars.[78] Such theoretical work has not distinguished very clearly between hopes (what people want to see) and expectations (what they think will probably happen), or between people's attitudes regarding their personal future and their views on the societal future. Most of the empirical research has been on personal hopes and expectations. Such studies typically show no interest in discerning the societal contexts people hope or expect to live in, but rather take the continuation of the present institutional context for granted. The resulting impression – that the ways of life individuals foresee for themselves seldom differ from the ways of life lived in the present – is therefore pre-ordained by the research design. It is at least questionable that all attitudes about personal futures are confined within such narrow extrapolative views of future society.[79] Careful understanding of personal attitudes toward the future, and of the relationship between personal and societal futures, requires more explicit attention to attitudes concerning the *societal* future.

There have been several empirical studies of the most general future expectations or hopes of particular groups,[80] and several studies that have related people's future aspirations or expectations to their social backgrounds.[81] A few inquiries have examined the interplay between such general societal hopes and expectations and related both to respondents' social position.[82] But almost none have dealt with future social policy questions and been able to convey any substantive notion of ordinary people's preferred images of the societal future. As Galtung *et al* observed in 1976, in the study that still constitutes the major exception:

> There are still no large-scale efforts to use education to raise general future consciousness, at least not regarding the social future and how to make the future basically different from the past ... The various agents of socialization ... have all too often stressed the *status quo* or at least a future defined and to be accepted in advance. There were hardly any steps towards improving the capacity for utopias and imagination, except in small groups often labeled 'sectarian'. It is certainly no chance phenomenon that the majority of futurological books written during the last ten years are not dealing with the social future but with the technological prospects, and that there is not a single research project which comes close to the present one.[83]

Since so little critical scholarly attention has been paid to popular orientations to the social future, my purpose here is merely to draw on the results of the Galtung *et al* opinion survey (subsequently called the World Images 2000 Project)[84] and a somewhat similar survey that I conducted in Ontario (to be termed The Ontario Images 2000 project)[85], in order to suggest *very* tentatively some possible tendencies and class differences in contemporary popular images of the societal and educational future. It should be noted that most of these findings are quite dated. The World Images 2000 Project surveys occurred primarily in 1967–68 in various countries, and the Ontario Images 2000 Project was conducted in 1973. However, I know of no more recent directly comparable surveys. Needless to say, most of the general limitations of opinion surveys discussed in Chapter Four apply here as well. Inter-country comparisons of expressed opinions must be even further limited because of the differing material contexts, and numerous cultural differences in interpretation of concepts. In the present instance, there are also methodological differences in sample composition and the type of survey instrument.[86] Finally, it can be argued that the various surveys were conducted in two different political conjunctures within the world capitalist system, divided most graphically by May 1968.

Most of the World Images 2000 Project country surveys were conducted during 1967. This was a year of great international tension, highlighted by the escalation of Vietnam War, the Six Days War in the Middle East, the Greek army coup, and Sino-Soviet border disputes. However, 1968 saw a marked rise in social and political unrest *within* many of the advanced capitalist societies themselves, as well as in Czechoslovakia. Of the World Images 2000 Project surveys referred to here, only the Japanese and West German studies occurred in the wake of this domestic instability, which in some respects marked the onset of the current protracted capitalist crisis. As Ornauer notes in this respect, the responses to these surveys ' . . . *may* have been influenced by 1968's heavy student unrest in many countries of the world and by the events in Czechoslovakia'.[87] It may perhaps be argued that popular views on broad social structures in the distant future may be less malleable to current events than are current social attitudes. But certainly, as the World Images authors themselves suggest, 'there are good reasons to suspect that opinions on some problems surveyed in 1967/68 have undergone substantial changes since then . . . '[88]

Popular Images of the Societal Future

Among the most discernible general aspects of popular orientation to the societal future are the matters of how often people think about the future, how clear an image of future society they think they have, and – particularly in light of the previous discussion of predominant tendencies in intellectuals' views of the future – the extent to which popular futures thinking is dominated by technological extrapolations. A closely related issue is the anticipated amount of popular influence in future public affairs. Finally, we can review expressed opinions about one central substantive issue, the expected and desired degree of economic inequality. Again, the intention here is simply to suggest broad profiles in popular orientations to the future.

The first basic finding of the World Images 2000 Project was that popular concerns for the future and the tendency to think about the future were poorly developed.[89] However, as Table 35 indicates, there may have been a substantial increase in concern about the future in advanced capitalist societies since early 1968. The Japanese survey, which was conducted late in 1968, showed a notably higher frequency than the earlier studies. In the 1970 West German and 1973 Ontario surveys the majority of respondents indicated frequent thinking about the future. Table 36 summarizes the class differences expressed in frequency of thinking about the future in the most recent, Ontario survey. While majorities in all class positions indicated much concern, capitalists appear to have been most completely disposed to thinking about the future. On the other hand, productive proletarians and the chronically unemployed exhibited more preoccupation with immediate conditions than most others, along with pensioners – who very frequently offered the rationale that they had very little personal future left.

Table 35   Frequency of Thinking About the Societal Future, International Comparisons

	Much or very much %	Little or not at all %
Great Britain 1967	32	67
Netherlands 1967	20	79
Norway 1967	23	77
Japan 1968	43	58
West Germany 1970	56	44
Ontario 1973	64	35

Sources: ORNAUER, H. *et al* (1976) *Images of the World in the Year 2000: A Comparative Ten Nation Study* Paris: Mouton, p. 639; and LIVINGSTONE, D.W. (1976) *Ontario Images 2000 Project* files.

Predictably, a lot fewer respondents claimed to have achieved any considerable clarity in their images of the future. As Table 37 shows, corporate capitalists, along with managers and professional employees were more likely than most others to think that they do have at least a moderately clear image of future society. Certainly within the capitalist labour process, people in these three positions exercise much of the total societal control over the technical planning of future production, while small employers along with most others have generally become quite dependent on such corporate and state agents' initiatives, at least in this narrow economic sense. At the other extreme, the chronically unemployed expressed the greatest future disorientation. While at least a quarter of respondents in all other class positions said they had a moderately clear image of the future, the extent to which such images contain active and/or critical elements which relate to social practice is perhaps the key question.

Table 36   Frequency of Futures Thinking, Ontario 1973

	Much or very much %	Little or not at all %	N
Corporate Capitalists	100	–	8*
Small Employers	93	7	16*
Petty Bourgeoisie	70	30	96
Managers	79	21	65
Supervisors	70	30	55
Professional Employees	79	21	123
Non-Productive Proletariat	69	31	201
Productive Proletariat	54	46	304
Housewives	62	38	439
Chronically Unemployed**	50	50	27
Pensioners	53	47	163
Students	77	23	108
Total 18+ Population	64	36	1625

Source: LIVINGSTONE, D.W. (1976) *Ontario Images 2000 Project* files.
*   Extreme caution must be used in interpreting percentage distributions for both capitalist class positions in the 1973 Ontario sample because of these very small numbers. It should also be noted that rentier capitalists, who also comprise a very small proportion of the population, could not be distinguished from pensioners in this survey.
** Only those who have been unemployed for most of the previous year are counted here. Again, the small numbers of this group must be kept in mind.

Table 37   Clarity of Image of the Future, Ontario, 1973

	Moderately or very clear image %	Vague or no image %
Corporate Capitalists	67	33
Small Employers	33	67
Petty Bourgeoisie	36	64
Managers	52	48
Supervisors	31	69
Professional Employees	48	52
Non-Productive Proletariat	32	68
Productive Proletariat	28	72
Housewives	26	74
Chronically Unemployed	7	93
Pensioners	37	63
Students	36	64
Total 18+ Population	33	67

Source: LIVINGSTONE, D.W. (1976) *Ontario Images 2000 files.*

A second major finding of the World Images 2000 Project was that technological extrapolation was the predominant way of thinking about the future. Open-ended questions most frequently drew comments about technical progress and development. In the advanced capitalist societies, such comments were often combined with considerable pessimism and scepticism expressed on many items about the future benefits of science and technology. Galtung concludes that:

> ... [F]or the nations in our sample the future seems somehow to be synonymous with a technological future. The future is seen in technical terms, not in terms of culture, human enrichment, social equality, social justice, or in terms of international affairs ... People may also think in terms of social future but regard it as unchangeable. But it seems more probable that they have only been trained to think technologically and have no other types of thoughts as a response to the stimulus 'future'; or have at least not been trained to *express* any other thoughts. And this will then become self-reinforcing since no one will be stimulated by others to think about social futures.[90]

In the Ontario Images 2000 Project, people were asked how much influence they expected scientists and technologists would have in society by the year 2000. As Table 38 indicates, over four-fifths of respondents expected them to have more influence and the majority foresaw *much* more influence. This is only the most explicit of numerous indications of technological extrapolationist thinking expressed in this survey. It is interesting to note that, in addition to

Table 38   Influence of Scientists and Technologists in Society by the Year 2000, Ontario 1973

	Less %	Some %	More %	Much more %
Corporate Capitalists	–	12	12	76
Small Employers	–	8	22	71
Petty Bourgeoisie	–	6	38	51
Managers	5	15	28	52
Supervisors	–	12	30	58
Professional Employees	4	9	28	57
Non-Productive Proletariat	1	9	34	50
Productive Proletariat	3	9	27	59
Housewives	3	11	31	45
Chronically Unemployed	–	–	10	90
Pensioners	6	16	37	32
Students	2	11	31	54
Total 18+ Population	3	10	31	51

Source: LIVINGSTONE, D.W. (1976) *Ontario Images 2000 Project* files.

pensioners who for the most part would not be around to experience the future impact of technology, housewives whose work process has been least affected by modern technology were least likely to expect a much greater technological influence. Conversely, the chronically unemployed have already experienced the most direct negative consequences of automation; they were even more likely to expect increased future technological impact than capitalists, who as major beneficiaries to date expressed the most positive expectations of further technical 'progress'.

However, the association of pessimism and scientific scepticism with technological futures thinking generally remained much as was found in the earlier World Images 2000 Project. The most prominent type of comment among the vast majority who expected increasing influence for scientists and technologists concerned the need for remedial actions to counteract physical problems, problems often recognized as consequences themselves of technical 'progress'.

A female clerical proletarian, for example, subscribed to such a 'science to save us from science' view:

> Scientists will be the men attempting to solve the problems, like air pollution, that were caused by technology in the first place.

A teacher professional most clearly expressed the heightened concern for environmental problems in Ontario by 1973, and the presumption of technological solutions:

> With the need for pollution control, increased food production by whatever means possible, dwindling natural resources, etc., science and technology must of necessity play a major role.

A manager with an engineering background, while acknowledging a need for remedial uses of science, expected enlightened expansion of technological control of the natural environment:

> The goal is to control the environment and ensure proper adaptation to new technologies.

Others simply expected an increasing influence of scientists and technologists as an obvious prerequisite for maintenance and expansion of industrial society. While many specific items were cited – food, medicine, transportation, etc. – all illustrated a general belief in continuity of rapid technological development. As one productive proletarian, a welder, put it:

> They will be controlling the country due to the complexity of providing energy, synthetics, etc. to replace our natural resources [which] will have run out.

The tiny minority who expected diminishing roles for science and technology may also be worthy of brief comment here. Their views were very much focused on *social* reactions against technological domination. There was some questioning of the benefits of technology-based consumerism. As a student commented:

> People will start to realize that they don't need any more 'new' things than they have already.

There were also sentiments that scientists have overstepped ethical limits. This view, commonly based on religious conviction, was most bluntly expressed by a female pensioner:

> I think those men overestimate themselves and thereby will harvest great disappointment.

A proletarian machinist most clearly stated the general concern underlying this rare expectation of diminished technological control of society, but not without the ambivalence characteristic of most popular expressions of technological futures thinking:

> I expect ordinary intelligent people to insist on more control over scientists and technologists to insure happier results – cannot decide whether this would be good or bad.

In all of these surveys, respondents were also asked about the related issue of how much influence they anticipated for themselves in public affairs. The results are summarized in Table 39. What is most apparent is that very few of the respondents in these liberal democracies saw themselves playing a significant role in the public sphere. There was no indication that this expectation was reversed after early 1968. The fact that the majority in most countries expected very little or no influence is not suggestive of ardent pluralist political dispositions in advanced capitalism. Table 40 suggests how pervasive this passive expectation was among different class positions in Ontario. The majority in all classes said they expected little or no influence in public policy making in the future. About a third of small employers and managers did

Table 39   Expected Future Influence in Public Affairs, International Comparisons

	Great deal %	Moderate amount %	None or very little %	Can't say %
Great Britain 1967	1	28	69	3
Netherlands 1967	1	39	55	6
Norway 1967	–	50	46	3
Japan 1968	4	12	56	28
West Germany 1970	–	35	63	1
Ontario 1973	4	18	73	6

Sources: ORNAUER, H. *et al* (1976) *Images of the World in the Year 2000: A Comparative Ten-Nation Study* Paris: Mouton, p. 688; and LIVINGSTONE, D.W. (1976) *Ontario Images 2000 Project* files.

Table 40   Expected Future Influence in Public Affairs, Ontario 1973

	Moderate or great deal %	None or very little %	Can't say %
Corporate Capitalists	21	79	–
Small Employers	3<u>8</u>	62	–
Petty Bourgeoisie	16	78	6
Managers	<u>37</u>	54	9
Supervisors	26	66	8
Professional Employees	24	74	2
Non-Productive Proletariat	22	74	4
Productive Proletariat	20	76	4
Housewives	19	75	6
Chronically Unemployed	20	69	11
Pensioners	19	72	9
Students	25	61	14
Total 18+ Population	21	73	6

Source: LIVINGSTONE, D.W. (1976) *Ontario Images 2000 Project* files.

expect moderate future political influence, a slightly higher proportion than in other class positions. This is perhaps consistent with their relatively visible spheres of social authority as small company owners and direct controllers of all subordinate personnel in the production process. But the technological rationalist view that the shaping of 'post-industrial' society is beyond the capacity of ordinary people is more widely accepted by those in other positions. This includes corporate capitalists, whose vested interests in repro-ducing dominant social structures is generally served very well by technological extrapolationist thinking; it also includes most proletarians, whose political capacity this mentality serves to repress.

Thus, the most general findings from the Ontario Images 2000 Project about class differences in popular orientations to the societal future are in accord with the final major conclusion of the World Images 2000 Project, which is based on an analysis of 'centre' and 'periphery' social positions. As the authors sum up:

> [There is] a *division of labor* in nearly all human societies with regard to the future. All societies have elites, whose task it is to be concerned with the future, and all societies have non-elites whose task it is to challenge the elites but only at a superficial level and not on really fundamental issues. The fundamental issues are not presented as something wanted by the elite as a result of their vested interest – but as dictated by immutable social laws, even by natural laws ... Is it strange that populations, who are never really given a say when it comes to social future, start seeing social future as immutable and hence have a low level of future imagination? ... This tendency is one

more way in which the elites in the more developed countries direct the politics of the future. This does not mean that these elites have a high consciousness of the future; they have probably much more consciousness of their interest in the present.[91]

However, there are indications that – without consciously rejecting this encapsulating, immutable 'post-industrial' image – people in the post-1968 period are becoming more concerned about the *social* future. The 1973 Ontario Survey findings suggest not only that the frequency of thinking about the future is increasing, but that more of this thinking is focused on social problems without any apparent technological solutions. A thematic analysis of respondents comments showed that, in contrast with the World Images 2000 Project responses to open-ended questions,[92] social problems were just as likely to be at the centre of people's images of the future as were aspects of technical 'progress' and development *per se*. Among the many social futures concerns expressed, some of the most common themes were: the disintegration of the family; increasing social alienation and identity problems; changes in the degree of social equality; decline of moral values and increasing need for social order or, conversely, expectations of greater social freedom and concern about the imposition of restrictive moral codes; and, most generally, expectations of increasing social conflict on the bases of either growing cultural intolerance, overly centralized political power, or increasing economic inequalities.

In community group discussions and preliminary open-ended interviewing leading up to the 1973 survey, many participants raised issues of social equality as central concerns in talking about the social future. Whether they are posed directly or deflected by intellectuals (for example, equality of condition, meritocracy), social equality issues are likely for the foreseeable future to constitute major substantive dimensions of popular thinking about the social organization of society. We therefore asked survey respondents to express both expectations and preferences regarding the extent of future social equality in several respects, including income, sex, and ethnicity. In Table 41 the results concerning *expected* economic inequality are compared with those found on a similar question in the World Images 2000 Project, as well as with those found on the same question included in the 1978 Ontario survey referred to in Chapter Four.[93]

Keeping in mind the substantial variations in the material contexts of these countries, the major pattern that emerges is of quite diverse expectations within each case. In all countries, more respondents expressed expectations of changes in the extent of economic inequality than of a continuation of the *status quo*. But there were generally substantial numbers expecting change in each direction. Ontario respondents in 1973 appear to have had relatively high expectations of diminishing economic inequality, but such expectations had dropped notably by 1978.

A more detailed summary of expected and desired future equality of incomes in Ontario by class position appears in Table 42. With regard to expectations, nearly half of the respondents in 1973 expected increased equality. Corporate capitalists and proletarians appear to have held the most opposed views. Proletarians were much less likely to anticipate increasing economic equality. While proletarian expectations of more equality appear to have diminished

Table 41   Expected Future Equality in Society, International Comparisons

	More %	About the same %	Less %	Can't say %
Netherlands 1967	28	22	47	3
Norway 1967	23	28	48	1
Japan 1968	47	18	26	10
West Germany 1970	20	39	27	14
Ontario 1973	45	31	18	6
Ontario 1978	25	37	23	15

Sources: ORNAUER, H. *et al* (1976) *Images of the World in the Year 2000: A Comparative Ten Nation Study* Paris: Mouton, p. 639; and LIVINGSTONE, D.W. (1976) *Ontario Images 2000 Project* files, and LIVINGSTONE, D.W. (1979) *Public Attitudes Toward Education in Ontario 1978* Toronto: OISE Press, p. 24.

Table 42   Expected and Desired Future Equality of Incomes, Ontario, 1973 and 1978.

	Expected Income equality by year 2000 % expecting more equality		Desired future income equality % preferring more equality	
	1973	1978**	1973	1978**
Corporate Capitalists	67	58	33	26
Small Employers	58	17	50	30
Petty Bourgeoisie	44	25	64	63
Managers	57	33	50	41
Supervisors	50	42	68	76
Professional Employees	46	20	55	61
Non-Productive Proletariat	34	27	65	69
Productive Proletariat	37	21	70	65
Housewives	43	26	64	63
Unemployed*	35	17	72	70
Ponsioners	52	28	72	61
Students	44	20	66	52
Total 18+ Population	45	25	64	62

Sources: LIVINGSTONE, D.W. (1976) *Ontario Images 2000 Project* file, and LIVINGSTONE, D.W. (1979) *Public Attitudes Toward Education in Ontario 1978* Toronto: OISE Press, p. 24.
*   All unemployed in 1978, but only chronically unemployed in 1973.
** For the numbers in each class position in this sample see Table 34.

even further by 1978, they were by then shared by the rest of the respondents – with the exception of corporate capitalists who continued to verbalize anticipations of 'galloping egalitarianism'. The most precipitous drop in equality expectations seems to have occurred among small employers, perhaps reflecting the fact that the relative prospects of small business most evidently worsened as the economic crisis persisted – with both sharply declining profit margins and increasing bankruptcies.

With regard to desired future income equality, the pattern is markedly different. In 1973 nearly two thirds of respondents expressed preferences for greater future economic equality. Only among corporate capitalists were such hopes clearly a minority view. In 1978, capitalists were joined by small employers and by managers, both of whom expressed tendencies to become more interested in protecting their own relative advantages as economic conditions worsened. But overall, expressed desires for increased equality remained about as high as they were five years earlier. The most significant general aspect of these findings, therefore, is the *widening gap* between economic desires and expectations. The expressed discrepancy between hopes and expectations has grown greatly among those in most subordinated class positions. By 1978, this gap was about as large within the petty bourgeoisie and professional employee positions and among those dispossessed people not directly engaged in hired labour, as it was in the proletariat. Hence, the most tentative conclusion of the World Images 2000 Project receives a more explicit confirmation ten years later:

> There is something stifling and stale about the entire way in which images are here woven into the social structure, something unreleased, unborn. It is like a crust of [elite] complacency and scepticism mixed with some gradualist social technology, thrown over a dormant volcano of wishes and aspirations with some small eruptions here and there – but with too little oxygen to thrive and develop into a cascade of new images and new actions reaching out for a new future. In short, it is like a dormant giant waiting for something to release it into action ... and if that should happen the [elites] in the world might be in for many surprises, for the total variation in images of the year 2000 is considerable and not easily reconciled into order and quiet ... [94]

The tremors have increased.

Popular Images of the Educational Future

To simply assume *a priori* that there is a close identity between views of the educational future and attitudes expressed on current educational issues – even if such attitudes concern organizational alternatives, as do those discussed in Chapter Four – would be to inflict yet another version of the extrapolationist thinking for which I have previously criticized most other intellectuals. To my knowledge, the Ontario Images 2000 Project is the only opinion survey that has attempted to probe popular images of the educational future in any detail.[95] The basic orientations that were found can be conveyed here by considering expressions of general expectations and desires regarding future educational change, as well as the central substantive issue of the desired degree of freedom of choice in future education.

The predominant pattern of association between expectations and desires regarding future educational structures in the 1973 Ontario survey is suggested by Table 43, which summarizes the responses to general questions on the extent of future change in educational institutions. Nearly two-thirds of the respondents expected a great deal of change, whereas the majority preferred to see no more than a moderate amount of change. When hopes and expectations concerning change in educational institutions were cross-tabulated, over 40 per cent of the respondents expected to see more change than they hoped for, while only 12 per cent hoped for more institutional change than they expected. Therefore, there appeared to be very substantial numbers who expected to see changes in educational institutions being imposed against their preferences. Respondents in general tended to expect that educational institutions would change greatly with the continuation of currently perceived trends, whereas the educational future they would like to see would involve more gradual rates of change in line with various educational philosophies. In all class positions the majority *expected* a great deal of educational change, whereas notably lower proportions expressed a preference for so much change.

Table 43   Expected and Desired Extent of Future Change in Educational Institutions, Ontario 1973.

	Expected educational change by year 2000 % expecting much change	Desired future educational change % preferring much change
Corporate Capitalists	69	31
Small Employers	75	44
Petty Bourgeoisie	65	33
Managers	61	48
Supervisors	60	37
Professional Employees	73	49
Non-Productive Proletariat	66	34
Productive Proletariat	61	37
Housewives	59	30
Chronically Unemployed	66	53
Pensioners	53	35
Students	68	46
Total 18+ Population	63	37

Source: LIVINGSTONE, D.W. (1976) *Ontario Images 2000 Project* files.

It should be noted here that the 1973 survey was conducted in the context of continuing criticism, led by the corporate mass media, of the Hall-Dennis Commission proposals to establish a more child-centred curriculum in Ontario schools. The respondents themselves generally indicated a relatively low degree of satisfaction with the services that schools were currently providing.[96] Thus, the expressed views on educational futures may involve personal resistance to such attempted current changes, or perhaps unreflective acceptance of the dominant media rhetoric opposing them. However, child-centred education also had many articulate 'new middle class' defenders in this period. Indeed, the immediate appearance of educational instability may itself have had a wide influence on expectations of future educational change. But the general tenor of respondents' comments suggests that encapsulation within the technological extrapolationist way of thinking about the social future was a still more pervasive, and more enduring, factor in such views.

Thematic analysis of the respondents' comments revealed a variety of specific views on both expected and desired educational change. With regard to *expectations*, the most common theme was that education – along with society in general – was perceived to have been changing rapidly and would continue to do so in the future. This general attitude conditioned most of the responses, but especially among the majority who expected a great deal of educational change (fifty-three per cent). The comment of a retired minister was typical:

> There will be a great deal of educational change if we can go by the rate of change in just the last decade.

Similarly, a young proletarian machine operator noted:

> Because they have changed a great deal already.

Within such extrapolations to the educational future three substantive concerns were evident among those anticipating a great deal of change. Many of this group perceived increasing specialization and expected education to become much more moulded to society's technological needs. As a young tool-and-die apprentice put it:

> Technology is accelerating rapidly and education must keep up.

Others emphasized an increasing person-centredness in education. They cited a decreasing stress on such external criteria as centrally structured curricula and degrees, and saw an increasing extension of personal choice along with such related trends as the growth of lifelong learning to meet individual needs. As a middle-aged sales professional observed:

> Students will have more and more to say about their education.

A third major concern was expressed especially by those with a more cyclical view of educational trends. They saw a current wave of permissiveness to be followed by a return to more traditional discipline in schooling. A retired manager commented:

> I would expect that the pendulum will swing back to more traditional forms of education – higher standards, less freedom of choice of curriculums, greater stress on higher education, better qualified teachers.

The anticipations of those who expected total reform of present forms of schooling (ten per cent) were also based on extrapolation of perceived rapid changes, but more particularly on views of educational institutions as currently lagging in the generally pervasive change toward a more technologically oriented *or* a more person-centred society. The technological orientation was well expressed by a young lathe operator who said:

> Educational institutions will need to be drastically reorganized to accommodate increased need for the increase in technological knowledge and longer years spent in school.

Another young proletarian electrician exemplified the person-centered view:

> Future school will be orientated more towards what the student wishes to learn since the school's main purpose will not be to get people ready to work in industry.

Among those who foresaw total reform of existing institutions there were some who, while they expected the established roles of schooling to continue, saw a necessity for more economical modes of organization. As an elderly housewife put it:

> There will have to be much less waste of public tax money. Taxpayers are getting fed up with providing plush nurseries without seeing better results.

The one-quarter of respondents who expected only a moderate degree of educational change seemed to be more aware of obstacles to change in today's schools. A middle-aged professional said:

> I think there will be an increasing trend toward mediocre education but the structure of the educatinal institutions will not change. It's too entrenched to change radically.

Among the moderates, the same three general sorts of concrete issues again emerged – expectations of more emphasis on practical, job-oriented curricula, an increasing degree of choice for students, or a re-emerging priority for the '3R's'.

The very small numbers who expected little or no change (six per cent) were more preoccupied than the moderates with an immutability of the structures and functions of education. The general perspective was expressed by a secondary teacher professional in her early thirties:

> Education has never really changed much from Socrates or Plato to Rousseau, Dewey, and now Hall-Dennis!

Reasons cited for the expected stability ranged from the view that trustees are rigid, and will be slow to implement change to the general attitude that educational institutions are 'always the last to change in any society'. The familiar concrete concerns with job-oriented education, student choice, or traditional discipline were once more apparent. But the tone of these comments differed markedly from that of respondents who expected greater educational change. For example, an aging petty bourgeois prospector foresaw distinct limits to expanding educational opportunities:

> We'll always need workers, and US couldn't get soldiers from their educated masses. We'd be in big trouble if education makes you feel above a pick and shovel, or fighting for your country.

And a sales professional in his late fifties expressed a common belief of those with a traditionalist orientation when he commented that:

> No significant change in schools is possible if teachers have not got a better way of teaching discipline.

But overall, the public's *expected* images of the educational future appear to have been based on anticipation of quite unrestrained, largely unguided societal change. While the expected images varied considerably in both concrete and thematic concerns, few people were as overwhelmed by such perceived and expected rates of change as 'future shock' hypotheses[97] suggest. Indeed, even expectations of 'drastic reorganization' of education seemed to assume the established institutional structure of state schooling and advanced capitalist society in general.

In view of the general expectation of unrestrained change it is not surprising that many *preferences* were for more gradual educational changes guided by particular human values. The desire for incremental value-based change was, of course, most evident among the largest group (forty-one per cent), who wanted 'moderate' educational change. A university student, for instance, felt that:

> Schools should move with the future personal needs; and children should be learning more at an earlier age but without having too much forced on them too early.

The specific changes the moderates wanted to see ranged from 'more personal attention in smaller classes', and increased emphasis on learning how to learn, to greater emphasis on basic skills and more discipline. But the changes suggested were typically limited to gradual modifications within existing educational programmes, as this comment of a middle-aged housewife indicates:

> I sincerely wish that we will be able to control the situation. What we need is more personal attention, smaller classes, more teachers.

In contrast, those who wanted 'a great deal' of educational change (thirty-seven per cent) usually showed a greater concern for discrepancies between human needs and educational services. There was a notable polarity between those who desired freer, more flexible forms of education and those who preferred more highly structured, specialized forms. The preference for greater freedom was clearly stated by a middle-aged professional:

> I would like to see a system that is more stimulating intellectually, more exciting, and *much* less regimented.

The desire for more structured education was commonly expressed in terms of either basic skills or vocational training. An elderly housewife said:

> There should be much more emphasis in the future on spelling and reading. I think the small schools were much better and gave the child a feeling of security.

And a young manager asserted:

> There should be a much greater emphasis on job specialization and training in trades. Today's young people are ill-equipped to fit specific jobs and have little or no skills to offer in the job market.

Generally speaking, those who wanted a great deal of future educational change were much more likely than the moderates to suggest specific changes that would make a discernible difference in forms and content of schooling, such as extensive work-study programmes, a purely Canadian curriculum, or rigorous moral training. The underlying sentiment of those who wanted a great deal of educational change was perhaps expressed by a middle-aged supervisor:

> Since the present system is an unqualified disaster it is a great temptation to opt for abolition. But it isn't wise to throw out the baby with the bathwater.

The very small group (five per cent) who wanted total reform of the present form of schooling were more occupied than other respondents with links between education and other aspects of life, and they seriously questioned the social, economic, and political relevance of contemporary schooling. For example, a middle-aged proletarian mechanic aruged:

> Schools are obsolete. They're run by an establishment who have spent their lifetime in a school atmosphere and know little of what's going on in the real world.

The persistent freedom-discipline polarity was most evident within this group's preferences. A young professional artist felt that:

> Something drastic should happen. We need a very flexible lifelong learning system, because as it's set up now there aren't enough returns to justify the imaginations and creativity that are being stunted.

Conversely, a university student stated:

Schools are now worse than ever. The high school student choosing his own subject is a false concept. At those ages most students will choose subjects which require less work and initiative. They are allowed too much freedom, therefore constantly revolting against the system. Computerized schools should be allowed.

At the other extreme, those who would like to see little or no change in schools (ten per cent) usually offered no elaboration of their position. There were some general extrapolationist comments on 'continuing to keep up-to-date', but the basic attitude was probably best reflected by an elderly housewife who stated:

Schools are so wonderful compared to the little red schoolhouse.

In some respects, educational institutions have remained more vulnerable to direct popular pressure than many of the other major social institutions of advanced capitalist societies. This appears to be reflected in the finding that a considerably larger proportion of respondents expected more future public influence in educational planning than expected greater influence in public affairs generally. It is true that, as Table 44 indicates, only the minority expected any greater educational influence than at present, while the majority would prefer a greater say in the future. This was the case for nearly all class positions. However, the discrepancies between such educational hopes and expectations remained less pronounced than on a variety of general societal futures issues.

Table 44   Expected and Desired Future Public Influence in Educational Planning, Ontario 1973

	Expected future say in educational planning % expecting greater say	Desired future say in educational planning % wanting greater say
Corporate Capitalists	25	58
Small Employers	7	26
Petty Bourgeoisie	37	61
Managers	33	50
Supervisors	37	60
Professional Employees	41	60
Non-Productive Proletariat	38	59
Productive Proletariat	33	54
Housewives	43	64
Chronically Unemployed	47	77
Pensioners	43	60
Students	41	64
Total 18+ Population	39	60

Source: LIVINGSTONE, D.W. (1976) *Ontario Images 2000 Project* files.

The most prominent themes in comments on these questions concerned the role of 'experts'-qualified educational 'authorities'- and the need for 'expert knowledge'. Among those expecting less future public influence (twenty-five per cent), many based their opinions on a perception of the general public as incapable of understanding and dealing with issues in education, and less commonly on the capacity of government bureaucrats to dominate educational decision making. The most pessimistic respondents often referred to specific educational issues on which central planners overrode popular local sentiments. Those expecting more future public influence (thirty-nine per cent) commonly based this less on perceived trends than on notions of what ought to occur. Some comments referred to imminent changes in the school system as a result of public pressure, but most stated that greater public input was necessary to budge an inbred educational establishment or to ensure democratic representation. A key point to note is that participation was generally regarded in terms of officials' responsiveness rather than public control – in short, the right to be consulted by the expert authorities. Similar comments were found regarding preferred future public influence in educational planning; those who wanted less public influence typically cited the 'ignorance of ordinary people', while the majority preferring increased future influence generally expressed quite strong desires that 'representative educational institutions be made to work'.

There was, to be sure, little questioning of the dominant historical form of state schooling in advanced capitalism (as discussed in Chapter Three), and a widespread acceptance of the assumption that current technological trends affecting schooling would remain beyond the capacity of ordinary people to influence. But, as the preceding thematic analysis may suggest, public influences in relation to the future substantive form and content of *the learning process itself* were matters on which strong differences of opinion were expressed, with regard to future expectations as well as preferences. In view of this *relatively* activist popular orientation to education futures, it is interesting to note that the majority of corporate capitalists – in contrast to the posture of relying on technological rationality and appeals to expertise which they expressed on many social and political issues – similarly desired greater future say in educational planning. This might perhaps be indicative of how keenly corporate capitalists perceived an isolation of their views from those of state educational policy makers on substantive requirements of the learning process in 1973, and how strategic many of them felt it was to continue to ensure that 'education be cut to the job market cloth'. The state initiatives toward a child-centred curriculum in this period may have been regarded by small employers as equally at odds with their similar needs for adaptive, 'steady' workers. But as their influence in public affairs was highly localized, they tended, in the face of a strong central state commitment, to lapse into an extreme pessimism concerning influence in educational planning.[98]

In any case, both our preliminary community-level discussions and the thematic analysis of comments on the general questions about the future extent of change in educational institutions suggest that the extent to which 'freedom' or 'discipline' should prevail within the learning process was the central dimension of most popular thinking about desired educational futures. The most specific survey question in this regard asked about the freedom of choice respondents would prefer to see in future education, particularly for young-sters in deciding what they want to learn. The results appear in Table 45. Overall, the plurality preference was for a greater degree of freedom of choice than was generally perceived to be allowed in 1973. Less than one quarter preferred to see less freedom of choice in the future. The views of capitalists did tend to be quite distinct from others, particularly in their lack of enthusiasm for greater future educational freedom, and in corporate capitalists' definite preference for more restricted choice in the future. In all other class positions there was at least plurality support for greater freedom in future education. Such support was most notable among the chronically unemployed, who typically had been 'turned off' and dropped out of school and now had few substantial prospects of obtaining further formal education.

Table 45   Desired Freedom of Choice in Future Education, Ontario 1973

	More %	Same %	Less %	Can't Say %
Corporate Capitalists	8	8	67	8
Small Employers	12	56	29	3
Petty Bourgeoisie	50	20	28	2
Managers	36	25	30	9
Supervisors	51	26	18	5
Professional Employees	46	19	30	5
Non-Productive Proletariat	42	29	23	6
Productive Proletariat	51	25	21	3
Housewives	44	31	20	5
Chronically Unemployed	67	3	30	–
Pensioners	40	29	27	4
Students	49	24	18	9
Total 18+ Population	45	26	23	6

Source: LIVINGSTONE, D.W. (1976) *Ontario Images 2000 Project* files.

While all those who chose the same pre-coded response on this item certainly cannot be presumed to have held the same conception of educational freedom, cross-tabulations indicated that the degree of freedom desired in future learning processes was related to other future educational preferences. The desire for greater freedom was associated with a lower evaluation of the future impor-tance of compulsory education, a greater interest in ensuring the rights of organized social groups to set up their own educational programmes, and a preference for much greater future public influence in educational planning.[99] The associations of these other aspects of preferred educational futures with each other were less notable than the association of each with the educational freedom question. Thus, the degree of freedom for learners was further confirmed as the central organizing dimension in most people's preferred images of the educational future, at least at that particular moment in Ontario. However, it must be stressed that these are tendencies within responses to discrete questionnaire items; the respondents' comments contain very few explicit articulations of coherent images of preferred educational futures.

In this regard, it should be noted that mass opinion surveys on *current* educational issues that were conducted in the early 1970s found similar patterns of preferences on questions concerning the amount of choice that current students should have in course selection.[100] However, as noted in Chapter Four, our own most recent survey (see Table 28) finds widespread consensus on *requiring* current high school students to take language, mathematics and career preparatory courses, with only some optional courses. If current and future educational preferences remain closely associated in the more recent period, this dramatic shift would suggest that popular orientations to the educational future have not only responded to perceived worsening of economic conditions, with an increased concern to ensure that students are well prepared for the job market. It would also suggest that even the most strongly expressed central features of future educational preferences are merely diffuse sentiments quite devoid of any practical concept of an alternative future. In any event, the marked shift of such popular attitudes toward closer apparent accord with capitalist views on restricting freedom of choice indicates that mass sentiments abour educational alternatives have been highly vulnerable to ideological manipulation by dominant class interests since 1973.

While technological extrapolationist thinking prevailed with regard to both general societal and educational expectations in the 1973 Ontario survey, there was an evident tendency for different preferences concerning future freedom of choice in education to be associated with preferences regarding future social equality. Most notably, those people with a stronger desire for freedom of choice in learning expressed a stronger preference for future economic equality. In spite of the general absence of coherent inspirational images of the future in the public sphere of advanced industrial societies, popular sentiments about preferred futures for education did therefore appear to be thought of in relation to similar preferred conditions in the social context of education.[101] However, the more recent Ontario survey results regarding current orientations on freedom and equality issues again lead one to question the durability of most popular desires concerning the educational future, as well as their relation to practical activity. As we have seen, clear majority preferences for greater economic equality have continued to be expressed by those in most subordinate class positions. But the greatly increased popular acceptance of a need for compulsory core curricula (see Table 28) suggests that any link between preferences for future educational freedom and economic equality may have weakened considerably. Even more directly indicative of disjuncture between popular economic preferences and general sentiments toward educational futures is the finding that, in spite of such continuing desires for greater economic equality, most of those in subordinate class positions express the belief that substantial equality of educational opportunity already exists in higher education (see Table 22).

While these attitude trends may suggest a widespread acceptance of persistent corporate demands concerning a more restrictive social form for the learning process, and reflect a growing disjuncture with persistent popular economic egalitarianism, the disjuncture is by no means complete. Greater continuity and connectedness with economic preferences appears with regard to the *content* of the learning process desired by different classes. Analyses of expected and desired curricular priorities in the Ontario Images 2000 Project survey indicated that respondents generally expected a more narrowly specialized technical content in future education than they would like.[102] Many people expressed a desire for a curriculum that would place emphasis on personal and social concerns with the provision of technical skills integrated into that context. Corporate capitalists expressed a stronger priority for basic skills than for job training, while productive proletarians displayed opposite tendencies. In all of these respects, similar patterns are discernible in our recent surveys of current educational attitudes. The differences in capitalist and proletarian curricular priorities have become much more pronounced. But the continuity of expressed popular differences on such priorities lends further credence to the view that the technical content of the learning process is the real centre of contemporary class conflict over the current and future character of educational provisions. This is further supported by the finding in the 1973 survey of a strong positive association between support for future automation in the workplace and curricular priority for basic skills training among corporate capitalists, and a similarly strong negative association of automation and priority for job training among proletarians. The later surveys offer no indications that such associations have weakened.

Concluding Remarks

The Ontario Images 2000 Project survey elicited an *extraordinary* amount of written commentary from respondents in comparison with the later, present-oriented surveys. There is hardly sufficient evidence in this survey or the earlier World Images 2000 surveys to presage the imminent emergence in advanced capitalism of clearly articulated images of possible and preferable alternative educational and social futures. But there are strong indications that the 'latent potentialities' whose historical existence Ernst Bloch has so richly illustrated[103] do continue to exist. Indeed, popular images may have more diversity and vibrancy than the explicit images of the technological and social future produced in recent times by either bourgeois or socialist intellectuals. But they must be opened and explored if they are to have significant creative implications for future society.

Socialist intellectuals have a profound responsibility to engage in sensitive efforts to understand the images of potential futures that are inherent in practical activities and expressed sentiments of the members of subordinate social groups. They also have the equally important task of articulating and disseminating *related* normative visions of possible societies, consistent with such basic socialist principles as self-management, equality in social relations, and diversity of social development.[104] Both tasks have been largely ignored.

A large-scale opinion survey at a single point in time cannot offer deep insight into the stability or dynamics of people's images of the future. It is possible also that a largely pre-coded questionnaire can impose overly-rationalistic, reified interpretations of images of the future. More sensitive, smaller-scale studies, using such methods as the oral history approach, are needed to deepen understanding of the cognitive and emotional issues involved especially in subordinate group interpretations of the world, whether in recalling the past or imagining the future. The relevance of large-scale surveys is in locating very general patterns of orientations in large populations.

In spite of the prevalence of technological extrapolationist tendencies in popular thinking about the social and educational future, one clear implication of the 1973 Ontario survey is that, in order to respond to currently held popular preferences, the educational provisions of the future must be organized on a thorough-going principle of economic, political and cultural pluralism. However, some of the major differences in preferred social and educational futures suggested by our Ontario surveys, as well as by those of the World Images 2000 Project, reflect deep class divisions of interests and of power in advanced capitalism. That is not to deny the possibility of a non-violent transition to a more liberated future society, however historically unprecedented this would be. In any event, wide dissemination of undistorted information on subordinate groups' preferences regarding the social and educational future would provide at least a marginally more salutary condition for popular action than one in which the only legitimate 'knowledge' about the future is created and controlled by an established elite and a small collection of assorted experts. Whether or not such undistorted communication occurs, many other objective factors of course influence the shape of future society. But it should be clear, in light of the demonstrated diversity in the public's preferred images of the social and educational future, that the guiding question for socialist intellectuals and activists, traditional intellectuals, and the lay public alike should *not* be how to adapt to any simple range of predicted or prescribed types of future. It is rather, how can we act to realize a future of alternative choices for all people?

Notes

1 An earlier version of parts of this section appeared in LIVINGSTONE, D.W. and LAKE, D.G. (1977) 'Preferred images of the future: Twentieth century bourgeois and socialist visions', *McGill Journal of Education* 12 (1) (Spring), pp. 95–110.

2 POLAK, F. (1973) *The Image of the Future*, San Francisco, Jossey-Bass, p. 14.

3 ARBLASTER, A. and LUKES, S. (1971) *The Good Society*, London, Methuen, pp. 1–21, *et passim*.

4 By 'bourgeois' I refer here to all those intellectuals organically aligned with capitalist interests as well as traditional intellectuals who profess neutrality and non-alignment. However, any dividing line between bourgeois and socialist modes of *thought* remains somewhat arbitrary.

5 It is true that utopian *fiction* writing has now almost disappeared. See ARMYTAGE, W.H.G. (1968) *Yesterday's Tomorrow: A Historical Survey of Future Societies*, London, Routledge and Kegan Paul, for a review, and SHKLAR, J. (1967) 'The political theory of Utopia: From melancholy to nostalgia' in MANUEL, F. (Ed) *Utopias and Utopian Thought*, Boston, Beacon, pp. 101–115, for an explanation for the demise of classical utopian writings. Compare MANUEL, F. and MANUEL, F. (1979) *Utopian Thought in the Western World*, Cambridge, Harvard University Press. Dystopian fiction literature has proliferated, including several works which can serve as powerful negative visions for approaching the future. See, for example, SARGENT, L. (1972) 'Utopia and dystopia in contemporary science fiction', *The Futurist*, VI. (3), pp. 93–98. My primary interest here is rather in visions that are put forward as *realizable* preferences.

6 See LIVINGSTONE, D.W. (1976) 'On hegemony in corporate capitalist states', *Sociological Inquiry*, 46 (3–4), pp. 240–242. For a more detailed summary, see MARKELY, O.W. (1980) *The Images of Man*, Elmsford Park, Pergamon Press.

7 KAHN, H. and WEINER, A. (1967) *The Year 2000: A Framework for Speculation on the Next Thirty Three Years*, London, Collier-Macmillan, p. 7. Compare the more muted technological optimism in KAHN, H. (1979) *World Economic Development: 1979 and Beyond*, Boulder, Westview Press. The most evident Canadian spin-off is DROUIN, M.J. and BRUCE-BRIGGS B. (1978) *Canada Has a Future*, Toronto, McClelland and Stewart.

8 BELL, D. (1973) *The Coming of Post-Industrial Society: A Venture in Social Forecasting*, New York, Basic Books.

9 See especially McLUHAN, M. and FIORE, Q. (1967) *The Medium is the Message: An Inventory of Effects*, Toronto, Bantam Books.

10 For a distillation see MARIEN, M. (1972) 'The basic, long-term multifold trend in education', in Committee on Education and Labor, House of Representatives, *Alternative Futures in American Education*, Washington, U.S. Government Printing Office, p. 3. For overviews of the educational futures literature of this period, with emphasis on variants of technological forecasting, see, for example, MARIEN, M. (1971) *Alternative Futures for Learning*, Syracuse, Educational Policy Research Centre, Syracuse University, and TOFFLER, A. (Ed) (1974) *Learning for Tomorrow: The Role of the Future in Education*, New York, Vintage Press, as well as STEVENSON, H. and HAMILTON, W. (1972) *Canadian Education and the Future*, London, University of Western Ontario, and Commission on Educational Planning (1972) *A Future of Choices, A Choice of Futures*, Edmonton, Queen's Printer. Both Marien and Stevenson have continued to produce broad ranging annotated bibliographic reviews of futures and social policy research with considerable emphasis on educational issues. The most sustained and systematic educational forecasting efforts were made by the Stanford Research Institute Educational Policy Research Center. See especially HARMON, W. et al. (1973) 'The forecasting of plausible alternative future histories: Methods, results, and educational policy implications' in OECD *Long-Range Policy Planning in Education*, Paris, OECD, pp. 299–385.

11 See, for example REDD, K. and HARKINS, A. (Eds) (1980) *Education: A Time for Decisions*, Washington, World Future Society, and JENNINGS, L. and CORNISH, S. (Eds), (1980) *Education and the Future*, Washington, World Future Society.

Compare NEWITT, J. (1979) *Future Trends in Educational Policy*, Lexington, D.C., Heath.

12 I have presented a more detailed critique of these limitations in LIVINGSTONE, D.W. (1972) 'Inventing the future: Anti-historist reflections on *Toward 2000*', *Interchange* 3 (4), pp. 111–119, which focuses on one of the most influential Canadian educational forecasts of this period. As direct illustrations of post-industrial society advocates' failure to grasp such points, see the following exchange between John Porter and myself (1972) (*Interchange* 3 (4), pp. 120–23), as well as that between Daniel Bell and Stephen Berger (1974) (*Contemporary Sociology* 3 (2) pp. 101–5, 107–9).

13 WAGAR, W. (1972) *Good Tidings: The Belief in Progress from Darwin to Marcuse*, Bloomington, Indiana University Press, p. 10.

14 MARIEN, M. (1976) *Societal Directions and Alternatives: A Critical Guide to the Literature*, Lafayette, NY. Information for Policy Design.

15 STEVENSON, H. (1975) *Canadian Policy Issues, Ideas and Alternatives: A Select, Annotated Guide to Current Literature*, New York, World Institute Council.

16 TEILHARD P. DE CHARDIN (1959) *The Phenomenon of Man*, New York, Harper. For a more concrete vision in the same spirit, see GARCIA, J.D. (1971) *The Moral Society*, New York, Julian Press.

17 SOROKIN, P. (1948) *The Reconstruction of Humanity*, Boston, Beacon, SKINNER, B.F. (1971) *Beyond Freedom and Dignity*, New York, KNOPF, and WILSON, E.O. (1975) *Sociobiology: The New Synthesis*, Cambridge, Harvard University Press.

18 GOLDSMITH, E. et al. (1972) *A Blueprint for Survival*, London, Tom Stacey, FERKISS, V. (1974) *The Future of Technological Civilization*, New York, Braziller.

19 BORSODI, R. (1929) *This Ugly Civilization*, New York, Simon and Schuster; SCHUMACHER, E.F. (1973) *Small is Beautiful*, New York, Harper and Row; ILLICH, I. (1973) *Tools for Conviviality*, New York, Harper and Row.

20 FALK, R. (1975) *A Study of Future Worlds*, New York, Free Press. See also WAGAR, W. (1971) *Building the City of Man*, New York, Grossman.

21 ROCKEFELLER, J.D. (1973) *The Second American Revolution: Some Personal Observations*, New York, Harper and Row. Compare HARMAN, W. (1973–4) 'Humanistic capitalism: Another alternative', *Fields Within Fields*, 10 (Winter), pp. 3–15.

22 McKENZIE KING, W.L. (1918) *Industry and Humanity*, Toronto, T. Allen.

23 While market-centred economists such as Von Hayek and Friedman have provided much of the technical rationale, George Gilder (*Wealth and Poverty*, New York, Basic Books, 1981) most effectively expresses this rationale in combination with normative appeals. For example: 'The crucial rules of creative thought can be summed up as faith, love, openness, conflict, and falsifiability. The crucial rules of economic innovation and progress are faith, altruism, investment, competition, and bankruptcy, which are also the rules of capitalism. The reason capitalism succeeds is that its laws accord with the laws of the mind. It is capable of fulfilling human needs because it is founded on giving, which depends on sensitivity to the needs of others. It is open to faith and experiment because it is also open to competition and bankruptcy. Capitalism accumulates the capital gains not only of its successes but also of its failures, capitalized in new knowledge. It is the only appropriate system for a world in which all certitude is a sham.' (p. 265).

24 HARDIN, H. (1974) *A Nation Unaware: The Canadian Economic Culture*, Vancouver, Douglas. Compare the scattered examples in CLARKSON, S. (Ed) (1970) *Visions 2020: Fifty Canadians in Search of a Future*, Edmonton, Hurtig.

25 One of the more elaborate of such efforts is SHERMAN, V. (1970) *Two Contrasting Educational Models: Applications and Policy Implications*, Menlo Park, Educational Policy Research Center, Stanford Research Institute.

26 The weight has clearly been on the more liberal, open end of this continuum. For

recent examples, see WAGSCHAL, P. (Ed) (1979) *Learning for Tomorrows: Commentaries on the Future of Education*, New York, Praeger, as well as the annotated bibliography in GLINES, D. (1980) *Educational Futures V: Creating and Foresighting*, Millville, Anvil Press.

27 See especially ILLICH, I. (1970) *Deschooling Society*, New York, Harper and Row; and REIMER, E. (1971) *School is Dead: Alternatives in Education*, New York, Doubleday.

28 One of the most incisive economic critiques is GINTIS, H. (1972) 'Toward a political economy of education', *Harvard Educational Review* 42 (1) (February). For a more wide-ranging critique, see LIVINGSTONE, D.W. (1971) 'Educational revolution: Problems and prospects', *Interchange* 2 (1), pp. 36–43, as well as Everett Reimer's response in the same issue.

29 ILLICH, I. (1976) *After Deschooling, What?* London, Writers and Readers Publishing Cooperative, p. 53. An introduction by Ian Lister alludes to the Ontario experience.

30 See for example, WITTKE, C.F. (1950) *The Utopian Communist: A Biography of William Weitling*, Baton Rouge, Louisiana State University Press; MANUEL, F. and MANUEL, F. (Eds) (1966) *French Utopias: An Anthology of Ideal Societies*, New York, Free Press, COLE, G.D.H. (1927) *The Life of William Cobbett*, London, W. Collins and Sons, COLE, G.D.H. (1965) *The Life of Robert Owen*, London, Frank Cass, and BUBER, M. (1949) *Paths in Utopia*, London, Routledge and Kegan Paul.

31 See especially ENGELS, F. (1970) 'Socialism: Utopian and scientific' in MARX, K. and ENGELS, F. *Selected Works*, Vol. 3, Moscow, Progress, p. 119; and ENGELS, F. (1970) 'The housing question', *Selected Works*, Vol. 2, pp. 368–369.

32 For further details on this point, see CASTLES, S. and WUSTENBERG, W. (1979) *The Education of the Future: An Introduction to the Theory and Practice of Socialist Education*, London, Pluto Press, pp. 32–42 and *passim*.

33 *Ibid.*, pp. 6–7, 33. Compare SHAPIRO, H.S. (1979) 'Radical movements, ideology, and the sociology of educational ideas', *Social Praxis* 6 (3–4), pp. 193–215, as discussed in Chapter Three.

34 Cited in CASTLES, S. and WUSTENBERG, W. (1979) *op. cit.*, p. 39.

35 See *Ibid.*, pp. 33–39.

36 See for example, TROTSKY, L. (1934) *The History of the Russian Revolution*, London, Gollancz. For recent examples of Russian social forecasting see SAIFULIN, M. (Ed) (1973) *The Future of Society*, Moscow, Progress.

37 CASTLES, S. and WUSTENBERG, W. (1979) *op. cit.*, pp. 99–100.

38 For intellectual expressions see, for example, HORVAT, B. et al. (Eds) (1975) *Self-Governing Socialism*. 2 Volumes, White Plains, International Arts and Sciences Press, and BAHRO, R. (1978) *The Alternative in Eastern Europe*, London: New Left Books. This is *not* to suggest that political revolutionary potential is necessarily greater in such societies than in some peripheral capitalist societies.

39 For recent overviews see OAKESHOTT, R. (1978) *The Case for Workers' Co-ops*, London, Routledge and Kegan Paul, and CARNOY, M. and SHEARER, D. (1980) *Economic Democracy: The Challenge of the 1980s*, White Plains, M.E. Sharpe. With more explicit regard to education see, for example, SHAPIRO, H.S. (1979) *op. cit.* and the work of Celestin Freinet as discussed in CASTLES, S. and WUSTENBERG, W. (1979) *op. cit.*, pp. 182–89.

40 See ANDERSON, P. (1976) *Considerations on Western Marxism*, London, New Left Books.

41 *Ibid.*, pp. 88–89.

42 See, for example, BLOCH, E. (1970) *A Philosophy of the Future*, New York, Herder and Herder, and (1971) *Spirit of Utopia*, New York, Herder and Herder. Bloch's most important work, *Das Prinzip Hoffnung* (The Principle of Hope), although completed in the late 1940s, has apparently not yet been published in English.

43 BLOCH, E. (1971) *On Karl Marx*, New York, Herder and Herder, p. 172.

44 See however RUHLE, J.R. (1963) 'The philosopher of hope: Ernst Bloch', in LABEDZ, L. (Ed) *Revisionism: Essays on the History of Marxist Ideas*, London, Allen and Unwin, GROSS, D. (1972) 'Ernst Bloch: The dialectics of hope', in HOWARD, D. and KLARE, K. (Eds) *The Unknown Dimension: European Marxism Since Lenin*, New York, Basic Books, and the several articles in *Telos*, No. 25 (Fall 1975).

45 WOODCOCK, G. (1972) *Pierre-Joseph Proudhon: His Life and Work*, New York, Schocken Books.

46 KROPOTKIN, P. (1899) *Fields, Factories and Workshops*, London, Hutchinson. See also the suggestive scenario by PATAUD, E. and POUGET, E. (1913) *Syndicalism and the Co-Operative Commonwealth (How we shall bring about the Revolution)*, London, New International Publishing.

47 GOODMAN, P. and GOODMAN, P. (1974) *Communitas*, New York, Vintage, BOOKCHIN, M. (1971) *Post-Scarcity Anarchism*, San Francisco, Ramparts, and WARD, C. (1974) *Anarchy in Action*, New York, Harper and Row.

48 See for example, GOULET, D. (1974) *A New Moral Order: Development Ethics and Liberation Theology*, Maryknoll, New York, Orbis.

49 See BUBER, M. (1949) *op. cit.*, pp. 139–49. Compare the similarly technologically advanced workers' co-operatives and education programmes of the Mondragon system in the Basque nation in Spain. This system is based on a socialist vision derived largely from Robert Owen by an activist Catholic priest; a good account appears in OAKESHOTT R. (1978) *op. cit.*, pp. 165–214.

50 See GARAUDY, R. (1972) *The Alternative Future: A Vision of Christian Marxism*, New York, Simon and Schuster.

51 BLAND, S.C. (1973) *The New Christianity or the Religion of the New Age*, Toronto, University of Toronto Press, PARTRIDGE, E. (1926) *A War on Poverty*, Sintaluta, Saskatchewan, E. Partridge.

52 See CROSS, M. (Ed) (1974) *The Decline and Fall of a Good Idea: CCF-NDP Manifestos 1932–1969*, Toronto, New Hogtown Press.

53 See NELLES, V. and ROTSTEIN, A. (Eds) (1973) *Nationalism or Local Control: Responses to George Woodcock*, Toronto, New Press.

54 See for example, GRAND'MAISON, J. (1970) *Vers un nouveau pouvoir*, Montreal, Editions HMH.

55 With regard to *historical* significance I must concur with Hobsbawn that ' ... the number of articles, books and authors which a political tendency produces is notoriously a poor measure of its practical importance, except of course among intellectuals. Guild socialism, an articulate and much described creed, deserves at best a footnote in the actual history of the British labour movement.' See HOBSBAWN, E. (1973) *Revolutionaries*, New York, Pantheon, p. 130.

56 For indicative works, see COLE, M. (1971) 'Guild socialism and the labour research department' and 'Guild socialism: The Storrington document', in BRIGGS, A. and SAVILLE, J. (Eds), *Essays in Labour History*, Vol. 2, London, Macmillan, CARPENTER, L.P. (1973) *G.D.H. Cole: An Intellectual Biography*, Cambridge, Cambridge University Press, GLASS, S.T. (1966) *The Responsible Society: The Ideas of the English Guild Socialists*, London, Longmans Green, COLE, M. (1971) *The Life of G.D.H Cole*, New York, Macmillan; PENTY, A.J. (1906) *The Restoration of the Guild System*, London, Swan Sonnenschein, HOBSON, S.G. (1917) *National Guilds: An Inquiry Into the Wage System and the Way Out*, London, G. Bell and Sons (2nd ed.); RUSSELL, B. (1918) *Roads to Freedom: Socialism, Anarchism and Syndicalism*, London, George Allen and Unwin, COLE, G.D.H. and MELLOR, W. (1918) *The Meaning of Industrial Freedom*, London, The Herald, TAWNEY, R.H. (1966), *The Acquisitive Society*, London, Fontana Library, COLE, G.D.H. (1917) *Self Government in Industry*, London, Hutchinson Education reprint from 1917 edition in

1972; COLE, G.D.H. (1923) *Workshop Organization*, London, Oxford COLE, G.D.H. (1920) *Guild Socialism Re-stated*, London, Leonard Parsons, COLE, G.D.H. (1923) *Social Theory*, London, Methuen, (3rd ed.); COLE G.D.H. (1920) *The World of Labour: A Discussion of the Present and Future of Trade Unionism*, London, G. Bell and Sons.

57 The strongest critique of capitalism is in HOBSON, S.G. (1917) *op. cit.*, pp. 1–108.

58 COLE, M. (1972) 'Introduction to the edition of 1919', in COLE, G.D.H. (1917) *op. cit.*, p. xii.

59 COLE, G.D.H. (1917) *op. cit.*, p. 13.

60 COLE, G.D.H. (1920) *Guild Socialism Re-Stated*, *op. cit.*, pp. 174–188.

61 COLE, G.D.H. and MELLOR, W. (1918) *op. cit.*, p. 20.

62 COLE, G.D.H. (1920) *The World of Labour*, *op. cit.*, p. 17. See also CRAIK, W.W. (1964) *The Central Labour College*, London, Lawrence and Wishart.

63 COLE, G.D.H. and MELLOR, W. (1918) *op. cit.*, pp. 6–7.

64 COLE, G.D.H. (1920) *Guild Socialism Re-Stated*, *op. cit.*

65 COLE, G.D.H. (1923) *Social Theory*, *op cit.* and (1920) *Guild Socialism op. cit.*

66 See for example, COLE, G.D.H. and MELLOR, W. (1918) *op. cit.*

67 For the details involved see COLE, M. (1971) 'Guild socialism: The Storrington document', *op. cit.*

68 See, for example, MANDEL, E. (1975) *Late Capitalism*, London, New Left Books; BRAVERMAN, H. (1974) *Labor and Monopoly Capital*, New York, Monthly Review Press; and ANDERSON, P. (1974) *Lineages of the Absolutist State*, London, New Left Books.

69 GRAMSCI, A. (1971) *Selections from the Prison Notebooks*, New York, International Publishers. For a recent overview see JESSOP, B. (1980) 'The Gramsci debate', *Marxism Today* (February), pp. 23–25.

70 See especially RASKIN, M. and BARNET, R. (General Editors) (1973) *Draft Prospectus for the Encyclopaedia of Social Reconstruction: Plans and Practices for a New Society*, Washington, Institute for Policy Studies; CAMPEN, J. (1974) *Materials Relevant to Constructive Thinking about Socialist Alternatives for America: A Bibliography*, Ann Arbor, Michigan, Union for Radical Political Economics. See also THOMPSON, E.P. (1976) 'Romanticism, moralism and utopianism: The case of William Morris', *New Left Review*, 99 (Sept -Oct), pp. 83–111. The corpus of work produced by Johan Galtung, one of the most eminent and prolific peace researchers, also deserves mention here. An intellectual who has long been actively committed to issues of social justice and equality, Galtung has recently produced an extensive vision of preferred global futures, under the aegis of the World Order Models Project (1980) *The True Worlds: A Transnational Perspective*, New York, Free Press. His analysis goes beyond that of FALK, R. (1975) *op. cit.* in beginning to specify some of the historical relations of exploitation and domination, and associated strategic problems, that stand in the way of such preferred futures. Galtung has also offered insightful observations about the unstated assumptions underlying most bourgeois and socialist thinking about education; see, for example, his 'Educational planning and educational research: Some unstated assumptions' in OECD (1973) *op. cit.*, pp. 229–52.

71 An earlier version of parts of this section, with more detailed attention to educational images, appeared in LIVINGSTONE, D.W. (1976) 'Images of the educational future in advanced industrial society', *Canadian Journal of Education* 1 (2), pp. 13–29.

72 A fuller indicative listing appears in STEVENSON, H. (1980) *Public Policy and Futures Bibliography*, Toronto, Ministry of Education/Ministry of Colleges and Universities.

73 For example, HODGETTS, B. (1968) *What Culture, What Heritage?* Toronto, Ontario Institute for Studies in Education; HURTIG, M. (1975) *Never Heard of*

Them ... They Must Be Canadians : A Report on the Results of a Canadian Student Awareness Survey, Toronto, Canadabooks, and the various reports of the US National Assessment of Educational Progress.

74 Quoted in BANTAM, J. (1974) 'UBC Group Analyses GVRD Attitudes', *UBC Reports* 20 (14), p. 3. It may be of interest to note here that Hardwick later was appointed deputy minister of education in British Columbia, and presumably became more sceptical about such views.

75 For indicative earlier examples, in addition to those cited in Chapter Four, see PARKER, D. (1970) *Schooling For What?* New York, McGraw-Hill; and LAUWERYS, J. (1973) *The Purposes of Education: Results of a CEA Survey*, Toronto, Canadian Education Association.

76 See, for example, KNOEPFLI, H. and SAUL, D. (1973) *Learning For Change: A Study of the Learning Needs and Interests of Ontario Adults*, Toronto, Ontario Educational Communications Authority.

77 See especially HAMILTON, R. (1972) *Class and Politics in the United States*, New York, John Wiley.

78 For example, BOULDING, K. (1965) *The Image: Knowledge and Life in Society*, Ann Arbor, University of Michigan Press; BOORSTEIN, D. (1964) *The Image: A Guide to Pseudo-Events in America*, New York, Harper-Colophon, and BELL, W. and MAU, J. (1971) 'Images of the future: Theory and research strategies' in BELL, W. and MAU, J. (Eds), *The Sociology of the Future*, New York, Rusell Sage. Compare BLOCH, E. (1971) *op. cit.*

79 Alvin Toffler, author of the 'pop psychology' best seller, *Future Shock*, has conducted one of the few impressionistic empirical studies bearing on this issue. See 'The psychology of the future' in TOFFLER, A. (1974) *op. cit.*, pp. 3–18. Toffler found that among a small group of high school students there was a lopsided emphasis on non-personel matters in their various views of the future, while the respondents 'made no provision for change in themselves, no provision for adaptation to a world exploding with change' (p. 11). But he also noted that he expects different groups to formulate quite different images of the future and to reflect different degrees of personal connectedness with societal change (p. 11).

80 For example, VIEILLE, P. (1969) 'Les Jeunes et l'an 2000' *2000: Revue de l'Amenagement du Servitoire et du developpement regional* 14 (October), pp. 45–53; YANKELOVICH, D. (1969) 'What they believe', Editors of Fortune (Eds) *Youth in Turmoil*, New York, Time-Life Books; and DILLMAN, D. and CHRISTENSON, J. (1972) 'Towards the Assessment of Public Values', paper presented at the annual meetings of the American Sociological Association, New Orleans, August.

81 For example, GILLESPIE, J. and ALLPORT, G. (1955) *Youth's Outlook on the Future*, Garden City, Doubleday, TUMIN, M. and FELDMAN, A. (1961) *Social Class and Social Change in Puerto Rico*, Princeton, Princeton University Press; and MAU, J. (1968) *Change and Images of the Future*, Cambridge, Schenkman. One of the richest Canadian sources is Grant Maxwell's adaptation of the oral history method to record views on a number of general current and future social issues expressed by a cross-section of the public identified by occupation; see his (1976) *Attitudes at the Canadian Grassroots*, 5 volumes, Ottawa, Canadian Catholic Conference.

82 The major empirical study in this regard has been CANTRIL, H. (1956) *The Pattern of Human Concerns*, New Brunswick, Rutgers University Press.

83 GALTUNG, J. et al. (1976) 'The future: Forgotten and to be discovered', in ORNAUER, H. et al. (Eds), *Images of the World in the Year 2000: A Comparative Ten Nation Study*, Paris, Mouton, pp. 579–80. Willener's study of the image of the future emerging in France during May 1968 provides one other case; see WILLENER, A. (1970) *The Action Image of Society*, London, Tavistock.

84 For details of the history, sample composition, and questionnaire of the World Images 2000 Project surveys, see ORNAUER, H. *et al* (1976) *op. cit.*, especially pp.

589–612, 637–710. The ten countries included were: Czechoslovakia, Spain, Great Britain, India, Japan, Norway, The Netherlands, Poland, Finland, and West Germany. I am indebted to Helmut Ornauer for providing me with some of the findings of the project prior to publication.

85 The Ontario Images 2000 Project was funded by the Ontario Institute for Studies in Education. Only results pertaining directly to educational issues previously have been published. Basic descriptive information about the survey is presented in LIVINGSTONE, D.W. (1976) *op. cit.* The questionnaire is available from the author.

86 It is most pertinent to note that the World Images 2000 Project country surveys were limited to fifteen to forty years age groups, while the Ontario survey was based on the entire population over eighteen years of age. Secondly, the surveys were variously based on face-to-face interviewing and mail questionnaires, with the Japanese and Ontario studies using the latter; a general discussion of effects of these different types of instruments appears in LIVINGSTONE, D.W. and HART, D.J. (1981) *Public Attitudes Toward Education in Ontario 1980*, Toronto, OISE Press, pp. 44–45.

87 ORNAUER, H. (1976) 'The basis and background of data interpretation', in ORNAUER, H. et al. (Eds) *op. cit.*, p. 611. Ornauer here also gives a slightly more detailed account of current events.

88 ORNAUER, H. et al. (1976) *op. cit.*, p. vi.

89 GALTUNG, J. (1976) 'The future: A forgotten dimension', in ORNAUER, H. et al. *op. cit.*, pp. 52–53.

90 *Ibid.*, pp. 56–57. See also pp. 641–42.

91 GALTUNG, J. et al. (1976) *op. cit.*, p. 581. For discussion of this concept of social position, see VAN DER VEER, K. (1976) 'Social position, dogmatism and social participation as independent variables', in ORNAUER, H. et al., *op. cit.*, pp. 621–36; and GALTUNG, J. (1976) 'Social position and image of the future', in ORNAUER, H. et al. *op. cit.*, pp. 381–400. This relational and multi-dimensional notion of the social power structure distinguishes 'top dogs', some intermediate positions, and 'underdogs'. It has some similarities with my own identification of class circles, which is referred to in Chapter Two and developed more fully in LIVINGSTONE, D.W. *Class and Class Consciousness in Advanced Capitalism* (to be published).

92 See especially ORNAUER, H. (1976) et al., *op. cit.*, p. 641.

93 LIVINGSTONE, D.W. (1979) *Public Attitudes Toward Education in Ontario 1978*, Toronto, OISE Press, p. 24.

94 GALTUNG, J. (1976) *op. cit.*, p. 400.

95 LIVINGSTONE, D.W. (1976) 'Images of the educational future', *op. cit.*

96 Comparisons with later expressed levels of satisfaction with school services appear in LIVINGSTONE, D.W. (1979) *Public Attitudes, op cit..*, pp. 5–7.

97 This thesis has been popularly conveyed by TOFFLER, A. (1970) *Future Shock*, New York, Random House, in an admixture of technological extrapolationist, psychologistic, and liberal populist forms of 'post-industrial' thought.

98 These interpretations of corporate capitalists' and small employers' views on future educational planning are *highly* speculative, especially in light of the small numbers of cases for each group in this sample.

99 The determination of important patterns of association has been based initially on detailed inspection of marginal distributions and cross-tabulations of responses in close conjunction with the respondent's own comments. All associations cited here have also been subjected to ordinal level correlation analysis (with unscalable coded responses removed) and have been found to be statistically significant at the .001 level.

100 See, for example, ADAMS, M. (1972) *Quality Education in Ontario*, Toronto, Environics Research Group, pp. 73–76. A more extensive discussion of expressed parent, teacher and student support in the early 1970s for greater student

participation in school decision-making appears in ADAMS, M. et al. (1976) *Educational Perspectives: A Survey of 10,000 Ontario Students, Teachers and Parents*, Toronto, Ministry of Education.

101 LIVINGSTONE, D.W. (1976) *op. cit.*, pp. 24–26.

102 *Ibid.*, pp. 17–18.

103 BLOCH, E. (1971) *op. cit.*

104 One of the few recent systematic efforts among socialist intellectuals in advanced capitalism appears in ALBERT, M. and HAHNEL, R. (1978) *Unorthodox Marxism: An Essay on Capitalism, Socialism and Revolution*, Boston, South End Press, pp. 253–96. My only published attempt to date is LIVINGSTONE, D.W. (1973) 'Man and community: A radical humanist perspective' in FARINA, J. (Ed), *The Social Development Papers*, Volume 2, Toronto, The North Pickering Development Project, pp. 1–13. As stated there: 'Therefore the fundamental principle in humanist planning is that institutional forms should permit people maximum opportunity to determine individually and collectively the ways in which they seek to gratify their needs for food, clothing and shelter, protection against pain and danger to life, intimate relatedness to others, and a consistent view of the world. To suggest more specific values as universal principles for normative planning would be just as doctrinaire and restrictive of people's capacities for self-determination as to resort purely to "tactical" planning which takes human nature for granted and deals essentially with technological feasibility.' (p. 4). It should be noted that neither of these general visions is explicitly related to progressive aspects of the practical activity and expressed sentiments of subordinate social groups.

Chapter Six

Notes For Educational Praxis in Advanced Capitalism

The materialist doctrine concerning the changing of circumstances and upbringing forgets that circumstances are changed by men and that it is essential to educate the educators themselves ... The philosophers have only *interpreted* the world, in various ways; the point is to *change* it.

Karl Marx *Theses on Feuerbach*(1845)[1]

To think in terms of a socialist alternative in education is purely illusory unless this alternative includes the liberation of the teachers. This transformation could only take place within the practice of a mass socialist movement – so that the problem of the teachers immediately repercusses back on the general problem of creating a hegemonic socialist party with beachheads in the teaching profession. Such a practice could only be founded concretely on demands which arise from the teachers' situation.

Quintin Hoare *New Left Review* (1965)[2]

Our analysis of the situation has shown that teachers who are ideologically workers must of necessity join ranks and build solidarity with the working class, because teachers share their condition. For, with the greatest will in the world, we teachers cannot bring about profound change in the *status quo* by ourselves.

Yvan Charbonneau, President of Quebec Teachers' Union (CEQ) (1972)[3]

The educational theoreticians who pose radical ideas have failed to present practical strategies for action. Ideas are worthless if they don't include a plan for their application – not an idealistic one, but a practical one which takes account of the concrete situation that teachers find themselves in here and now.

Nigel Grant, Rank and File member (1976)[4]

It has been one of the primary conceits of twentieth century intellectuals in advanced capitalist societies to presume the inherent power of ideas – whether disseminated by the mass media, vanguard parties, or not at all. As we have seen, intellectuals' ideas have had little impact unless they have responded to the social interests of some powerful group. Many committed socialist intellectuals have, of course, recognized this and made profound efforts to engage themselves in genuine working class and other subordinate group organizations and movements. The manifest failure of nearly all such movements to achieve anything more than minor concessions with regard to fundamental class interests indicates how massive an obstacle capitalist hegemony still presents to efforts to unify socialist theory and practice. While a great deal of attention has been paid in this text to ideological aspects of capitalist hegemony, it must be stressed here that this system of domination in advanced capitalism is *always* based on a combination of material concessions to and repression of the proletariat, other subordinate groups, and their aligned activists. Norman Geras has expressed the essential character of this system very well:

> Bourgeois democracy's strength in eliciting [support from working classes, etc.] derives from mechanisms of ideological legitimation and political integration incomparably more powerful than those available to the alternative, overtly repressive forms of bourgeois rule and for want of which the latter employ systematic terror. All bourgeois democracies, to be sure, also possess an armed, repressive apparatus which they use not only as a last resort, when these other mechanisms begin to fail decisively, but also on a more regular basis: piecemeal or in generous doses depending on the nature of the case. They rely upon a combination of repressions and concessions. But the basic pillar of their strength is a dense and complex structure of institutions and practices, many of them external to the state apparatus itself – of elections, legislative, executive, and advisory bodies, political parties, pressure groups and trade unions, newspapers and other mass media, etc. – through which the needs and demands of the masses are processed. This structure has a dual character. On the one hand, it does provide the workers' movement with the organizational and political means for opposing the more blatant forms of exploitation and oppression, for defending the workers' most immediate interests and for winning material gains on their behalf. This provision is the source of bourgeois democracy's self-legitimating power, and explains why it is no *mere* fraud and why an attitude of sectarian ultra-left abstentionism towards it will not win the confidence of politically conscious workers. On the other hand, this structure largely succeeds in sublimating and neutralizing, or sabotaging, such genuinely anticapitalist demands and initiatives as do emerge, by taking them through its many 'competent' and 'specialized' channels, that is, away

from the masses, out of their direct control and sight – generally with the assistance of reformist workers' parties and trade union leaders.[5]

However, in periods of accumulation crisis with diminished capacity to grant material concessions, capitalist groups and their allies must necessarily rely more heavily on forces of repression and 'public order'. The tendencies toward increased use of repressive measures, and particularly new technologies of political control, in the current crisis should by no means be underestimated.[6] But it is also at such moments that subordinate groups become most predisposed to be mobilized to create a socialist society. While there is now much dissatisfaction and social protest, working class circles and other subordinate groups have, to date, exhibited little inclination to reject the basic institutional structure of bourgeois democracy. The futility of small revolutionary vanguards relying on tactics of counter-violence under such conditions has been amply demostrated by the isolation of such groups as the Weathermen in the US, and the Red Brigades in Italy.[7] As Abraham Guillen, a foremost Latin American systematizer of the strategy or urban guerrilla movements, has observed:

> If the bulk of the population does not support an action for liberation, as in the case of Che Guevara in Bolivia, then every tactical victory leads to an ultimate strategical defeat.[8]

Therefore, on strategic as well as philosophical grounds, a socialist movement must be democratically constituted in order to be successful. The fundamental issue now in advanced capitalist societies is how to build such movements into material forces which are capable of transforming existing institutions into socialist ones. We are in a situation in which the opposition between active class forces is, in Gramsci's terms, primarily an intricate 'war of position'.[9] That is, for socialists it is pre-eminently a matter of drawing on progressive aspects of mass predispositions to establish a *popularly-based* political and ethical counter-hegemony. One of the major weapons in such a struggle is education. Education should be regarded most broadly to include the transmission – especially among young people – of cultural and technical knowledge, the dissemination of information about current affairs, and the articulation of world views consistent with the social interests of different groups. The major organized instruments of education in advanced capitalist societies are the schools and communications media. Their effects pervade social consciousness in all other major social sites – workplaces, households, and communities. The control of such instruments and the content of their messages are clearly central to the contemporary exercise of ideological hegemony.

The most immediate tactical issues for socialist movements are therefore how to democratize control of schools and mass media, and how to ensure that educational content is generated and distributed 'dialogically' (that is, through two-way communications) rather than imposed by remote specialists. The tactics that are most appropriate will vary immensely with particular circumstances. As Saul Alinsky, the great American community organizer, noted:

> The greatest barrier to communication between myself and would-be organizers arises when I try to get across the concept that tactics are not the product of careful cold reason, that they do not follow a table of organization or plan of attack. Accident, unpredictable reactions to your own actions, necessity, and improvization dictate the direction and nature of tactics. Then, analytical logic is required to appraise where you are, what you can do next, the risks and hopes that you can look forward to. It is this analysis that protects you from being a blind prisoner of the tactic and the accidents that accompany it. But I cannot overemphasize that the tactic itself comes out of the free flow of action and reaction, and requires on the part of the organizer an easy acceptance of apparent disorganization.[10]

What I can do here is simply to raise several of the underlying *strategic* issues involved in the constituting and development of socialist movements in advanced capitalist societies – many of which have been largely ignored in most such movements to date. These are reference points for reflective analysis which may aid in generating action plans; specific tactics must remain responsive to the 'flow of action and reaction'.

Some Basic Strategic Questions for Educational and Social Movements[11]

Even in turbulent times most of us take for granted innumerable things about the social contexts in which we live. On the one hand, incessant questioning of what we 'know' as 'reality' in our everyday lives can be immobilizing; when our routines are interrupted we usually try to use common-sense knowledge to integrate the problem into the unproblematic sector of everyday life and go on about our practical activity. But, on the other hand, to seek fundamental social change is to try to transcend the boundaries of the reality of everyday life and to point to other potential realities; when problems that give rise to a desire for fundamental social change are reacted to in purely *ad hoc* or doctrinaire ways, too much of the context is taken for granted for creative action to be sustained. What sort of strategic framework can facilitate continuing questions of the social context and yet be usefully related toaction? I would like to suggest a set of five basic questions:

1   What are the fundamental values and objectives on which our collective action is based?

2   Who should be actively involved in such a movement for fundamental social change?

3   Do we consider a wide array of alternative programmes and carefully assess their *desirability* in terms of fundamental and popular objectives?

4   Do we have an accurate critical understanding of the real social forces supporting, opposing, and indifferent to our programmes and contending programmes?

5   Have we selected an action plan which is both most desirable for society as a whole and feasible in light of the current array of social forces?

Group reflection with reference to such general questions should not necessarily proceed in any given sequential way. Of course, any itemization of essential strategic questions is quite open to dispute. My main concern is to emphasize the importance of critical reflection on such strategic issues, and in particular to point both to a few of the available ways and means of facilitating such reflections as well as to limitations progressive social movements often impose on themselves by ignoring some of these issues.

Clarifying Values and Objectives

Any effort to create an alternative future is based in part on underlying general values or ethical principles. Socialist activists have often taken such general principles as self-management, equality or social diversity for granted. While one can agree with Gramsci that such principles are implicit in some of the practical activities of subordinate groups, they are seldom explicit. Common-sense understanding of these principles has typically been associated with such ubiquitous general themes of dominant bourgeois ideology as 'individual freedom', 'opportunity', and 'democracy', with little and very selective connection to practical activity. Values have often been dismissed as too vague and elusive to be usefully discussed within social movements. But our preferences on such matters as views of human nature, relation to the natural environment, and such aspects of social relations as bases of superiority and subordination and the relative significance of the individual and the collectivity, unavoidably underlie both our actions and our judgements about more specific issues. The social animation work of Paulo Freire in Latin America and Danilo Dolci in Sicily, for example, has shown that popular dialogue about such values and everyday common sense concepts can serve as a strong incentive to thinking about preferable futures in practical terms.[12] More generally, the concrete reality of subordinate groups and their *own* experience of this reality should always be a point of reference for progressive change efforts. Such dialogues can serve not only to clarify fundamental values but to identify real, widely-experienced social problems. It is the formulation through open group discussion of specific objectives to resolve such common problems consistent with lived values, that can generate a compelling sense of a desirable alternative future, and provide the basic impetus for sustained collective action.

The common tendency, however, in progressive change movements in most advanced capitalist settings has been to formulate objectives entirely within the context of existing institutions, with only the most superficial reference to real values. My education surveys have found, for example, growing expressions of conflicting curricular objectives among capitalists and proletarians, sentiments which are presumably linked with different lived values and which imply alternative preferred forms of education. The real problems underlying such expressed objectives need to be widely discussed within subordinate groups in relation to lived values, in order to open the door to educational futures that are more than merely extensions of or *ad hoc* reactions against current school institutions. But, these 'codification' and 'problematization' processes, which have been very effective in animating peasant literacy movements in several peripheral capitalist settings where forms of oppression are relatively overt,[13] have met with very limited success to date in the few serious efforts that have been made to apply them in the more complex hegemonic conditions of bourgeois democracy. Such attempts are worthy of careful attention by those wishing to go beyond them.[14] A central difficulty in these 'conscientization' efforts has been a preoccupation with the familiar everyday concepts in which social problems are typically expressed. Particularly in advanced capitalist settings, where commodity fetishism is very highly developed, and many forms of oppression are indirect and cloaked within intricate institutional structures, more incisive codifications of popularly expressed social problems by aligned intellectuals are needed. The historical materialist method of inquiry discussed in Chapter One can be used in intimate contact with rank and file members of subordinate groups to apply established determinate abstractions and identify additional ones that can both resonate the contradictory relations of social existence in advanced capitalism and *penetrate* beneath the simple abstractions of 'common sense' understanding.[15] Declining material concessions can make these contradictions more apparent, and social animation work somewhat more straightforward. But, whatever method is used, sensitive clarification of the progressive values implicit in the practical activities of subordinate groups is likely to remain the critical lynchpin of sustained collective action to create a genuine socialist society on an advanced technological base.

Who Should Be Involved?

The prior analyses suggest that on the bases of shared material conditions and of class interests, as well as in terms of expressed subjective dispositions, the productive proletarian core of working class circles is likely to constitute the primary membership of any effective socialist movement in current advanced capitalist societies. There are also indications that the allegiance of numerous of those in intermediate class positions to capitalist interests has weakened somewhat in recent years. Effective alliances with such intermediate elements are likely to be critical fòr either the maintenance of capitalism or the emergence of socialism. With regard to maintenance of the established order or fundamental change in education, the role of teachers is clearly of central strategic importance. Both corporate and labour leaders perceive this. But the discourse analyses in Chapter Three suggest that corporate leaders have a greater sense of urgency and initiative.[16]

Certainly, any successful movement toward a socialist alternative in education will have to involve a concrete understanding of the situation of teachers. The Birmingham Education Group offers a useful general characterization, which also reflects some of the tendencies frequently discussed in this text with regard to professional employees in general:

> Teachers, especially where they are also active in trade unions and professional bodies, are obviously central to the popular politics of schooling, not least because they combine the two levels of struggle: struggles in and struggles over schools. Their relation to other popular constituencies, especially working-class parents, is peculiarly contradictory. But this goes for the other professionals too, especially educational researchers and educational experts in universities . . . This 'educational interest' belongs to a broader social *milieu* with two major characteristics: first, a relative distance from the management and control of economic activity, whether financial activity or productive industry; second, a high degree of dependence on personal skills which are closely associated with formal education and certification. Such groups have a particularly intimate stake in the education system, both in terms of their own employment (many are employees of the state if not of the education system) and in terms of family strategies for their own children. They are likely to be more knowledgeable than others about the internal working of schools and about the complexities of individual advancement by this route. They are likely to play a particularly important – and also highly ambiguous – role in educational politics as a whole.[17]

The most detailed critical studies of teachers' situation in current advanced capitalist settings, and particularly in working class communities, have found that the general institutional arrangements of the school, the enduring ideologies of school knowledge and professional competence, and the immediate constraints of practical work activity, have '. . . effectively precluded the majority of teachers from the possibility of challenge or even the possibility of much critical reflection about their own activities.'[18] While teachers have been mobilized for direct political action in several countries in recent years, salary and work load matters have typically been of such central concern that issues of teacher self-management and general educational change have scarcely been raised. Most teacher organizations remain hung on the horns of professionalism versus unionism. On pay and work conditions they increasingly rely on trade union actions, but as professional associations they have commonly been resistant to any criticism of current teaching practices and generally closed to any close alliances with working class organizations to press for progressive change in educational provisions. An analysis of the attitudes of the teachers included in our recent Ontario surveys, for example, suggests that their tax dollar priority for public education versus other government expenditures may have doubled since 1978 and that their sentiments of support for the social democratic party (NDP) which most strongly supports education spending has also increased. But, on educational matters their expressed views are strongly in favour of giving school principals greater authority as opposed to supporting greater community control, and only a minority would support giving labour perspectives any greater emphasis in the curriculum.[19] Generally, radical teacher movements inside established professional associations have had very marginal effects. It would appear that such movements would be better advised to put more of their efforts into forming their own direct alliances with subordinate group organizations and communities, while continuing to try to put their ideas into widespread circulation within their still predominantly conservative professional bodies.[20] It should be noted here, however, that in Quebec, as a direct result of the 'school crisis' of 1966–67 in which the government imposed firm spending ceilings and harsh back-to-work legislation against striking teachers, the major teacher organization (CEQ) did form a close alliance with organized labour and fought strongly for progressive educational changes in the early 1970s.[21]

In any case, it is fairly clear that both proletarian organizations and radical educators will have to establish effective alliances with other dispossessed and intermediate social groups in order to accomplish progressive educational and social change in advanced capitalist settings. Reflecting the 'centuries of childhood', young people and especially those under eighteen have been largely ignored in this text, as they have been by all sides in most analyses of the influences on educational policies. But the support of students, as well as other school workers, is likely to be decisive for the fate of locally-based progressive change initiatives. The women's movement, minority ethnic organizations, and retired people – who are often more organized than those outside their contact realize – are other major political constituencies whose particular interests and potential support must be considered.

The second basic issue here is the form of command structure involved in directing fundamental change movements. Elite centralist, populist, and grass-roots decentralist approaches may be distinguished. In the elitist approach, a small group of people effectively define themselves as having sufficient powers and knowledge to impose substantial alterations in educational or other social provisions for the mass of the population. The variants of this predominate style of directing deliberate social change range from formal commissions that have their terms of reference set by central governments or by corporate interests, to small bands of disaffected professionals and intellectuals who are strongly opposed to dominant institutions. In the case of expert commissions, which typically take the established power structure for granted, there may be a great degree of attention to trying to accommodate mass grievances and aspirations within that structure. In social movements that are initiated without much mass participation, as in the social revolutions in Meiji Japan, Kemalist Turkey, and several current transitional socialist societies, mass grievances and aspirations may be more taken for granted, and greater attention given to redesigning and trying to redistribute institutional goods and services in accord with such assumed needs. In all instances, however, the characteristic problem of the elitist approach remains the same – how can the relevance of change efforts to actual mass grievances and aspirations be assured when the directing group remains limited to a presuming few?

In the populist approach, instead of aligning themselves with or addressing any clearly identifiable groups, some would-be change agents merely offer their critiques and/or proposals to humanity as a whole to use as it sees fit. In the past decade, this approach was exemplified by such radical critics of schooling as Ivan Illich. Such humanist intellectuals have found it inimical to their principles to align themselves with any specific groups, hoping rather that by publicly proclaiming existing institutional contradictions and suggesting more sane alternatives they will convince sufficient numbers of people to facilitate educational or cultural revolution. The recent free school movement in North America has been stimulated at least in part by writings of these radical critics. While not wittingly elitist at the outset, the movement has attracted mostly the affluent, with many free schools being even more discriminatory than the state schools. In the populist approach to change, self-segregating groups can always take over and diminish the wider aims of the initial change agents.[22]

In the grass-roots approach, groups of people take action to try to change their own immediate educational or social conditions, not because they define themselves as particularly powerful or knowledgeable but simply because they are very dissatisfied with such conditions. The basic participation criteria in the 1970s movements in North America for community control of schools, for example, were dissatisfaction and community residence. While the community control and conscientization movements still appear full of promise, grass-roots change efforts have historically had great difficulty in achieving anything but the narrowest of objectives in small, isolated areas. Indeed, the characteristic problem of this approach is whether such locally-based movements can became sufficiently aware of extra-local forces beyond their own immediate situation to avoid being co-opted at the local level or suppressed in any attempts to coordinate their efforts with other groups beyond their own locality for mutual benefit.

Only a decentralist approach is ultimately compatible with essential socialist principles of self-management, equality in social relations, and the fostering of human diversity. There has been much rhetorical hand-wringing over the purported failure of leadership in decentralized social movements. The critical missing element in many instances has actually been the lack of adequate *inter-locality networks* of communication and coordination. In the past decade, both the co-operative movement and community control groups have made significant steps toward establishing such networks in many countries.[23] As a critical reading of bourgeois military strategists can confirm, such decentralized networks have a much greater political mobilization potential than conventional centralist or vanguard organizations within subordinate populations.[24] As the current crisis continues, rank-and-file movements within organized labour are increasingly throwing up popular, progressive leaders, and attracting more socialist intellectuals into alignment. But without the maintenance of decentralist communication and control networks, such movements remain prone to Michels' 'iron law' of oligarchy, and highly vulnerable to the defusing of top leaders.

A third, most vital issue, is how to gain the sympathy of the oppressed majority who remain outside active participation in the movement. This is centrally a matter of getting the movement's ideas into wide circulation. While the immense encapsulating power of capitalist control of the major means of cultural production should never be underestimated, the production and distribution of critical pamphlets, newspapers, magazines, and books, as well as the use of public speakers and mass media events can be effective.[25] But to be able to continue in such activity, any liberation movement must establish bases or 'liberated zones' which enable it to grow as a material force. Co-operative activities in the workplace and between households in working-class communities, and community-based education practices in such contexts, offer the most potent grounding for organized socialist politics, as well as the most compelling demonstration effects of a viable socialist alternative. This is a point on which central intelligence agencies of the state are often most paranoid – to the extent of making extraordinary efforts to infiltrate some of the most democratically-constituted community groups. The only effective antidote to such efforts at subversion is *open* assessment, in both recruitment and internal work efforts, of the extent to which individuals and groups are committed or sympathetic to the movements' developing objectives. Any movement that established pat answers to these questions is probably signing its own death warrant.

Envisaging and Evaluating Alternatives

As I have illustrated in Chapter Five, we now have only one general image of the societal future that has been envisaged in much detail. This possible future is essentially a technological extrapolation, and a main contribution of corporate and state planners, futurists, and policy scientists has been to objectify this image. Of course, no professional forecaster would argue that trend is destiny. But the general preoccupation with contingencies within a generalized trend to 'post-industrialism' underlines the point that the envisaging of an array of *alternative* possible futures is more fundamentally an expression of value-based imagination than of trend projections.

Value-based envisaging of the future remains rare. Subordinate groups may express a wide array of values and opinions on various future-related issues, but they have had very limited access to tools for systematic speculation. If we are actually to create the future, in the sense of generating an array of desirable images and trying to implement the most practical ones, then the varieties of existing human values and of speculative techniques must both be involved in a highly interactive way.

There is something of an array of alternative educational programmes in various stages of implementation today within advanced capitalist societies – such as several patterns of community control of schools, programmed learning, voucher systems, and open universities. But such alternative provisions continue to be conceived in a piecemeal fashion. There are, on the other hand, many speculative techniques such as gaming, scenario-building, brainstorming, relevance trees, contextual mapping, and morphological analysis that could serve as useful aids to thinking about alternative educational and related social provisions, working out their practicability, and revealing unintended consequences.[26] While these techniques require little experise to use, at least in rudimentary form, their use for policy and programme-making has remained largely the preserve of professional forecasters. The main difficulty in using such techniques is one that is common to most group problem-solving strategies – discouraging negative evaluations of any alternative until all those that have been suggested have been fully described. Change-oriented groups typically devote much of their early effort to designing a single alternative to established programmes and, in the process, develop a high degree of commitment to this alternative programme, thereby excluding serious consideration of other alternatives.

Matrix thinking can help overcome such 'premature closure'. Regarding education, for example, when *activities* (such as educational goal setting, acquisition and allocation of education resources, control and co-ordination of resources use, curricular design, and the learning process itself) on the one hand, and *resources* (such as human participants, materials, space, and time) on the other, both serve as dimensions that must be described and interrelated, then possible educational alternatives immediately become both more concrete and more distinctive than when the task is simply to think up an alternative socialist programme that is 'better' than existing institutional provisions. In my own efforts to aid several groups in working class communities as well as teacher groups to envisage a variety of concrete alternative educational futures, we have relied mostly on a variant of contextual mapping that consists of a matrix of activities involved in and resources required for various possible educational futures. This encourages people to relate all potential activities and resources in 'cross-impact' format for each alternative.[27] Working with the aid of even the most simple matrices, such groups can go through wider ranging, more systematic efforts to imagine alternative programmes than *ad hoc* methods can ever facilitate.

It is true that in thinking about desirable socialist futures there is much that can be learned through study of the brief historical successes from the Paris

Commune of 1871 onward, from small-scale current successes such as the *kibbutzim* movement and the Mondragon co-operatives, as well as from the large practical heritage of failures. But, although heavy reliance on matrix techniques can encourage ahistorical thinking, desirable alternative futures for subordinate groups in advanced capitalist settings must come largely from themselves.

With regard to the *evaluation* of alternative possible programmes of action, it is often a particular type of proposed alternative to established conditions that has brought a change-oriented group together. However, terminating the normative evaluation process before the particular alternative programme is collectively worked through quite thoroughly in terms of the resources and activities involved may be hazardous. *Ad hoc* positive evaluation leads almost inevitably to piecemeal implementation efforts in which many negative consequences are largely a result of premature normative support for an alternative that has been only narrowly conceptualized. Proposals for educational voucher systems that have been put forward by various progressive intellectuals, for example, may be evaluated much differently in isolation than when activity and resource changes required for adequate implementation are taken into account.

There is also a common tendency for normative evaluations of the desirability of proposed alternatives to be ignored almost entirely in concrete change efforts. In general, the concrete predominates over the abstract in human thought. It is very difficult to use concrete experiences as criteria to evaluate entire institutions. Therefore, if the group is not committed to clarifying and using more abstract values and objectives as evaluative criteria, then the existing institutions themselves tend to provide the criteria for, as well as the objects of, evaluation. Conversely, if values and objectives which substantial parts of the population are likely to support can be made more perceptible through carefully worked out concrete alternative programmes that are compatible with them, then the evident discrepancies between such lived values and existing institutional provisions can become a resource in itself for attracting supporters to the movement. In any case, for a change-oriented group to presume the popular desirability of *ad hoc* alternatives over the *status quo* is to deny both bourgeois domination of most existing institutions in advanced capitalism as well as the institution-bound nature of most people's conscious evaluation criteria.

The relevance of such concretely-posed alternatives for a socialist politics of education has been expressed by Simon Frith and Paul Corrigan:

> There has always been a strange reluctance on the left in Britain (none such as the Right) to get stuck into the details of what schooling should involve ... Political activists, in placing education in the wider context of political struggle, must focus on the questions of education *content* and *control*. The point is this: the state does monopolize educational resources, and these resources must (as Marx pointed out) be used by the working-class. If, then, schools are to be used in the context of

political struggle, an explicit link has to be made between education and the future – the content of education has to be given socialist (and not just capitalist) relevance (it is not enough simply to press for an expansion of educational resources or to call for 'relevant' education' – relevant for the working-class within capitalism). It is necessary to make education relevant in a new way and for an alternative future . . .

Secondly, there is the problem of creating an alternative education, outside the state system. Again, the point of such alternatives must be political. There is no point in setting up echoes of state schools, more efficient or more sympathetic but with the same ultimate purposes (cf. Free Schools) – the purpose of alternative socialist education must be revolutionary, revolutionary both in challenging bourgeois norms and in creating new, socialist, institutions . . . Too many 'progressive' educational ideas are progressive only by reference to bourgeois values; education can only be progressive when we know what are progressing to, when it is, in a revolutionary sense, political. We must take educational debates out of their exclusively educational contexts (where the bourgeoisie still set the limits of discussion) and place them in the context of organized socialist politics. It is only there that a truly radical educational politics can be constructed.[28]

In Britain and elsewhere, neo-conservative forces have become adept at linking proposals for reprivatization of the educational system and the economy to traditional bourgeois values that are still little questioned.[29] Socialists must become more adept at appealing to the lived progressive values in subordinate groups' practical activities.

Understanding Real Social Forces

Since much of the text is addressed to the question of which real class forces are reproducing and modifying advanced capitalist societies in general and educational institutions in particular, I will be very brief here. The basic question a change-oriented group must continually ask is 'what are the forces that will help and that will hinder us in pursuing our purposes?'.

Many simple techniques are available to aid any group of non-experts in conducting such an analysis. As an illustration consider force-field analysis.[30] The basic process is as follows. Group members are asked to list all the present influences they are aware of that they believe will help to achieve a given programme, as well as all those things they think will prevent achieving such a programme. Next, they are asked to indicate the relative strength of respective driving and restraining forces. Then the group is asked to try to think of ways to diminish, remove, or reverse the influence of restraining forces, and to strengthen, combine, or create new driving forces.

If such analyses are collectively reviewed and modified as a result of continuing experience with existing programmes and careful observation of the effects of change efforts, they can become invaluable aids to future group practices. But it is vital to persist in drawing openly on the collective experience of the group as well as any possible outside sources of information, and to test every notion against practice. Aligned intellectuals can play a useful role here in suggesting possible indirect influences. Critical analysis in subordinate group movements for social and educational change is necessarily a more intricate matter than counting those who take 'pot shots' at you – as Alinsky sometimes seemed to think. But it is in the interplay between the subordinate group's own critical reflection and its own practice that the identification of real social and environmental forces impinging on social change programmes emerges. Such analyses can never be complete in a dynamic social world, and aligned intellectuals in particular must be wary of inadvertently conveying closed theoretical perspectives. This is certainly the case for analyses of class relations and class alliances. To presume the continuation of the current array of class forces, or to accept uncritically 'objective', 'neutral' analyses that assert or infer such, is to exhibit yet another version of extrapolationist thinking, and to limit unnecessarily the group's range of possible actions.

Creating Practical, Desirable Futures

Do we select the most practical desirable alternative for action? If alternatives have not been explicitly linked both with values and objectives and with facilitating and impeding forces in group dialogues, it makes little sense to ask this question. However, no matter how graphic the description of an alternative future that we find desirable, and how incisive the analysis supporting the feasibility of such a future, others may still not want to act upon it. Diversity of interests among group members is likely to become most apparent when free decisions about commitment to action are involved. In addition, there is no easy formula for balancing off desirability and feasibility. But as long as group members feel that their views have been heard in the selection process and continue to be seriously considered by others, action can be taken to implement programmes without dissension immobilizing the group. Conversely, the unanimity that prevails when only one alternative programme to existing provisions is considered makes it much more difficult for the change-oriented group to continue to address any of these strategic questions or even to remain a viable movement when elements of its proposed programme are taken up by defenders of the capitalist social order.

However questions of selecting practical, desirable alternatives may be resolved at a given moment by any change-oriented group, the selection of particular educational and social programmes should lead to further reflection on the other strategic questions. To recognize humanity's potential for creating educational and social futures is also to realize that there are no final answers to what such futures should or will be.

The current moment in human history is fraught with unprecedented dangers. The generalized recession deepens and social contradictions become increasingly explosive. As Ernest Mandel suggests:

> ... [I]t is possible that the imperialist bourgeoisie during the next several years may for a second time have recourse to the 'remedies' with which it 'resolved' the crisis of the 1930s. It will then seek to inflict a very heavy defeat on the working class, to raise the rate of profit through superexploitation of the workers, to stabilize this system through a 'strong state' or even through a ferocious dictatorship. It would once again take the course of war. These would be 'remedies' infinitely more catastrophic during the epoch of nuclear and biological weapons than they were during the epoch of Hitler. Thus, the generalized recession also recalls the timeliness of the burning alternative: socialism or barbarianism.[31]

Indeed, even without nuclear war, the continuation of a world economy driven by capitalist accumulation imperatives may well be making us vulnerable to an ecological holocaust of even more devastating proportions. We are slowly being forced to recognize that the cumulative impact of the massive, interactive array of pollutants generated by the capitalist form of production (and similarly by the chosen forms of production in most transitional socialist states) can threaten not only the biological survival of humanity and other living species, but the biosphere itself.[32]

In any event, the overriding assumption of this discussion is that proletarian and other subordinate groups must now make concerted efforts to build sane alternative futures in advanced capitalist societies. If we do not meet this challenge, both the peoples of the advanced capitalist world and the rest of humanity are likely to inherit from ourselves social and educational futures that we do not want – or none at all.

Notes

1 MARX, K. (1845) 'Theses on Feuerbach' in MARX, K. and ENGELS, F. *The German Ideology* New York, International Publishers, 1970 pp. 121, 123.

2 HOARE, Q. (1965) 'Education: Programmes and men' *New Left Review* 32 p. 52.

3 CHARBONNEAU, Y. (1972) 'A strategy for the CEQ' in MARTELL, G. (Ed) *The Politics of The Canadian Public School* Toronto, Lorimer, 1974.

4 GRANT, N. (1978) 'Teacher politics and educational change' in WHITTY, G. and YOUNG, M.F.D. (Eds) *Explorations in the Politics of Knowledge* Driffield, Nafferton Books, p. 251.

5 GERAS, N. (1977) 'Luxemburg and Trotsky on the contradictions of bourgeois democracy' in BLACKBURN, R. (Ed) *Revolution and Class Struggle: Reader in Marxist Politics* London, Fontana, pp. 309–10.

6 For valuable documentation of some of these developments, see ACKROYD, C. et al. (1977) *The Technology of Political Control* Harmondsworth, Penguin Books.

7 For a detailed account of the recent development of such vanguard groups in Italy

and of their varied conceptions of the use of counter-violence see NEGRI, T. et al. (1979) *Working Class Autonomy and the Crisis: Italian Marxist Texts of the Theory and Practice of a Class Movement, 1964–79* London, Red Notes and CSE Books.

8 GUILLEN, A. (1973) *Philosophy of the Urban Guerrilla* (Edited by D.Hodges) New York, William Morrow, p. 257.

9 For a discussion of the distinction between war of position, war of manoeuvre or movement, and underground warfare particularly with reference to 'civil society', see GRAMSCI, A. (1971) *Selections From the Prison Notebooks* New York, International Publishers, especially pp. 229–39.

10 ALINSKY, S. (1972) *Rules for Radicals* New York, Vintage Books, p. 165.

11 An earlier effort along these lines appeared in LIVINGSTONE, D.W. (1973) 'Some general tactics for creating alternative educational futures' *Interchange* 4 (1) pp. 1–9.

12 For examples of the processes and dialogues in such 'culture circles', see FREIRE, P. (1968) *The Pedagogy of the Oppressed* New York, Herder and Herder, 1970, and (1968) *Education for Critical Consciousness* New York, Seabury Press; DOLCI, D. (1956) *Poverty in Sicily* Harmondsworth, Penguin Books, 1966, and (1965) *A New World in the Making* Westport, Greenwood Press, 1976.

13 This is not to suggest that such approaches to popular dialogue as they have been practised to date in peripheral capitalist settings have not suffered from serious limitations. In particular, the critical development of Friere's 'conscientization' techniques, in both Latin American and African settings, appears to have been constrained both by his continuing allegiance to the broad Catholic tradition of syncretism and by a related lack of concrete analyses of societal forces. For an important critique along these lines, see WALKER, J. (1980) 'The end of dialogue: Paulo Freire on politics and education' in MACKIE, R. (Ed), *Literacy and Revolution: The Pedagogy of Paulo Freire* London, Pluto Press, pp. 120–50.

14 In North America one of the most substantial efforts has involved the Movement for a New Society, centred in Philadelphia. This avowedly socialist, 'middle class'-centred movement has developed many techniques for facilitating group discussion and integrating critical dialogue about social problems with social practice. The most useful document in this regard is *Organizing Macro-Analysis Seminars: A Manual* which is available in several printings from the Philadelphia Macro-Analysis Collective, 4719 Cedar Avenue, Philadelphia, Pa. 19143.

15 For significant attempts to develop such determinate cultural abstractions on the basis of dialogues in working-class communities, see WILLIS, P. (1977) *Learning to Labour: How Working Class Kids Get Working Class Jobs* Westmead, Saxon House, especially part 2; and SIEGEL, S. (1980) *Towards an Analytical Model of the Situated Working Class Individual*, Ph.D. dissertation, University of Toronto.

16 The following quotations, from business and labour spokespersons respectively, may be most indicative, at least for English Canada: 'Education is too serious a matter to be entrusted to educators. There is an existing demand from teachers generally for some association with business ... In the larger sphere of education, businessmen can reach out for contact with members of boards of education and of trustees, associations of teachers and businessmen can be formed to discuss mutual problems. The exchange of teachers with people from industry can be worked out ... Thus people in business will learn more of the educators' problems and aspirations, and work together towards common goals.' (G. Temple (1976) 'What Business Can Do About Education' *Canadian Business* June, p. 46.

'I notice that the teachers are not in the Ontario Federation of Labour. I wish they were, and I think it would be a step toward convincing them that they ought to be in it, if we did show solidarity and have a resolution calling for a reduced number of pupils per teacher.' (C. Beeman, Delegate Remarks in Education Debate. *Ontario Federation of Labour Convention Proceedings 1977*, p. 75).

17 Education Group, Centre for Contemporary Cultural Studies (1981) *Unpopular*

Education: Schooling and Social Democracy in England Since 1944 London, Hutchinson, p. 31.

18 GRACE, G. (1978) *Teachers, Ideology and Control: A Study in Urban Education* London, Routledge and Kegan Paul, p. 218.

19 While these statements must again remain tentative, especially because of the small numbers of teachers among the respondents – approximately thirty in each survey – the results do appear to be consistent with observed tendencies in practice.

20 Nigel Grant's (1978) *op. cit.* critical reflections on the efforts of Rank and File to influence the National Union of Teachers in England are most insightful in this regard.

21 A helpful comparative analysis is provided in HARP, J. and BETCHERMAN, G. (1980) 'Contradictory class locations and class action: The case of school teachers' organizations in Ontario and Quebec' *Canadian Journal of Sociology* 5 (2) pp. 145–62. One of the central documents of this Quebec teacher movement is 'Phase One: CEQ Manifesto' in DRACHE, D. (Ed) (1972) *Quebec-Only the Beginning: The Manifestoes of the Common Front* Toronto, New Press, pp. 97–148.

22 For a more detailed discussion of the difficulties with the populist approach, see my critique of the work of Illich and Everett Reimer in (1971) 'Educational revolution: Problems and prospects', *Interchange*, 2(1), 36–43, as well as Reimer's response in the same issue.

23 In the United States, for example, representative cases are the Industrial Co-operative Association (2161 Massachussetts Avenue, Cambridge, Mass. 02140) which provides advice and publishes guides on setting up worker co-ops, and Vocations for Social Change (353 Broadway, Cambridge, Mass., 02139) which produces the Greater Boston area People's Yellow Pages.

24 See, for example, McCUEN, J. (1966) *The Art of Counter-Revolutionary War* London, Faber and Faber; PAGET, J. (1967) *Counter-Insurgency Operations* New York, Walker and Company; and especially KITSON, F. (1971) *Low Intensity Operations* London, Faber and Faber. For critical readings, see ACKROYD, C. *et al* (1977) *op. cit.* and BUNYAN, T. (1976) *The History and Practice of the Political Police in Britain* London, Julian Friedmann.

25 For some of the dangers involved in trying to use current mass media, see, for example. GITLIN, T. (1980) *The Whole World is Watching: Mass Media in the Making and Unmaking of the New Left* Berkeley, University of California Press.

26 Many of these techniques are described in fairly straightforward terms in ROSOVE, P. (1967) *A Provisional Survey and Evaluation of the Current Forecasting State of the Art for Possible Contributions to Long-Range Educational Policy-Making* Santa Monica: System Development Corporation. In fact, most of these thinking aids essentially amount to arraying possible activities and resources to deal with a problem into a matrix, grid, or chart.

27 Detailed illustrations of the early development of this approach appear in LIVINGSTONE, D.W. (1970) 'Alternative futures for formal education' *Interchange* 1 (4), pp. 13–27. A report on the work of the largely *ad hoc* teacher groups was prepared and discussed with the executive body of the major Ontario teacher organization. ('Teachers and the Future of Education'. Report on the Educational Futures Workshop Series jointly sponsored by the Ontario Teachers Federation and the Ontario Institute for Studies in Education, February, 1974). This report was quite prescient in identifying some current problems of the teaching profession and proposing alternative solutions, including many possible new roles for teachers, especially as community-based resource co-ordinators. I presume the report has now been relegated to the dustbin of history!

28 FRITH, S. and CORRIGAN, P. (1977) 'The politics of education' in YOUNG, M.F.D. and WITTY, G. (Eds) *Society, State and Schooling*, Lewes, Falmer Press, pp. 265–66.

29 See especially Education Group (1981) *op. cit.*, pp. 169–265.
30 This technique has been used extensively by largely 'middle class' community groups in the United States. See especially SCHINDLER-RAINMAN, E. *et al.* (1973) *Toward a Human Society: Images of Potentiality in the School and Community*, Washington, Institute for Applied Behavioural Science.
31 MANDEL, E. (1975) *The Generalized Recession of the International Capitalist Economy*, Toronto, Forward Books, p. 24.
32 Particularly with regard to the impact on human biology, see EPSTEIN, S. (1979) *The Politics of Cancer*, Garden City, Doubleday and, from a more global and apocalyptic perspective, DESHUSSES, J. (1982) *Life on the Edge of Human History*, Toronto, Deneau.

Author Index

Abercrombie, B and Turner, B., 138n63
Ackroyd, C. *et al.*, 239n6, 241n24
Adams, M., 176n24, 177n27 and n30, 223–4n100
Agh, A., 83n22
Aglietta, M., 39n55
Ahier, J. *see* Flude and Ahier
Albert, M. and Hahnel, R., 224n104
Alinsky, S., 228, 238, 240n10
Allport, G. *see* Gillespie and Allport
Althusser, L., 36n32 and n36
Amin, S., 52–3, 63, 83n21, 85n45
d'Amour, P., 141n101
Anderson, P., 37n46, 39n55, 189, 219n40, 221n68
Anyon, J., 102–3, 136n41, 138n53 and n54
Apple, M.W., 37n38, 87n69, 133n2, 136n35, 137n50
Arblaster, A. and Lukes, S., 217n3
Archer, M., 136n36
Arièss, P., 38n53
Armytage, W.H.G., 217n5
Arnot, M. and Whitty, G., 133n2
Aronowitz, S., 25–6, 38n52
Attali, 40n65
Auld, D., 176n17
Axworthy, L., 177n40

Bahro, R., 83n16, 219n38
Balbus, I., 138n61
Baltzell, E.D., 85n52
Banaji, J., 37n45, n46 and n47, 83n22, 142n131
Bantam, J., 222n74
Barnes, B. *see* Shapin and Barnes
Barnes, D. *et al.*, 137n44
Barnet, R. *see* Raskin and Barnet
Barrett, M., 38n53
Barrett, M. *et al.*, 40n59, 134n11
Barsodi, R., 183
Barton, L., 34n6
Barton, L. *et al.*, 136n35
Baurdrillard, J., 132n1
Becker, J., 37n44

Beeman, C., 126, 240n16
Bell, D., 181, 217n8, 218n12
Bell, W. and Mau, J., 222n78
Bendix, R. and Lipset, S.M., 135n31
Berger, S., 218n12
Bernstein, B., 35n22, 36n34, 139n65, 156
Betcherman, G. *see* Harp and Betcherman
Beverley, J., 41n70
Birmingham Cultural Studies Centre, 40n64
Birmingham Education Group, 108, 231
Blackburn, R., 239n5
Bland, S.C., 190, 220n51
Bleasdale, G., 138n56
Bloch, E., 189, 193, 215, 219n42 and n43, 222n78, 224n103
Bloomfield, J.J., 134n13, 138n64
Boggs, G., 135n22
Bookchin, M., 189, 220n47
Boorstein, D., 222n78
Borsodi, R., 218n19
Bottomore, T., 175n9
Bottomore, T. and Nisbet, R., 35n24, n25 and n26
Boulding, K., 222n78
Bourdieu, P. 35n22, 36n34, 136n42, 137n42, 156
Bourdieu, P. and Passeron, J.-Cl. 135n32, 139n65
Bowles, S. and Gintis, H., 7, 34n5 and n6, 36n34, 76, 87n69 and n72, 102, 135–6n35, 136n41, 138n52
Bradford, R., 142n130
Braverman, H., 38n55, 82n10, 135n35, 136n36, 177n36, 221n68
Briggs, A. and Saville, J., 220n56
Brighton Labour Process Group, 48, 82n11 and n14
Brodie, M.J. and Jenson, J., 139n75
Brook, E. and Finn, D., 67, 86n56
Brown, R., 108, 139n67
Bruce-Briggs, S. *see* Drouin and Bruce-Briggs
Buber, M., 219n30, 220n49

Buci-Glucksmann, C., 133n1
Bullock, C., 141n102
Bulmer, M., 82n5
Bunyan, T., 241n24
Burawoy, M., 38n55, 106, 138n60
Burris, V., 59–61, 70, 84n33, n38 and n40

Callaghan, R., 35n32
Cameron, D., 176n19
Cameron, K., 134n15
Campen, J., 221n70
Canadian Labour Congress, 110
Cantril, H., 222n82
Carchedi, G., 82n9, 83–4n24, 84n25
Carlton, R. *et al.*, 141n102
Carnoy, M. and Levin, H., 136n39
Carnoy, M. and Shearer, D., 219n39
Carter, M., 99, 136n39
Castells, M., 37n44, 40n65
Castles, S. and Wustenberg, W., 135n30, 138n55,
    186–7, 188, 219n32, n33, n34, n37 and n39
CEA Task Force, 176n25
Centre for Contemporary Cultural Studies,
    University of Birmingham, 18–19, 37n37,
    133n3, 139n68 and n70, 176n10, 177n40,
    241n17
Charbonneau, Y., 225, 239n3
Chardin, T.P. de, 182, 218n16
Christenson, J. *see* Dillman and Christenson
Clarke, J., 93–4
Clarke, J. *et al.*, 134n10 and n18
Clarke, J.R., *et al.*, 134n17
Clarkson, S., 218n24
Clement, W., 63, 71, 77, 79, 85n44 and n52,
    86n61, 88n76 and n79
Cobb, J. *see* Sennett and Cobb
Cole, G.D.H., 191, 219n30, 221n58–n66
Cole, G.D.H. and Mellor, W., 191, 220n56,
    221n61, n63 and n66
Cole, M., 220n56, 221n58 and n67
Coleman, J.S. *et al.*, 87n67, 135n31
Commission on Educational Planning, 217n10
Committee on Education and Labour, House of
    Representatives, 217n10
Connell, R.W., 138n54
Cornish, S. *see* Jennings and Cornish
Corrigan, P. *see* Barrett *et al.*; Frith and Corrigan
Craik, W.W., 221n62
Craven, P., 139n73
Cross, M., 220n52
Crouch, C. and Pizzorno, A., 82n8, 175n6
Crouse, J. *see* Olneck and Crouse
Cumbler, J., 85n52
Curran, J., 82n5
Curti, M., 7–8, 34n7 and n9

Dale, R., 34n6
Dale, R. and MacDonald, M., 40n62
Dale, R. *et al.*, 40n62, 137n49

David, M., 41n67
Dawe, A., 15, 35n24
Della Volpe, G., 40n61
Deppe, R., 175n6
DES, 133–4n7
Dillman, D. and Christenson, J., 222n80
Dobb, A.E., 139n68
Dobbin, L. 115, 140n88
Dolci, D., 229, 240n12
Domhoff, G.W., 86n64
Donald, J., 133n4
Drache, D., 140n75, 241n21
Draper, H., 82n7, 83n24, 84n26 and n31, 86n53,
    87n65, 138n59
Drouin, M.J. and Bruce-Briggs, B., 217n7
Drummond, R. *see* Fletcher and Drummond
Dumont, F., 139n73
Dunn, T. *see* Jones and Dunn

Edwards, R., 38n55, 48, 82n12 and n13
Elam, S., 176n24
Elsht, J., 137n45
Employment and Immigration Canada, 177n40
Engels, F., 20, 186–93, 219n31 *see also* Marx and
    Engels
Enzensberger, H., 132n1
Epstein, S., 242n32
Esland, G. and Ferguson, 40n62 *see also* Dale
    et al.
Ewen, S., 132–3n1

Falk, R., 183, 218n20, 221n70
Farina, J., 224n104
Feldman, A. *see* Tumin and Feldman
Fenwick, M., 123, 141n114
Ferguson *see* Esland and Ferguson
Ferkiss, V., 183, 218n18
Finn, D. *et al.*, 133n4 *see also* Brook and Finn
Fiore, Q. *see* McLuhan and Fiore
Fleming, B., 115
Fleming, D.B., 140n90, 141n106
Fletcher, F. and Drummond, R., 176n15
Flude, M. and Ahier, J., 135n34, 137n44
Foreign Investment Review Agency, 63
Form, W. *see* Huber and Form
Foster, J., 86n62 and n63
Foster-Carter, A., 83n22
Fox, B., 84n27
Frank, A.G., 83n22
Frank, R., 95
Freinet, C., 219n39
Freire, P., 229, 240n12, and n13
Friedman, A., 38n55
Frith, S. and Corrigan, P., 236, 241n28
Fry, J., 85n50

Galtung, J., 136n37, 221n70, 223n89, n91 and
    n94
Galtung, J. *et al.*, 195–6, 222n83

Garaudy, R., 220n50
Garcia, J.D., 218n16
Genovese, E., 39n56
Geras, N., 226–7, 239n5
Gilder, G., 218n23
Gillespie, J. and Allport, G., 222n81
Gintis, H., 219n28 *see also* Bowles and Gintis
Giroux, H., 37n38
Gitlin, T., 241n25
Glaberman, M., 148, 166, 176n13, 177n31
Glass, S.T., 220n56
Glines, D., 219n27
Goldsmith, E., *et al.*, 218n18
Goldthorpe, J., 70, 86n57, n59 and n63
Gonick, C. *et al.*, 140n76
Goodman, P. and Goodman, P., 189, 220n47
Gordon, D., 37n44
Gorelick, S., 87n72, 136n35
Gorz, A., 82n9, 137n49, 138n57
Gough, I., 84n25
Gouldner, A., 133n1
Goulet, D., 220n48
Grace, G., 137n45, 241n18
Gramsci, A., 13, 18–19, 30, 34n16, 36n36, 38n39,
    39n56, 91, 93–4, 133n1, 148–9, 176n14, 193,
    221n69, 227, 229, 240n9
Grand' Maison, J., 190, 220n54
Grant, N., 225, 239n4, 241n20
Gray, R., 138n64
Gross, D., 220n44
Gross, N. *see* Herriott and Gross
Guettel, C., 115, 140n86
Guillen, A., 227, 240n8

Hainey, A., 140n86
Hall, E.m. *et al.*, 141n102
Hall, S., 18–19, 34n6, 36n36, 134n13
HALL, S. AND JEFFERSON, T., 133n3, 134n17
Hall-Dennis Commission Report, 118
Halsey, A.H. *et al.*, 88n77 *see* also Karabel and
    Halsey
Hamilton, R., 222n77
Hamilton, W. *see* Stevenson and Hamilton
Hardin, H., 184, 218n24
Hardwick, W., 194
Harkins, A. *see* Redd and Harkins
Harman, W., 218n21
Harmon, W. *et al.*, 217n10
Harp, J., 87n67, 176n23
Harp, J. and Betcherman, G., 241n21
Harp, J. and Hofley, J., 87n67, 176n23
Harrison, J., 139n68
Hart, D.J. *see* Livingstone and Hart
Heap, S., 40n66
Heller, A., 138n59
Hernstein, R., 87n69
Herriott, R. and Gross, N., 36n33
Herriott, R. and Hodgkins, B., 36n32
Hiller, P., 82n5

Hirschman, A.O., 35n17
HMSO, 87n67
Hoare, Q. 225, 239n2
Hoare, Q. and Nowell-Smith, G., 34n16, 37n39
Hobsbawn, E., 220n55
Hobson, S.G., 220n56, 221n57
Hodgetts, B., 221n73
Hofley, J. *see* Harp and Hofley
Hogan, D., 34n6, 139n69
Hoggart, R., 17–18, 36n35 and n36
Holly, D., 100–1, 136n35, 137n46 and n47,
    139n67
Hopkins, T. and Wallerstein, I., 37n44
Horton, J., 35n27
Howard, D. and Klare, K., 40n61, 220n44
Howat, B. *et al.*, 219n38
Hoyles, A., 178n45
Huber, J. and Form, W. 176n20
Hughes, A.S., 175n8
Hurn, C., 16, 17, 35n31, 36n34
Hurtig, M., 221n73
Husen, T., 7–8, 34n4 and n8, 87n68
Hyman, H., 135n31

Illich, I., 34n12, 36n34, 183, 184–5, 218n19,
    219n27 and n29, 234, 241n22
ILO, 59–60
Industrial Cooperative Association, 241n23
Irvine, J. *et al.*, 176n11
Isbester, F. *see* Miller and Isbester

Jalee, P., 37n43
Jamieson, S., 85n50
Jarolunek, J., 36n33
Jefferson, T. *see* Hall and Jefferson
Jeglum, A., 136n41
Jencks, C., 87n69
Jencks, C. *et al.*, 87n69, 88n78
Jennings, L. and Cornish, S., 217–18n11
Jenson, J. *see* Brodie and Jenson
Jessop, B., 174, 175n4, 178n44, 221n69
Johnson, C., 134n13
Johnson, L., 64–5, 85n46, n47, n48, n49 and n50
Johnson, R., 39–40n59, 90–1, 97, 134n10, n11
    and n18, 135n33
Johnston, W., 60
Johnston, W. and Ornstein, M., 84n37
Jones, D. and Dunn, T., 135n29
Juster, T., 87n69

Kahn, H., 181, 183, 217n7
Kahn, H. and Weiner, A., 217n7
Kanzow, E. 102 *see* also Roth and Kanzow
Karabel, J. and Halsey, A.H., 35n22, 137n42,
    139n65
Karier, C. *et al.*, 36n34
Katz, M., 6, 34n3, 36n34, 135n27, 139n69
Katznelson, I., 39n55
Kautsky, 187–8

Kealy, G., 139n72
Kielty, F. *et al.*, 175n8
Kitson, F., 241n24
Klare, K. *see* Howard and Klare
Kloskowska, A. and Martinotti, G., 135n23
Kluckhohn, C., 134n14
Knoepfli, H. and Saul, D., 222n76
Kogan, M., 133n7
Kolakowski, L., 38n51
Konrad, G. and Szelenyi, I., 37n39
Kropotkin, P., 189, 220n46
Krupskaya, 188
Kuhn, A. and Wolpe, A., 134n9 *see also* Barrett *et al.*
Kuhn, T., 35n30
Kusterer, K., 38n55, 83n15

Labedz, L., 220n44
Lake, D.G. *see* Livingstone and Lake
Lauwerys, J., 222n75
Laxer, R., 87n66
Lazonick, W., 39n55, 94, 134n20
Lefevre, M., 44–5
Lenin, V.I., 51, 83n19
Levidow, L., 37n49
Levin, H. *see* Carnoy and Levin
Levine, R., 35n21
Levitas, M., 40n62
Lind, L., 138n54
Lindsey, J.K., 76–7, 79, 87–8n74 and n75
Lipset, S.M. *see* Bendix and Lipset
Lipton, C., 87n66
Lister, I., 219n29
Litchfield, R., 140n83, 142n122
Litt, E., 138n54
Livingstone, D.W., 34n2, 38n54, 60–2, 83n23, 84n36 and n39, 85n41, 86n54, n55, n57 and n58, 134n8 and n16, 136n36 and n40, 138n56, 175n7 and n8, 176n21 and 22, 178n42, 197, 198, 201, 202, 204, 206, 211, 213, 217n6, 218n12, 219n28, 221n71, 223n85, n91, n93, n95 and n96, 224n101, n102 and n104, 240n11, 241n27
Livingstone, D.W. and Hart, D.J., 84n39, 86n57, 176n7, n12 and n24, 177n29, n33 and n37, 178n43, 223n86
Livingstone, D.W. and Lake, D.J., 216n1
Livingstone, D.W. and Mason, R.V., 35n19, 138n51
Lockhart, A., 137n48, 141n102
Lomax, B., 178n45
Lopreato, J. and Hazelrigg, L., 82n5
Lukacs, G., 39n56
Lukes, S. *see* Arblaster and Lukes
Luria, A.R., 39n56
Luxton, M., 86n52

McCuen, J., 241n24
McDermott, D., 115–16, 140n91

MacDonald, K., 111, 140n80 and n83, 141n111
MacDonald, M. *see* Dale and MacDonald; Dale *et al.*
McKenzie King, W.L., 139n73, 183, 218n22
Mackie, R., 240n13
McLellan, D., 82n6
McLuhan, M., 181
McLuhan, M. and Fiore, Q., 217n9
McNally, D., 82n42
McNeill, W., 134n15
Macpherson, C.B., 35n17, 138n62
McRobbie, A., 137n43
Mailer, P., 178n45
Mandel, E., 37n43 and n44, 40n61, 221n68, 239, 242n31
Mann, M., 175n4
Manuel, F. 217n5
Manuel, F. and Manuel, F., 219n30
Marcuse, H., 138n62, 175n3
Marien, M., 182, 217n10, 218n14
Markely, O.W., 217n6
Martel, G., 40n62, 138n54, 141n102, 176n23
Martin, B., 35n19
Martin, R., 175n6
Martinet, R., 125, 142n119 and n120
Martinotti, G. *see* Kloskowska and Martinotti
Marx, K., 20–31, 37n42 and n48, 38n52, 39n57, 40n61, 46, 49, 50, 58, 82n6 and n7, 83n15 and n18, 84n24, 87n65, 91–2, 134n8 and n19, 146, 186–93, 225, 239n1
Marx, K. and Engels, F., 134n12, 138n59, 219n31, 239n1
Mason, R.V. *see* Livingstone and Mason
Matas, R., 177n39 and n41
Mau, J., 222n81 *see also* Bell and Mau
Maxwell, G. 222n81
Maxwell, S., 142n121
Mellor, W. *see* Cole and Mellor
Mellos, K., 109, 112, 139n71 and n74, 140n82
Mepham, J. and Ruben, D.-H., 40n60
Messinger, E., 39n57
Metro New Democrats – Labour Council of Metrolopitan Toronto, 119, 123, 126, 140n77, 141n93, n94, n97, n105 and n107, 142n115 and n125–9
Miliband, R. 133n5
Miliband, R. and Saville, J., 88n80
Millar, J.P., 139n68
Millar, R., 83n24
Miller, R. and Isbester, 139n75
Ministry of Education (Canada), 176–7n26
Monière, D., 139n73
Montano, M., 40n61
Montgomery, C., 177n40
Movement for a New Society, 240n14

Nasaw, D., 135n25
National Energy Policy (Canada), 63
Naylor, T., 85n42

Nearing, S., 136n41
Negri, T., 38n53, 239–40n7
Nelles, H.V., 86n64
Nelles, H.V. and Rotstein, A., 220n53
Nelson, R. and Nock, D., 40n62, 138n56,
    141n102
Newitt, J., 218n11
Nisbet, R. *see* Bottomore and Nisbet
Nock, D. *see* Nelson and Nock
Novarro, J., 45
Nowell-Smith, G. *see* Hoare and Nowell-Smith
Oakeshott, R., 219n39, 220n49
O'Brien, M., 38n53
O'Connor, J., 34n14, 84n25 and n32, 133n6
OECD, 9, 12, 34n13, 217n10, 221n70
Offe, C. and Wiesenthal, H., 175n5
Okraku, I. *see* Rinehart and Okraku
Olneck, M. and Crouse, J., 87n71
Olson, D., 133n6
Ontario Federation of Labour, 110, 140n77,
    141n93, n95–7, n99, n103, n104, n106 and
    n114, 142n116, n123 and n124
Ontario Public Service Employees' Union,
    177n38
Ontario Survey of Educational Issues, 145–6,
    149–72
Opinion Research Index, 175n8
Ornauer, H. *et al.* 197, 201, 204, 222–3n83 and
    n84, 223n87–92
Ornstein, M.D., 60, 86n60, 87n71, 88n78 *see also*
    Johnston and Ornstein
Ossowski, S., 45, 82n4
Owen, R., 220n49
Oxford Social Mobility Group, 70

Paget, J., 241n24
Paige, J., 83n17
Panitch, L., 85n50, 135n25, 140n76
Park School Community Council, 176n23
Parker, D., 222n75
Parkin, F., 87n70
Parrot, J.-Cl. 141n91
Parsons, T., 356n32
Partridge, E., 190, 220n51
Passeron, J.-C., 35n22, 36n34 *see also* Bourdieu
    and Passeron
Pataud, E. and Pouget, E., 220n46
Penner, N., 139n75
Pentland, H.C., 85n45
Penty, A.J., 220n56
Perdue, W. *see* Reasons and Perdue
Perrone, L. *see* Wright and Perrone
Phillips, A. and Putnam, T., 135n23
Pike, R. and Zureik, E., 137n48
Pizzorno, A. *see* Crouch and Pizzorno
Plowden Report, 87n67
Polak, F., 217n2
Popkin, J.W., 111
Porter, J., 63, 71, 218n12

Pouget, E. *see* Pataud and Pouget
Poulantzas, N., 82n9, 84n29, 133n5
Poulantzis, M., 58
Prentice, A., 138n56
Proudhon, 189
Provincial Committee on Aims and Objectives
    of Education in Schools of Ontario, 176n26
Przeworski, A., 65–6, 85n51
Putnam, T. *see* Phillips and Putnam

Quinney, R., 177n35

Rapp, R., 86n52
Raskin, M. and Barnet, R., 221n70
Reasons, C. and Perdue, W., 35n27–9
Redd, K. and Harkins, A., 217n11
Reimer, E., 34n12, 135n27, 184–5, 219n27,
    241n22
Rey, P.P., 37n41
Rinehart, J. and Okraku, I., 176n20
Robin, M., 139n75
Rockefeller, J.D., 183, 218n21
Rosdolsky, R., 40n61
Rosove, P., 241n26
Ross, L., 43–4
Roth, K.H. and Kanzow, E., 137n49
Rotstein, A. *see* Nelles and Rotstein
Rowbotham, S. *et al.*, 40n65
Royal Commission on Corporate
    Concentration, 63, 85n42
Royal Commission on Relations of Capital and
    Labour, 139n72
Ruben, D.-H. *see* Mepham and Ruben
Rubin, B., 95, 135n21, n24 and n26
Rudé, G., 39n56, 175n4
Ruhle, J.R., 220n44
Russell, B., 220n56
Rutter, M. *et al.*, 87n69
Ryerson, S., 85n42

Saifulin, M., 219n36
Salter, B. *see* Tapper and Salter
Samuel, R., 85n52
Sanoff, A., 177n34
Sargent, L., 217n5
Sartre, J.P., 105, 138n58
Sarup, M., 40n62
Saul, D. *see* Knoepfli and Saul
Saville, J. *see* Briggs and Saville; Miliband and
    Saville
Sayer, D., 40n60 and n61
Schechter, S., 135n25, 136n38, 138n56
Schindler-Raminau, E. *et al.*, 242n30
Schmidt, A., 38n54
Schultz, R. *et al.*, 140n76
Schneider, M., 138n59
Schumacher, E.F., 183, 218n19
Schwendinger, H. and Schwendinger, J., 35n18

Schwendinger, J. *see* Schwendinger and
    Schwendinger
Seccombe, W., 39n55, 134n9
Seeley, J.R., *et al.*, 134n14
Seiden, S., 34n14
Sennett, R. and Cobb, J., 36n35
Sève, L., 39n58, 138n59
Shapin, S. and Barnes, B., 137n49
Shapiro, H.S., 96, 135n23, n28 and n29, 219n33
    and n39
Sharpe, R., 133n2
Shearer, D. *see* Carnoy and Shearer
Sherman, W., 218n24
Shklar, J., 217n5
Siegel, S., 240n15
Signal, B., 126, 142n123
Simon, B., 34n11, 40n63, 41n68, 135n25, 139n68
Sinclair, S., 141n98
Skinner, B.F., 183, 184, 218n17
Sklar, H., 35n20
Smith, D., 38n53
Smith, D.N., 136n41
Sohn-Rethel, A., 23–4, 37n39, n46 and n49
Sorokin, P., 182–3, 218n17
Spring, J. *see* Karier *et al.*
Stalin, J., 187–8
Stevenson, H., 182, 184, 218n15, 221n72
Stevenson, H. and Hamilton, W., 217n10
Syzmanski, A., 51, 83n20
Szelenyi, I. *see* Konrad and Szelenyi

Taliani, E., 135n23
Tapper, E. and Salter, B., 8, 34n10, 142n132
Tawney, R.H., 220n56
Teeple, G., 85n46
Temple, G., 111, 124, 140n81 and n84, 141n112,
    142n117, 240n16
Terkel, S., 82n1–3
Therborn, G., 24, 37n40, 38n50, 39n55, 133n1
Thompson, E.P., 36n36, 40n63, 81, 85n52,
    88n80, 134n15, 136n41, 221n70
Timpanaro, S., 38n54
Toffler, A., 217n10, 223n79 and n97
Trotsky, L., 219n36
Tumin, M. and Feldman, A., 222n81
Turner, B. *see* Abercrombie and Turner

UNESCO, 9, 11
Useen, E. and Useem, M., 36n34
Useem, M. *see* Useen and Useem

Vaisey, G.D., 85n52
Van Der Veer, K., 223n91
van der Veldon, J.H., 141n102

Vieille, P., 222n80
Violas, P., 36n34 *see also* Karier *et al.*
Vocations for Social Change, 241n23

Wagar, W., 182, 218n13 and n20
Wagg, L., 141n95 and n100
Wagschal, P., 219n26
Walker, J., 240n13
Walker, P., 82n9
Wallerstein, I., *see* Hopkins and Wallerstein
Ward, C., 189, 220n47
Warren, B., 83n22
Warren, P.J., 175n8
Warwick, D., 137n44
Weiner, H. *see* Kahn and Weiner
Weiss, H., 175n9
Wesolowski, W., 138n61
Whitty, G. and Young, M., 35n23, 137n45,
    239n4 *see also* Arnot and Whitty; Young and
    Whitty
Wiesenthal, H. *see* Offe and Wiesenthal
Willener, A., 222n83
Williams, R., 34n15, 36n35 and n36, 108, 139n66,
    166, 177n32
WILLIAMSON, B., 98, 135n34, 136n36
Willis, P., 37n37, 40n64, 133n3, 137n43, 240n15
Wilson, E.O., 218n17
Wittke, C.F., 219n30
Wolfe, A., 133n1
Wolfe, D., 85n50
Wolff, J. *see* Barrett *et al.*
Wolpe, A. *see* Kuhn and Wolpe
Woodcock, G., 220n45
World Bank, 12, 33n1
Wright, E.O., 57–8, 60–1, 79, 82n9 and n10,
    84n28, n30, n34 and n35, 87n73, 88n78, 102,
    138n61
Wright, E.O. and Perrone, L., 87n73
Wrigley, J., 34n11, 139n69
Wustenberg, W. *see* Castles and Wustenberg
Wyatt, H.E., 120, 124, 140n77 and n85,
    141n108–10 and n113, 142n118, 156, 176n18

Yankelovich, D., 222n80
Young, M., 14–15, 35n23, 108, 139n67 *see also*
    Whitty and Young
Young, M. and Whitty, G., 35n23, 136n35,
    241n28
Young T.R., 143, 146–7, 175n1 and n2, 176n10

Zeitlin, M., 34n11, 139n69
Zeleny, J., 40n61
Zureik, E. *see* Pike and Zureik

Subject Index

accumulation crises
  in capitalist societies, 32–3, 172, 173–4, 227
age
  and class position, 1, 68
authority
  in schools, 162–3, 172

Bolsheviks, 187–8
bourgeois intellectual traditions
  and visions of the future, 180, 181–6

Canada, 2–3, 20, 60–75, 77–81, 84n39, 85n45
  and n52, 86n64, 87n66 and n67, 90, 104, 107,
  108–32, 136n38, 138n56, 139n73, 139–40n75,
  140n76 and n77, 143–78, 182, 184, 190,
  193–224, 232, 240n16, 241n21 see also OECD
  countries
capital accumulation, 51, 52–66
  see also accumulation crises
capitalist society, passim
choice
  in education, 164, 213–14
class
  and capitalism, 43–50
  and educational attitudes, 151–72
  and educational crisis, 143–78
  and educational ideologies, 89–142
  and images of educational and social future,
    179–224
  and material production, 43–56
class conflict, 2, 46, 94–105
class relations, passim
  and schooling, 1, 3, 120–4, 151, 155–6, 161–6
class structure, 2, 43–88
Chartists, 20
community colleges, 157
conflict perspectives, 15–19
consensus perspectives, 15–17
contested subordination approach, 19, 26
cores
  and social classes, 2, 66–75, 86n57, 173, 202–3
  see also peripheries

corporate business, 129–31, 140n77, 144–5,
  151–72, 177, 193–215
  and cultural ownership, 111–14
  and school discipline, 120–2
  and skill requirements, 124–6
corporatism, 140n76
cosmic evolutionism, 182
crisis
  in education, 2, 5–12, 31–3, 143–78
cultural capital, 136–7n42
cultural ownership, 1, 3, 151, 155–61
curriculum, 33, 136n41, 155, 158–9, 168–9, 207,
  208, 210, 214

decentralism, 183, 184
deschooling, 34n12, 184–5
discipline
  in schools, 120–2, 161–2

ecological limits, 183
economic performance
  indicators of, 9–12
education, passim
  content of, 151, 155–72 see also curriculum
  form of, 151, 155–72
  relations of, with society, 5–41
educational change
  and mass opinion, 143–78
educational future
  images of, 3, 179–224
educational ideologies, 2, 89–142
educational management technologies, 36n33
educational objectives
  in secondary schools, 167–8
educational organizations
  development of, 136n36
educational planning
  public influence in, 211–12
educational practices, passim
educational praxis
  in advanced capitalism, 3, 225–42
educational reform, 6–12, 17, 205–15

educational relations
   and class conflict, 2, 94–105
educational technologies, 124–9
   see also technology
employment, 9–11, 33
   see also job opportunities
equal opportunity
   in education, 157–8, 214–15
ethnicity, 1, 26, 38n53, 69

feminism, 38n53
   see also gender; sex
financial priorities
   for education, 3, 151–5
   see also public expenditure
France, 96
   see also OECD countries
Freinet movement, 96

gender, 26
   see also feminism; sex
Geneva Resolution, 187
German Democratic Republic, 188
guild socialism, 190–3

hegemony, 2, 18–19
historical materialism, *passim*
human agency approach, 15–17, 19

ideologies
   and social reality, 90–4
images
   of educational and social futures, 3, 179–224
individual liberty, 181–6
intellectual interpretations
   and educational facts, 2, 5–41
intellectual traditions
   and the future, 179–93
intellectuals, 3, 12–19, 34n16, 37n39, 179–224
International Working Men's Association, 20
Italy, 82n10, 135n23, 239–40n7

job opportunities
   and educational system, 10, 170–1, 172–4
   see also employment

labour, 140n91
   and cultural ownership, 114–20
   and school discipline, 122–4
   and skill requirements, 126–9
less developed countries
   see Third World economies
lumpen class, 57, 84n26

marriage
   and class position, 71–4, 86n62
Marxism, 1, 6–7, 16, 20–31, 38n53 and n54,
   39n56, n57 and n58, 40n61 and n62, 76, 82n10,
   98, 138n61, 142n131, 188–9

mass opinion, 2, 143–78

OECD countries, 33, 52–3
Ontario, 2–3, 65–6, 67–75, 77–81, 84n39,
   86n64, 145–78, 193–224, 232
Ontario Images 2000 Project, 196–216, 223n85
   and n86
opinion surveys, 2–3, 145–74, 175n7 and n8,
   194, 216
   limitations of, 146–9
organization
   of learning process, 5–12, 166–7

participation rates
   in education, 8–9
peripheries
   and social classes, 2, 52–3, 66–75, 86n57,
   202–3
   see also cores
piecemeal change perspectives, 183–4
popular images
   of the future, 193–215
production, *passim*
proletarianization, 51–2
public expenditure
   on education, 9–11, 33, 151–5
public opinion
   see mass opinion

Quebec, 139n73, 140n75, 232, 241n21

reconstructed humanism, 182

schooling
   and capitalism, *passim*
sex
   and class position, 1, 69
   see also feminism; gender
skill requirements
   in learning, 124–9, 166–72
social classes, *passim*
   and cores and peripheries, 66–75
   in Marxism, 23–31
   see also class
social equality, 204
   see also equal opportunities
social future
   images of, 3, 179–224
socialism, 83n16, 180, 186–93, 225–42
socialist intellectual tradition
   and visions of the future, 180, 186–93
societal future
   popular images, 196–205
society
   educational relations with, 5–41
state education commissions, 141n102
state schooling
   and educational ideologies, 89–142
strike

right to, 164–5
structural-functionalism, 16
'surplus' teachers, 155, 172
surveys
    see opinion surveys
systemic subordination appraoch, 18–19

technical relations
    of schooling, 1, 3, 151, 155–6, 166–72
technology
    and the future, 181–6, 199–202, 216
Third World economies, 52, 83n22
trade unions, 47, 74, 87n65 and n66, 95, 114–20,
    122–4, 126–9, 129–31, 135n23, 144–5,
    151–72, 232
    and class position, 74–5
    see also labour
Trilateral Commission, 14

Union of Soviet Socialist Republics (USSR),
    187–8

United Kingdom (UK), 8, 70, 82n10, 85n52,
    87n67, 94, 97, 101, 108, 134n18, 135n23, 166,
    182, 190–3
    see also OECD countries
United States (US), 6–7, 60–3, 82n10, 85n52,
    86n64 and n67, 94–5, 96, 135n23, 139n69, 184,
    241n23
    see also OECD countries
utopianism, 186–7, 192

West Germany, 47, 102, 104–5
    see also OECD countries
working class, 2, 3, 17–18, 23, 25, 26, 30, 36n34
    and n35, 38n52, 40n64, 56, 85n52, 86n52 and
    n57, 95, 102–3, 104, 114–20, 122–4, 132,
    135n25, 139n68 and n69, 159–61, 174, 177n42,
    232, 240n15
World Images 2000 Project, 195–216, 222–3n84
    and n86
world order models, 183